A STUDY PREPARED UNDER THE AUSPICES OF THE
NEW YORK UNIVERSITY INSTITUTE OF COMPARATIVE LAW

THE CODE NAPOLEON AND THE COMMON-LAW WORLD

STUDIES IN COMPARATIVE LAW

NEW YORK UNIVERSITY

INSTITUTE OF COMPARATIVE LAW

THE CODE NAPOLEON AND THE COMMON-LAW WORLD

EDITED BY

BERNARD SCHWARTZ

THE SESQUICENTENNIAL LECTURES DELIVERED AT
THE LAW CENTER OF NEW YORK UNIVERSITY
DECEMBER 13–15, 1954

GREENWOOD PRESS, PUBLISHERS
WESTPORT, CONNECTICUT

Library of Congress Cataloging in Publication Data

Schwartz, Bernard, 1923- ed.
The Code Napoleon and the common-law world.

Reprint of the ed. published by New York University Press, New York, in series: New York University, Institute of Comparative Law. Studies in comparative law.
Bibliography: p.
Includes index.
1. Civil law--France--Addresses, essays, lectures.
2. Law--Codification--Addresses, essays, lectures.
3. Civil law systems--Addresses, essays, lectures.
4. Common law--Addresses, essays, lectures. I. Title
II. Series: New York University. Institute of Comparative law. Studies in comparative law.
[Law] 340'.09744 73-16951
ISBN 0-8371-7250-0

Originally published in 1956 by New York University Press, New York

Reprinted with the permission of New York University Press

Reprinted by Greenwood Press, Inc.

First Greenwood reprinting 1975
Second Greenwood reprinting 1977

Library of Congress catalog card number 73-16951
ISBN 0-8371-7250=0

Printed in the United States of America

Contents

Preface

On March 21, 1804, there occurred one of the most notable events in all legal history. For it was on that day that the Code Napoleon was voted into law. The French Civil Code is the first great modern codification of the law. It abrogated the law of the *Ancien Régime*—based largely on local custom, and anything but the unified system demanded by a large national State—and substituted for it a coherent code, logically arranged and clear and precise in its terms.

It should be noted that the popular title of this monumental work, the *"Code Napoleon,"* is no mere figure of speech. Attempts at codification had been made for many years, and even the Revolution had not seen them come to fruition. It was the all-powerful will of the First Consul that was the necessary catalyst. It was his energy that brought to completion the work so long awaited.

Napoleon himself realized from the beginning the monumental significance of the codification that bears his name. At Saint Helena, near the end of his life, he wrote: "My glory is not to have won forty battles, for Waterloo's defeat will destroy the memory of as many victories. But what nothing will destroy, what will live eternally, is my Civil Code."

The framers of the Code Napoleon were dominated by the desire to present the law in a form readily accessible to all. Like Jeremy Bentham, they sought to be able to say: "Citizen, what is your condition? Are you a farmer? Then consult the chapter on Agriculture."

Of course, they did not wholly succeed in their aim. But the instrument that they drew up as a codification of all of the private law is remarkable for its brevity and lucidity of style. The entire Code contains only 2,281 sections and, even in its modern form, can readily be printed in a convenient pocket-size volume. The Code itself, after six short preliminary sections, is divided into three parts. The first deals with Persons; the second with Property; and the third with the different ways whereby property may be acquired.

The French Civil Code today is in its essentials what it was when Napoleon ordered it drawn up, because its dominant characteristic was the spirit of moderation with which it was drafted. Though it was a product of the French Revolution, its provisions were anything but revolutionary. But neither was it a reactionary document seeking to undo the work of the men of 1789. On the contrary, it sought to preserve the sound portions of their work—such as the equalitarian ideal, so vital to a democratic legal and economic system—while renouncing the radical and violent measures of the later Revolution.

As noteworthy as its effect on French law has been the territorial expansion of the Napoleonic Code. It has served as the model for similar codes in most countries outside the Anglo-American world. In countries so diverse as Belgium and Japan, Italy and Egypt, the French Code has served as the basis for analogous codifications. And the Code itself has been not without influence in the common-law world. In both Canada (Quebec) and the United States (Louisiana) there are jurisdictions whose law is based on its provisions.

The sesquicentennial of an event as important to the history of law as the promulgation of the Code Napoleon is one that should be marked by appropriate celebrations throughout the legal world. And it is fitting that the largest public celebration was that held at Arthur T. Vanderbilt Hall on December 13, 14, and 15, 1954, under the sponsorship of the New York University Institute of Comparative Law. Few lessons that comparative law has to teach us are of greater significance than the experience under the French Code. This is particularly true for the Anglo-American world. In all the common-law countries there has been, during the past century, an ever-increasing stream of legislation to supplement, and even to supersede, the law made by the courts. Since Bentham, informed jurists have questioned whether we could not bring some order out of the chaos of statute and case law by the use of the method of codification. The recent attempts at restatement of the law and at uniform state laws are manifestations of our concern with this problem. Certainly, in our attempts to deal with it, we should be aided greatly by an understanding of the first great modern Code and of the experience with it in practice.

That is why the theme of the sesquicentennial celebration was *The Code Napoleon and the Common-Law World.* What are the lessons for our system of a hundred and fifty years of the French Code? This theme was particularly emphasized during the third day, but it was present as the underlying motif in all three sessions. The participants were all eminent jurists, drawn from countries throughout the world. Their subjects were selected as those calculated to be of special interest to an American audience. The celebration itself, one of the largest public manifestations in this country of interest in comparative law, was decidedly a notable event in contemporary legal history.

The present commemorative volume contains, with one notable exception, the papers delivered by the participants in the Code Napoleon celebration. The exception is that of Dean Boris Mirkine-Guetzévitch, whose untimely death occurred before his paper could be completed. It is, however, gratifying, especially to the present writer, that Dean Mirkine could personally participate in the first session on December 13, as the last public event of a career so noted in the field of comparative law. In the place of Dean Mirkine's paper there is printed a short contribution by M. René Cassin, whose duties as head of the *Conseil d'Etat* made it impossible for him personally to attend the celebration.

Public thanks should be paid to all those who helped make the celebration a success, particularly to the participants and the chairmen of the three sessions, M. Pierre Donzelot, Director of the Cultural Services of the French Embassy, Dr. Ivan Kerno, of the United Nations, and Russell D. Niles, Dean of the New York University Law School. This volume, which makes the result of their efforts more than merely transitory, should constitute a permanent contribution to comparative law.

Bernard Schwartz

Director, New York University
Institute of Comparative Law

I

The Ideological and Philosophical Background

C. J. FRIEDRICH

VOLTAIRE, in a famous exclamation, demanded the total destruction of all existing law. "Do you want good laws? Burn yours and make new ones!"—"Voulez-vous avoir des bonnes lois? Brûlez les vôtres, et faites-en des nouvelles." The radical discontent with existing legal institutions under the *Ancien Régime* was here linked to the goal of radical reform, indeed a chiliastic hope that truth and goodness were known and ready to hand, and that all that was needed was the will to make a clean sweep of the past and to start afresh. Voltaire's dramatic demand symbolizes the revolutionary attitude that underlay the ardent search for a code of laws during the revolution that followed.

I do not propose to discuss in the following pages the content of these efforts at codification, the substantive law and how and to what extent it was in fact changed; for that is the concern of others contributing to this symposium. What I wish to explore is the background of political thought and ideas for the notion of codification as such. What made the revolutionaries think in those terms, and what instilled in Napoleon Bonaparte, the executioner in a double sense of the Revolution and of its ideology, the wish to see this task through? The content itself was, of course, bound up with, and to some extent expressive of, the aspirations of the spirit of 1789: all citizens are legally equals; primogeniture, hereditary

C. J. FRIEDRICH *is Eaton Professor of the Science of Government at Harvard University*

nobility, class privileges, and executions are unjust; private property is sacred; the conscience is or ought to be free; government employment should be available to all, indeed general opportunity should be equal for all citizens; laws should be simple and legal proceedings public, efficient, and inexpensive; to put it all in a nutshell, personal liberty and civil rights should be inviolable[1] As Albert Sorel has said: "The *Code Civil* has remained, for the peoples (of the world), the French Revolution—organized. When one speaks of the benefits of this revolution and of the liberating role of France, one thinks of the *Code Civil,* one thinks of this application of the idea of justice to the realities of life."[2]

New laws, yes, but why a code? The idea of uniting all law in one great body or corpus is, of course, an old one. Indeed, Western legal development had been taking place through centuries under the shadow of the *Corpus Juris* of Justinian, and considerable parts of France, more especially the South, had lived by it for a long time. Perhaps, then, one should rather ask: Why not a code?

It is, however, easily overlooked that the idea of a code and of codification appears in at least three clearly distinguishable forms. The Justinian Code just mentioned represents one of these types. It tries to bring together and "digest" a body of existing law, clarifying and systematizing it, but not intending to altar it in any significant way.[3] A second form tries to codify the law in terms of a natural law that provides a pattern for the systematization; that is to say, the clarification and therefore to some extent the reformation of the law. Reason is here assigned a distinctive role. This is the kind of code which the "Common Code for the Prussian Lands" *(Allgemeines Preussisches Landrecht)* and the "Common Civil Law Code" *(Allgemeines Bürgerliches Gesetzbuch)* of the Hapsburg Empire sought to be. Such codes were in line with the thinking of enlightened despotism and of the "heavenly city of the eighteenth century philosopher," to use Carl Becker's happy phrase.[4] Finally, there is a type of codification essentially inspired by the idea of lawgiving, which sets out to remake the law in the image of a new and better society.

The original French Revolutionary codes are of this type of "rationality." The lines between these three types of code may at times be a bit blurred, but the types embody nonetheless valid distinctions that are particularly important for an understanding of the ideological background of the *Code Civil.* For, as will appear in the sequel, the *Code Civil* was inspired by thinking along the lines of the third type, but was actually shaped into the second type. It is this fact that justifies A. Esmein in asserting that the drafters of the code, the commissioners of the Consulate and the members of the *Conseil d'Etat,* were simply those who did the final work, that they "built solidly the building the plan of which had been drawn before and the materials for which had been chosen and prepared by previous generations."[5] He quotes the commissioners themselves as saying: "The codes of people develop in time; properly speaking, one does not make them."[6] Whether this assertion is in fact true may be doubted. But the observation expresses well the sentiments of the historical school of jurisprudence. Actually, the Code embodied *in extenso,* as we have already noted, some of the very explicit lawmaking of the Revolution.

As bearing on certain notions common among American lawyers, it may be of interest to recall in this connection that Francis Bacon, as Lord Chancellor, at least twice raised the question of the possible wisdom of codifying the laws of England. And although he phrases his thought as if he had in mind merely the first type, a pure digest, the very heading of his proposal "for amending the laws of England" shows that he had the second type in mind. His well-known interest in a rational law of nature reinforces this conclusion. This is how he put it (in part): "The work which I propound, tendeth to the pruning and grafting the law, and not to the ploughing up and planting it again; for such a remove I should hold indeed for a perilous innovation. . . . But in the way that I shall propound, the entire body and substance of the law shall remain, only discharged of the idle and unprofitable or hurtful matter; and illustrated by order and other helps, towards the better understanding of it, and judgment thereon."[7] The proposal came to naught, for it encountered the fierce opposition of the law guilds and more especially of Sir Edward Coke, always alert to their special interests and concerns. But its existence helps us appreciate the link between this kind of rational reform code and enlightened absolutism, since even in England the idea was thus projected.

In summing up this preliminary analysis we may say, then, that there are three types or forms of code: the digest type, the reform type, and the revolutionary type, and that the *Code Civil* appears to be not the revolutionary, but the reform type, though partaking through its revolutionary predecessors to some extent of the revolutionary inspiration. To elucidate and confirm this hypothesis, we now turn to a more detailed examination of its ideological antecedents.[8]

In raising this question we are approaching the Civil Code as historians. The codification is itself seen as part of that ebb and flow of ideas by which the law is molded as it evolves. The seamless web of history is seen not as torn apart by a code, but as merely reinforced. It is important to keep this difference in mind, because of the lingering prejudice that once upon a time was so forcefully urged by Karl von Savigny in his celebrated *Of the Calling of our Time for Legislation and Legal Scholarship*.[9] He there sharply attacked the Civil Code for its rationalizing radical alteration of existing law. But involved in Savigny's attack, precipitated as it was by a proposal for a German code along similar lines, was the great German scholar's belief in the importance of legal learning for the shaping of the law. The time seemed to him not ripe for the kind of codification that is defensible and sound; it is clear that he would not have objected to the digest type of code, and his lifelong interest in and concern with the *Corpus Juris* demonstrates that fact, confirmed as it is by his conviction that the Roman law was the best law, something of a model for all times. Recent clarifications of Savigny's outlook[10] have not basically affected this aspect of the matter. But since Savigny did not appreciate the extent to which custom had been conserved in the French Code, one may wonder whether he might not have rendered a different verdict had he been more fully cognizant of the tradition-related character of the *Code Civil*, [11] which is not only universally acknowledged today, but is the ground for insistent demands that the Civil Code be altered and reformed.

Let us briefly review the historical development. The original draft of a code (1793) was strictly revolutionary in both intent and content. As the editors of the preparatory work pointed out, it was an enterprise meant to change everything at once, in education, in manners and customs, in the spirit and in the laws of a great people. They invited the Assembly to which the draft was submitted (August 9, 1793) to look at the Code as the fruit of liberty. "The nation will receive it as the guarantee of its happiness, and it will offer it one day to all the peoples...." In the style of all good revolutionaries, they recognized only one truth, and this truth was now revealed in the proposed code.[12] But the Assembly did not share their confidence; if truth it was, it was still too complicated, too hard to comprehend for the ordinary citizen, and therefore a still shorter one was prepared by Cambacérès[13] and his collaborators, which they presented on September 9, 1794. It was composed of only 297 articles containing very general principles. It has been aptly remarked (Esmein) that this was much more a manual of practical morals than a code of civil law. It failed of adoption.

But after the 18th Brumaire, the project did not go into the limbo; quite the contrary. With the vigorous support of Napoleon Bonaparte, the project of a code was pushed forward until finally it achieved definitive form in a draft presented to the *Conseil d'Etat*, there vigorously and minutely discussed with the steadfast participation of the First Consul, and eventually adopted on March 21, 1804, in the form in which it has endured. Having abandoned the revolutionary position, the draftsmen were now content to say. "We have much less the pretension of being novel than that of being useful. We have consulted jurists who were recommended by public opinion and general esteem (Jacqueminot)." [14] And in the famous introductory discourse (*Discours Préliminaire*) it was declared that "laws are not pure acts of power." The draftsmen added that it is necessary to be "sober" in face of proposed innovations in the law. In good Aristotelian manner and harking back to the perennial French liking for *bonne mesure,* they pontificated that "it would be absurd to adopt absolute ideas of perfection in matters which are susceptible only to relative goodness."[15] Here clearly the lawyers are speaking, the technicians who know and appreciate the weight of tradition and of the intellectual inertia that in all times and places supports it. But they do not by any means abandon the notion of useful reform. Indeed, this utilitarian standard, so characteristic of enlightened despotism, is the beacon light of their labors.

In this work of retrenchment they were aided enormously by the work of a great jurist of the previous generation, Pothier.[16] Purely in the spirit of a digest code, he had labored to demarcate the "area of agreement," as we nowadays say, of the many legal rules that had currency in the different parts of France. "While the commentators on the local customs had generally emphasized the originality of the [local] institutions . . . Pothier bringing to the study of the whole of French legislation the method of exposition . . . [of the Roman jurists] . . . , dwelt upon the central ideas and the elements of cohesion common to all customs. . . . His texts were often literally incorporated in the Code."[17] There were, of course, many other sources; but Pothier is not only the most outstanding by far, but also the one whose work most nearly approaches a codification by digest. It lacks, therefore, those ideas that only a rational natural law could superimpose upon the work. The Civil Code combines the reformist with the traditionalist outlook, progress with stability, justice with order. This balancing of countervailing values is no doubt the secret of its success.

But the analysis so far still leaves us without an answer to the question: Why a code? If the revolutionaries had a ready answer, they failed to carry through to realization the inspiration that Jacobin enthusiasm about Rousseau and the *volonté générale* had generated for law and legislation. Why did Napoleon succeed where the revolutionaries had failed? In putting this question we intend to concern ourselves, not with practical politics, but rather with those ideas that were demonstrably alive in the thought of Napoleon as a heritage. The present writer believes that there are three clusters that ought to be analyzed separately: (a) those of Rousseau and the *philosophes* of the eighteenth century; (b) the ideology and the impetus of the revolutionaries, more especially the Jacobins; and (c) the rivalry with monarchical absolutism (enlightened despotism) and more especially with Frederick the Great.

Let us turn first to Jean Jacques Rousseau and the *philosophes.* Bonaparte's devotion to Rousseau, his intimate youthful acquaintance with the "Newton of the moral world," as Kant had called him, is well known.[18] But he developed the side of Rousseau that finds its most effective expression in the *Contrat Social,* rather than the Rousseau of the sentimental views in the essay on the *Inequality of Man.* Indeed, Bonaparte judged that the latter, which he read in the summer of 1791, was nonsense. "I do not believe any of this," he commented. And he proceeds to write down what he believes to have been the state of nature: sociable, focused on love and friendship, with village communities; one senses the background of rural Corsica. Napoleon's main point is that sentiment and reason are natural to man and the mainstay of his nature. It is clear that his views are close to the notions of Rousseau, when seen in their entirety, but with a decided stress on the national, collective, authoritarian side of Rousseau, the side that in our day has even been called "totalitarian."[19] Indeed, Napoleon's response to Rousseau's teaching might be made a mainstay of this argument, which I nonetheless consider in error. Neither Rousseau nor Bonaparte was a totalitarian at all, and the best and most convincing proof lies in the field with which we are here concerned: they were both convinced believers in the law and considered legislation the most important activity of government. As Napoleon was to write on Saint Helena: "My true glory is not to have won forty battles. . . . What nothing will efface, what will live forever, is my *Code Civil,* the records of the proceedings in the *Conseil d'Etat.*"[20] Though this judgment is no doubt affected by the thought of posterity, it is really very much in line with what Napoleon said in the *Conseil d'Etat* while the Code was under consideration.

We know that Napoleon tried to apply the ideas of the *Contrat Social* to the officers of his regiment; the idea of everyone's commitment to the whole was the essence of his conception of morale. Indeed, there is alive in Rousseau, especially in the *Contrat Social,* something of the spirit of ancient Rome, with its emphasis on the soldier and the marching column. But the crucial point is another one.[21] At the very heart of Rousseau's teaching we find the doctrine of the legislator who gives the political community its basic form. In Book II, Chapter VII of the *Contrat Social* Rousseau exclaims: "Gods are needed to give laws to men." To him the legislator is the engineer who invents the machine, whereas ordinary government merely operates it. In this connection Rousseau cites Montesquieu, who had written (in the *Grandeur et Decadence des Romains,* Chapter I) that at the birth of societies "the rulers of Republics establish the institutions, while afterwards it is the institution that molds the rulers." But not only the rulers: the laws will shape the entire citizenry. The man who makes these laws "ought to feel himself capable of changing human nature, of transforming each individual into a part of a greater whole. . . ." Rousseau repeats here his doctrine of man as oscillating between the poles of solitary independence and complete absorption in the political community, "from which in a way he receives his very life and being." The legislator who does this is akin to the gods, because he transforms a physical, brutal being, independent man, into a moral being who cannot exist without other men. And the more interdependent men become, the better: "if each citizen is nothing and can do nothing without the rest, . . . it may be said that legislation is at the highest point of perfection."

This notion is a far cry from the individualism and emphasis on self-reliance characteristic of Roman law as contained in a considerably diluted form in the *droit écrit* of southern France, but it bears some strong kinship (if we may note this in passing) to the customary law of the north. In any case it shows the lawmaker as the molder of men and states; he "is, in all respects, an extraordinary man in the state." The reason is that his office is neither that of an executive (*souverain*) nor of a judge (*magistrat*). It is clear that what Rousseau has in mind is really the constituent power,[22] in the sense in which the lawmaker in the tradition of Lycurgus and Solon and *The Laws* of Plato is the builder of the political community. There is a contradiction here in Rousseau's thinking, as there often is; for the general will presumably continues to act as the source of some laws, though Rousseau's discussion of the legislator creates serious doubt whether he ever thought of the legislative power as a continuing activity in the political community. At the end of Book II, in a curious chapter dealing with the division of laws, he draws a distinction between the fundamental "political" laws (evidently the constitution), the civil laws, and criminal laws, all of which he refers in the last analysis to "the true constitution of the state," which is not (to quote his famous phrase) "graven on tablets of marble or brass, but on the hearts of the citizens."[23] This set of notions, which consists of "morality, custom, public opinion," is the "secret" concern of the great legislator; it forms the "immovable keystone" of the particular rules that the lawmaker formulates. And because this is so, the legislator cannot appeal to either force or rational argument, and he must therefore have recourse to an authority of a different order, "an authority which can lead without violence, and persuade without convincing." It is the appeal to the gods, the "intervention of heaven," as more particularly illustrated by the case of Lycurgus. But Rousseau also mentions specifically Calvin. This "divine reason" which rises above vulgar men is by the legislator imputed to the immortal gods.

It is not without interest that Rousseau here refers to Machiavelli, who in the *Discourses* had pointed out that there had not been an outstanding lawgiver in any country who had not had recourse to God.[24] But, Rousseau adds, not every man can appeal to the gods and be believed. The true miracle is *la grande âme du legislateur,* and only wisdom makes the laws endure. It is not a question of being an impostor; the political theorist and philosopher admires in such institutions "the great and powerful genius which presides over a lasting establishment." There is little doubt that the Napoleon who wrote at the end of his life that his laws would endure, rather than the glory of his battles, was a true pupil of Rousseau and of the ancients.

Rousseau was, of course, the great and universally admired *inspirateur* of the Jacobins.[25] And although they simplified and in simplifying distorted Rousseau's thought, the Jacobin creed that expressed itself in the revolutionary codes of 1793 and 1794 was Rousseauism in action, and even the *Terreur* still embodied the general will, or was believed to do so—a far cry from the systematic and "scientific" exploitation of anxiety and fear under modern totalitarianism. But Rousseau's stress on will and emotion, on the genius of the legislator and the patriotic sentiment of the citizen, was implemented and to some extent even superseded by the stress on rational discourse, the heritage of the philosophers of the eighteenth century. Within this context, the task of legislation appeared as calling for neither the mysterious working of the general will[26] nor the transcendent good fortune of the wisdom of a single great *nomothetes.* It appeared rather in the everyday garb of the common sense of the citizen, the common man of later American parlance, whose rational capacity was celebrated in ringing phrases by Thomas Paine.[27] To such writers—and let us not forget that indefatigable drafter of codes, Jeremy Bentham, whom the Jacobin revolutionaries hailed as one of theirs—the codification of law was indeed a good thing, because it would enable every man to read and understand the "principles of his conduct," as indeed Bonaparte himself phrased in one of his numerous comments to the *Conseil d'Etat.* This had been the sentiment of the radicals of the Convention when they demanded a new and simpler draft in 1793; and when Cambacérès introduced his new draft in September 1794 he stated in the introductory *Discours* that the committee had reduced the Code to precepts wherein everyone could find the rules for his conduct in civil life. It was a recurrent theme of Napoleon when he participated in the work of the *Conseil d'Etat*.[28]

Related to this idea was the more technical one that the judges ought to be left enough leeway to apply these principles of rational conduct. This criticism was leveled at the Civil Code, and Napoleon himself recognized it. In the discussion he himself said at one time that in general the project of the *Code Civil* did not leave enough latitude to the courts and seemed not sufficiently "dogmatic." What Bonaparte here means by "dogmatic" is, of course, this emphasis on principles, on "what is the end that the law wishes to attain." In short, to the rational man corresponds the rational judge who is not misled by legal technicalities in his search for true justice. "Injustice," to quote Napoleon once more, "can be found in judges because they are men; but it is against the nature of things that it should never be found in the law, and that the law should force the judge to be unjust against his own better judgment (*malgré lui*)."

The belief in rational man, more or less alike in all times and places, was not, to be sure, a peculiar thought of the Revolution; it was growing throughout the century. The idea, derived from it, that all those interested should be invited to participate in the making of a code of laws had made a great appeal to monarchs like Frederick the Great and his successor in Prussia. It was a kind of substitute for a representative assembly such as otherwise might, as in England, participate in an orderly way in the lawmaking. To start with, the drafting of these codes is often entrusted to philosophically trained and inspired laymen, rather than to lawyers, judges, or learned professors.[29] Christian von Wolff and Immanuel Kant were among the molders of the mind and thought of these men. The plans and projects of these laymen were then made available to a wider public of interested persons and to the general public.

The Prussian government published a draft code in 1787 and invited comments from all those interested; it even offered a prize for the best comment.[30] Once again we have the idea that laws are somehow moral precepts, a trend that Kant specifically applauded in his essay "What is Enlightenment?" in which we read: ". . . a head of state who favors freedom in the arts and sciences . . . understands that there is no danger in legislation permitting his subjects to make *public* use of their own reason and to submit *publicly* their thoughts regarding a better framing of such laws together with a frank criticism of existing legislation."[31]

The desire for simplicity is a central concern of the code makers of the period. In contrast to Montesquieu (and most of the British), who inclined to the view that the multiplicity of laws provided protection against royal absolutism—as of course it did for those whom the older feudal law favored—eighteenth-century rationalism wanted unity, clarity, simplicity. The natural-law doctrines developed in the preceding generations were now coming to fruition. The common sense that John Locke celebrated found its juristic echo in the doctrines of Christian Thomasius. A work like *Fundamenta juris naturae in quibus secernuntur principia honesti justi ac decori* (1705) inspired an interest in codification among princes. This was more especially true of Thomasius' own king, Frederick William I, the father of Frederick II, who in fact set up a commission for this purpose. To be sure, the work bogged down, but largely because Thomasius himself was not too happy about it, perhaps because of political apprehensions. In any case Thomasius, building on the foundation laid by Grotius and Pufendorf, sought to develop a complete system of law on the basis of a rational natural law capable of being comprehended by common sense (*sensus communis*). Anyone, he thought, could feel within himself what matters for the moral nature of man, and though morals and law should be clearly differentiated (along lines later made famous by Kant's distinction between the inner and the outer obligation, but in a crude form), ordinary human experience seems to him quite sufficient for the purpose of the general precepts in terms of which a system of law should be constructed. Like Hobbes and Rousseau, Thomasius considered the command of the legitimate authority the source of law (*lex* is the source of *jus*).[32] He was, in his very generality and lack of originality, a true son of the Enlightenment, a fighter for tolerance and religious freedom, a passionate enemy of every kind of prejudice from the belief in witches to that in the evidential value of torture. In turn, Christian von Wolff, who produced perhaps the most celebrated of the compendious and soporific systems of natural law,[33] strove to systematize the various antecedent trends; his was the inspiration not only of the Common Code for the Prussian Lands, but also of the Bavarian, Austrian, and related codes.

It is within this setting of ideas that the position of Frederick II must be seen and understood. As we said earlier, Bonaparte was animated by a vivid sense of rivalry with the great monarch to the East, as indeed with the legitimate rulers throughout Europe. It is well known how deeply he felt the problem of making his rule legitimate. Thus the sense of rivalry with enlightened absolutism gradually seems to take the place, in the thought of Napoleon, of the revolutionary inspiration. Would it be too much to say that the Civil Code is intended to do in the field of legislation what the marriage to the Hapsburg princess was to accomplish in the strictly dynastic realm? One does not wish to push any such reflections too far, but is it an accident that, in his notes as a young man, when he read Frederick's historical accounts (in 1788) he noted that Cocceji had edited the *code Frédéric*?[34] There is ample evidence that Napoleon, eager to excel the king on the battlefield, also recognized the king's often stated insistence on the importance of clear and simple laws. Thus we find that the Testament of 1752 opens with a discussion of *Rechtspflege,* of the cultivation of the law. Frederick, after recalling the confusion he had found in the law, states that he requested Chancellor Cocceji[35] to work out a reform. He adds: "It would be well, if princes would give special care to putting the right man into the office of Chancellor," for the king cannot attend to the judicial business. "To decide questions of law [as a judge] himself, is a task which no ruler can undertake"—this is the premise of Frederick's remarks. It ties in neatly with an aside of Napoleon's in the *Conseil d'Etat:* "Nothing more barbarous exists than the idea of the kings of France judging under a tree."[36]

The inspiration of Frederick and his penchant for the ideas of the Enlightenment came, of course, as everyone knows, in the first place from Voltaire. But it is perhaps even more interesting that at the very time (1749) when Cocceji was working on the draft of a code Frederick wrote an essay on "the Reasons for introducing and abolishing Laws"[37] that appears to be clearly in line with Montesquieu's *Spirit of the Laws,* which had appeared the previous year. The king speaks of the importance of relating laws to the "spirit" of a nation; he reviews the legislators of old, notably Lycurgus, Solon, the Twelve Tables, and Justinian; he refers to the efforts of Louis XIV to collect the laws, which gave rise to the Codex Ludovicensis. The essay closes with a sentiment typical of the more sober rationalists of the Enlightenment: "He who realizes that all men are neither good nor bad, and who rewards good acts above merit and punishes bad ones with lenience, he who shows forbearance for weaknesses and acts humanely toward everyone, acts as a sensible man should act." It was sentiments such as these that inspired the codification of the enlightened absolutism. Voltaire and Montesquieu and the English philosophers to whom they are akin thus affected the work of the Civil Code not only in various direct ways, as they helped mold particular provisions of the law, but also indirectly, because they helped shape the thought of rulers throughout Europe with whom Napoleon Bonaparte wished to be on an equal footing.

Actually, the Code had become an inescapable necessity through the very work of the Revolution. Not only had it strengthened the nation's consciousness of its unity but it had removed many of the vested local interests that had obstructed the unification of the law under the *Ancien Régime*. Moreover, the feudal law was gone.

Whether one agrees with Philippe Sagnac's classical analysis or not,[38] whether or not one therefore divides the period during which the Code evolved into two sharply separated periods, 1789–1795 and 1795–1804, during one of which the *esprit philosophique* reigns supreme, whereas during the other the *esprit juridique* is in the ascendant, whether or not one relates these to such dichotomies as liberty and authority, progress and reaction, it is clear that the ideological and philosophical background of the idea of a code combined with the urgent needs of a country revolutionized in its social and governmental structure and firmly united into one modern nation, to bring about the magnificent structure of the *Code Civil.* Its qualities of superior style and lucidity are the result of this combination of the old with the new, not as a patchwork of discordant elements, nor yet as a doctrinaire and mechanical uniformity, but as a living and organic whole. The fellowship (*Genossenschaft*) conceptions of the traditional customs (*droit coutumier*) are combined with the lordship (*dominium-Herrschaft*) conceptions of Roman law (as found, though somewhat altered, in the *droit écrit*), as are their respective equalitarianism and individualism, while the feudal and the canon law are largely superseded by the new spirit of citizenship in a modern nation. But unity calls for a certain largesse of spirit, for a tolerance of divergent notions, for a sense of accommodation. Between the divergent groups in the *Conseil d'Etat* the voice of moderation was that of Portalis, who at one point observed: "The spirit of moderation is the true spirit of the legislator; the political as well as the social good is always found between two extremes."[39]

But the idea of unity and simplicity was soon compromised by new argument and new gloss. Napoleon in 1807 had the gratification of having the Code called the Code Napoleon, thus joining the Justinians, the Louises, the Fredericks in the procession of great monarchical lawgivers. Not long afterwards, however, he commented a bit ruefully that the scribes had taken over once more: "The Code had hardly appeared when it was followed almost immediately, and as a supplement, by commentaries, explanations, developments, interpretations, and what not. . . . I was in the habit of saying to the *Conseil d'Etat:* Gentlemen, we have swept out the stable of Augeas; for Heaven's sake, let us not clutter it anew!" This has been the fate of the makers of codes at all times—that their work is merely the start for new transformations. Animated by the ideas of unity, order, common sense, they hope to build a permanent structure from the institutional accumulations of the past. But life, the life of the law, never stands still, and another day brings new problems and new attempts at solutions. One reason why the idea of a code seems so strange to us today is that we, deeply imbued with the sense of history as a never-ending chain, are far from the clarity, simplicity, and optimism of eighteenth-century rationalism. These provided both the ideology and the philosophy for the Civil Code, which remains as the most beautiful instance of this constructive spirit that we admire, but cannot emulate.

NOTES

[1] See Philippe Sagnac's classical treatment *La Législation Civile de la Révolution Française* (1789–1804). Summaries of this sort are found in most works on Napoleon I, notably Fisher, *Napoleon* (1913).

[2] See his Introduction to *Le Code Civil 1804–1904* XXX (1904). This work, published in 1904, contains numerous valuable articles, among which, for our purposes, Esmein, Boistel, Salcilbe, and Gény may be especially mentioned. It will hereafter be referred to as *Cent.* (Centenary volume).

[3] The work of the American Law Institute appears to be of this type.

[4] See Carl Becker, *The Heavenly City of the Eighteenth Century Philosophers* (1932); the idea of codification is, however, not fully recognized here.

[5] A. Esmein, "Originalité du Code Civil," *Cent.* 5, 18.

[6] *Id.,* at 20.

[7] *The Works of Francis Bacon,* Vol. II, 231 (ed. Basil Montagu, 1842).

[8] Ideology should not be confused with systems of ideas, when the test of truth is primary, as tends to be the view of Mannheim. Regarding this matter, see my paper "Political Philosophy and the Science of Politics" at the Conference on Political Philosophy at Northwestern University, to be published presently. Ideology is, typically, a system of ideas offering a criticism of existing society and suggesting a reform of it; a revolutionary ideology is one in which the reforms proposed are radical and revolutionary, and a totalitarian ideology is one in which both critique and change are total. This, at any rate, would seem the way of employing these words most concordant with prevailing usage.

[9] *Vom Beruf unserer Zeit für Gesetzgebung und Rechtswissenschaft* §7 (1814) and the comment by Saleilles, "Le Code Civil et la Méthode Historique" in *Cent.* 97 et seq.

[10] See especially Adolf Stoll, *Friedrich Karl von Savigny. Ein Bild seines Lebens,* in three volumes (1927, 1929, 1939) and Franz Zwiglmeyer, *Die Rechtslehre Savigny's* (1929). A balanced assessment is to be found also in Erik Wolf, *Grosse Deutsche Rechtsdenker,* Vol. II, 436–507 (2d ed. 1944).

[11] This is pointed out by Wolf, *op. cit. supra* note 10, at 476: "Den deutschrechtlichen, konservativen und volkstümlichen Gehalt erkannte er nicht."

[12] See F. A. Fenet, *Receuil Complet des Travaux Préparatoires du Code Civil,* Vol. I, II (in 16 vols.—1836–) (hereafter cited as Fenet): "Voyez le Code que le Convention prépare pour la grande famille de le nation comme le fruit de lá liberté. La Nation le recevra comme le garant de son bonheur; elle l'offrira un jour à tous les peuples . . ."

[13] J. J. Regis de Cambacérès (1753–1824).

[14] Fenet, Vol. I, 330 Jacqueminot stresses the code of Bonaparte, *id.* at 331.

[15] Fenet, Vol. I, 466–7: "Les lois ne sont pas de purs actes de puissance . . . qu'il faut être sobre de nouveautés en matière de legislation . . . qu'il serait absurde de se livrer à des idées absolues de perfection dans des choses qui ne sont pas susceptibles que d'une bonté relative . . ." The same point is made by Esmein, *supra* note 5, at 12–13.

[16] Robert Joseph Pothier (1699–1772); regarding him see the study by L. H. Dunoyer, *Blackstone et Pothier* (1927) and J. E. G. Montmorency's study in *Great Jurists of the World* (ed. S. J. MacDonald and E. Manson, 1914).

[17] Dunoyer in the *Encyclopaedia of the Social Sciences,* article "Pothier."

[18] One receives the most vivid impression of this relationship from the material published by Frédéric Masson under the title of *Napoléon Inconnu—Papiers inédits 1786–1793* (1895) in two vols. Napoleon in his youth often made lengthy and very revealing summaries of his readings. The volumes also include a defense Napoleon wrote of Rousseau's idea of a civil religion and of the adverse effects of Christian (Catholic) doctrine on a civil polity (against a certain Roustan); this piece is significant for our purpose here, because it shows the emotional attachment of Napoleon to Rousseau. Purest Rousseauism is also displayed by Bonaparte in a *Discours de Lyon* in which he deals more especially with the importance of emotion for politics and government in a very lively fashion; see Masson, *op. cit.,* Vol. II, 292–332. "J. J. l'auteur de l'Emile, du Contrat Social, cet homme profond et pénétrant . . ." *Id.,* Vol. I, 150.

[19] This remark of Napoleon's is found in his comments on Rousseau's essay on *The Origin of Inequality,* Masson, *op. cit. supra* note 18, Vol. II, 286. For the totalitarian argument see J. L. Talmon, *The Rise of Totalitarian Democracy* (1952), especially Pts. I, III.

[20] "Ma gloire n'est pas d'avoir gagné quarante batailles . . . Ce que rien n'effacera, ce qui vivra éternellement, c'est mon (sic!) Code Civil, ce sont les procès-verbaux du Conseil d'Etat."

[21] I cannot attempt here to sum up Rousseau's political thought; see my *Inevitable Peace* (1948) for the development of those aspects bearing on natural law, the common man, and peace. See also Charles W. Hendel, *Jean-Jacques Rousseau—Moralist* (1934) and Robert Derathé, *Jean-Jacques Rousseau et la Science Politique de son Temps* (1950) for the more recent interpretation of Rousseau as in many ways strongly in the tradition of eighteenth-century rationalism. References to Rousseau will be to the 20-volume edition *Oeuvres de J. J. Rousseau* (Werdet et Lequien Fils 1827). The *Contrat Social* is found in Vol. V. Most of the quotations are from Bk. II, Ch. VII.

[22] Rousseau says at the end of Book II of the *Contrat Social* that he is in that work only

concerned with "political" laws (constitutional, in our parlance); hence technically the *Contrat Social* does not bear upon the Civil Code. It does bear, however, upon the idea of codification, with which we are here dealing. For the doctrine of the constituent power see *Constitutional Government and Democracy,* Chs. VII and VIII (new ed. 1950).

[23] " . . . une quatriême loi . . . qui ne se grave ni sur le marbre, ni sur l'airain, mais dans les coeurs des citoyens; qui fait le véritable constitution de l'Etat. . . . " Vol. III, p. 159.

[24] *Discorsi sopra la Prima Deca di Tito Livio,* Bk. I, Ch. 11. This is, of course, an ancient idea. Plato's notion of a "noble lie" belongs here. Cicero restated it in Roman perspective. And of course the more recent tendency to refer to nature (when used dogmatically as in Marxism) is merely the substitution of yet another deity.

[25] See Crane Brinton, *The Jacobins* (1930).

[26] See Friedrich, *Inevitable Peace* 172 et seq. for an analysis of the complexities of the doctrine of the general will.

[27] See e.g. Thomas Paine, *Common Sense* (in Patriots Edition, 1925, Vol. II), and *The Rights of Man* (*ibid.,* Vols. VI–VII). For an evaluation in perspective see my *New Image of the Common Man* (1941, 1951).

[28] Besides the record of the *Conseil d'Etat* as given in Fenet, and in Locré, *La Législation Civile, commerciale, et criminelle de la France* (in 31 vols., 1827). See also the anonymous *Mémoires sur le Consulat 1799–1804* (actually by Comte A. C. Thibaudeau) published in 1827; Ch. XIX deals with the *Code Civil* and gives an interesting critique of the published record, which in spite of its inaccuracies it defends against the charge of being subservient to Napoleon.

[29] See for this Ch. XIII of my *Philosophie des Rechts in historischer Perspektive* (1955), and for fuller accounts Franz Wieacker, *Privatsrechtsgeschichte der Neuzeit,* Part III, §14–18 (1952); S. Thieme, *Das Naturrecht und die europäische Privatrechtsgeschichte* (1947).

[30] These have been published as *Materialien zum Allgemeinen Landrecht.*

[31] See my *Philosophy of Kant* 139 (1949) and *Werke,* Vol. IV, p. 175 (ed. E. Cassirer).

[32] See my study, cited *supra* note 29, Ch. XIII for more detailed references. Cf. also Erik Wolf, *op. cit. supra* note 10, Vol II, 339–393.

[33] Christian von Wolff (1679–1754), *Jus naturae methodo scientifico pertractatum,* Bk. I, Ch. 1, §26 (1748/9, 9 volumes).

[34] Masson, *op. cit. supra* note 18, Vol. I, 427. Masson says that he does not know which work Bonaparte had been reading. It seems reasonably clear that he read *Histoire de mon temps* and *Histoire de la Guerre de 7 Ans,* and this is the more probable since these two works were readily available. They form Vols. I–III of the *Oeuvres Posthumes de Frédéric II* published in Berlin 1789. There is an English version available.

[35] See *Werke,* Vol. VII, pp. 118–19. Cf. also Max Springer, *Die Cocceijische Justizreform* (1910) and the works cited *supra* note 29.

[36] Thibaudeau, *op. cit. supra* note 28 at 425.

[37] *Oeuvres de Frédéric le Grand,* Vol. IX, 11 et seq. (1846 and later). "Dissertation sur les Raisons d'Etablir ou Abroger les Lois." This essay was prepared for and read to the Berlin Academy of Sciences in 1750. It was later edited slightly by the king.

[38] See *op. cit. supra* note 1, 381–398.

[39] See Locré, *op. cit. supra* note 28, Vol. I, 327. Albert Sorel, *op. cit. supra* note 2, at XIX, observes: "Le code civil, c'est la jurisprudence du droit romain et l'usage des coutumes combinés ensemble et adaptés a la Declaration des droits de l'Homme, selon les moeurs, convenances, et conditions de la nation française."

2

The Grand Outlines of the Code

ANDRÉ TUNC

1. THE promulgation of the Civil Code in the year 1804 is, historically, the legislative response to a desire expressed during many centuries by the French people.[1]

Traditionally, during French history, there had been some distrust of the administration of justice. Justice had been rendered first by lords in a more or less arbitrary fashion. The royal authority, later on, established regular courts charged with rendering justice according to law, and it engaged in a fight against the seignorial courts that led to their disappearance. Still, if there was great confidence in the justice of the king, there often was less confidence in the royal officers and even in the royal judges. People complained quite commonly that the law was so confused that nobody, including the judges, was able to know it with certainty, and that they were at the mercy of the courts. On the eve of the Revolution the dictum was still valid: God save us from the equity of the courts—Dieu nous protège de l'équité des Parlements!

In England, protection against an arbitrary administration of justice was sought in two rules that became fundamental principles of the common law: the rule of *stare decisis* and the rule that prescribes the determination of the facts by a jury after public trial.

In France also those protections were sought. But appeal was made very early to the idea that the law should be written, and written in clear and ordinary language, so that everybody should know his rights and that no discretion should be left to the judge. As early as 1453 Charles VII gave satisfaction to this popular desire

ANDRÉ TUNC *is Professor of Law at the University of Grenoble*

when he ordered a compilation of the customs.[2] The task was not immediately accomplished. In the *Etats Généraux* of 1484 the *Tiers Ordre* requested again that the customs be expressed in written form. This was done, as far as most of the customs were concerned, only at the beginning of the sixteenth century.[3] And the criticisms that some legal writers, among them Charles Dumoulin and Bertrand d'Argentré, directed at this first version of the customs led to a revision of most of them in the following fifty or sixty years.[4]

2. From that time—the sixteenth century—a codification was sought for an additional purpose: to unify the law of France.[5] The customs were local or, at most, regional. As Voltaire remarked two centuries later in a famous sentence, the traveler changed laws as often as he changed horses. No valid reason could be given for this diversity. Some forward-looking writers said that codification was the key not only to protection against arbitrary action, and to clarity of the law, but also to its unification. They received such popular support that the *Etats Généraux* of 1560, at the request of the *Tiers Ordre,* expressed the wish that a restatement be made of the rules that should henceforth be kept and observed by the subjects of the king, and similar wishes were expressed, sometimes by all three *Ordres,* in 1576, 1614, and at later dates.[6]

3. The popular desire was not to receive a complete satisfaction before 1804. Some earlier achievements, however, should not be forgotten. As Bonaparte was to do a hundred and thirty-five years later, Louis XIV appointed, in 1665, a commission of codification and personally attended some of its meetings.[7] The result was the Great Ordinances of Colbert. It is true that Colbert and Louis XIV did not dare to deal with private law and codified only admiralty, adjective law, criminal law, and commercial law. In the eighteenth century, however, Chancellor Daguesseau undertook a complete codification of the law and obtained from the king, between 1731 and 1747, three important ordinances on donations, successions, and

substitutions.[8] If he did not succeed in codifying the law on a broader scale, the limitations of his achievements did not come from a change of mind on his part, nor from a lack of popular support. Nor did they come from obstacles raised by the king. They came only from the opposition of the *Parlements,* which felt that codification would be an encroachment on their privileges.[9]

4. Throughout the long and intricate Revolution codification remained a constant objective of the successive governments.[10] The Constituent Assembly in 1790, the Convention in 1793 and 1794, and the *Directoire* in 1796 all promised the French people that they would draw up a code, and some even appointed commissions for that task. Furthermore, they actually passed some very important and comprehensive statutes. Finally, in 1800, the First Consul, Bonaparte, appointed and led the commissions that drew up the Civil Code.[11]

5. In the light of this perspective the Code appears, not as the result of an arbitrary decision, as it is too often thought of, but as the fulfillment of a promise made to the French people both by their kings and by their revolutionary governments. It appears as the result of a long evolution, an evolution that runs from the earliest times of feudalism to the eve of the Empire, through royal absolutism and the Revolution. Bonaparte saw it as a token of peace, as an instrument of reconciliation among the citizens.

Two questions, then, emerge and require an answer. First, what is the French concept of a codification? What were the French people expecting from codification and how did they conceive the desired codification? Secondly, what is the position of the Code, an instrument of peace and reconciliation, between traditional law and revolutionary law? Those are the two questions that we shall try to answer. Our answers should not be personal ones. Both questions were answered by Portalis in his marvelous *Discours Préliminaire,* and nobody can expect to find a better guide to the Code or a more powerful master in the process of codification.[12]

I. THE FRENCH CONCEPT OF CODIFICATION

6. The need for a Code as an instrument of unification of the law was a temporary one. What a French lawyer sees as the permanent basis of a Code, and what David Dudley Field sees in the same light,[13] is the principle that was also historically its first justification: that the law should be clear and should be stated in written form, so that, as far as possible, every citizen may know what his rights and his duties are. Only by such clarity can litigation be decreased,[14] injustices avoided, and freedoms preserved. This idea appears in Article 4 of the Declaration of Rights of 1791: "Freedom consists in doing those things that do not harm others; therefore the exercise of the natural rights of each man has no limits other than those that ensure to other members of society enjoyment of those same rights. *These limits can be determined only by statute.*"[15]

7. Portalis, it is true, while stressing the impact of law on society,[16] understood very clearly that the law could not usually be so clear as to be known fully by the layman.[17] Still, the idea that the law should be so clear as to be known by the citizen has practical value. Those engaged in the practice of law in France are often surprised to see to what extent the law is known by ordinary people, or at least the law of property by the owners of land and persons living in the country, the laws of business by businessmen, and the law of the family by everybody. People are often ignorant of the details and sometimes mistaken. On the whole, however, they have a surprising knowledge of the law. The reason may be that the Frenchman likes to exercise his rights and therefore makes the effort necessary to know them. It may be that the law of property has not undergone any important change from 1804, and that it is therefore learned by country children just as they learn how to farm land and take care of animals. It may be that French law is clear enough for popular comprehension, if we disregard many recent statutes, often poorly drafted or at least very complicated, and wisely left outside the Code. Whatever the reason, the result is there: the idea that the

law should be accessible to everybody and generally known has to a great extent materialized. In exceptional circumstances the idea may even recover the political force that it had from the very beginning. If an arbitrary measure is taken by the government, public opinion will be very sensitive to legal arguments and will require that the legal process be followed and the law strictly observed by everybody.

8. This justification of a code may explain the traditional French approach to codification. A code, a Frenchman thinks, should be complete in its field; it should lay down general rules; and it should arrange them logically. These are, in fact three of the most important features of the Civil Code. We shall consider them separately. A fourth important feature should also be mentioned: viz., the fact that the Code is grounded on experience.

9. (A) A code should be complete in its field. There is no need to elaborate on this point. If the law should be clearly stated in a written document, this document should be complete, lest it be misleading.

10. From this point of view the Civil Code as enacted in 1804 was certainly satisfactory. The law of persons, including the law of the family; the law of property, including the law of mortgages; the law of torts and of contracts and the specific rules governing all the common contracts; the law of donations and the law of successions, were all encompassed within its 2,281 articles. Nor did any serious gap appear when the Code actually came to be applied. Probably one matter only had not been dealt with in the Code that should have been: the law of mines, which, only referred to in Article 552, required a special statute as early as 1810. The Code was so complete that the legislature, when it sought to draft a rural code during the nineteenth century, could hardly find any matter not already contained in the Civil Code.

11. It should, however, be pointed out that revision of the Code—which has, in fact, been entrusted to a Commission since 1945—now appears highly desirable because of the number of important

statutes passed during the nineteenth and twentieth centuries and left outside the Code. The present situation is not so unfortunate as it might be, for many publishers present in a single volume the text of the Code and the text of the relevant private law statutes. In fact, the yearly *Code civil* published by *Librairie Dalloz* is a very satisfactory working tool. Still, the task of giving a clear and complete statement of the law should not be left to publishers; it is the duty of the legislature itself.

12. (B) A code, in the traditional French approach, should also in the main state general rules. A well-drafted code should not contain too many detailed provisions or too many exceptions to the principal rules. "L'office de la loi," Portalis wrote, "est de fixer, par de grandes vues, les maximes générales du droit; d'établir des principes féconds en conséquences, et non de descendre dans le détail des questions qui peuvent naître sur chaque matière."[18] Such general rules are considered in France to be the best technical means of preventing litigation by stating to the ordinary citizen what he may and what he may not do, as well as the best means of resolving litigation when it does arise. Portalis was even obliged to defend the draft of the Commission against the popular feeling that a code should not have more than a few hundred articles.[19]

The justifications for this approach are aptly expressed by Portalis.[20] First, a too bulky code would not be clear enough. Conciseness is a factor of clarity. More important, however, is the consideration that the legislature cannot reasonably hope to foresee all the applications of the basic principles it wishes to embody. If it tried to foresee everything it would probably foresee circumstances that do not arise, and thus leave the parties and the judge, for the decision of actual difficulties, with a bulk of details and exceptions very difficult to use. Of equal importance is a last consideration: the legislature should not "bind the action of the future and oppose the course of human events."[21] Only in general rules can sufficient flexibility be found. That an American scholar could write in 1940 that the Code "left open many avenues for growth and change, as new pressures and new ethical standards emerged in French society,"[22] should be gratifying to the memory of Portalis, for that was his express desire.

13. These views may appear strange in the United States, where the famous words of Justice Holmes, "General propositions do not decide concrete cases," are so often quoted to mean that a code is unworkable. Yet these ideas represent daily experience for all civilians. The article requiring a man to be at least eighteen years old and a woman at least fifteen before contracting marriage (Article 144) is a general rule that has governed all marriages for one hundred and fifty years without the slightest difficulty. The article preventing anybody from entering into a second marriage before the dissolution of the first (Article 146) is also as certain as possible if the time of the dissolution of marriage is clearly defined in the law.

It is true that one can also find in the Code extraordinarily broad statements, such as the one in Article 146: "There is no marriage when there is no consent." Such statements can be found either as general explanations of more precise rules—the law of duress, for instance, is made precise in Articles 1111–1115—or where the draftsmen felt that precision was impossible and that decision should necessarily be left, in any concrete set of circumstances, to the courts. The rule of Article 146, for instance, governs the marriage of insane persons. But there are various mental diseases that alter the ability to consent. These sicknesses are of various degrees. A person may have periods of insanity alternating with periods of sanity of various length. All these particular circumstances cannot, it is true, be decided upon by general rules. But neither can they be decided by detailed statutory rules or by precedents. Any case of this kind raises a question of fact—whether there was consent—and must be decided on the basis of its particular merits and only by remote application of a rule of law, whatever its form.

14. Even if we disregard these exceptionally broad rules designed for exceptional circumstances in which no authority can give the

judge a reasonable ruling, the codification of law in general rules leaves the courts with a specific responsibility, which Portalis feels obliged to stress at some length. The Revolutionary trend was to strip the courts of any power except mere application of the statute.[23] Portalis understood that this view was unrealistic, and he tried to balance the task of the legislature and that of the courts.[24]

Quite normally, general rules apply to concrete circumstances so easily that no litigation arises. Many provisions of the Code settled problems that had been discussed for years or even centuries and did it so clearly that these matters ceased to be problems.

In many cases, however, the application of the general rules to concrete circumstances reveals a difficulty. The task of the courts is then to penetrate the spirit of the rules in order to apply or to extend the proper one to the case, so as to bring about the solution that would have been desired, or, if necessary, the one that would be desired today, by the legislator. Such is Portalis' view: "L'office de la loi est de fixer, par de grandes vues, les maximes générales du droit; d'établir des principes féconds en conséquences, et non de descendre dans le détail des questions qui peuvent naître sur chaque matière. *C'est au magistrat et au jurisconsulte, pénétrés de l'esprit général des lois, à en diriger l'application.*"[25] "Il y a une science pour les législateurs, comme il y en a une pour les magistrats; et l'une ne ressemble pas à l'autre. La science du législateur consiste à trouver dans chaque matière, les principes les plus favorables au droit commun: *la science du magistrat est de mettre ces principes en action, de les ramifier, de les étendre par une application sage et raisonnée, aux hypothèses privées.*"[26]

In thus applying the law, the courts create a new body of law, although a secondary one. For it is very clear that, for Portalis, precedents should usually be respected. He draws the contrast between a nation that respects its judicial precedents and Turkey, where the *bacha,* to the terror of his subjects, could then decide cases arbitrarily.[27] Obedience to precedents, however, should not be servile. For this secondary body of law, this "supplement to the statute," is in the process of being made and should be tested every day by practical experience. Every day a concrete case will suggest a new rule that may appear unfortunate or unsound in the light of tomorrow's case.[28]

The secondary place of the law made by judges and lawyers, and its relationship to the statute law, must be well understood. It is a subordinate body of law developing "beside the sanctuary of the statutes and under the control of the legislature."[29] The task of this living law is threefold. First, by developing the full impact of general rules on concrete circumstances it adds to the statutory rules a precision, a sharpness, that its draftsmen, for the reasons already explained, could not give them. Secondly, it will fill, year by year, the gaps of the Code: "c'est à l'expérience à combler successivement les vides que nous laissons. Les codes des peuples *se font avec le temps;* mais, à proprement parler, *on ne les fait pas.*"[30] Finally, it will adjust the Code, to the extent consistent with the respect due to its provisions, to new social circumstances.[31]

15. If one seeks to find to what extent Portalis' conceptions of the relations between statutory law and judge-made law materialized in practice, one cannot fail again to admire the genius of that jurist.

To give an example at random, one will find in Article 442 of the Code an enumeration of the persons who cannot be guardians. Foreigners are not expressly excluded. The question arose in the nineteenth century whether guardianship should not be reserved to citizens. The courts decided, on the contrary, that a foreigner could be a guardian. This is a typical ruling that added precision to the statutory article. But it was reasonable not to include the precision in the article itself, for ten precisions of the same kind could be added to any article, and a code of 22,810 articles instead of 2,281 would no longer be a code, not to mention the greater chance of contradictions among the various articles. Another question arose: somebody argued that the provision eliminating from guardianship the parties to a lawsuit on the result of which the condition of a minor or of part of his fortune may depend should be applied to anyone who, having been a party to such a lawsuit, might be prejudiced against the minor. The argument, although it had some merits, was rejected by the courts. Again a precision was thus added to the law, but one that could not reasonably be placed in the Code. It will appear from these examples that Portalis' conception of the respective tasks of the legislator and of the courts materialized and that it was a wise one. It will also appear that, usually, judge-made law is no more, as Portalis said, than a prolongation of the rules set forth in the articles of the Code. The courts make explicit the law in particular circumstances, according to the general rules declared by the legislator. As was said by Planiol, and nearly said by Portalis,[32] courts are legislators in particular cases: *les juges sont le législateur des cas particuliers.* Judge-made law is a "supplement to statutory law," and the French lawyer is able to find in the same pocket-size book, the *Code civil Dalloz,* the articles of the Code and, under each, the main relevant decisions.

It is true, finally, that the courts did to a certain extent adjust the law to modern circumstances. They did it, however, with the feeling of their subordinate position. They recognized that any important change in the law was the province of the legislature, not of the judge, the judge being only able, according to the words of the great American judge, "to legislate interstitially." This recognition did not prevent them from giving to the law a progressive and general adaptation to modern conditions of life. They even took great liberties with certain articles. They recognized, for example, the general validity of stipulations on behalf of a third party, notwithstanding the restrictive language of Article 1121. And, when the legislator, in the difficult matter of liability for damages "caused by a thing," failed to respond to the general wish for a new law, they used a few words found in Article 1384, *un lambeau de phrase,* as a platform from which to launch a completely new set of rules.

16. One may ask, if there is a case law supplementing the Code, has not the purpose of codification been defeated? The answer is clearly No. As has been previously said, many provisions of the

Code are so clear that they have not even been the subject matter of any litigation. There were no "particular circumstances" in which their application needed any clarification. As for the many provisions that did give rise to litigation, the courts found in the Code all the basic principles giving a lead to the decision of concrete cases. The discussion was therefore greatly clarified and narrowed. The question was often which of two principles, apparently conflicting on the given occasion, should prevail over the other; but at least the two principles themselves could not be a matter for discussion. The law had received a frame. Very little litigation, for instance, occurred on the basis of the fifty-two articles that embody the law of evidence. They put an end to the endless litigation under the ancient law in this field. So little litigation has arisen, in fact, that many provisions could now be eliminated.

17. (C) It would be unjust to the drafters of the Code not to stress their reliance on logic as an essential factor of the judicial process.[33]

Again, this view may cause some surprise in a country in which the famous words of Holmes are nearly always quoted with approval: "The life of the law has not been logic: it has been experience."

The drafters of the Code would certainly not have challenged the dictum that the life of the law has been experience. In fact, some of them said it in so many words. But they would have been surprised by the contrast drawn between logic and experience. For they certainly considered life as having logic. This is, I think, the French approach to law and to life. You may remember the proof of the existence of God offered by Voltaire: "I cannot believe that such a watch exists and that there is no watchmaker." For him, the world clearly ran as logically as a watch. It may not be inappropriate either to recall the cult of Queen Reason that was celebrated during the French Revolution. For the Reason thus deified was not the reason of the reasonable man, but the cold Reason of clarity and logic. Most French people would still consider that there is no possible contrast between life and logic. The religious minds will agree on this point with Voltaire, Bergson with Broussais, the psychoanalysts with Condillac. The dissent that may be voiced by Jean Paul Sartre seems not to be a clear one; and the physicists, however fascinated by the apparently fortuitous internal life of the atom, will agree that at the human level life seems governed by logical rules. In the field of law the draftsmen of the Code certainly considered that the natural development of any legal system leads it to a point of logical consistency at which it can be codified.[34] A code, to them, was not a mere collection of rules, but a collection of rules with such inner consistency that logical reasoning could be a part of legal reasoning.

18. Although many authorities in the common-law world took another view, it may be submitted, with respect, that the view of the drafters of the Code was a sound one.[35] Logic should be an important factor in the development of law, and it can play a much more important role in the judicial process, both in civilian countries and in common-law countries, than is usually admitted. Only logic brings clarity and justice. The question whether a particular set of circumstances should be governed by precedent A or precedent B (or by Article A or Article B) is of no consequence if precedents A and B (or Articles A and B) are logically consistent. The question will not even arise. Litigation will arise, on the contrary, if the precedents or articles are inconsistent. The decision will even be a third precedent that will make the law more complicated than it was. Logic, therefore, is an essential need of law, as of any other intellectual experience, and it is submitted that it would do injustice to the common law, as well as to the civil law, to consider them as collections of rules without connection and without consistency. With different techniques, each of these legal systems forms a co-ordinated body of orderly organized rules.

19. The French lawyer, it may be true, will give more importance to logic than the common lawyer. In very happy terms Dean Roscoe Pound has characterized the common lawyer's frame of mind as

"a frame of mind which habitually looks at things in the concrete, not in the abstract; which puts its faith in experience rather than in abstractions; . . . which prefers to go forward cautiously on the basis of experience from this case or that case to the next case, as justice in each case seems to require, instead of seeking to refer everything back to supposed universals; . . . the frame of mind behind the sure-footed Anglo-Saxon habit of dealing with things as they arise instead of anticipating them by abstract universal formulas."[36] The French lawyer, on the contrary, as Dean Pound has cogently stated in other writings, looks at the articles of the Code not as mere rulings, but as particular expressions of more general rules.[37] Therefore, if no express answer to a certain problem is found in the Code, it is not improper to consider various articles in order to induce from them a more general rule and to apply this rule if it can give a solution, or, if not, to combine it with other rules to arrive at a solution. It has sometimes been said that articles of a code are not only law, but sources of law.[38] This is true, not only in the sense that the courts may, by deduction, decide on the implications of a certain article, but also in the sense that the courts may, if necessary, use induction to discover the general rules implied in the provisions of a code and then, reverting to deduction, develop the full potential of these rules in the solution of the problem at hand. If all the rules were sound and no mistake was made in the reasoning, the result should be fortunate. If it fails to be so, the reason may be only that one of the rules is not in accord with social needs. But in that event it should be amended, not only in the particular circumstances of the case, but more generally. To respond to modern conditions of life the French courts may sometimes slightly distort the will of the drafters of the Code—although they will consider that the primary responsibility for amendment rests with the legislator—but they will always try to maintain the consistency of the solutions and the logical value of the body of law with which they are entrusted.

19. (D) No contrast, therefore, should be drawn, in the French approach, between logic and experience. And if the Code is a work

of logic, it is also, and in the main, a work of experience. The draftsmen never meant to create a new law. They wanted only to restate the law, having to make a choice on the basis of experience when the Revolutionary law was at variance with the previous law. "Les codes des peuples *se font avec le temps,*" Portalis wrote in a passage already cited, "mais, à proprement parler, *on ne les fait pas*";[39] codes require time to be made, but, actually, one does not make them. And elsewhere: "Il est utile de conserver tout ce qu'il n'est pas nécessaire de détruire: les lois doivent ménager les habitudes, quand ces habitudes ne sont pas des vices. On raisonne trop souvent comme si le genre humain finissait et commençait à chaque instant, sans aucune sorte de communication entre une génération et celle qui la remplace."[40]

The formulas are striking, and Portalis' elaboration of them is most convincing. "Laws are not pure acts of will; they are acts of wisdom, of justice, and of reason. The legislator does not so much exercise a power as fulfill a sacred trust. One ought never to forget that laws are made for men, not men for laws; that they must be adapted to the character, to the habits, to the situation of the people for whom they are drafted; that one ought to be chary of innovations in matters of legislation, for if it is possible, in a new institution, to calculate the merits that theory may promise us, it is not possible to know all the disadvantages, which only experience will reveal; that the good ought to be kept if the better is dubious; that in correcting abuses, one must also foresee the dangers of the correction itself; that it would be absurd to indulge in absolute ideas of perfection in matters capable of a relative value only. . . ."[41]

The spirit of the French Revolution may have been a spirit of pride, justified to a certain extent—a spirit of discovery of a new world. Portalis' spirit appears, on the contrary, to have been one of moderation. "He governs badly who governs too much," he wrote, almost in Jefferson's words.[42] And elsewhere: "We have too much indulged, in recent times, in changes and reforms; if in matters of institutions and laws the periods of ignorance witness abuses, the periods of philosophy and enlightenment too often witness excesses."[43] In 1804 the period of illumination was over, and some disillusionment had already been experienced. The Revolution, however, was not repudiated. For Portalis, as well as for Bonaparte, France needed a return to normality, not a return to the *Ancien Régime*. The Revolution had been excessive, not unsound. Its moral conquests deserved consolidation, a consolidation based on the avoidance of any radicalism.[44]

The drafting of a code was, then, a particularly difficult task. Portalis knew that codes must be based on experience; but France's recent experience had been twofold. "Laws must be adapted to the character, to the habits, to the situation of the people for whom they are drafted." But the French people had beloved excessively their kings and their Revolutionary rulers—and been somewhat disappointed by both; for a hierarchical society they had substituted a society based on equality[45]—and discovered the danger of a direct popular government; they had persecuted religion, which they had previously respected—and been horrified by, for example, the great number of easy divorces; they had created a new order—and become anxious to find some peace. Both the Revolution and the tradition were a part of the immediate heritage of the French people. The drafters of the Code were anxious to keep the best of each.

II. BETWEEN REVOLUTION AND TRADITION

20. If the historical context of the Code placed on its draftsmen an exceptional responsibility, it provided them also with exceptional experience. They had experienced the law of ancient France and the law of the Revolution, which had been, in certain fields, a wide departure. They did not feel any propensity to innovations: they were in a period of disillusionment. For the same reason they were not prejudiced for or against any of the previous experiences. The past few years had been rich in achievements and heavy in errors. Matured as the draftsmen were by these years of trial and efforts, they were ready to admit any rule or any philosophy that

would seem to them, on the basis of the facts, the best suited to the French people. This pragmatic approach explains why in certain matters they kept the traditional views, why elsewhere they appear ardent supporters of the Revolution, and why on many points they tried to work out a compromise between the different views.

21. The Code, after a few introductory articles on law and its application, is divided into three parts according to a logical scheme. The first part deals with persons, the second with goods considered in themselves, and the third with the means of acquiring a right in goods, either by succession or donation, by contract or matrimonial arrangement. Torts and quasi contracts are the subject of a few articles after the treatment of contracts. The various usual contracts are considered separately after contracts in general. Legal and conventional mortgages, and after them limitations, are considered at the end of this last part.

22. One of the first problems that the drafters had to consider was the organization of records of births, marriages, divorces, and deaths.

For centuries these records had been kept by the Roman Catholic Church. Without any spirit of hostility toward the Church, but considering the diversity of religions in France and the right of everybody not to profess any religion, the draftsmen decided to maintain the public organization of records set up by the Revolution in 1791–1792.[46] In every city the mayor or someone under his control is in charge of the records, copies of which may be obtained according to certain rules. These records are the only official evidence of births, marriages, divorces, and deaths. The idea was certainly most reasonable, and it seems not to have been challenged.

23. The first main institution dealt with by the Code was marriage. In this matter also, they had to make a decision between the two experiences of France. Marriage as such had never been attacked by the Revolution. But it had been diminished in importance by being secularized; it had been weakened by the disappearance of family control over it and by the introduction of divorce, which very quickly led to an abuse of divorce.[47]

The drafters of the Code regarded the family as the fundamental institution of a civilized society; an institution imposed by nature itself, but still one that needed to be protected against human passions and weaknesses. Considering again the diversity in the religious feelings of the French people, they kept the secularized view of marriage. Consequently, and for the purpose of having a public and uniform system of records, they reserved to public officers—viz., the mayor of the city or an alternate—the right to celebrate marriage under the law. Priests and ministers of the various cults may, of course, perform religious marriages, but those marriages are disregarded by the law, and in order to avoid misunderstandings they may not be celebrated before the official marriage.

24. The control of families over prospective marriages had become—against the desire of the Church—very strong during the last centuries of the *Ancien Régime.* A son could not contract marriage against the will of his parents before he was thirty years of age, a daughter before she was twenty-five. Even then marriage could not be performed without the consent of the parents if the parents had not been notified by two "respectful summonses." The Revolution, on the other hand, had considered that families could not prevent even an inconsiderate marriage when the children had reached the age of majority. All control over children of twenty-one or older was eliminated.

It is interesting to find in the Code a restoration, at least a partial one, of the traditional view of the family. A son cannot contract marriage against the will of his parents if he is not twenty-five years old; before thirty he will have to notify his parents in three "respectful and formal acts." After that age one of these acts will still remain necessary. For a daughter, the corresponding ages are twenty-one and twenty-five. The law on this point remained in effect until 1907. In that year and in 1922, 1927, and 1933 statutes were enacted that gradually returned the French law to the Revolutionary rule.

25. The organization of the family is one of the matters on which the draftsmen of the Code did not have the benefit of a double

experience. The family of the *Ancien Régime* had been organized under the strong authority of the husband, heir of the powers of the old *paterfamilias*. The trend over the centuries had been to give greater power to the husband over his wife. The Revolution, it is true, considered in the abstract that women were equal to men. Few practical consequences, however, were derived from this view.[48]

The drafters of the Code did not see any reason to change the law. Indeed, Bonaparte's authoritarianism went very far in the idea that the married woman should be subordinated to her husband. The Code expressly states that she owes him obedience. Furthermore she is made incapable of almost any act without the written consent of her husband: she can neither sell, give, or mortgage, nor buy, or even receive by gratuitous title. On all these points, except for some changes of small effect, her condition was not changed by statute until 1938 and 1942.

26. The wife's condition was also subordinate in the field of property relations. The legal arrangement creates a community property that receives all the earnings of the spouses—an arrangement, it must be underlined, usually favorable to the wife. The husband, however, chief of the family, is also the chief of the community, the idea being that he has normally more experience in business than his wife. In 1804 he received almost all power over the community property. He was even given the power of administering his wife's separate property—a power confined to mere administration. The protections given to the wife by the law were purely passive ones. Institutions such as the legal mortgage given to her on her husband's immovable property partly restored her, however, to a position of partnership; and a statute of 1942 restored her, if not to equality with the husband, at least to a more reasonable position.

27. A very important matter on which the drafters of the Code had to pass was the question of divorce.

The *Ancien Régime* had authorized only separation from bed

and board. The Revolution had had much experience with divorce, including divorce by mutual agreement, and had had to recognize, as is often said, that "the door open to divorce is the door open to abuse of divorce."[49]

The matter was very carefully considered by the draftsmen of the Code. Portalis gives it twelve pages out of the forty-two that he devotes to special matters.[50] He considers marriage to be, by reason of its purpose, a perpetual contract. The laws, however, should never be perfectionist beyond the capacities of the people that they govern. The question is not whether divorce in itself is good or bad, but whether it should be permitted in the given circumstances.

The drafters answered it in the affirmative. Diversity of religious views permits many persons to seek divorce if they desire it. The legislature should not, then, oblige unhappy spouses to live together for life, or even to live separate, unable to contract a more fortunate union. The legislator should, however, for the sake of the people, apply some check to the passions. "The most sacred of contracts should not become the toy of caprice." Many of the grounds for divorce accepted by the Revolution were therefore rejected. The only grounds kept were adultery, condemnation to an exceptionally severe and "infamous" punishment, and excesses, cruel treatment, or serious insult. The procedure was made a long and somewhat discouraging one. The general idea, as expressed by Portalis, was to protect marriage against an abuse of divorce: *on va au mal par une pente rapide; on ne retourne au bien qu' avec effort.*

Under the personal pressure of Bonaparte divorce by mutual agreement was introduced in the final text of the Code, but only as a means of keeping private an actual ground for divorce. It was very far from a divorce at will. It was acceptable only under certain conditions of age, after two years of marriage and not more than twenty, with the consent of the parents of the spouses or with the "respectful and formal acts" required for a marriage. The parties had to make provisions for education of the children and for the support of the wife. They were obliged to appear, assisted by two notaries, before a judge who would try to reconcile them. The same procedure was repeated four times, the parents having, each time, renewed their consent in a public act. Finally, one year after the first appearance before the judge, a last attempt of reconciliation was to be made by the judge and two friends of each spouse—friends at least fifty years old. A new marriage could not be contracted until six years later. One half of the property of each of the spouses was immediately to be devoted to the children.

After repeal in 1816, divorce was reintroduced in 1884, the approach of the legislator remaining that of the original drafters. Only divorce by mutual agreement was not reintroduced, being too complicated and too costly, as regulated, to be practiced.

28. In dealing with property the draftsmen took over the clear concepts of the Revolution.[51]

Feudalism can be characterized as a hierarchy of persons tied to a hierarchy of lands or of rights in land. No trace of feudalism appears in the Code. The Code regulates, on the one hand, persons who are the subjects of rights and are equal[52] and, on the other hand, things, which are the objects of rights and subject to no other distinction than the physical one between movable and immovable property. The normal relationship between persons and things is ownership, which is a complete, absolute, free, and simple right. It is true that mere usufructs or servitudes are possible, but they never involve a personal duty on the part of the persons who have only a limited right in a thing. The Code expressly states that a servitude "is a charge laid on an estate for the use and utility of another estate belonging to another owner" (Article 637) and that "servitudes do not establish any pre-eminence of an estate over another" (Article 638). The Louisiana Civil Code adds: "One of the characteristics of a servitude is, that it does not oblige the owner of the estate subject to it to do anything, but to abstain from doing a particular thing, or to permit a certain thing to be done on his estate" (Article 655). The Code therefore adopted completely, in this field, the Revolutionary approach, which had rid the French law of property of all the previous complications inherent in feudalism. It failed, however, to maintain the Revolutionary statutes that had organized a system of publicity by registration of all conveyances of immovable property. The gap thus left was filled only partially by the Code of Practice, and more fully by statutes in 1855 and 1935.

29. The Revolutionary approach was also kept in the field of successions and donations.[53]

Three kinds of property had been previously distinguished in the estate and subjected to particular rules: the *fiefs et alleux nobles* on one hand, the *meubles et acquêts* on the other, and finally the *propres*. The Revolution had unified the rules governing all the parts of estates and abrogated the privileges of the firstborn and of the males that were the rule as far as *fiefs et alleux nobles* were concerned. It also appears to have favored as much as possible the younger generations.

The drafters of the Code maintained the basic idea of equality among all persons that are of the same degree of kindred. The estate is devolved according to the assumed wishes of the defunct: to his children and grandchildren if he has any; if not, to his parents, brothers, and sisters and, in default of them, his grandparents; and, finally, if he does not have any grandparents, to his cousins.

Wills are possible. Even an informal will is perfectly valid as long as it is entirely written, dated, and signed by the hand of the testator (Article 970). Freedom of will or of donation is, however, far from complete. The family must be protected against excessive liberalities. A parent may not bring about any important inequality among his children by means of donations and legacies. A person who leaves one child may therefore dispose of only one half of his estate: if he leaves two children, one third; and if three or more children, one fourth (Article 913). Legacies with the duty in the legatee to keep the object of the legacy and transmit it to somebody else at his death (substitutions) are as a rule prohibited (Article 896), except within very narrow limits (Articles 1048, 1049). Properties must be free from any kind of restraint.

The spouse was not made an heir unless the defunct did not leave any child or grandchild, parent or grandparent, or cousin up to the twelfth degree. The drafters of the Code professed the traditional idea that properties should be kept in the family. They considered, therefore, that it should be left to each spouse to make sufficient donations or legacies to the other. They even provided for a greater freedom for gratuitous disposition made for the benefit of a spouse. They thought, furthermore, that the division of community property at the death of one spouse would leave the other with sufficient financial means. As a matter of fact, however, the surviving spouse was often left, by the lack of foresight of the other, with inadequate means, and the law had to be changed by statutes in 1891, 1917, 1925, and 1930.

30. The matter of contracts, quasi contracts, and torts was by no means a political one. The law was left untouched by the Revolution. The drafters of the Code therefore had no important decision to make. They were satisfied to restate the law of contracts in general, quasi contracts, torts, and the law of the various contracts as they had developed through the centuries. Although they did not express the principles of freedom of contract and of informality of contract that had emerged under the influence of the canonists, they meant to imply them in the striking formula: "Agreements legally entered into have the effect of laws on those who have formed them" (Article 1134), and they did not place limits on the freedom of contract other than those arising from public policy. The law of contracts is clearly designed for a period of liberalism. Notwithstanding the numerous and unavoidable present interventions of the legislature in this field, the law certainly remains a very valuable framework.

31. One of the weakest parts of the Code was one of the last: the chapter dealing with legal and conventional mortgages.

This field of law had been the subject matter of an excellent statute in 1798—one that organized a complete system of publicity by registration for every transfer of land or creation of a mortgage.[54] The buyer of land could thus be certain that he was buying from a regular owner, and he could know whether the land was mortgaged. If it were, he was authorized to clear his title by offering the price to the mortgagee.

The drafters of the Code may have failed to understand the full value of these provisions, or at least to resist the pressure of certain landowners for their repeal. As has been stated, they did not require continued publicity by registration for all conveyances of immovable property. Although they kept this publicity for the creation of mortgages, they failed to create any serious sanction for default of publicity in the case of legal mortgages. Finally, they kept certain legal mortgages covering all the immovable property of the mortgager. The main reforms came in 1855 and 1935, when the legislature organized a general system of publicity for conveyances of immovable property.

32. The last part of the Code, dealing with limitations, is, on the contrary, a successful effort to put order and clarity into this field of law. Actions at law are limited to thirty years, or to shorter periods specified in special provisions. The person who occupies premises or land as owner becomes owner in thirty years unless he bought the property in good faith from someone whom he mistakenly considered as the owner, in which event he may become owner in ten years, or in from ten to twenty years. Furthermore, the bona fide purchaser of movable property becomes the owner immediately unless the property has been lost or stolen. In that event the thing may be recovered by the true owner, provided, if it has been bought in a store or a market or at a public sale, that the true owner reimburses the bona fide purchaser with the price.

33. Such are the main principles embodied in the 2,281 articles of the Code. Nobody would maintain that they were perfect and sufficient. On many points the courts not only had to make precise their impact in special circumstances, but also to clarify and even improve them. On some points an intervention of the legislator was necessary or would have been desirable. No one would maintain, either, that all the provisions of the Code were so reasonable and so

flexible that no change appeared necessary in one hundred and fifty years. Again, the permanent work of adaptation done by the courts did not render unnecessary, on some matters, the intervention of the legislator.

Still, one has to admire the efficiency and the flexibility of French Civil Code as he has to admire the efficiency and the flexibility of the American Constitution. Old as it is, there is now certainly much less dissatisfaction with the law in France than in many other countries. The main source of dissatisfaction is the bulk of recent and more or less temporary statutory law. Even if the Code now has to be improved and adjusted to modern conditions of life, it remains highly satisfactory. That the forty-eight states of the most powerful nation should be governed today by the same Constitution agreed on in 1787 by the representatives of thirteen small agricultural states isolated from the rest of the world must be a source of amazement to everyone. Hardly less surprising is the permanent value of the French Code throughout the extraordinary changes in the conditions of life that resulted from the development of industry and from two world wars. The explanation of the permanence of the two documents is certainly to a great extent the same. The drafters of both were men not of systems, but of experience. They had sufficiently mastered the lessons of the past to let their constructive spirit work without danger of losing ground. They had a clear feeling of the limitations that they ought to impose on themselves. Whatever their intellectual strength, the clue to their genius may have been their modesty.

NOTES

[1] See E. Van Kan, *Les efforts de codification en France. Etude historique et psychologique* (1929). For a bibliography on the Civil Code, see Kurt H. Nadelmann, annotations of Julliot de la Morandière's article, *The Reform of the French Civil Code*, 97 University of Pennsylvania L. Rev. 1 (1948). *Adde:* Association Henri Capitant pour la culture juridique française et Société de législation comparée, *Travaux de la semaine internationale de droit, Paris, 1950: L'influence du Code civil dans le monde* (1954). On the evolution of French Law since 1804, see:—on changes of substance: *Le droit privé français au milieu du*

XXème siècle. Etudes offertes à Georges Ripert, 2 vols. (1950); Savatier, *Les métamorphoses économiques et sociales du droit civil d'aujourd'hui* (2ème ed., 1952); on matters of techniques, most of the reports published in the *Travaux de la semaine internationale,* or the reports published in the *Travaux de l'Association Henri Capitant pour la culture juridique française,* Vol. VI (1950), 1952, pp. 37–69; Eugène Gaudemet, *L'interprétation du Code civil en France depuis 1804* (1935); and other works listed in André et Suzanne Tunc, *Le droit des Etats-Unis d'Amérique. Sources et techniques,* n° 84, footnote 1 (1955). See also David, *French Bibliographical Digest* (1952).

[2] Van Kan, *op. cit. supra* note 1, at 16 *et seq.*—The same popular desire was to find an expression in England in the proposal for a codification of the common law made by Chancellor Bacon and, in America, in the colonial movement for codification that starts from the Massachusetts Bay Colony as early as 1634.

[3] Dawson, *The Codification of the French Customs,* 38 Mich. L. Rev. 765–800 (1940).

[4] *Ibid.*

[5] Van Kan, *op. cit. supra* note 1, at 32–63. It should be noted that, as early as the eighteenth century, Beaumanoir had tried to restate the "common law" of France, *i.e.,* "the law common to all people in the Kingdom of France."

[6] Van Kan, *op. cit. supra* note 1, at 56 *et seq.*

[7] *Id.* at 64 *et seq.*

[8] *Id.* at 101 *et seq.*

[9] Cf. E. Caillemer, *Des résistances que les Parlements opposèrent à la fin du XVIème siècle à quelques essais d'unification du droit civil,* in *Le Code civil, Livre du centenaire,* Vol. 2, 1077–1108 (1904).

[10] Van Kan, *op. cit.,* p. 208 *et seq.* and 267 *et seq.;* A. Esmein, *L'originalité du Code civil,* in *Le Code civil, Livre du centenaire,* 1904, Vol. 1, 5–21; Philippe Sagnac, *La législation civile de la Révolution française (1789–1804),* th. Lettres Paris 1899, pp. 47–55.

[11] See Tucker, *Legislative Procedure in the Adoption of the Code Napoleon* (1935); Sorel, Introduction to *Le Code civil. Livre du centenaire,* Vol. 1, XV–L 1904.

[12] The *Discours Préliminaire* is reproduced in Fenet, *Recueil complet des travaux préparatoires du Code Civil,* Vol. 1, 463 *et seq.* (1827–1828) (hereafter cited as Fenet) and Locré, *Législation civile, commerciale et criminelle de la France,* Vol. 1, 243 *et seq.* (1827–1832), (hereafter cited as Locré). On Portalis, see Capitant, *Portalis, le père du Code civil,* in Revue critique de législation et de jurisprudence 187–200 (1936).

[13] See *David Dudley Field. Centenary Essays,* ed. by Alison Reppy, introd. Russell D. Niles (1949).

[14] Cf. Voeux des Etats d'Orléans de 1560, Noblesse, 201, art. 3, reproduced in Van Kan, *op. cit. supra* note 1, at 57.

[15] Italics supplied. French text: "La liberté consiste à pouvoir faire tout ce qui ne nuit pas à autrui: ainsi, l'exercice des droits naturels de chaque homme n'a de bornes que celles qui assurent aux autres membres de la société la jouissance de ces mêmes droits. Ces bornes ne peuvent être déterminées que par la loi." The words *"la loi,"* in this context, refers exclusively to statutory law. The point was often made in the revolutionary period that there should be no judge-made law of any kind.

[16] Fenet, Vol. 1, 465–466; Locré, Vol. 1, 255.

[17] Fenet, Vol. 1, 469–472, 471; Locré, Vol. 1, 258–261, 260.

[18] Fenet, Vol. 1, 467–470; Locré, Vol. 1, 255–258.

[19] Fenet, Vol. 1, 467–469; Locré, Vol. 1, 255–257.

[20] Fenet, Vol. 1, 467–470; Locré, Vol. 1, 255–258.

[21] Fenet, Vol. 1, 469; Locré, Vol. 1, 257–258.

[22] Dawson, *supra* note 3, at 800.

[23] Cf. Van Kan, *op. cit. supra* note 1, at 304 *et seq.*

[24] Fenet, Vol. 1, 469–474; Locré, Vol. 1, 257–262. See also Fenet, Vol. 1, 476 or Locré, Vol. 1, 265: "on ne peut pas plus se passer de jurisprudence que de lois."—A reminiscence of the Revolutionary theory might be found in a dictum by Chief Justice Marshall: "Judicial power, as contradistinguished from the power of the laws, has no existence. Courts are the mere instruments of the law, and can will nothing" (Osborn v. Bank of the United States, 9 Wheat. 738, 866 (U.S. 1824). The context, however, suggests an approach much closer to Portalis than it may seem. And, as well known, Justice Marshall's approach to the interpretation of the Constitution was a very progressive one. See especially McCulloch v. Maryland, 4 Wheat. 316, 415. (U.S. 1819).

[25] Italics supplied. Fenet, Vol. 1, 470; Locré, Vol. 1, 258.

[26] Italics supplied. Fenet, Vol. 1, 475–476; Locré, Vol. 1, 264.

[27] Fenet, Vol. 1, 472; Locré, Vol. 1, 260–261.

[28] Fenet, Vol. 1, 470; Locré, Vol. 1, 258: "De là, chez toutes les nations policées, on voit toujours se former, à côté du sanctuaire des lois, et sous la surveillance du législateur, un dépôt de maximes, de décisions et de doctrine qui s'épure journellement par la pratique et par le choc des débats judiciaires, qui s'accroît sans cesse de toutes les connaissances acquises, et qui a constamment été regardé comme le vrai supplément de la législation."

[29] Fenet, Vol. 1, 470; Locré, Vol. 1, 258.

[30] Fenet, Vol. 1, 476; Locré, Vol. 1, 265.

[31] Cf. *supra,* n° 12.

[32] Fenet, Vol. 1, 476; Locré, Vol. 1, 265.

[33] Cf. Fenet, Vol. 1, 476; Locré, Vol. 1, 265: "le jugement, dans le plus grand nombre des cas, est moins l'application d'un texte précis, que la combinaison de plusieurs textes qui conduisent à la décision bien plus qu'ils ne la renferment." See also Ray, *Essai sur la structure logique du code civil français* (1926).

[34] See Pound, *Sources and Forms of Law* 145–149, (1946), Williston, *Some Modern Tendencies in the Law* 60–106 (1929). Cf. André et Suzanne Tunc, *Le droit des Etats-Unis. Sources et techniques,* n° 211, pp. 451–456 (1955).

[35] André et Suzanne Tunc, *op. cit. supra* note 34, n° 79, p. 205 *et seq.*

[36] *What is the Common Law?* in *The Future of the Common Law* 3–23, 18–19 (1937). Cf. Denning, *The Changing Law* 50 (1953).

[37] Cf. Pound, *The Theory of Judicial Decision,* 36 Harv. L. Rev., 641–662, 802–825, 940–959, 647 (1923).

[38] Cf. Portalis, quoted in text cited, note 33.

[39] Fenet, Vol. 1, 476; Locré, Vol. 1, 266.

[40] Fenet, Vol. 1, 481; Locré, Vol. 1, 272.

[41] Fenet, Vol. 1, 466–467; Locré, Vol. 1, 254–255: "Les lois ne sont pas de purs actes de puissance; ce sont des actes de sagesse, de justice et de raison. Le législateur exerce moins une autorité qu'un sacerdoce. Il ne doit point perdre de vue que les lois sont faites pour les hommes, et non les hommes pour les lois; qu'elles doivent être adaptées au caractère, aux habitudes, à la situation du peuple pour lequel elles sont faites; qu'il faut être sobre

de nouveautés en matière de législation, parce que s'il est possible, dans une institution nouvelle, de calculer les avantages que la théorie nous offre, il ne l'est pas de connaître tous les inconvénients que la pratique seule peut découvrir; qu'il faut laisser le bien, si on est en doute du mieux; qu'en corrigeant un abus, il faut encore voir les dangers de la correction même; qu'il serait absurde de se livrer à des idées absolues de perfection, dans des choses qui ne sont susceptibles que d'une bonté relative. . . ."

[42] Fenet, Vol. 1, 514; Locré, Vol. 1, 307: "On gouverne mal, quand on gouverne trop."

[43] Fenet, Vol. 1, 482; Locré, Vol. 1, 272: "Nous avons trop aimé, dans nos temps modernes, les changements et les réformes; si, en matière d'institutions et de lois, les siècles d'ignorance sont le théâtre des abus, les siècles de philosophie et de lumière ne sont que trop souvent le théâtre des excès."

[44] See Chevallier, *Histoire des institutions politiques de la France de 1789 à nos jours* 115–170, (1952).

[45] See Garaud, *Histoire générale du droit privé français (de 1789 à 1804)*, Vol. 1: *La Révolution et l'égalité civile* (1953). On this point, as well as on all the Revolutionary law, see Sagnac, *La législation française de la Révolution française (1789–1804)* (th. Lettres Paris 1899).

[46] See Sagnac, *op. cit. supra* note 45, at 259–276.

[47] See *id.* at 277–293.

[48] See Garaud, *op. cit. supra* note 45, at 178–179; Sagnac, *op. cit. supra* note 45, at 294–314, 362–379.

[49] See *id.* at 282–293.

[50] Fenet, Vol. 1, 487–498; Locré, Vol. 1, 278–289.

[51] See Sagnac, *op. cit. supra* note 45, at 57–243, 330–354.

[52] Cf. Garaud, *op. cit. supra* note 45.

[53] See Sagnac, *op. cit. supra* note 45, at 213–239, 347–354.

[54] See *id.* at 201–207, 345.

3

Codification and National Unity

RENÉ CASSIN

I. NOT even the most ardent adversaries of codification have been able to deny that the Civil Code of 1804, among its other noteworthy achievements, contrived to accomplish that unity of laws demanded in almost all of the *Cahiers* drawn up in 1789 on the eve of the Revolution. But this extremely difficult task could not be accomplished, even after an evolution of several centuries, without much work and some extraordinary decisions.

Diversity of laws was actually the dominant characteristic of the *Ancien Régime*. There was such diversity, first of all, with regard to the sources of law. The written Roman law governed in the south of France; in the northern part of the country (including Paris), the customary law, developed originally after dim, distant Frankish and Germanic invasions and then from feudal rules, controlled; in addition, marriage and the family were entirely within the domain of the Church and canon law; and, starting with the sixteenth century, a growing number of matters were governed by royal edicts and ordinances or by the case law of the *Parlements* (supreme courts).

From a territorial point of view the diversity of laws was particularly evident. Although as early as the end of the fifteenth century the kings had issued ordinances to reduce the uncertainty of the law and to commit the various customary laws to writing (as well as to revise them from time to time), and though in the long

RENÉ CASSIN *is Vice-President of the French Conseil d'Etat and a member of the Advisory Council of the New York University Institute of Comparative Law*

run the revised Custom of Paris had exercised a predominant influence, there were still, on the eve of the Revolution, about sixty general and three hundred local sets of customary laws.

Nor was the diversity of laws less, considered from the point of view of persons and property. The nobles and their property had their own large number of privileged rules; and so did the clergy. As far as the common people were concerned, there were no longer many serfs by the end of the eighteenth century, but the laws governing the citizens of the free cities, and especially the members of the professional guilds, were wholly different from those affecting people in the country, who were still under feudal servitudes on their property and even on their persons.

The jurists imbued with Roman law, those who served the centralizing monarchy, like Domat and Pothier, and Parisian lawyers, like Dumoulin, were the great partisans of the unification of law. But if such unification could be brought about, as early as the seventeenth century, in the field of commercial and maritime law, as well as to some extent in contracts and civil and criminal procedure, it was quite another matter when the kings began to intervene in the law of marriage, left till then to the Church, or to unify the law of property or succession. Here they met the obstinate resistance of the judges of the *Parlements,* who, in invoking provincial liberties and "privileges," had checked all attempts at codification between 1625 and 1789 except in the fields of gifts, wills, and charities.

Among the most important causes of the Revolution must be placed the overwhelming need of the French nation to have a single system of law—"a written law common to all Frenchmen." And that is why, even while occupied with foreign and civil war, the great number of lawyers and jurists who were part of the different Revolutionary legislatures constantly sought to attain that goal.

However, the necessary political, economic, and social changes that directly affected the laws governing persons, the family, property, and contracts did not permit the legislatures that enacted them to attempt at the same time an over-all codification. Several projected attempts got nowhere. Such codification could not reasonably be accomplished until the great reforms were carried out and the basic principles of the new regime were accepted by the country.

The great merit of Bonaparte, then First Consul, was that he seized the propitious occasion, as soon as it arose on the eve of 1800, to establish the Council of State, composed of men trained in the pre-Revolutionary manner, versed in the written law (like Portalis and Cambacérès) or in the customary law (like Treilhard, Maleville, and Bigot de Préameneu), but including many who had sat in the Revolutionary assemblies. Nor did Bonaparte content himself with delegating to the Council the task of drafting the future Code. He himself, though a soldier and a mathematician, assumed the presidency of most of the sessions of the Council of State, and once the work of draftsmanship was accomplished, it was he who overcame the resistance of the *Tribunat* (the legislative assembly of the time), which sought to slow the adoption of the Civil Code. The law of 30 *Ventôse* of the year 12 of the Revolutionary era (1804) united all of the civil law into one body of laws and repealed all of the Roman law, the ordinances, the general and local customary laws, and all statutes and regulations, which were covered by the new French Civil Code.

II. If the preparation of the Civil Code (like that of the other great French codes—Commerce, Civil Procedure, Criminal Law and Procedure) was the crowning achievement of the evolution toward the unification of the laws, its completion and its operation in practice had the equally important effect of cementing national unity.

True, such unity had been slowly forged by the trials that all had undergone during the monarchy—one need only mention the names of Joan of Arc, Louis XI, and Richelieu—and it had been reinforced by the victorious resistance to foreign invasion of the Revolutionary armies. But the fall of Napoleon and the restoration of the monarchy in 1815 could perhaps have jeopardized national unity if the country had not already had the time to become accustomed, not only to the specific provisions of the Civil Code, but even more so to the great principles that had inspired such provisions, and especially to these three:

1) Freedom of the person and of contract, as well as equal right to engage in professions and to possess property;

2) Suppression of all the old privileges and equality of all Frenchmen, regardless of status, sex, or social condition;

3) Freedom of civil society from all ecclesiastical control.

Later on, the Code could properly be criticized because it was too "bourgeois"; because it placed the married woman in too dependent a position by comparison with the husband; because it was too favorable to the dispersion of rural property; and, finally, because it was too individualistic. On the technical level, proponents of the historical school could criticize the codification for having ossified the rules of civil law and prevented certain necessary developments. But none of these criticisms—that they were inadequately based was revealed only after half a century—could deny that the Civil Code was a useful work of practical compromise; that it was designed to suit a people greatly attached to their traditions; or that it enabled individuals to modify certain of the traditional arrangements, thereby helping to consolidate the most important reforms of the Revolution. The legal foundations of nineteenth-century France, a democratic country, more rural than industrial, have a remarkable solidity.

III. The spectacle of strong national cohesion thus obtained so impressed the governing classes of both new and old nations that the nineteenth was, at one and the same time, the century of national emancipations and that of codification. It is hardly necessary to recall that the countries of Europe (Austria, Netherlands, Serbia, Italy, Romania, Portugal, Spain) were not the only ones to promulgate civil codes. All the countries of Latin America gave way to the same impetus to codification, and it was felt as well in Turkey, Egypt, and Japan.

The situation of federal states should be underlined with particular emphasis. In 1861 the German Confederation unified its commercial law. Soon after the establishment of the German Empire as a result of several victorious wars, there appeared in 1871 a penal code, a code of criminal procedure, and a code of bankruptcy. In that Empire, still federal in structure, it was nevertheless the unification of civil law that was the most important legal achievement of the latter nineteenth century. In 1896 the *Bürgerliches Gesetzbuch* was adopted, which left to the federal states the power to regulate only a small number of matters.

The example of Switzerland is at least as striking. As early as 1880 a uniform code of obligations was adopted (revised in 1912). In 1907, under the influence of Huber, the twenty-two Swiss cantons, jealous as they were of their autonomy, abandoned their own codes to adhere to a common civil code that left little scope to the separate laws of each.

Great Britain, a very old nation that has escaped foreign invasion for nine hundred years, has, it is true, also escaped this movement, at least in part. The national unity of the country has been so great that it has not seemed necessary totally to unify her private law. The law of Scotland is maintained as a separate entity. In Canada the province of Quebec remains faithful to French law. In South Africa Roman-Dutch law holds its ground alongside English law. But the immense role of the common law should not be forgotten, especially in the field of commercial law and in that of the law of obligations. Besides, during the present century a great number of new laws have unified large areas. In the fields of contracts, the law of property, corporations, bankruptcy, and bills of exchange, statute law has taken on the aspect of partial codification.

IV. If we turn now to the United States, we cannot avoid the question of the extent to which its unification of law and its national unity could be strengthened by codification.

The complexity of American law is a well-known fact. It is due not only to the continental dimensions and the diversity of territory, but also to the large number of immigrants of different origins and cultural backgrounds who have peopled the country as well as to the different dates of development of each of the states and sections of the country. The federal character of the country has permitted the particularisms of local laws to continue and even, in certain instances, to be strengthened.

This stated, it is impossible to deny the immense influence exerted by the acceleration of the means of communication and, in a more general way, by the great changes caused by the industrial revolution. The intermingling of large groups of peoples and the uniformity of laws demanded by modern life in certain fields, notably those of health, safety, rates, monopolies, labor relations, and the like, have already greatly augmented the unity of that great reservoir of men and of economic resources. It would be wrong, too, to underestimate the ever-increasing part played by the uniformity of language, of education both scholastic and civic, and by the means of transmitting ideas—the press, the cinema, and radio, and television. And, finally, if a European may say so, we must emphasize the two great world wars, in which the American people took so effective a part, and the considerable changes in mentality that have resulted from them in every family and in every citizen, while at the same time the federal government and administration have so greatly increased in powers and means of action.

All of these have greatly promoted national unity. And they can promote the unification of law, which will in turn be an agent to strengthen the common beliefs, comportment, and habits of Americans.

V. The principal institutions and influences that tend directly to promote the unification of law in the United States correspond in a striking manner to those that prepared the unification of French civil law, even when we bear in mind the difference between monarchical France and a federal republic.

In the first place there is legal education, which, through teaching and writing, tends to give jurists the concept of a common law. The uniform federal legislation, ever more abundant in the fields of economics, health, and demography, correspond, as far as the objects dealt with are concerned, to the royal ordinances of the *Ancien Régime.* Moreover, the activities of the various bar associations in the United States have a much greater importance than the *conférences de coutumes* and synthetic expositions of the pre-Revolutionary French lawyers. Nor was there, in the old France, a National Conference of Commissioners on Uniform State Laws like that founded in the United States in 1890, which has sought to have each state adopt the same law governing a given part of the law; for example, negotiable instruments.

We must finally recognize the effectiveness of the great work accomplished by the American Law Institute, without official governmental sanction, in unifying the common law. The Restatement of the Law is an example of a codification of customary law in its most advanced stage and far superior to the written drafting of customary law in France, which all too often crystallized local opposition to unification and consolidated the differences that existed.

The Restatement has already dealt in many volumes with nine major subjects, such as contracts, conflict of laws, torts, trusts, suretyship, and property. All the same, as Professor Yntema pointed out in an address in Paris in October 1953, the work of the American Law Institute contains important gaps. It has still not touched certain important areas of the common law, notably persons, contracts concerning personal property, conveyances of property, sales, evidence, insurance, and corporations and partnerships. And above all one must note the inadequacy of the sanctions behind such a customary codification, which not all of the case law respects.

VI. The American Law Institute has consequently found it necessary to go beyond the unification of the customary law and to sponsor uniform laws to submit to the different state legislatures. The most advanced law of this type thus far is the Uniform Commercial Code prepared in collaboration with the Conference of Commissioners on Uniform State Laws, which represents a substantial consolidation and revision of a number of uniform laws approved in most of the states. In reality, in its fundamental conception and the degree of its integration it constitutes perhaps the most ambitious effort that can be attempted in the United States outside of a federal codification undertaken from Washington.

The interventions of the latter have multiplied in an extraordinary manner in all the domains not reserved to the states by the federal Constitution. A true federal law has thus grown up which covers, among other things, advertising, competition, protection of investments, labor relations, power, transport, and radio regulation.

The manner in which the application of these laws is controlled by the courts is beyond the scope of this paper. The case law of the United States Supreme Court has, in many cases, used the federal Constitution to invalidate state legislation, even in the field of private law, contrary to these federal laws. The Court has also recognized in the federal government the power to bind the states by treaties signed by it in areas not otherwise covered by federal laws.

VII. We have thus come to the crucial question whether American jurists will not soon have exhausted all methods of obtaining uniform laws in the different states and of developing the domain of federal legislation consistently with the Constitution. Will the day not come when national unity, whose strengthening, at least to some extent, has been noted, will be invoked (as it was in Switzerland in the face of cantonal autonomy) to give the federal government the accepted means of legislating directly in certain fields of the law heretofore reserved to the states?

A European is hardly qualified to pose, still less to answer, such a question. In his attachment to the great American democracy, however, he does wish at least to present to all those who see in the laws of a people a faithful expression of that people's ideas and way of life an exposition of the way in which the unity of French civil law was prepared and established by the Civil Code of 1804, as well as a summary picture of the influence that the movement for unification of the law and for codification can have upon a nation that, though geographically complex, is economically, politically, and morally one unit.

4

The Code and the Case Law*

ANGELO PIERO SERENI

1. THE legislative enactment to which Napoleon was to entrust his greatest and most lasting claim to fame was not the first body of written law in Europe to be characterized as a code. As early as 1683 Christian V had promulgated for Denmark a civil code that was later extended to Norway and Iceland; in 1734 a civil code was enacted in Sweden; and in 1786 a body of family laws that were to be the first part of a civil code was issued in Austria. The Prussian *Allgemeines Landrecht of* 1794 also predates the Code Napoleon

* On the various problems considered in this article, see: Allen, *Law in the Making* 151–224 (1946); Amos, The Common Law and the Civil Law in the British Commonwealth of Nations, 50 Harv. L. Rev. 1249 (1936); Ancel, Case Law in France, 16 Journ. of Comp. Law 1 (3rd Ser., 1934); Ascarelli, *Studi di diritto comparato* (1952); Cohn, E. J., Precedents in Continental Law, 5 Cambridge L. J. 366 (1937); David, *Introduction à l'étude du droit privé de l'Angleterre* (1948); Deak, The Place of the "Case" in the Common and the Civil Law, 8 Tulane L. Rev. 337 (1934); Eder, *A Comparative Survey of Anglo-American and Latin American Law* (1950); Friedmann, W., Re-examination of the Relations between English, American and Continental Jurisprudence, 30 Can. Bar Rev. 175 (1942); Goodhart, Precedent in English and Continental Law, 50 Law Quart. Rev. 40 (1934); Grunhut, English Law and the History of Continental Legislation, 20 Journ. of Comp. Legisl. (3rd Ser., 1938); Gutteridge, *Comparative Law* (1946); Ireland, Precedent's Place in Latin-American Law, 40 West Virg. L. Rev. 1195 (1934); Lipstein, Doctrine of Precedent in Continental Law, 28 Journ. of Comp. Law 34 (3rd Ser., 1946); Lobingier, Precedent in Past and Present Legal Systems, 44 Mich. L. Rev. 955 (1946); Micheli, *Contributo alla formazione giudiziale del diritto; case law e stare decisis* (1938); Rheinstein, Common Law and Civil Law; A Comparison, 12 Penn. Bar. Ass. Quart. 7 (1940); Sereni, La "Common Law" negli Stati Uniti d'America, Riv. Ital. Sc. Giur. 98 (1950); Smith, Interpretation in English and Continental Law, 9 Journ. of Comp. Legisl. 153 (3rd Ser., 1927).

ANGELO PIERO SERENI *is Professor of Law at the University of Ferrara and Adjunct Professor of Law at New York University*

by ten years. To a superficial observer, therefore, the French Civil Code might appear to be little more than a link in a chain of similar enactments (some of them considerably older) that were to become quite common in Europe and to spread to other continents during the nineteenth and twentieth centuries.

Nor could it be maintained that the substance of many of the Code Napoleon's provisions was startlingly original. To a considerable extent the Code adopted and organized pre-existing French law as mainly developed through the *coutumes* and the decisions of the various *Parlements;* also, in many instances, it almost literally embodied provisions of previous statutes, such as the famous *Ordonnances* of Daguesseau on Gifts (1731), Wills (1735), and Substitutions (1747). By the time work started on the Code these various bodies of law had been systematically organized and authoritatively construed by Pothier and the other great commentators of pre-Napoleonic French law.

Unquestionably, however, the Code Napoleon was far superior to its predecessors as to style, legislative technique, and the spirit that pervades it. The style of the Code is a literary as well as a legal masterpiece; its language is clear and precise, concise and direct. Likewise, the legislative technique followed by its drafters, although by no means immune from defects, still commands considerable respect. The provisions of the Code are neither vague nor subtle; they proceed from reality to reality and not from reality to abstraction; qualifications, limitations, and exceptions are kept down to a bare minimum; confusing casuistry and sterile abstractions are entirely absent. Moreover, the drafters of the Code Napoleon were able to express legal concepts and to formulate legal provisions in the language currently employed by the French people in its everyday life and therefore generally understood; literal interpretation was thus made easy, and the definition of technical legal terms was avoided except in a comparatively small number of instances. Finally, as far as its spirit is concerned, the Code Napoleon did away with France's feudal structure; its provisions are neither too reactionary nor too revolutionary and strike a successful balance between a prudent liberalism and an enlightened conservatism; they assert human dignity and equality while preserving the authority and protecting the rights of the head of the family, the property owner, and the employer. Thus, the Code, as amended and implemented, was able to guide France for a century and a half through many political upheavals and during her transition from an agricultural to a modern capitalistic country.

2. But apart from the inherent qualities and peculiar merits that make the Code Napoleon far superior to its predecessors, it chiefly differs from prior enactments that were also characterized as "codes" by virtue of its ideological premises and purposes. For a proper understanding of the relationship between the Code and the case law, analysis of the premises and purposes of the Code Napoleon is indispensable. Pre-Napoleonic codes were only a more or less systematic collection and conglomeration of prior usages, statutes, and judicial decisions; in principle they purported, not to supersede pre-existing law, but rather to co-ordinate, clarify, and restate it. The Code Napoleon, on the other hand, was the product and image of a rationalistic age that believed in enlightenment and progress: the moral justification of the rule of law was in its alleged conformity to reason, and ancient origin and past compliance were no longer held to be proof of the inherent value of legal rules. Prior laws were held to be the expression of a political and legal system thought contrary to reason and enlightenment; hence they were to be superseded. Ideologically at least, the Code was meant to be a break with past law. And even though the contents of many of its specific provisions might actually be the same as those of the pre-existing legal rules, yet the new code operated a "legislative novation"[1] in that the validity and binding force of its various provisions was exclusively dependent on the fact that they had been merged with the new enactment and were part of it.[2] Also, it was felt that laws were to be uniform throughout France and well settled; the only remedy against the vagaries and arbitrariness of

the courts, the best answer to the quest for certainty and uniformity of the law, was to be found in the enactment of a body of written law systematically organized into a code whose provisions the courts should administer without power of amendment. And since human reason had, according to the ideology then prevailing in France, the inherent ability fully to regulate legal relations, a code could and should be complete,[3] so as to supply the solution for any legal problem that might arise with regard to the matters regulated by it.[4] Being the embodiment of human reason, the code could and should also be self-sufficient; within its four corners an answer could and should be found to each question arising in connection with any topic covered by the code itself without resorting to other sources or to any method of implementation of its provisions. To sum up, the ideological premises and purposes at the basis of the Code Napoleon were novelty and certainty of its provisions, and completeness and self-sufficiency of the Code itself.[5] Hence the Code Napoleon chiefly differs from preceding codes and is the first modern code according to the meaning of that expression in civil-law countries, in that it is in fact a systematic collection of co-ordinated legal precepts covering a substantial body of legal relations and formulated in general terms wherein a solution may be found to each and every legal problem arising in connection with any of the subject matters regulated by it.

3. By reason of the above-mentioned characteristics, the Code Napoleon and the codes enacted under its influence in other civil-law countries are inherently different from most common-law statutes, including those entitled codes. As a rule a common-law statute does not propose completely to supersede the pre-existing traditional law governing the topics covered by it, nor does it propose to lay down general principles of its own; on the contrary, it presupposes the existence of general principles, relating to the topic covered by it, that are part of the traditional common law predating the statute itself, and that may or may not have crystallized into precise legal rules.[6] The statute is meant to be understood and con-

strued against the background and to operate within the framework of such prior law. Thus, the general principles underlying the statute are to be found within the realm of the traditional unwritten law, while the main function of the statutory provisions is that of clarifying doubtful points, settling the law with regard to particular questions relating thereto, and implementing pre-existing rules and principles. This relationship explains the particular technique adopted in the drafting of common-law statutes: rather than broadly outlining in a general and systematic manner the basic features of the particular legal topics to which they refer, they consider a great number of different situations that at times are only loosely connected, they go into many details, and they are replete, therefore, with exceptions, distinctions, and qualifications. By attempting to offer adequate solutions to a substantial number of specific problems of a very particular sort, common-law statutes seek to avoid, to some extent at least, the need for judicial legislation. On the other hand, the nature and function of the statutory provisions explain and justify the familiar common-law rule that statutes are to be strictly construed in the absence of specific provisions to the contrary.

4. In modern civil-law countries code provisions have been implemented by an increasing number of statutory provisions. The fictions of completeness and self-sufficiency at the basis of the Code Napoleon now constitute the fundamental premises of a modern civil-law system considered as a whole. The body of provisions (code and statutory) constituting the written law of the country is held to be complete and self-sufficient. A technical problem of legal draftsmanship arises therefrom: it consists of adequately covering and regulating the whole field of relations and transactions to which these legislative enactments apply, without enacting, however, an excessive number of particular provisions that would make them too cumbersome and abstruse. The solution adopted in civil-law countries is to frame the provisions of the written law in general and comprehensive terms. They do not necessarily offer a direct and

specific solution for the particular problems that may arise in the course of human relations and especially before the courts; rather, they lay down the general rules constituting the major premises from which the solution of each particular problem may be derived by means of a process of logical deduction.[7]

This legal technique is closely connected with the particular type, structure, and function of the legal rules contained in civil-law systems.[8] David and other modern civil-law writers have appropriately pointed out that the Anglo-American concept of "legal rule" is not the exact equivalent of the French concept of *règle juridique*. The differences are due to historical reasons. In common-law countries most legal rules were originally laid down by courts in connection with specific cases to be decided by them. Hence legal rules were enunciated with great particularity and with reference only to the specific questions submitted to the court. An effort was and is still made to limit the holding to the particular case decided. A case is authority only for what it actually decides.[9] A case based on slightly different premises can be easily distinguished and differently decided.

In civil-law countries, on the other hand, the *règle juridique* is not judge-made. From earlier times and to a much greater extent than in common-law countries, it has been laid down in the form of a legislative enactment based on the doctrines of legislators and legal scholars rather than on the practice of the courts.[10] The doctrine of the supremacy of the legislature over the courts in the law-making process is centuries old in civil-law countries; it was predominant in France at the time of the enactment of the Code Napoleon.[11] Also, the natural inclination of legislators and legal scholars in civil-law countries is to think in general and universal terms; hence they make a constant attempt to set forth the law in the form of clear and unequivocal principles and to express legal rules in a general and comprehensive manner. As a result of such different approaches and trends, an English or American legal rule might often appear to a civil-law lawyer to be so particularized as to constitute a *solution d'espèce;* that is, the application of a legal provision to the solution of a particular case rather than a legal provision of general scope and authority. On the other hand, the civil-law *règle juridique* may appear at times to an Anglo-American lawyer to be nothing more than an abstract precept or at most a general directive rather than an actual legal provision.[12]

Whether codification was made possible in France and thereafter in other civil-law countries by reason of the widespread acceptance of such a concept of the *règle juridique* or whether, instead, it developed from the broad language of the code provisions—this is a problem that cannot be considered here. In all probability there was considerable interaction between the concept of the *règle juridique* and the trend toward codification, and both were the result of certain political premises. Be that as it may, the technique of the civil-law codes is predicated on and made possible by the broad concept of the *règle juridique* prevailing in civil-law countries.

5. The legislative technique adopted in the drafting of the codes and other statutes and the type of legal rules embodied in such enactments determine the kind and scope of the function performed by the courts in civil-law countries. Since code and other legislative provisions usually consist of broad statements expressed in general terms and do not go into details to the same extent as common-law statutes, it is for the courts to proceed to the implementation, in connection with the particular cases submitted to them, of the general principles laid down by the legislature; as a result the administration of the law by the courts in civil-law countries presupposes the exercise of judicial discretion to a greater extent than is customary in common-law countries. This power was granted to the courts not by accident, but deliberately and avowedly, for the purpose of avoiding excessive particularization of the provisions of the written law. Portalis, one of the main drafters of the Code Napoleon, had clearly in mind and admirably defined in his *Preliminary Discourse of the Commission of the Year VII* the respective tasks of the legislature and the judiciary in a country in

which the law is codified or, more generally, written. "The function of the law is to determine, by means of basic concepts, the general precepts of the law, and to establish principles fertile in consequences, rather than to go into the details of questions that may arise with regard to each particular matter. It is for the judge and the lawyer, who are imbued with the spirit of a legal system, to attend to its implementation." And he added: "Those changing and petty details with which the legislator ought not to be preoccupied and all those matters that it would be futile and even dangerous to attempt to foresee and to define in advance, we leave to the courts. It is for them to fill in the gaps that we may leave. The codes of nations shape up with the passage of time; properly speaking, they are not drawn up by the legislature."

6. The discretionary power thus granted to the courts is subject, however, to certain limitations inherent in the ideological premises on which the written law is predicated in civil-law countries. The first of such limitations is that, whenever the law is reduced to a system of written principles and rules, the discretionary power granted to the courts is to be exercised within the scope of the written law and in the manner provided for it. Codes, together with the statutes whereby they are implemented or amended, constitute the framework within which the solution of each particular problem is to be found by the courts.[13] Since the written law is self-sufficient, courts may not rely on legal principles that are not in the written law itself or to which reference is not made by it. As we have repeatedly pointed out, courts must find the rule of decision for each particular case in the written law and through the written law, not beyond it. Since the written law is complete, the judge may not abstain from deciding a case on the ground that it contains no provision covering the particular matter or that the law is obscure;[14] whenever the express provisions of the written law seem to have left open a gap, it is to be filled by the process of either expanding the meaning of some provision or of reasoning by analogy from one or several provisions. But the judge is never permitted to

add to or go beyond the provisions of the written law; written law constitutes, therefore, the fountainhead of, but also the limit to, any creative function that the courts may have in the decision of cases.

The dogmas of the completeness and self-sufficiency of the written law and of a civil-law system not only affect the scope and the limits, but also the method of interpretation, of the legal rules on the part of the courts. An important corollary of these dogmas is that each decision of a court must find its ultimate justification in some specific provisions of the written law. The broad statements embodied in the various provisions of the various legislative enactments constitute a co-ordinated group[15] of major premises from which the solution of each particular legal problem may be derived by means of a process of deductive reasoning.

Moreover, a civil-law court, inasmuch as it is dealing with written provisions only, will place considerably more emphasis than a common-law court on the specific language of the various provisions; it will seek to determine the meaning of particular expressions used in the code and the statutes by reference to the use of the same or other expressions in other provisions of the same enactment; it will treat a code or a statute as a whole whose provisions are to be construed together and in relation to each other; and, most important, it will rely to a much greater extent than a common-law court on liberal construction and analogy.

The duty of the interpreter to take into consideration the whole of a code or other legislative enactment for the purpose of construing its particular provisions is based on the premise that each of them, and more generally each legal system,[16] must be treated as the expression of an organic and consistent body of legal doctrines and principles. Thus the French speak, for instance, of the *esprit du Code Civil,* and Jhering analyzed the spirit of Roman law. This is, of course, a fiction, inasmuch as the various groups of provisions constituting a legal system were enacted at different times and often on the basis of different needs and motivations; it is a useful fiction, however, in that it justifies an evolutionary interpretation of the law. Furthermore, codes and other statutory enactments in civil-law countries often embody among their provisions specific rules of construction. It may well happen, therefore, that two civil-law codes may be construed according to different rules of interpretation.[17] A further consequence to be derived from the embodiment of rules of construction in the codes is that statutory rules of construction, to the extent to which they are in conflict with logical rules of interpretation, prevail over them.[18]

7. Because of the particular structure of the legal systems within which common-law courts operate, they resort to other techniques in deciding cases. Since a common-law system consists of both traditional unwritten law and statutory law, courts in common-law countries are frequently confronted at the outset with the problem of determining whether a particular case submitted to them for decision falls within a specific statutory provision or whether it is governed by traditional principles and rules of the common law that have not been superseded or modified by statutory provisions.[19] The coexistence of unwritten and written law affects the processes of interpretation and creation of the law by the courts in two respects. The first is that a common-law court seeking to exercise its creative power with regard to a particular cause submitted to it for decision, and involving a matter that may be held to be specifically covered by a statutory provision, will probably attempt to take the cause out of the statute and decide it in accordance with some unwritten rule of traditional law that would leave more room for judicial discretion.[20] Escape into the realm of traditional unwritten law is a device to which a civil-law court may not resort, since its discretion must be exercised within the bounds of written law.[21] The second effect of the coexistence of written and unwritten law is that a common-law court, for the purpose of determining whether a matter is governed by traditional or statutory law, may not resort to a deductive process based on major premises, since there are no such major premises to which resort may be had; it can decide only by a process of comparison of the case in issue with

and distinction from prior cases that have been found to be respectively governed by either traditional or statutory law. Hence the inductive method based on comparison with and distinction from precedents, which is a typical common-law technique for the decision of cases, is indissolubly connected with the coexistence of traditional and unwritten law. The same method is also the most appropriate one for the finding of the rules of traditional law. Common-law courts also resort to it in construing and applying statutory provisions, partly because of the traditional inclination of courts and lawyers to rely on methods traditionally followed, but much more frequently because of the great particularization of the provisions of common-law statutes.

It appears from the foregoing not only that the methods of interpretation resorted to by the courts in civil-law and in common-law systems are basically different, but also that the relationship between legal rules and the judicial function is differently understood.

8. The second limitation imposed upon the courts in civil-law systems by the existence of a complete and self-sufficient body of written law is that, in the absence of enabling statutory provisions, they may not adopt judicial precedents as rules of decision. The principle is expressly stated in the Code Napoleon[22] and penal sanction is given to it.[23] But the principle of nonrecognition of the rule of *stare decisis* applies, as a rule, in civil-law countries even in the absence of an express provision to that effect. Its rationale is to be found in the dogma that in civil-law countries the written law is complete. Since the solution of each legal problem can be found in the provisions of the written law, there is no reason why a court, in deciding a case submitted to it, should rely on the holding of a prior court; the solution is to be derived directly from the written law itself by means of a process of legal reasoning and interpretation.

Actually, the foundation of the civil-law principle denying binding force to judicial precedent is historical and political rather than strictly logical. To attribute binding force to the precedent is tantamount to recognizing a substantial amount of lawmaking power in the courts. In fact, the practical effect of *stare decisis* is that of vesting courts with the power to determine in a general manner and to implement by regulations, as the Code Napoleon states, the contents of statutory provisions. The will of the courts is thus substituted for that of the legislature; this trend was opposed in civil-law countries at the time of the enactment of the Code Napoleon and is still opposed in them in principle.

In common-law countries the rationale of the rule of *stare decisis* seems to be that a court in deciding a case does not create but merely finds the law; hence, precedent is merely proof of the legal rule that it enunciates; it is to be followed in that it does not create law but merely declares what the law is. The rule of *stare decisis,* however, is of comparatively recent origin; it developed slowly in England during the seventeenth and eighteenth centuries; it was finally established there at a time when the law was almost entirely unwritten and precedents were few.

In the United States the rule of *stare decisis* was never rigidly followed, probably because of the fact that the vesting of the legislative power in Congress from the very origin of the Republic was not challenged by the courts, and because of the substantial number of statutes enacted in this country since its early days. Furthermore, the great number of cases officially reported tends somewhat to impair the binding force of judge-made law, and the increasingly rapid pace at which the law changes tends to shorten the period during which most cases may be considered as authorities.

It may very well be that the validity of *stare decisis* in common-law countries is being constantly weakened; yet the principle of the binding force of precedent has never been expressly repudiated. Precedents are therefore properly characterized in Anglo-American legal systems as "case law"—that is, law made by cases; also, concededly, the content of statutory provisions is not authoritatively established unless and until they have been construed by the courts.

In civil-law countries, on the other hand, decisions of the courts are, to use the French expression, nothing more than *jurisprudence;* that is, the explanation or demonstration of the law by the judiciary. True, as will be seen hereafter, precedents, and especially those of the higher courts, tend to acquire growing authority. Thus precedents in civil-law countries may be highly persuasive; but they are never conclusive.[24] The distinction between the value of precedent in Anglo-American law and in the civil law thus still remains in existence and is a substantial one.

9. The basic civil-law principles (1) that the solution of each case is to be found in the provisions of the written law, (2) that precedents, however authoritative, are not binding, and (3) that the deciding court must demonstrate that its decision is based on provisions of the written law and not merely on precedent—these are the justification for the principle almost generally accepted in civil-law systems, that decisions of the courts are to be supported by opinions. Its purpose is to compel the court to reach the solution of the case through an independent process of legal reasoning and to offer a legal justification for the result obtained. The opinion is the test of the validity of such reasoning and of the correctness of the result. Inadequacy of the court's opinion, including the failure on its part to meet the legal arguments advanced by the parties, are in most civil-law countries grounds for appeal, which may be invoked even when error of law, and not also error of fact, is the sole ground on which an appeal may be taken. True, a court may adopt by incorporation the reasoning followed by another court in a prior case in which the same question arose; and a higher court on appeal may adopt the reasoning of a lower court; but a court, by incorporating in its opinion the reasoning of another court makes that reasoning its own and takes full responsibility for it. Hence, although precedent may be actually followed in both groups of legal systems, the basic difference between them, from a conceptual viewpoint, is that in civil-law countries a precedent, weighty as it may be, will exercise its influence on future courts not by reason of its hold-

ing, but only by reason of the inherent validity and persuasiveness of the reasoning whereby the holding is supported. Subsequent courts will not decide according to precedent unless they approve and accept the reasoning of the prior court. Hence, in civil-law systems the existence of a consistent line of identical decisions (*jurisprudence constante*) will have greater persuasive force than a single decision, because it is highly improbable that a substantial number of courts could have misconstrued the law. Yet even a *jurisprudence constante* does not excuse a subsequent court from the duty of writing an opinion in support of its holding, nor does it prevent it from reaching a different conclusion. In some civil-law countries it is not even permissible to cite or quote verbatim prior decisions in an opinion; it is only permissible to follow and repeat their reasoning. Should the persuasiveness of the reasoning of preceding opinions be impaired in the course of time, subsequent courts may follow a different line of reasoning and may reach different or even opposite results.

10. The emphasis on the logical aspects of prior court decisions rather than on the holding serves also to explain the importance that at least until recently was attributed in civil-law countries to the opinions of text writers or, to use the French expression, to *doctrine*. In common-law countries most textbooks are merely a restatement of the law as set forth in the cases. Even in commenting on statutory provisions, textbooks in common-law countries often do nothing more than restate in a concise and systematic form the holdings of cases in point. A text writer would seldom dare to assert opinions unsupported by court decisions, nor would a court ordinarily overrule a precedent in reliance solely on the contrary opinion of text writers. In civil-law countries text writers do not hesitate to assert opinions in conflict with court adjudications and even with a *jurisprudence constante,* or to criticize decisions whose holding or reasoning they deem to be unsound. Since courts rely on the reasoning rather than on the holding of precedents, they may at times follow the reasoning of a text writer rather than that of a

prior decision. Thus, in civil-law countries *doctrine* does contribute to the evolution of the law through decisions more directly than in common-law countries.

11. Another consequence of the different conceptual significance of precedents is that a civil-law court will show much less hesitancy than a common-law court in overruling a precedent of another court or even of its own. The overruling of a case in a common-law country is deemed to constitute a change in the law; but in a civil-law country a *revirement de la jurisprudence* is not deemed to constitute, theoretically at least, such a change, for the law consists only of the written provisions to which reference is made in the opinion. Furthermore, each decision is binding only with regard to the particular case decided and, theoretically at least, should not influence the decision of other cases.[25]

12. Codification and case law are legal techniques through which the various legal systems seek to solve, among other problems, the basic problem of retaining the flexibility of a legal system while securing a reasonable amount of certainty with regard to the solution of legal problems and of predictability for the event of litigation. The devices to which common-law and civil-law systems resort in seeking to solve the problem of flexibility and that of certainty and predictability are basically different. The problem of flexibility will be examined first.

Flexibility in all legal systems is chiefly obtained through the grant to the courts of a certain amount of discretion. The legal justification for such grant and the devices through which discretion is exercised are not the same in the various legal systems.

Since the basic principles of the common law have not been reduced to writing, flexibility in common-law systems is secured through the devices previously mentioned: namely, the grant to the courts of a substantial lawmaking power which they exercise under the pretense of finding and setting forth pre-existing unwritten law, and the process of limiting each holding to the particular facts of the case decided, thus enabling a court to distinguish the case which it is called to decide from previous holdings.[26] Moreover, courts, at least in the United States, would not hesitate in extreme cases expressly to overrule a precedent. On the other hand, the particularization of common-law statutes is also a device tending to reduce the need for flexibility of the law by supplying a specific legislative solution for each situation that may arise.

Civil-law systems, instead, consist almost exclusively of written rules, and the legal provisions are usually set forth in the form of broad propositions expressed in general terms. In relation to these particular characteristics, flexibility in civil-law systems is chiefly attained through the characterization as questions of fact of various questions that in common-law systems would be characterized as legal issues, the nonrecognition of the rule of *stare decisis,* and the adoption of the legal fiction according to which the meaning and contents of written provisions may vary although their language remains unchanged. These three devices will be separately analyzed.

Concerning the characterization of the various questions that courts are called on to decide, it should be noted that the provinces of law and fact do not coincide in common-law and civil-law systems.[27] Because of the existence of the jury system and of the distrust of judges toward jurors, many questions that from a logical point of view should be characterized as problems of fact are treated in common-law countries as problems of law.[28] On the other hand, the great particularization of statutory provisions, and especially the characterization of judicial precedents as *law,* bring about the result that there is much more law in common-law than in civil-law systems. Conversely, in civil-law countries the lack of particularization of the legislative provisions enables the courts to treat as issues of fact, which they may decide in their discretion, many questions that in common-law countries would be characterized as questions of law.[29] Thus the sphere of discretion of courts in civil-law countries is greatly broadened.

Nonrecognition of *stare decisis* leads to the result that courts in civil-law countries, while bound ultimately to rely on some provision of the written law as authority for their pronouncements, may depart from an earlier construction of the provision invoked and reach different results on the basis of different reasoning. The broad language of the code and of the statutory provisions facilitates the exercise by the courts of the discretion thus granted them.

Finally, courts in civil-law countries may find that the meaning of written provisions has evolved although the language has remained unchanged. Such a finding may be justified on two grounds. The first is that the current meaning of some of the terms contained in such provisions has changed. As has been stated, the Code Napoleon and other civil-law codes that have followed its pattern contain no definitions of several important terms used in them. Concededly, words are to be construed as a rule according to their ordinary meaning. Courts may find, however, that the meaning of a particular term has undergone a change that may in turn result in a change of the meaning of the legal provisions in which it is embodied and of others to which it is related. Moreover, a change may have taken place in the social climate and the social concepts to which reference is made in a particular provision. For instance, the concepts of *ordre public et bonnes moeurs* (public policy) have greatly changed. An agreement that would not have been held contrary to public policy a century ago may be held invalid on that ground now; this change in social concepts took place in various civil-law countries with regard to the validity of combinations in restraint of trade.[30] Likewise, the continuing expansion of the concept of public interest has affected the construction and administration of legal provisions; matters that were once held to be exclusively within the province of private law are now held to be subject to certain provisions of the public law formerly considered inapplicable to them.[31] The second ground on which a change in the meaning of legal provisions may be predicated is that the various provisions of a legal system are interrelated and that each of them is connected with and dependent on the others.[32] Now the provisions of a legal system are in a state of perpetual change; old ones are repealed or amended and new ones enacted. Since the meaning of each legal provision is to be understood within the context of the legal system in which it belongs, any change in this affects in a sense the meaning of all its particular provisions; that is, not only of the particular ones that have been expressly repealed or amended, but also of others connected with them. Ultimately any change affects the whole structure of the system, since its various components are thereafter to be seen in a different perspective. Thus, in addition to the changes in the social climate previously examined, there are continuous changes in the legal climate. They are made easier by the fact that legal terms used but not defined in the legal rules may be given an entirely different construction at different times.[33] Such changes have been invoked by the courts as justification for the development of entirely new doctrines and rules of law, based on written provisions to which a new construction has been given although their language has remained unchanged. For instance, the principle of the *responsabilité du fait des choses* has been developed in France by the *Cour de cassation* through dramatic changes in the construction of Article 1384 of the Code Napoleon, although the language of the article has not changed.

13. In France and most civil-law countries the doctrine has thus come to be generally accepted that law, even though codified, changes constantly through its own internal processes. Courts, it is argued, have power, not to make or to change the law, but only to administer it; it is their duty, however, to perceive changes and to take them into consideration in deciding cases. Obviously this doctrine is a mere fiction, for the law is being actually changed through its administration by the courts.[34] Obsolescent provisions of the written law are rejuvenated through new court interpretations in keeping with social and legal developments. The older code and statutory provisions become, the bolder the courts grow in modifying the contents of their provisions under the guise of mere construction. It is only by means of this process of rejuvenation that codes in civil-law countries are enabled to remain in force over

long periods of time, notwithstanding substantial changes in the social and legal climate. The one-hundred-and-fifty-year-old Code Napoleon is a case in point. It could survive, with a comparatively small number of changes only, because the French courts, and especially the Court of Cassation, have exercised broad discretion in actually modifying it.

The increasing boldness of the French judiciary in changing the meaning of the written law, and especially of those of the Code's provisions that would otherwise have become obsolete, has led Savatier to the conclusion that in some particular fields French civil law has ceased to consist of written law and has become common (unwritten) law. According to the French scholar, the traditional and spectacular opposition between the sources of English and of French law has been surprisingly reduced.[35] Savatier's position may sound far-fetched; it is certainly correct, however, to the extent to which it runs counter to Savigny's well-known theory that codification entails of necessity an unhealthy crystallization of the law.[36] The lawmaking function performed by courts in France and a few other civil-law countries justifies Capitant's remark that "codification should not be repeated too often. It is preferable, rather, to live under an old code and through special statutes, which may be more easily drafted, to amend those parts of it that no longer correspond to present conceptions, while leaving to the courts, under the guidance and with the assistance of text writers, the task of working on this body of written law, retouching it, and modifying it by imperceptible steps."[37]

14. Certainty and predictability are, in addition to flexibility, the basic goals of all legal systems. As is pointed out above, common-law systems seek to achieve them, to some extent at least, through the particularization of statutory provisions and, to a greater extent, through the operation of the rule of *stare decisis;* but it was also noted that the increasingly rapid tempo of social and legal change tends to shorten the period during which a case may be held to be a precedent.

In the absence of *stare decisis,* certainty and predictability in civil-law countries are sought through the adoption of particular techniques in the drafting and construction of the written law. The basic principles of a legal system are not only reduced to writing in the form of general propositions but also set forth in an organic and systematic manner; they are co-ordinated among themselves and implement each other. Thus, in the absence of specific provisions, the solution of a particular problem may be derived by means of the deductive process from the general premises set forth in writing. Unquestionably the solution of a particular problem can be more easily found by way of deduction from a series of co-ordinated general premises than by way of distinction from and comparison with other particular rules; the latter system leaves, in fact, a much wider area of uncertainty and ample room for casuistry. Reliance on logical and legal reasoning for the purpose of drawing from principles clearly established their ultimate and almost inevitable conclusions tends to secure a reasonable amount of predictability in civil-law systems, even in the absence of prior holdings in point; in common-law systems, on the other hand, lack of a precedent in point may constitute a major problem. It has been argued, therefore, that civil-law systems are not only more flexible but also afford a larger measure of predictability than common-law systems.[38]

It would seem, however, that the two groups of systems differ in the relative strength and impact of the various factors on which predictability depends rather than in the ultimate measure of predictability that they offer. Chiefly because of the reduction to writing and the systematic co-ordination of the general applicable rules and of the resort to the deductive method, the legal provisions governing a particular matter or situation can be more easily found within the purview of a civil-law than of a common-law system. Unquestionably much less research is required for the finding of the applicable rules of law within the scope of a civil-law system. Hence the consequence, among others, that legal assistance is much less expensive in civil-law countries, and the further consequence that there is less inequality between the rich and the poor as far as legal assistance is concerned. Conversely, since a greater number of questions to be decided are treated by civil-law courts as questions of fact, a greater area of uncertainty exists in this respect within the scope of civil-law systems. Thus, the correct conclusion would seem to be that while the rules of law governing a particular situation may be more rapidly, accurately, and unequivocally determined within the purview of a civil-law system, greater predictability of the outcome of a dispute does not necessarily follow from it.

15. Human relations, as they grow increasingly complex and articulate, require more detailed and diversified regulation. In civil-law countries, however, the legislative technique of formulating legal rules in broad and general terms still prevails; it is generally felt that it would be hard, if not impossible, for the legislator to anticipate and regulate the specific problems that may come before the courts. Hence the trend is toward leaving to the courts the power of implementing the broad provisions of the written law through the decision of particular problems involved in each dispute. In contradiction to the ideology of the Code Napoleon, courts are thus vested in fact with a broad regulatory power within the scope of the legislative enactments.

To secure stability in legal relations, higher courts in civil-law countries are inclined to perform their task by uniformly deciding recurrent questions, and lower courts tend to follow the lead of the higher courts. The law thus develops a uniform line of decisions, a so-called *jurisprudence constante,* which, by some French legal scholars, has been likened to customary law, in that it is unwritten; such customary law, however, exists only within the scope of the provisions of the written law and is not inconsistent with them. Furthermore, it is a mere usage in that it is not binding in a technical legal sense. It has been intimated that the growing tendency on the part of the courts in almost all civil-law countries to follow precedents is due, in part, to intellectual laxity and to an unhealthy trend toward conformity. It has been asserted that judges of the lower courts, when confronted with difficult problems, may prefer to choose the easy way out of relying on the reasoning of prior decisions of the higher courts rather than do their own independent thinking. It is to be noted, however, that in various civil-law countries, including France, one of the main tasks specifically entrusted to the highest courts (in France, to the Court of Cassation) is to establish and preserve uniformity in the administration of justice by the courts. Furthermore, uniformity is a necessity under modern conditions. Conflicting holdings, especially by lower courts, would not only create uncertainty, but would also entail an unnecessary expenditure of money and time for the litigants if a lower court were to take an isolated stand contrary to that of the highest court of the country on a matter that the latter has repeatedly and uniformly adjudicated: the inevitable result would be in fact a reversal. On the other hand, lower and intermediate courts have not hesitated to dissent from the higher courts on basic issues until a *jurisprudence constante* was established, and higher courts have no hesitation in reversing themselves should they deem it appropriate. Also, the influence of text writers, although now somewhat reduced, is still much greater than in common-law countries.

In common-law countries, or at least in the United States, there is, it should be noted, a noticeable tendency to limit the importance of precedents and to consider instead the broad legal principles and issues involved in each case.

A certain rapprochement is thus discernible between the two groups of legal systems as far as practical results are concerned. It would be a serious error and a dangerous one, however, to minimize the basic differences that still exist between common-law and civil-law systems with respect to the respective value and function of codification and case law.

NOTES

[1] Gény, "La Technique Législative dans la Codification Civile Moderne" in *Le Code Civil, 1804–1904, Livre du Centenaire,* Vol. II, 987 (1904).

[2] Thus, the Law of the 30th of Ventôse, year XII (1804), which consolidated thirty-six prior statutes into the Code, provided (Art. 7) that: "As of the day when these laws shall

become effective, Roman laws, ordinances, general and local usages, statutes and regulations shall cease to have the force and effect of general or particular laws with regard to the topics which are the object of the above-mentioned laws constituting the present Code."

[3] It does not follow therefrom, however, that a code must be the supreme law of the land. In many civil-law countries the validity of code provisions is conditional on their not being in conflict with provisions of the national constitution.

[4] Hence the Code Napoleon provides (Art. 4) that "a judge who shall refuse to decide a case under pretext that the law is silent, obscure or inadequate, may be prosecuted for denial of justice." See also Art. 185 of the French Penal Code.

[5] Furthermore, the Code Napoleon was based on the premise that since its basic provisions were, to some extent at least, the lasting embodiment of human reason, the principles asserted therein were universal. This was one of the ideological justifications of the efforts tending to introduce the Code in the foreign territories that came under French rule.

[6] For a demonstration of the existence of such principles see Lawson, *The Rational Strength of English Law* (1951).

[7] For problems relating to legislative drafting in civil-law countries, see Angelesco, *La Téchnique législative en matière de codification civile* (1930).

[8] David, *Introduction à l'étude du droit français* 125 et seq. (Paris, 1952) (mimeogr.).

[9] Lord Halsbury in *Quinn v. Leathem* [1901] A.C. 495.

[10] In this connection it may be pointed out that in common-law countries there is still a natural tendency to envisage legal rules, especially if not exclusively, as a guidance for the decision of litigated matters; in civil-law countries legal rules are primarily thought of rather as precepts governing basic human relations in ordinary life. There has been, however, in recent years a distinct trend in common-law countries toward the adoption of the civil-law conception.

[11] The historical reason for the doctrine is that in France the judiciary was, prior to the Revolution, a class organization and courts were responsible for many abuses; thus, it was felt that their power should be controlled. Further, from the doctrine of the sovereignty of the people and of the right of the people to enact its own laws through legislative bodies freely elected, it necessarily followed that the lawmaking power should be vested in the legislature only, which expressed the will of the nation, whereas courts, not being the expression of the will of the people, should administer, not create, the law. But legal provisions enacted by the legislature could only set forth basic principles couched in broad terms; hence the solution of each particular problem was to be found by the courts, by way of logical deduction, from the general principles set forth in the laws. Changes in the social structure of the judiciary whereby judges in present-day civil-law countries are no longer a separate class but only a body of civil servants drawn from all classes of the population have allayed the ancient fears and suspicions about them. Thus in modern times the judiciary in France and various other civil-law countries has met no opposition in its efforts to adapt written law to changing historical circumstances through its decisions.

[12] See, for instance, Article 1382 of the Code Napoleon, which not only is the fountainhead of the French law of torts but, together with Articles 1383 to 1386, also covers the whole topic. It reads as follows: "Every human fact which causes damage to someone else, obligates the one by reason of whose fault it occurred, to make reparation."

[13] A few civil-law systems expressly recognize a limited lawmaking power in the courts (Swiss Civil Code, Article 1). However, such power exists only because and insofar as it

is recognized by the written law itself, and furthermore the courts are reluctant to exercise it.

[14] See note 4 *supra.*

[15] Hence a code is meant to be a systematic collection of co-ordinated provisions, whereas a common-law statute need not be systematic.

[16] Thus, the Italian Code of 1942 provides, among other things, in Sec. 12 of the Provisions on the Law in General, that if other rules of interpretation set forth in said section are not adequate, a case is to be decided according to the general principles of the Italian legal system.

[17] The Italian Civil Code of 1942 sets forth some rules governing the interpretation of contracts (see for instance Article 1371) which are not to be found in the Code Napoleon.

[18] It is also a well-known fact that different methods of interpretation may apply to different branches of the civil law.

[19] In civil-law systems codes and statutes often provide that the provisions of prior statutes shall remain in force to the extent to which they have not been repealed or amended. It is for the courts to determine, in the event of dispute, whether a particular provision has been repealed or amended. In such a situation, however, the choice of the civil-law court is still limited as between statutory provisions only.

[20] Since the early development of the common law, courts in England have exercised a broad lawmaking power and have resisted attempts by the king to interfere with such power through the enactment of statutes. To justify their lawmaking prerogative the courts asserted the existence of an ancient law of the land (*lex terrae*) by which the king himself was bound and which could not be violated by his statutes. Actually the law of the land was merely a fiction; it constituted a limitation upon the king's lawmaking power imposed by the courts. Such purported law of the land consisted only of what a court would hold in each particular case to be the law of the land.

The circumstance that the largest part of the English law was originally unwritten law greatly facilitated the claim of the existence of the law of the land.

As parliamentary government developed and the enactment of statutes became more frequent, the fiction of the existence of a law of the land or natural law superior to the sovereign was less easily sustainable. There remained, however, a deeply rooted preoccupation that statutory provisions, because of their inability to foresee all possible contingencies, might unduly interfere with the exercise by the courts of their function of doing justice according to the particular circumstances of each case. The excessive particularization of common-law statutes lent some justification to that preoccupation. In order to preserve their lawmaking power, courts chiefly resorted to the device of taking a case out of a statute whenever justice would seem to require it. One may recall in this connection the equitable doctrines that courts developed for the purpose of taking cases out of the statute of frauds.

[21] As is shown above, it does not follow therefrom that civil-law courts are vested with a lesser amount of discretion than common-law courts; only, their discretion is exercised on the basis of different premises and by means of different techniques, consistent with the broad language of civil-law provisions.

[22] Article 5: "Judges are forbidden to decide in a general manner or in the form of regulations with regard to the cases submitted to them."

[23] French Penal Code, Article 127.

[24] Lord Mansfield in *Jones v. Randall,* 1 Comp. 37 (1774), stated: "Precedents serve

to illustrate principles and to give them a fixed certainty. But the law [of Francc] which is exclusive of positive law, enacted by statute, depends upon principles and these principles run through all the cases according as the particular circumstances of each have been found to fall within the one or the other of them."

[25] On the other hand, the principle of *res adjudicata* is much stronger in civil-law than in common-law systems. See Sereni, *Aspetti del processo civile negli Stati Uniti* (1954).

[26] For extreme applications of this device, see the recent decisions of the U.S. Supreme Court in *United States v. Schubert,* 348 U.S. 222 (1955) and *United States v. International Boxing Club of New York, Inc.,* 348 U.S. 236 (1955).

[27] On this point see Sereni, Basic Features of Civil Procedure in Italy, 1 Am. Journ. of Comp. Law 374, n. 6 (1952), and Sereni, *Aspetti del processo civile negli Stati Uniti* (1954).

[28] E.g., the question whether a statement is libelous *per se.*

[29] E.g., what amount of time constitutes a reasonable time within which a check should be presented.

[30] With specific reference to changes in French law, see Savatier, *Les Metamorphases economiques et sociales du droit civil d'aujourd'hui* (1952).

[31] With regard to the increase in the number of human relations held to be of public interest, see, especially in reference to France, Savatier, *Du Droit civil au droit public,* (1950).

[32] Such a relationship exists, of course, not only among the various provisions of a code, but also among all the provisions of a legal system. In France and other countries where the law is codified, an increasing number of basic legal provisions is to be found in enactments other than codes; the older codes become, the greater is the number of fundamental provisions embodied in separate statutes.

[33] In this connection, it should be noted that nowhere in the Code Napoleon may there be found a definition of such fundamental legal terms and concepts as *droits, actions, exceptions, actes, biens, choses, ayant cause, bonnes moeurs, ordre public,* and *faute.*

[34] David, *op. cit. supra* note 8, at 139: "In France what actually constitutes the creation of new legal rules is still characterized as construction of existing texts; in order to justify such results reference is made to certain [code] provisions which actually are used only as window dressing." David remarks, however, that this is the result not of a hypocritical attitude of French courts and lawyers, but of a sincere belief that the meaning of legal provisions changes as time goes by. Likewise, subsequent generations put a different interpretation on literary works.

[35] Destin du Code Civil Francais, in 16 Rev. Internat. de Dr. Comp. 637, 643–644 (1955).

[36] See Savigny, *Vom Beruf unserer Zeit fur Gesetzgebung und Rechtswissenchaft* (1814). It should be pointed out, however, that the amount of leeway granted to courts in civil-law countries is not uniform. It varies according to the legislative techniques adopted in drafting the codes. The German Civil Code, burdened as it is by definitions, is much more rigid than the Code Napoleon and limits the creative function of the courts to a much greater extent.

[37] *Introduction à l'étude du droit civil* 99 (5th ed., 1926).

[38] Cohn, Precedents in Continental Law, 5 Cambridge L. J. 366 (1937).

5

Techniques of Interpretation

SHELDEN D. ELLIOTT

1. PRE-CODE Views on Judge-Made Law and Interpretative Techniques

Before the adoption of the French Civil Code there were occasional similarities of viewpoint in England and France as to the respective authorities of courts and legislative bodies in lawmaking and statutory interpretation. The parallels are undoubtedly fortuitous, and certainly they were widely separated in time, but one can mention them as items of possible historical interest. Thus in 1748, Montesquieu in his *L'Esprit des Lois* commented: ". . . Judges are no more than the mouth that pronounces the words of the law, mere passive beings, incapable of moderating either its force or rigour."[1] A few decades later, in 1792, Jeremy Bentham in his polemic, or perhaps more fittingly his "jeremiad," against his pet anathema, judge-made law or "dog-law," vouchsafed a grudging and dubious compliment on what was then occurring in contemporary France. Though Bentham's point of view was a minority one, it established at least a point of rapport in England with the Continental approach to statute law.

> "The French have had enough of this *dog-law;* they are turning it as fast as they can into *statute law,* that everybody may have a rule to go by: nor do they ever make a law without doing all they can think of to let every creature among them know of it. The French have done many abominable things, but is this one of them?"[2]

SHELDEN D. ELLIOTT *is Professor of Law at New York University, and is a co-author of Nutting and Elliott,* Cases and Materials on Legislation *(2d ed., 1955)*

Another parallel, short-lived in both countries, was the technique of judicial resort to the legislature for advice on interpretation. The *référé legislatif,* introduced by the French National Assembly in 1790 during the first period of the Revolution, required the courts to apply to the legislature for an interpretation whenever doubts arose as to the meaning and application of a statute.[3] Though the *référé legislatif* was abolished by Article 4 of the French Civil Code, it must have had, for the longer-memoried of the common lawyers across the Channel, a certain *déjà vu* aspect. Campbell, in his *Lives of the Lord Chancellors,* refers to "the practice of the common law judges, when any question of difficulty arose before them in their several courts, to take the advice of Parliament upon it before giving judgment."[4] He cites instances during the reign of Edward III in the 14th century in which the King's Bench resorted to Parliament for advice as to the intended meaning of a statute, a custom that appears not to have survived these early excursions.[5]

The foregoing are, it is admitted, but fleeting instances, cited merely to show that perhaps the English and the Continental systems were not always and wholly antipodal in their views of the respective domains of court and legislature in statutory interpretation. Even in the post-Code era we find points of similarity in approach, but the Anglo-American pattern is a complex and often a confusing one. At the risk of oversimplification, this paper will offer first a comparative analysis and then certain illustrative examples.

2. Approaches to the Techniques of Statutory Interpretation

a. The "Traditional" Anglo-American Classification

In this category are the several standard groupings recognized by such authorities on statute construction as Black and De Sloovère. The groupings comprise, respectively, certain "basic" doctrines, intrinsic guides, and extrinsic aids—clusters that are not always mutually exclusive.

(1) *General Doctrines.* One guiding principle to which the courts

sometimes pay lip service is the "literalistic" rule: namely, that a statute must be construed according to its letter, with the chips falling where they may. Another, less drastic, is the so-called "golden rule" of construction, whereby the statute is given its plain and natural meaning unless manifest injustice or absurdity would result. A third, often referred to as the "mischief" rule, derives from a formula prescribed by Coke in Heydon's Case in 1584, which enjoined the courts to discern and consider: "1st. What was the common law before the making of the Act. 2nd. What was the mischief and defect for which the common law did not provide. 3rd. What remedy the Parliament hath resolved and appointed to cure the disease of the commonwealth. And, 4th. The true reason of the remedy."[6] Professor Friedmann has denominated these rules as the "pseudo-logical or text-book approach," and observes that "The mischief rule expresses both the oldest and the most modern approach."[7]

(2) *Intrinsic Guides.* These include rules and canons of construction as well as the component parts of the statute itself as guides or clues to legislative intent. Honored almost as often in their exceptions as in their application by the courts are the rules of strict construction of penal statutes or of statutes in derogation of the common law, as are also the formidable array of canons like *expressio unius, ejusdem generis, noscitur a sociis,* last antecedent, and *reddendo singula singulis.* Parts of the statute itself, which may or may not be relied upon to aid in its interpretation, include such elements as the context of the act as a whole, or its title, its preamble, its chapter and section headings, or even its punctuation.

(3) *Extrinsic Aids.* Here are grouped such external sources as the historical setting of the statute, its legislative history, including committee reports and debates, and the views and opinions of the draftsman. Also included here is the technique of resorting to statutes in *pari materia.* Again, the extent of judicial reliance varies both from jurisdiction to jurisdiction and often from case to case before the same tribunal.

b. The Conceptual Approaches

In a broader categorization, approaches to the techniques of statute construction may be grouped under three generic headings. Here the "logical" or "quasi-logical" approach would embrace the traditional classification above noted. The "social-policy" approach, corresponding to the French *but social,* directs the court in construing a statute to consider the social or economic needs of the community as a guiding principle. Finally, the "intuitional" approach allows the court to exercise its freewheeling judgment if it believes a statute is ambiguous or incomplete or calculated to lead to an injustice.

Commenting on these three possibilities, Professor Friedmann has observed:

> "None of these approaches is in itself sufficient. The analytical approach provides useful guides for the routine case but fails entirely in the solution of new situations or marginal problems which are quantitatively limited but qualitatively all-important. The social policy approach offers reasonably clear guidance only for the construction of those statutes which have a clear and definite social objective. The free intuition approach opens the way to uncertainty, prejudice and 'inarticulate major premises.'"[8]

c. Illustrative and Comparative Code Provisions

By way of contrast or comparison with the above theories, the following illustrative code provisions show the varied approaches of the codifiers to the techniques of interpretation:

French Civil Code, Article 4:[9] "A Judge who refuses to decide a case on the pretext that the law is silent, obscure or insufficient, may be prosecuted as being guilty of a denial of justice."

California Civil Code, Section 4:[10] "The rule of the common law, that statutes in derogation thereof are to be strictly construed, has no application to this code. The code establishes the law of this state respecting the subjects to which it relates, and its provisions are to be liberally construed with a view to effect its objects and to promote justice."

Swiss Civil Code, Article 1:[11] "The Code governs all questions of law which come within the letter or the spirit of any of its provisions.

"If the Code does not furnish an applicable provision, the judge shall decide in accordance with customary law, and failing that, according to the rule which he would establish as legislator.

"In this he shall be guided by approved legal doctrine and judicial tradition."

The first is in sharp contrast to the literalistic rule of the traditional approach; the second comes close to the social-policy view; and the third, derived from Aristotelian precedent,[12] markedly approximates the free-intuitional theory.

3. Selected Case Examples of Anglo-American Interpretative Techniques in Action

a. Equitable versus Literal Construction

As early as Plowden the English courts professed to recognize that a statute might, on occasion, be construed according to its equity rather than its letter.[13] This doctrine of equitable construction has fared variously in the American courts, as illustrated in the typical situation that might be referred to as "The Case of the Murdering Heir." It should be noted parenthetically that the French Civil Code anticipates the problem and resolves it by expressly excluding from succession one who has been found guilty of having killed or attempted to kill the decedent.[14] State statutes in this country have usually made no such express exception, and thereby have confronted the courts with the dilemma of either applying a statute literally or of judicially legislating into it the necessary exclusion.

In the leading case of Riggs v. Palmer[15] the New York court held that an heir who murdered a testator, even though not expressly prohibited by statute from taking under the law, should be precluded therefrom by reason of the statute's equity. To support its result, the court quoted from Bacon:

" 'By an equitable construction a case not within the letter of a statute is sometimes holden to be within the meaning, because it is within the mischief for which a remedy is provided. The reason for such construction is that the lawmakers could not set down every case in express terms. In order to form a right judgment whether a case be within the equity of a statute, it is a good way to suppose the law-maker present, and that you have asked him this question: Did you intend to comprehend this case? Then you must give yourself such answer as you imagine he, being an upright and reasonable man, would have given. If this be that he did mean to comprehend it, you may safely hold the case to be within the equity of the statute; for while you do no more than he would have done, you do not act contrary to the statute, but in conformity thereto.' 9 Bac. Abr. 248. In some cases the letter of a legislative act is restrained by an equitable construction; in others, it is enlarged; in others, the construction is contrary to the letter. . . ."[16]

The New York court's views here come close to the "intuitional" approach above referred to.

Some years later the Supreme Court of Kansas in McAllister v. Fair[17] allowed a husband who had murdered his intestate wife to succeed to her estate under a literal interpretation of the inheritance statute. The court stated:

"Although a theory cutting a murderer out of any benefits resulting from his crime appeals to the court's sense of justice, it cannot be overlooked that the Legislature has the power to declare a rule of descents; it has done so in language that is plain and peremptory, and no rule of interpretation would justify the court in reading into the statute an exception or clause disinheriting those guilty of crime."[18]

More recently the Connecticut court, in Bird v. Plunkett,[19] had before it a 1947 statute that expressly prohibits a "person finally adjudged guilty of murder in the first or second degree" from inheriting from his victim.[20] This, said the court, does not preclude inheritance by one convicted of *manslaughter*. The court reasoned from three premises: (1) the language of the statute is plain and means what it says; (2) since it has penal implications, the statute should be strictly construed; and (3) the legislative history shows that the intent was to have the statute apply only to "convicted murderers." By way of dictum, the court pointed out that under Connecticut law prior to enactment of the statute in 1947 a murderer could have inherited from his victim. A concurring judge, disagreeing on this point, referred to the Riggs v. Palmer doctrine, and stated: "I refuse to concede that equity would permit a person to profit from such an atrocious act as murder."[21]

b. Intrinsic Guides: Object and Purpose versus *Ejusdem Generis*

Similar contrasts may be observed in the weighing by American courts of the object and purpose of the statute as against a strict application of the canon of *ejusdem generis.* For example, in United States v. Alpers,[22] the Supreme Court had before it a statute making illegal the interstate shipment of any "obscene . . . book, pamphlet, picture, motion-picture film, paper, letter, writing, print, or other matter of indecent character.[23] The question was: Should the statute apply to interstate shipment of obscene phonograph records? In holding that the statute so applied, the majority relied on the "obvious purpose" of Congress to prevent interstate shipment of "any" obscene matter, and refused to invoke either strict construction or the *ejusdem generis* principle. "We are clear," said the Court, "that obscene phonograph records are within the meaning of the Act."[24]

An Ohio appellate court, in Rice v. Rinaldo,[25] considered a statute providing penalties for violation of civil rights by keepers of inns, restaurants, eating houses, barber shops, public conveyances, theaters, stores, ". . . or any other place of public accommodation."[26] The question was whether the statute should be applied to a dentist for refusal to render professional service because of the patient's race. The court here relied on *ejusdem generis,* holding that in light of the expressed enumerations a dentist was not a "place of public accommodation."

Apparently, therefore, a phonograph record can be impliedly *like* a "book . . . picture . . . or film" but a dentist cannot be impliedly like a "barber shop . . . theater, or store." While the difference may validly be one of degree, we might speculate as to how far a reliance on the object and purpose of the civil rights law, in line with the social-policy approach, would lead to a different result from that reached by the Ohio court.

c. Intrinsic Guides: Titles and Section Headings

At the outset there is a fundamental difference between the civil-law and the common-law approach to the function of titles and section headings of statutes. The traditional civil-law view accords them basic cognizance under such doctrines as *"a rubro ad nigrum"* —that statute construction proceeds from the rubric or title of a statute to the black-letter text—and *"nigrum nunquam excedere debet rubrum"*—that the text should never prevail over the rubric.[27]

American views are at variance both with the civil-law approach and with one another. In the leading case of People v. Molineux[28] the New York court held that where the text was ambiguous, chapter and section headings enacted as integral parts of the statute might be resorted to as valid aids to interpretation. Denoting a contrary view, the Military Justice Act of 1950 expressly provides that no inference of legislative construction is to be drawn by reason of the headings or catchlines in the new Uniform Code of Military Justice.[29]

d. Extrinsic Aids: Legislative History

In the matter of rejection or acceptance of legislative history as an aid to interpretation, the English view breaks sharply with the French doctrine. The latter, as is pointed out by Planiol,[30] readily permits the use of legislative history as an aid to interpretation where there is a doubt as to the meaning of a statute. But the English view firmly adheres to a policy of rejecting resort to such history in considering the meaning of a statute.[31] By way of recent example the Privy Council in the Canadian Wheat Board Case[32] completely disregarded legislative history as an aid to interpreting the Canadian National Emergency Transitional Powers Act of 1945.[33]

Though the American courts have been more liberal than the

English in recognizing legislative history as a permissible aid, the late Mr. Justice Jackson was frequently at variance with his fellow justices on this issue. In Schwegmann v. Calvert Distillers Corporation,[34] the Court had before it the question whether the Miller-Tydings Amendment,[35] exempting contracts under state resale price maintenance statutes from the Sherman Anti-Trust Act,[36] also exempted the enforcement of such statutes against nonsigners of fair trade contracts. The majority, relying on legislative history of previous attempts to amend the Sherman Act, held that such enforcement was not exempted. Three dissenting justices relied on "authoritative legislative history" to prove that enforcement of the nonsigner clause *was* intended to be exempted. Mr. Justice Jackson, in this concurring opinion, rejected legislative history as an aid, except to the extent that official committee reports might be of assistance. The gist of his objection was:

> "Aside from a few offices in larger cities, the materials of legislative history are not available to the lawyer who can afford neither the cost of acquisition, the cost of housing, or the cost of examining the whole congressional history."[37]

In a more recent case involving the Federal Power Commission Act[38] he reiterated the same point and amplified by specific illustration the difficulty of obtaining access to materials of legislative history.[39] In supporting his concurrence with the end result reached by the majority, he further announced:

> "I should concur in this result more readily if the Court could reach it by analysis of the statute instead of by psychoanalysis of Congress. When we decide from legislative history, including statements of witnesses at hearings, what Congress probably had in mind, we must put ourselves in the place of a majority of Congressmen and act according to the impression we think this history should have made on them. Never having been a Congressman, I am handicapped in that weird endeavor. That process seems to me not interpretation of a statute but creation of a statute."[40]

e. Extrinsic Aids: Draftsman's Views

As a final example, illustrative of the cyclical nature of Anglo-

American techniques, let us consider the matter of resorting to the views of the draftsman as to the meaning of the statute. Certainly in the early days, when the judges themselves were occasionally called upon the construe statutes they had drawn, the matter gave little difficulty. Thus, in the fourteenth century, Chief Justice Hengham in an argument as to the interpretation of the statute of Westminister II could abruptly silence counsel's arguments by observing sharply: "Don't gloss the statute; we know it better than you, for we made it."[41] And in Ash v. Abdy[42] Lord Nottingham commented on the Statute of Frauds: ". . . I had some reason to know the meaning of this law; for it had its first rise from me, who brought it into the Lords' House. . . ."[43]

But by the turn of the twentieth century, judges as draftsmen were less confident of their competence to construe their own handiwork. In the leading case of Hilder v. Dexter[44] the Earl of Halsbury stated:

> "My Lords, I have more than once had occasion to say that in construing a statute, I believe the worst person to construe it is the person who is responsible for its drafting. He is very much disposed to confuse what he intended to do with the effect of the language which in fact has been employed."[45]

His position has formed the basis for the doctrine in English and some American courts that the views of the draftsman should not be resorted to as an aid to interpreting statutes.[46]

Nevertheless there appears to be a discernible trend in the American decisions to consider such views as acceptable and authoritative guides. The trend is most clearly exemplified in the decisions of the United States Court of Military Appeals, where Professor Morgan as draftsman of the Uniform Code of Military Justice[47] is frequently quoted as a source authority for its proper construction.[48]

4. Need for Reappraisal of Interpretative Techniques

The foregoing illustrations, chosen at random from the plethora of Anglo-American materials on the subject of statutory interpretation, indicate that its techniques are varied and often conflicting.

The need for reappraisal is evident and the justification for it becomes increasingly cogent. For example, the growth of uniform laws and their increasing adoption by large numbers of states points up the need for consistent uniformity in the judicial interpretation of such laws.

"In the interpretation of a statute widely adopted by the states to the end of securing uniformity in a department of commercial law, we should be inclined to give great weight to harmonious decisions of courts of other states, even if we were less clear than we are in this instance as to the soundness of our own conclusions."[49]

If this is true as to uniform laws at the national level, will it not also become necessary, with the growth of international statute law, sooner or later to reappraise our techniques of interpretation on an international scale? If so, experience under the French Civil Code as well as in Anglo-American jurisprudence will inevitably receive careful scrutiny and revaluation.

NOTES

1 Montesquieu, The Spirit of Laws, Vol. I, Bk. XI, Ch. 6, p. 182 (D'Alembert ed., 1873).

2 Bentham, Truth v. Ashhurst Works, Vol. V, 236 (Bowring ed., 1834).

3 See Lenhoff, On Interpretative Theories: A Comparative Study in Legislation, 27. Texas L. Rev. 312, 320n. (1949).

4 Campbell, Lives of the Lord Chancellors, Vol. I, p. 274 (2d ed., 1846).

5 *Ibid.*, citing Y.B. 39 Edw. 3 (1366), Y.B. 40 Edw. 3 (1367). And see, Spencer v. State, 5 Ind. 41, 48 (1854).

6 Heydon's Case, 3 Co. 7a, 7b, 76 Eng. Rep. 637, 638 (1584).

7 Friedmann, Statute Law and Its Interpretation, 26 Can. B. Rev. 1277, 1279 (1948).

8 *Id.* at 1300.

9 (Cachard, rev. ed. 1930) 2.

10 (Deering's ed., 1951).

11 As reprinted in Schlesinger, Comparative Law Cases and Materials 276 (1950).

12 Aristotle, Nicomachean Ethics, Vol. 5, Ch. 10, Sec. I; and see Lenhoff, *supra* note 3, at 318.

13 Eyston v. Studd, 2 Plowd. 459, 464, 75 Eng. Rep. 688, 695 (1574): "Wherefore a man ought not to rest upon the letter of an Act, nor think that when he has the letter on his side, he has the law on his side in all cases."

14 Art. 727, *op. cit. supra* note 9, at 219.

15 115 N. Y. 506, 22 N. E. 188 (1889).

[16] 115 N. Y. at 510, 22 N. E. at 189 (1889).

[17] 72 Kan. 533, 84 P. 112 (1906).

[18] 72 Kan. at 540, 84 P. at 115 (1906).

[19] 139 Conn. 491, 95A. 2d 71 (1953).

[20] Conn. Gen. Stats., 1947 Supp. § 1316i, 1949 Rev., § 7062.

[21] 139 Conn. at 506, 95A. 2d at 78 (1953).

[22] 338 U. S. 680 (1950).

[23] U. S. Criminal Code § 245, 18 U. S. C. § 1462.

[24] 338 U. S. at 685 (1950).

[25] 119 N. E. 2d 657 (Oh. App. 1951).

[26] Ohio Gen. Code § 12940.

[27] Black, Interpretation of Laws 245 (2d ed., 1911).

[28] 53 Barbour (N. Y.) 9 (1868).

[29] Act of May 5, 1950, § 3, 64 Stat. 145.

[30] Planiol, Traité élémentaire de droit civil, Vol. 1, Par. 218, as quoted in Smith, Interpretation in English and Continental Law, 9 Jour. Comp. Leg. 3d ser. 153, 157 (1927): "La première chose à faire, pour lever le doute, est de consulter les travaux préparatoires de la loi (discussions des Chambres, rapports, exposés des motifs, etc.)."

[31] See, Regina v. Hertford College, 3 Q.B.D. 697, 707 (1878): "The statute is clear, and the parliamentary history of the statute is wisely inadmissible to explain it if it is not."

[32] Attorney-General for Canada v. Hallet & Carey Ltd., [1952] A. C. 427. For a vigorous criticism of the decision, see Davis, Legislative History and the Wheat Board Case, 31 Can. B. Rev. 1 (1953).

[33] 9–10 Geo. VI, c. 25.

[34] 341 U. S. 384 (1951).

[35] Act of August 17, 1937, c. 690, 50 Stat. 693, 15 U.S.C. § 1.

[36] Act of July 2, 1890, c. 647, 26 Stat. 209, 15 U.S.C. § 1.

[37] 341 U. S. at 396 (1951).

[38] Act of August 26, 1935, 49 Stat. 863, 16 U.S.C. §791a.

[39] United States v. Public Utilities Comm., 345 U. S. 295, 320 (1953).

[40] 345 U. S. at 319 (1953).

[41] The present writer, with more of simple faith than Norman blood, accepts this as a reasonable rendition of the original in Y. B. 33–35 Edw. 1 (R. S.) 83, as cited in Gutteridge, A Comparative view of the Interpretation of Statute Law, 8 Tulane L. Rev. 1, 10n. (1933): "Ne glosez point le statut; nous le savons [mieux] de vous, quar nous le feimes."

[42] 3 Swans. 664, 36 Eng. Rep. 1014 (1678).

[43] 3 Swans. at 664, 36 Eng. Rep. at 1014 (1678).

[44] [1902] A. C. 474 (H. of L.).

[45] [1902] A. C. at 477 (H. of L.).

[46] See, for example, Third District Land Co. v. Toka, 170 So. 793, 795 (La. App. 1936).

[47] Act of May 5, 1950, 64 Stat. 107, 50 U.S.C. §551.

[48] See, United States v. O'Neal, 1 USCMA 138, 151, 2 CMR 44, 57 (1952); United States v. Berry, 1 USCMA 235, 241, 2 CMR 141, 147 (1952); United States v. Norris, 2 USCMA 236, 239, 8 CMR 36, 39 (1953); United States v. Grow, 3 USCMA 77, 83, 11 CMR 77, 83 (1953).

[49] Union Trust Co. v. McGinty, 212 Mass. 205, 208, 98 N. E. 679, 681 (1912).

6

Territorial Expansion of the Code

JEAN LIMPENS

THE SPONSORS of this memorable conference have called upon a Belgian jurist to speak of the territorial expansion of the Code. I know not whether such a choice is merited, but I greatly appreciate the honor paid my country. As a matter of fact, Belgium may well be said to have some right to this distinction. Few countries have shown such strong adherence to the Napoleonic Code. Belgium retained the Code after Waterloo and even championed its cause before the parliament of the kingdom of Holland. It did so with such success, indeed, that, through the Hollando-Belgian project of 1830, the Code became the foundation of the Netherlands Civil Code of 1838. The French Code found its most ardent proponent in Belgium in the person of the great jurist François Laurent, Professor at the University of Ghent, whose work contributed greatly to the maintenance and prestige of French juridical culture in Europe. And, last but not least, Belgium has adhered more faithfully to the original text of the Code Napoleon than most other countries. In actuality, the changes made in the Code in Belgium have been less far-reaching than those made in France itself.

The expansion of the Code Napoleon was carried out in three ways: (1) by conquest, (2) by direct persuasion, (3) by inspiration. Something should be said about each method.

JEAN LIMPENS *is Dean of the Law School of the University of Ghent, Professor at the Law School of the University of Brussels, and Assessor of the Belgian Council of State*

I

CONQUEST

On the promulgation of the Code, March 21, 1804, it was naturally introduced into areas then a part of French territory. It was thus introduced into Belgium, Luxembourg, the German territories situated on the west side of the Rhine, the Palatine, Rhenan Prussia, Hesse-Darmstadt, Geneva,[1] Savoia, the duchies of Parma and Plaisance, Blemont, and the principality of Monaco. The greater part of these territories, it should be noted, conserved the Code for a long time: the German territories until 1900, Geneva until 1912, Belgium, Luxembourg, and the principality of Monaco until the present time. The Code was certainly nothing strange to them, for they were all territorially a part of France at the time of its promulgation.

As the Napoleonic armies swept through Europe they brought slavery to some and liberty to others, but to all they brought what Napoleon clearly thought of as the benefits of his new legislation. "Your statutes," he said to the Italian *consulte,* "extend the benefit of the Code whose drafting I myself presided over to the Italian people."[2] And in a similar vein he wrote to his brother Jerome, King of Westphalia, "The benefits of the Code will be of peculiar value to your monarchy."[3] Almost prophetically he dreamed "of a general European Code,"[4] and everybody—his brothers (Joseph in Naples, Jerome in Westphalia, Louis in Holland), his consuls (Lebrun in Genoa), his generals (Junod in Portugal, Murat in Madrid), his ambassadors (Champagny in Germany)—was urged to contribute to the success of the great undertaking of legal unification. The Emperor of Austria himself was threatened with the introduction of the Code in his own territories.[5] But Napoleon did not always get the proper help. While in exile he complained about this to Montholon: "If my brothers had followed me," he said, "we would have marched as far as the poles; we would have changed the face of the world."

Though Napoleon did not realize his grandiose scheme of an all-European legal system, the results achieved in that direction by his Code were far from mediocre. The Code was introduced in Italy (1805–1820), in the Netherlands (March 1, 1811), in the Hanseatic territories (December 13, 1810), and in the Grand Duchy of Berg (December 17, 1811).

Italy was then divided into a great number of harmless small states. If this situation weakened the political strength of the country, it also helped to make legal integration most difficult. It took no less than eight years to overcome this difficulty and to introduce the Code into the ten states that then made up the peninsula. (Genoa on July 4, 1805; Parma on September 23, 1805; Lombardy on January 16, 1806; Modena on January 30, 1806; Venice on March 30, 1806; Lucca and Piombino on April 21, 1806; Guastalla on August 12, 1804; Marches and Legations on April 2, 1808; Tuscany on May 1, 1808; Naples on December 26, 1809; the Papal States on January 16, 1812.)[6]

The Netherlands, on the other hand, accepted the Code, but proposed various amendments and asked for delay. The king, Louis Napoleon, who had dared to transmit these claims, was roughly castigated by his brother. "I don't see," said the latter, "why you need so much time or what changes must be made. . . . You are administratively immature if you think that the establishment of a specific code can worry the people or implant in the country a state of unhealthy confusion. The Dutch are telling you stories because they are jealous of all that comes from France. Moreover a nation of 18 hundred thousand cannot have a separate code. The Romans gave their laws to their allies—why should not France make hers adopted in Holland?" And also: "If you tamper with the Napoleonic Code, it will no longer be the Napoleonic Code."[7]

However, Louis followed his own ideas and promulgated a "Napoleonic Code in May 1809, as arranged for the Kingdom of Holland." This disagreement, among many others, was eventually to bring about his downfall. Holland was united to the Empire, and the Napoleonic Code was purely and simply imposed on Holland on March 1, 1811.[8]

II

PERSUASION

Napoleon's victories opened doors to the Code even beyond the conquered countries. The Code was literally adopted by several states of central Europe: Westphalia on January 1, 1808; Hanover (united to Westphalia in 1810); the grand duchies of Baden, Frankfort, and Nassau; the free town of Danzig; the grand duchy of Warsaw; certain Swiss cantons; and the Illyrian Provinces.

The persuasion that induced these countries to embrace the French law was, it is true, from time to time ably arranged by the Emperor himself, impatient to extend his domination over all of Europe. "Make no delay whatsoever in its establishment," he wrote to his brother Jerome, King of Westphalia, on November 15, 1807. "Undoubtedly objections will be made thereto; oppose them with a strong will. . . . The members of the Regency will make certain representations. Answer that it is none of their business."[9]

In many instances, however, it was local jurists themselves who persuaded their countrymen to adopt the Code. The German jurist Brauer recommended the adoption of the Code well before his state, the Grand Duchy of Baden, joined the Rhine Federation, to put an end to the deplorable state of legal decay that reigned in the small country of Baden at that time.[10] The Code, built on many Germanic customs, was not considered a foreign law by him nor by the other Rhenish jurists. Nothing proves this better than their long attachment to the Code, which remained in force in their provinces until 1900, giving rise to a remarkable brand of jurisprudence as well as to some works of exceptional value.[11]

Striking, although barely known, is the fact that Savigny himself, the great adversary of the Code, was brought to render formal, though indirect, homage to the Code. As there was a question in

1818 of replacing the Napoleonic Code by the Prussian Code of 1794, Savigny, questioned on the soundness of this reform, did not hesitate to condemn it.

III

INSPIRATION

Up to this point we have been considering countries into which the Code was completely introduced by means of conquest or persuasion. There are innumerable others, however, that, without having adopted the Code as such, were nevertheless deliberately inspired by it and therefore belong to the great legal family of the French Code whose genealogy we are now trying to trace.

In 1814 the direct expansion of the Code came to a halt. Indeed, at the outset the defeat of the Napoleonic armies brought with it attempts to do away with the law that they had imported.

A few sought entirely to destroy the usurper's New Law (Italy, except for Parma, Naples, Genoa, and Lucca, which maintained it respectively until 1819, 1820, 1838, and 1847; Switzerland, except for Geneva and the Berner Jura, which kept it until 1912).

Others were content to make some insignificant modifications (Baden and other Rhenish states).

Still others, like Belgium in 1831, limited themselves to the expression of a platonic wish to revise the Code—a revision, however, for which we are still waiting after more than a century.

The embers of reaction having sufficiently cooled, these countries, experiencing only legal chaos under the laws that they had substituted for the Code, soon regretted their post-1814 apostasy and returned to the Code. Others, more numerous, became interested in the Code or took inspiration from it.

This was the great era of dissemination of the Code throughout the world. One may say that its real expansion started at that time, *i.e.* around 1830.

Let us consider in order Europe, America, and the Orient.[12]

Europe.—The first attempt at adoption of the Code was made in *Greece* in 1827. This effort, however, was short-lived, for the jurist in charge of drafting the Code quarreled with the government and suddenly left Greece, taking with him all his documents. Nevertheless the Code was introduced into the Ionian Islands in 1841.[13]

The influence of the Code on the *Netherlands* is striking, but it did not come about without trouble and difficulty. Kempner, appointed by the king in 1815 to draft a new project, visualized a code of "pure Netherlandish inspiration." The Belgian delegates, on the other hand, wanted to maintain the Code as closely as possible in its original text. The inevitable result was sharp conflicts and bitter words. But the Belgians, supported by an important Dutch faction, were unyielding, and the kingdom of the Netherlands was thus developing toward a Code strongly resembling the Napoleonic Code when the Belgian revolution put an end to these efforts. The Dutch then decided to proceed to a revision of the project; but all in all, the modifications were very insignificant, and the Dutch Code of 1838 therefore preserved some resemblance to the Code Napoleon—a fact for which perhaps the Belgian delegates deserve some credit.[14] What will become of it in the future? It is difficult to say. The great jurisconsult Meijers, until his recent death, was in charge of drafting a new code. The code is now ready, and the first half has already been published.[15] Although each problem has been carefully thought out, one cannot say that it departs in a considerable manner from either the present Code or the original French example. However, some changes have been made, particularly in the integration by the new code of civil and commercial law.[16]

What happened in *Italy?* Suppressed in the majority of the Italian states, the Code soon reappeared in them by force of events. When it ceased to reign *"ratione imperii,"* as was so aptly remarked by Fiore, it reigned *"imperii rationis."*[17] In succession four codes (the civil code of the two Sicilies—1812; the civil code of Parma—1820; the civil code of Modena—1842; and the Albertine code of the

Sardinian States—1837) were promulgated, all of them almost entirely derived from the Code Napoleon.[18]

And finally, when the Italian kingdom (unified March 17, 1861) sought to promulgate a unified codification, the principal source of the code of 1865, though the Albertine Code was the working model, was once more the Napoleonic Code.[19]

In the same year (1865) *Roumania* adopted a code that is a mere translation of the French Code.[20] Although the prince, by edict of July 14, 1864, expressly advised the Council of State to take the Italian Code of 1865 as the model, M. C. Bozianu, the president of the Council, in utter disregard of this recommendation, deliberately followed the Napoleonic Code. Two months later the work was completed,[21] and from that time on the influence of the Code was so marked in Roumania that the new project, which was to come into effect on the eve of the last war, continued to bear witness to its French origin.[22]

The Iberian Peninsula, on the other hand, with its lands of ancient civilization, could not help displaying some originality.

The *Portuguese* Code of 1867, drafted by Seabra, is certainly not a simple translation of the Napoleonic Code. But of all the foreign codes considered it is undoubtedly the Napoleonic Code that most inspired the Portuguese legislator.[23]

In the *Spanish* Code of 1889 drafted by Goyenna, in addition to similarity of substance, one finds the clarity of thought and of drafting that was the trademark of the Napoleonic laws.[24]

America.—The dynamic influence of the Code did not stop at the borders of Europe. America, with its boundless territories, was to furnish new areas for expansion.

Strangely enough, it was in North America on the soil of the United States that the Code found its first foothold. *Louisiana,* a French establishment from 1682 to 1762, a Spanish possession from 1762 to 1800, a part of the United States from 1804, was first and foremost a land of French culture. The first code of 1808 amply demonstrated its heritage. Although it is not known if the drafters of the code were in possession of the definitive text of the Code Napoleon,[25] it is interesting to note that the divergences from it were not great. The second code of 1825, drafted by the great American codifier Livingston, is even closer to the Napoleonic Code.[26]

Although chronologically out of place, a few words should be said at this point of the Canadian experience. The *Quebec* Code of 1866 is certainly not a direct offspring of the Code Napoleon; it is above all—and the fact is worthy of attention—a codification founded on the Custom of Paris.[27] Nevertheless one is bound to note, in addition to certain striking borrowings, a great similarity of drafting in the matters common to both codes.

If we now turn our attention to Latin America, we find that the codes developed there during the nineteenth century were all more or less inspired by the French example.[28]

Moreover, there is one country in the Western hemisphere in which the original Code is still in effect: namely, the *Dominican Republic,* which was also the first to adopt it in 1825. Surprisingly enough, the Code was first introduced there in its original French text, although the current language of the country had been, from the early times of colonization, Spanish; the Code was not translated until more than half a century later (1884). And the short American occupation from 1917 to 1924, which, of course, left some traces in the legal field, did not even try to destroy French legal pre-eminence in the country.[29]

Second in chronological order came the *Bolivian* Code of 1831, which, except for a few minor details, was a simple translation of the French Code.[30]

The third was the *Chilean* Code of 1865, established by the great jurist Andres Bello, which, in spite of its incontestable originality, also belonged to the French family. Its arrangement is practically the same and many passages are literally borrowed from the French Code.[31] This code was nevertheless so remarkable that it was copied by some countries (Ecuador and Colombia, 1861 and 1873 respectively) and taken as a model in others (Uruguay and Argentina, 1867 and 1869).

The *Uruguayan* legislators took care to reveal the many sources of their new laws. "The European codes, those of America, the remarkable Chilean Code, the wisest critics of the Napoleonic Code, the project of Dr. Acevedo, that of Dr. Goyenna, that of Dr. Freytas, that of Dr. Sarsfield," they said, "were the precursors of the work we have revised, discussed and approved." But in spite of this diversity of inspiration and perhaps because of it—for these precursors themselves belong to the French family—the Uruguayan Code remains basically similar to the French Code.[32]

As for the *Argentinian* Code of 1869, drafted by the jurist Velez Sarsfield, a threefold source is generally attributed to it: the *Escobo* of Freytas for the first three books, Aubry and Rau and the Code Napoleon for the last three, Garcia Goyenna and the Chilean Code for the remainder.[33] As much directly as indirectly (through the Chilean conduit) the French influence is here again important if not preponderant.[34]

A new project drafted by Bibiloni in 1936 is at present under study. It cannot be denied that this project, though it gives much prominence to the German influence, still contains the teachings of the Napoleonic Code.[35]

At the turn of the century, however, the influence of the Code diminished. The German Code, born with the century, offered an indisputable attraction, despite its technicality and heaviness. The codes of Brazil (1916), of Mexico (1928), and of Peru (1936) are related to the German Code. However, if their exterior aspects plainly bear traces of German influence, many of their institutions still have their roots in the Napoleonic Code. Nor should one overlook the homage rendered the French Code by one of the most recent American legislatures (*Venezuela*), which in 1942, after an interval of 138 years, decided to adopt the French traditional tripartite division.

The Orient.—If we continue our itinerary beyond the Pacific, we find the first haven of French legal culture in *Japan.*

Thanks to the personal prestige of Boissonade and his colleagues in charge of teaching French law in Japan from 1872, the Code shone forth there with an exceptional brilliance. Boissonade, designated to draw up a local code, was naturally inclined to follow the Napoleonic example. And, a fact unique in legal history, his draft was applied in Japan from 1880 to 1896 without any official approval whatsoever.[36] This draft was, however, criticized for being too French and for not having paid any attention to the German projects already known at that time. A new commission was named, which drafted the Code of 1898. But although the plan was changed, a larger part of the dispositions of the first draft were maintained.[37]

As for *China,* she, aroused by the Japanese example, formed a commission in 1916 to take charge of preparing a code. The Chinese codes were promulgated from 1929 to 1931. Their format was borrowed from the German Code. Mr. Escarra himself, Professor of the Law School of the University of Paris, a member of the drafting commission, admitted that he did not seek to impose the *Code Civil* in China.[38] But all this belongs to the past. The Iron Curtain has been dropped over China. Without doubt her destinies have changed, and it is difficult to surmise what course her legislation will take.

If the Far East proved not too receptive to the Code, the Mediterranean area and the Near East have given French law, until very recent years, reasons for legitimate pride.

There is little to say of *Turkey.* She adopted four French codes (commercial code, code of civil procedure, criminal code, and code of criminal procedure). The Turkish civil code called *Medjelle* (1869) offers but fortuitous similarities to the Napoleonic Code. Moreover, in 1925 Turkey decided to adopt the Swiss Civil Code and the greater part of the Swiss Code of Obligations.

Egypt, on the other hand, extended a warm welcome to French law and culture. A mixed civil code and a National Civil Code were introduced (1876 and 1883). They were almost identical with the Code Napoleon. In 1948, however, Egypt adopted a new code, one of the most remarkable codifications of modern times. But this new legislation still carries on and pays respect to the great tradition of French jurisprudence; it has not left the sphere of influence of the Napoleonic Code.[39]

It was only natural for *Lebanon,* integrated with French culture, to turn toward France. A French judge, M. Ropers, and M. Josserand, Professor at the Law School of the University of Paris, were appointed to draft a code dealing with contracts and obligations. This code, which took effect in 1934, constitutes a simple acceptance, if not of the Code Napoleon, then at least of French law.[40]

The *Syrian* Civil Code of 1949, which is probably the most recent in the world, was modeled on the Egyptian civil code. To the extent that it departs from the latter, it reapproaches the French law.

Such, briefly, is the amazing trip that the Code Napoleon has made around the world. Introduced in thirty-five states, translated, copied, and adapted in thirty-five others, it might have been expected one day to have been extended throughout the entire world. "Founded on principles of civil equality and tolerance," Huc wrote in 1868, "the Napoleonic Code governs two-thirds of the civilized world; one may surmise that one day it will be adopted by all nations."[41]

Napoleon himself did not conceal his pride: "My true glory," he said to Montholon one night in St. Helena, "is not to have won forty battles. . . . Waterloo will erase the memory of so many victories. . . . But what nothing will destroy, what will live forever, is my Civil Code."[42]

Realism prevents one from believing that a code, perfect though it may be, can govern a nation for all time. However, by the same token, it can readily be assumed that the Napoleonic Code will dwell forever in the memory of men as a brilliant signpost on their journey toward social peace and liberty.

Once the success of the Code was established, scholars, in their avid desire to explain everything, tried to discover the reasons for its success.

Some argued that the Napoleonic Code is a *code,* emphasizing by this truism that only codified law can attain some penetration outside its own boundaries.[43] One can hardly imagine a body of case law such as the English common law, for example, seeking expansion. Of course, it can be applied wherever a judge may introduce it. But, generally speaking, it has no power of attraction whatsoever. Assuming that a foreigner can absorb a code, how can he be able, suddenly, even to understand the swarming diversities of a judicial tradition?

Others remarked that the Code was born at a most *opportune time.* If born before 1789, it would have been destroyed by the Revolution. If born the day after 1789, it would have been deemed a revelation of the "Supreme Being," the new God of the Revolution, and as such would have been swept away by the Restoration. It came instead to a world weary of the excesses of the Revolution, when the French people had found their traditional equilibrium once again.

The Code is indeed the most perfect expression of this equilibrium: equilibrium of sources, equilibrium of thought, equilibrium of form.

EQUILIBRIUM OF SOURCES

Enough has been said by others about how harmoniously the Code combined the customs of the northern part of the country with the Roman law that reigned in the southern part.

The make-up of the commission that drafted the Code was, indeed, a good omen. Old Tronchet, seventy-four years of age, president of the Supreme Court, former defender of King Louis XVI, and Bigot de Préameneu, attorney general at the Supreme Court, former member of the Parliament of Brittany, both men of the customary law, represented the northern provinces. Portalis, commissioner general of the Prize Court, former attorney of Aix, immortal drafter of the *exposé des motifs,* and Maleville, a member of the Supreme Court and former attorney of the Parliament of Bordeaux, both nursed by the written law, *i.e.* the Roman law, represented the southern provinces. Only a compromise could be the result of such a commission. But this aura of compromise was exactly what gave the Code its strength. For the northern neighbors, the Belgians, the Dutch, the Rhenish, recognized in it their own customs; conversely, the southern countries of Italy, Spain, Portugal, and Roumania recognized in it their own laws so far as these were derived from the Roman law.

EQUILIBRIUM OF THOUGHT

This included equilibrium between the principles of authority of the *Ancien Régime* and the individualism of the Revolution; between the religious conceptions of the Monarchy (in the field of domestic relations, for example) and the pagan conceptions of the Convention; between the protection of property and the distribution of individual wealth; between freedom of will and the public interest; and between rigid rules of law and legal standards, whose importance was so well pointed out by Napoleon himself when he said: "One should not burden oneself with overdetailed laws . . . law must do nothing but impose a general principle. It would be vain if one were to try to foresee therein every possible situation; experience would prove that much has been omitted. . . ."[44]

EQUILIBRIUM OF FORM

This appears at every moment in those clear, pregnant, carefully coined dispositions that plot the course of the Code and have been so rightly considered an exceptional success. For if, on the one hand, the Code is understandable to the layman, it also satisfies the talented writer. And even if we do not go so far as to make the Code daily reading, as Stendhal did, there is no doubt that it is a model of conciseness, clarity, and elegance.

Of course, the Code has its defects, but it would not be an exaggeration to say that rarely has a text been able to attain such a degree of perfection. The reason is worth mentioning. As it was so ably put by M. Le Roux, "The draftsmen of the Code knew that their text would pass under the eyes of a man of great intelligence, but a man foreign to their profession. . . . Tronchet and Portalis drew it up under the impression that their first reader would be Napoleon Bonaparte."[45]

Furthermore it would be incorrect to underestimate the time factor. Though it is true that a rule must ripen under the beneficent rays of experience, it is also true that it must be drafted without delay, once it is matured, in order to avoid the pitfalls of burdensome details and discriminations. It is well known that the draftsmen of the Code, goaded by the First Consul, succeeded in finishing their work within four months, which fact is certainly not the least surprising one in the wonderful history of the Code.

True, famous examples showed them the way—the Ordinances of Louis XIV, the remarkable works of Domat and Pothier. Nevertheless they must be lauded for having had the wisdom to borrow so many time-polished formulae from their ancestors. The law is a long tradition, and plagiarism becomes a virtue of humility for the legislator.

All these views tending to explain the success of the Code, certainly, contain an element of truth. But I for one should like to believe that the Napoleonic Code owes a great part of its success to Napoleon himself. What the kings of France tried to do for centuries without success, what the Revolution vainly inscribed on its programs, he, the short Corsican general, accomplished between two victories by a turn of the hand, and it is not true that he merely came at the right time to gather the fruits of a millennial elaboration. One needs only to glance through the history of the drafting to know that it was otherwise. Behind the Code stood a man gifted with tremendous will and energy, a man who wanted the Code and wanted it with obstinacy.

Nor was it an artificial work imposed on the people by an impulsive autocrat. Drafted by the most prominent jurists of the time, submitted for the judgment of the highest legal authorities, it was discussed for years in the sessions of the Council of State. It was even near defeat when, as early as December 1801, the preliminary title was rejected by the legislative body by 142 votes against 139. No fewer than 123 meetings, over 55 of which Napoleon himself presided, were necessary to pass the law that so many omens had apparently destined to failure.

Can one imagine a chief of state at the present day spending the greater part of his time drawing up a code? Such is nevertheless the striking picture of what took place a hundred and fifty years ago in the meetings of the French Council of State. Although the youngest by far—he was hardly thirty-two—Napoleon dominated the Assembly by his indisputable authority. Untiring, he presided over meetings that began at noon and often lasted until dawn. Pale, hollow-cheeked, with bright eyes, he followed the debates with avid interest and brought to them the spontaneous charm of his youth and enthusiasm. "He was," said Savatier, "the most natural, the only whimsical, the only spontaneous person in the Assembly; the only one in the field of marriage to talk about blondes and brunettes, of blue and black eyes and of the belief that such details could have any importance. He alone joked in this assembly of somber persons with youthfulness and a little bit of military liberty." "And I imagine," added Savatier, "that it was this naturalness; this informality, this passion, that formed part of his charm. For on this point, all who approached him were in agreement. Writing after his downfall, all his collaborators of the Council of State, Roederer, Locré, Thibaudeau, recall having been conquered by this fascinating young man."[46]

Almost ignorant of legal affairs, but gifted with extreme good sense and a superior intelligence, he knew by dint of reflection and vigil how to master the most delicate problems. His interventions were often decisive, at times disputable, but never mediocre. And it has often been deplored that his advice was not followed.

He had a vibrant faith that inflamed the imagination and stole all hearts. "I should like," he said in one of his moments of sublime inspiration, "a Frenchman of origin, even though of the tenth generation, still to find himself a Frenchman. . . . I want to raise the glory of the French name so high that it becomes the envy of all nations. I should like to see the day when, with the help of divine guidance, a Frenchman traveling throughout Europe could always find himself at home."[47]

After those words one cannot help thinking of the mockery of a fate that decreed that he, of all Frenchman of that time, was to die in exile on unfriendly soil. The only favor extended to his memory consisted in transporting his ashes to the borders of the Seine "in the midst of the people," as he himself wrote, "he loved so much."

It is pleasing to believe that, if the Code has had such success and such authority in the world, we must in all justice ascribe a part of this success to this "fascinating young man," gifted with a tremendous dynamism and with an immense love of his country, who knew how to mold these "masses of granite," as he used to call his Code, upon French soil.

He was the force that set loose the chain reaction of world-wide codification. He wished the French name to be the envy of all nations. At least we can say that all nations envied him the Code as being the very foundation of modern private law.

NOTES

1 Cavin, in Travaux de la semaine internationale de droit, 1950, 689 (1954).
2 Correspondance, Vol. 10, 599 (1858–70).
3 *Id.,* Vol. 16, 206.
4 Las Cases, Memorial de Sainte Hélène, Vol. 3, 298; Vol. 4, 153, 297 (1840).
5 Pérouse, Napoleon I et les lois civiles 330 (1866).

[6] Chironi, Le code civil et son influence en Italie, Le livre du centenaire, Vol. 2, 765 (1904); Berri, in *op. cit. supra* note 1, at 617.

[7] Letter of Napoleon of November 13, 1807. Correspondance, Vol. 16, 190.

[8] Asser, Le code civil dans les Pays-Bas, in *op. cit. supra* note 6, at 816.

[9] Correspondance, Vol. 16, 206.

[10] Boehmer, in *op. cit. supra* note 1, at 581.

[11] E.g., Zacharie, Treatise on the French Civil Code (1808).

[12] We shall not deal with French possessions and territories, in which, of course, one can expect the laws to be modeled on the French pattern.

[13] Ripert, Traité élémentaire de droit civil de Planiol, Vol. 1, 84 (1950).

[14] Van Dievoet, Het Burgerlyk recht in Belgie en in Holland tussen 1800 en 1940, 31–52 (1943).

[15] See Meyers, La revision du code civil néerlandais, Journal des Tribunaux 85 (1955).

[16] Limpens, De l'unification du droit civil et du droit commercial, Journal des Tribunaux 353 (1953).

[17] Fiore, Trattato di diritto civile, Vol. 1, 2 (1886).

[18] Berri, in *op. cit. supra* note 1, at 619.

[19] *Id.* at 622.

[20] Mazeaud, in *op. cit. supra* note 1, at 561.

[21] Constantinescu, in *id.* 673.

[22] *Id.* at 685.

[23] Mazeaud, *id.* at 560; de Magalhaes, *id.* at 636.

[24] Arminjon, Nolde, and Wolff, Traité de droit comparé, Vol. 1, 156 (1950).

[25] Dainow, Civil Code of Louisiana, The Louisiana Civil Law xix (1947).

[26] Morrow, Louisiana Blueprint: Civilian Codification and Legal Method for State and Nation, 17 Tulane L. Rev. 351, 388 (1943); Hubert, in *op. cit. supra* note 1, at 779; Franklin, Concerning the Historic Importance of Edward Livingston, 11 Tulane L. Rev. 163 (1937).

[27] David, Traité élémentaire de droit civil comparé 306 (1950).

[28] Cordeiro Alvarez, in *op. cit. supra* note 1, at 743.

[29] Galindez, in *op. cit. supra* note 1, at 805.

[30] Cordeiro Alvarez, *id.* at 743; Duran, *id.* at 771.

[31] Cordeiro Alvarez, *id.* at 742; Hurtado, *id.* at 816; Garcia-Lopez, *id.* at 822.

[32] Cordeiro Alvarez, *id.* at 744.

[33] *Id.* at 740.

[34] Garcia-Lopez, *id.* at 823.

[35] *Id.* at 730.

[36] Gorai, L'influence du code civil français sur le Japon, in *op. cit. supra* note 6, at 788.

[37] *Id.* at 789; Maury, in *op. cit. supra* note 1, at 849.

[38] Escarra, Le droit chinois 177 (1936).

[39] Chavagat, in *op. cit. supra* note 1, at 865.

[40] Maury, *id.* at 845; Chevalier, *id.* at 872.

[41] Huc, Le code civil italien et le code Napoleon, Vol. 1, 2 (1868).

[42] De Montholon, Recit de la captivité, Vol. 1, 401 (1847).

[43] Wigmore, L'avenir du système anglo-américain, in Introduction à l'étude du droit comparé, Recueil d'études en l'honneur d'Edouard Lambert, Vol. 2, 106 (1938).

44 "Is this fair, is this useful?" Napoleon constantly asked the members of the Council of State, referring to the "general interest" and "civil justice." Pérouse, *op. cit. supra* note 5, at 227.

45 Locré, Législation civile, commerciale et criminelle de la France, Vol. 4, 87, 89 (1827).

46 Savatier, Bonaparte et le code civil 21 (1927).

47 Mémoires de la Duchesse d'Abrantès, Vol. 4, 146 (1831–34).

7

The Code and Contract— A Comparative Analysis of Formation and Form

ARTHUR VON MEHREN

I

THE French Civil Code of 1804, however developed through judicial decision and legal writing, no longer represents, if only because of its relatively great age, the most advanced Continental thought on problems of contract law. Nevertheless there are many aspects of the subject of this paper, *The Code and Contract,* that could be considered with profit even by one not primarily interested in French law. It would be interesting to survey all of French contract law, examining its solutions for certain of the difficult and delicate problems that arise in this area. A detailed comparative investigation of one or more topics of contract law could be undertaken. The structure and techniques of contract law as developed by the *Code Civil,* by other continental codes, and by the common-law courts could be compared.

It would also be interesting to consider the problems that have arisen in the French law of contracts because of various defects in the Civil Code. For example, none of the problems of offer and acceptance are explicitly regulated by the Code. This omission can perhaps be explained on the ground that in 1804 commerce by cor-

ARTHUR VON MEHREN *is Professor of Law at Harvard Law School*

respondence had not yet developed to the point at which a detailed treatment of offer and acceptance was felt to be necessary. Whatever the explanation, the French courts had later to face without assistance from the Code the problem of developing satisfactory rules for handling contracts by correspondence.[1]

Other defects in the doctrinal structure of the Civil Code in the field of contract law result from commissions rather than omissions. Two examples of these can be noted here: Articles 1119 and 1121 contain what is, in appearance at least, a severe limitation on contracts for the benefit of third parties.[2] The granting of any form of specific performance in connection with contracts by which the obligor has assumed the obligation to do (or not to do) something would seem to be precluded by Article 1142 of the Code.[3]

A study of the handling in French law of these and other difficulties caused by defects in the structure of the Civil Code would furnish interesting examples of the judicial process at work in a codified system. Such a study would emphasize, however, the achievement of the French courts rather than the achievement of the codifiers of French law. It has, therefore, seemed more appropriate on this occasion to consider two basic areas of the law of contracts, formation and form, in which the structure of the Civil Code is superior to that of the common law. An attempt will also be made to suggest an explanation for this superiority.

II

In French law a contract is created, as a matter of general theory, by the parties' agreeing to a proposition.[4] The legal system sets, of course, limits to the power to create by agreement legally enforceable obligations. Thus, certain categories of agreements are not binding if formal requirements have not been met. And agreements that deeply offend the community's sense of justice are refused enforcement. In French law the question whether an enforceable contractual obligation has been formed is, however, approached by analyzing whether there was an agreement between the parties.

The general requirements for the formation of a contract at common law are more complex. The Restatement of Contracts states them to be "A manifestation of assent by the parties who form the contract to the terms thereof, and by every promisor to the consideration for his promise . . ." and "a sufficient consideration. . . ."[5] Of course, just as in French law, not all transactions meeting these requirements are enforceable, but the question whether a contract has been formed is ordinarily approached by the common law in terms of assent and consideration.[6]

The respective merits of the handling of the problem of formation in the two systems can be determined by examining how each treats several concrete situations.

The doctrinal mechanism of both systems functions easily and well for what can be called the normal contract situation; that is to say, where a bargained-for exchange of economic values by each side is contemplated. There is present the agreement required by French law and the assent and consideration which the common law emphasizes.

When the common law comes to deal with situations in which there is no present exchange of economic values, difficulties arise that are avoided in French law. This difference can be demonstrated in connection with two types of arrangements, the granting of an option and the situation in which a promise contemplates an acceptance in the form of an act of performance without the offeree assuming any commitment before performance, that is to say, the so-called offer for a unilateral contract.

In commercial life the option is a normal arrangement. A promises B to sell him certain property or goods for a stated sum if B indicates his willingness to buy within a fixed period. B knows of, and assents to, the option. Does B have an enforceable option contract? The solution of the French law is clear.[7] Agreement is present, and agreement is all that is required, as a matter of general principle, in order to form an enforceable contract. The solution is equally clear in the common law. B has given no consideration; consequently there is no enforceable contract, and A may revoke at any time before B exercises the option.[8]

If, as would seem to be the case, these option arrangements when clearly understood by both parties should be binding,[9] a general theory of contract formation that blocks enforcement is today, to this extent at least, unsatisfactory. The common-law courts have done what they could to improve the situation by enforcing option arrangements in which the recipient of the option gives something even though there is not a true exchange of values.[10] This solution necessarily puts a premium on legal sophistication.

Turn now to the handling of the offer for a so-called "unilateral contract." Here a party is said to seek not a promise, but an act, in return for his promise.[11] "I will pay you $15.00 if you paint (not *promise* to paint) my porch." Under the traditional common-law analysis, the promise to pay $15.00 does not become binding, because there is no consideration to support it (the act requested has not yet been performed, and the promisor does not wish or receive a promise of performance), until the porch has been painted. A result of this analysis is that the promisor can withdraw his promise to pay $15.00 at any time before the painting is begun (and possibly at any time before it is completed), even though he knows that the promisee has begun to prepare for performing.[12]

The whole approach of the common law to these situations is artificial. It eliminates from the court's consideration a perfectly normal interpretation of the parties' intentions and operates with the mechanical alternative that both parties are bound at once or neither party is bound until one party has completed his performance. French law avoids this Procrustean bed. Its theory of contract formation enables it to consider a third possibility, that of an option arrangement. By agreeing to the owner's proposition, the painter concludes a contract under which he is entitled to a certain sum of money if the porch is painted within a reasonable period of time. He does not, presumably, assume any obligation to paint until he has actually begun the job. The availability of this analysis avoids the difficulties that the common law has had in handling these "unilateral" situations and centers the court's attention on the basic functional problem: what did the parties intend?

In many situations the common-law courts have managed, of course, to avoid the consequences that an unsatisfactory doctrine would seem to require. They will find, in interpreting an ambiguous situation, that a present exchange of promises was intended, thus avoiding the injustice that would be caused by treating the arrangement as an offer for a unilateral contract.[13] Moreover, the doctrine itself has been modified. Today in many jurisdictions partial performance, or the tendering of partial performance, of the requested act in a unilateral contract situation will bind the promisor to the contract.[14] But, even after the passage of considerable time and the expenditure of much effort, the situation in the common law remains unsatisfactory.

III

A legal system's approach to contract formation foreshadows and, in considerable measure, determines the general outlines of its treatment of the problem of form. The functional problem of form is the same for all systems:[15] the usefulness of certain transactions must be balanced against considerations such as whether enforcing them may encounter unusual difficulties or costs and whether they present in practice special dangers to the person who contemplates entering into them. Formal requirements are indicated where such difficulties or dangers clearly outweigh the complications created by requiring formalities. The problem of form can be said to be successfully resolved if formalities are required only for appropriate categories of transactions, if these categories are clearly marked out, and if adequate and workable formalities are provided.

French law, with its theory of contract formation based on

agreement, approaches form as a problem analytically distinct from formation and imposes its formal requirements directly. The two most important categories of transactions in which the Civil Code requires formalities are agreements to confer a gratuitous benefit (gift) (Articles 931 and 932) and agreements in nonbusiness transactions[16] where the sum or value involved exceeds 5,000 francs (approximately fifteen dollars) (Article 1341).

In the common law, formal requirements are, in considerable part, implied in the system's theory of formation. The doctrine of consideration indirectly requires a form in all transactions in which there is not a bargained-for exchange of real economic values. In addition, formalities are directly imposed by statute-of-frauds legislation on a variety of transactions; for example, agreements to sell goods the value of which exceeds a certain amount (usually fifty, one hundred, or five hundred dollars), contracts to sell any interest in land, agreements not to be performed within one year from the making thereof, and suretyship agreements.

Considerable evidence exists that both the French law and the common law impose formal requirements upon transactions in which evidentiary or cautionary protection is today not needed. There appears to be little justification under modern conditions for the Civil Code's imposition of a formal requirement upon all nonbusiness transactions involving more than approximately fifteen dollars. In modern times this requirement of French law has been steadily watered down.[17]

The provisions of the Statute of Frauds relative to the sale of goods and contracts not to be performed within a year have recently been repealed in England on the ground, among others, that "they had outlived the conditions which generated and, in some degree, justified them. . . ."[18] Nor is the requirement, resulting from the doctrine of consideration, of a formality in option agreements justified.

The categories of transactions in which formalities are required are perhaps somewhat more clearly marked out in French law than in the common law. The broad scope and general form of Article 1341 avoids certain of the perplexing borderline cases that arise under statute-of-frauds legislation.[19] Furthermore, it is probably easier to mark off the limits of the formal requirements applicable to gratuitous transactions where the approach is, as in French law, through the concept of gift rather than through the doctrine of consideration. Many of the difficulties encountered in this area are, however, inherent in the subject matter. No structure of doctrine can completely avoid problems of the type discussed in the common law under the headings of moral consideration, past consideration, and charitable subscriptions.[20]

Various defects can be noted in the adequacy and workability of the formalities provided in each system. Under the Civil Code an agreement to confer a gift is enforceable if embodied in a notarial contract and expressly accepted by the donee.[21] The courts have also come in time to accept an alternative, party-developed formality—the disguised donation in which the gratuitous transaction is cast in the guise of an onerous transaction.[22] The formality provided by the Code is probably excessively strict in requiring an express acceptance by the donee.[23] This requirement is avoided by the use of the disguised donation.[24] In a transaction involving a sum or value of more than 5,000 francs, the formal requirement of French law can be satisfied either by a written instrument, executed in the presence of a notary or signed by the parties, or by a beginning of written proof (that is to say, a writing, emanating from the party sought to be held and indicating the existence of the obligation that is to be proved).[25] This last alternative has given rise, as was probably inevitable, to considerable litigation in the process of defining its scope.[26]

The common-law statute-of-frauds legislation provides adequate and workable formalities: a memorandum or note in writing, signed by the party to be charged or by his authorized representative, and, alternatively, for the sale of goods, the giving of "something in earnest to bind the bargain or in part payment." A major defect in the common law's handling of the problem of form exists, however, in its failure to provide an adequate and workable formality for those transactions in which the lack of consideration results in a promise unenforceable without form. In the older common law a satisfactory formality was available in the seal. Today, a gratuitous promise under seal is not enforceable in most jurisdictions.[27] The only formality available is nominal consideration —the casting of the gift transaction in the form of a bargained-for exchange of economic values.[28] The involvement of the question of available formalities with the general doctrine of consideration has complicated the judicial administration of this formality. It may, by obscuring the true function of nominal consideration, have led some courts to refuse, because of a misunderstanding of the real problem at issue, to accept certain types of nominal consideration. Thus, in the case of Schnell v. Nell, [29] where the gift promise of money was cast in the form of an exchange by the donee's promising one cent in return, the court refused to enforce the promise even though the parties had obviously used the technique of nominal consideration in an effort to find a formality by which the promise could be made binding. In some states there is, in consequence, no longer any legal device available that can be employed with the certainty that it will bind the promisor to a gratuitous promise.[30] Even when nominal consideration is recognized, it remains a formality less comprehensible to the layman than is the notarial contract of French law.

Thus the French Civil Code appears to be somewhat superior to the common law in its handling of the problem of form. The superiority here is not so marked, however, as with regard to contract formation.

IV

The superiority of the French Civil Code to the common law in these two basic areas of the law of contracts is not purely fortuitous. It would seem to be due, at least in part, to the fact of codification and to the habits of thought and patterns of development associated with codification on the continent of Europe. In both legal systems the law of contracts was, in its beginnings, primitive and unsuited to the commercial and industrial societies that were later to emerge.

The formless, fully executory agreement, so necessary for trade and commerce, was not enforced. The economic life of England and the Continent had to flow, even when a trading economy began to develop, within the legal framework of the formal contract and of the half-executed transaction, that is to say, a transaction fully performed on one side. In neither legal system was the task of developing a law of contracts appropriate for the emerging economic order simple or easy. Ultimately, both legal orders made available what was indispensable: a body of contract doctrine by which ordinary, executory business agreements, involving a future exchange of values, could be made enforceable.

The new law of contracts began to grow up on the Continent and in England through the practices of merchants, which early developed into a *jus mercatorum* administered by courts of merchants. The practices of merchants were at first devoid of all sanction by the legal order and could not be invoked in the existing law courts. But as early as about 1116 the Count of Flanders "instituted in most of his towns local courts of *échevins,* chosen from among the burgesses and alone competent to judge them. Sooner or later the same thing happened in all countries. In Italy, France, Germany and England the towns obtained judicial autonomy, which made them islands of independent jurisdiction lying outside the territorial custom."[31] Merchants came in the eleventh century to assert the force of their own practices against the customary law.[32] For example, they claimed that sales concluded at fairs should be binding regardless of whether they were made in the proper legal forms, for such was the custom of merchants.[33] Mercantile practices tended, in general, to develop informal and flexible transactions appropriate to active commercial life. And the merchant courts provided expeditious procedures and prompt justice administered by men who were themselves merchants and fully aware of mercantile problems and customs.[34]

In the twelfth and thirteenth centuries the development of the law of contracts on the Continent and in England began to diverge as different forces came into play in molding the common and the civil laws. In England the common law of contracts was to be developed pragmatically and judicially. Until the fifteenth century this development went forward in the King's and many other courts. Indeed, the Courts of the Boroughs, of the Fairs, and of the Staples administered a law of contracts more suited to the needs of business than that available in the King's courts.[35] In the fifteenth and sixteenth centuries the jurisdiction of the King's courts showed a pronounced tendency to become progressively more exclusive. It was perhaps logical and inevitable that, after an effective, centralized administration of justice had been established, it should seek to acquire an exclusive jurisdiction. In all events, with the decline of the Courts of the Fairs and other local courts in the second half of the fifteenth century, the common law of contracts entered upon a decisive stage in its evolution. It was not without importance for the law which developed that this stage was presided over by the common-law courts and the practicing legal profession.

From perhaps the thirteenth century the medieval common law had dealt with contractual problems primarily through two actions, debt and covenant.[36] Where a fixed sum of money was owed, under an express or implied agreement, for a thing or benefit given, simple debt lay to recover the sum. Debt on a specialty was available for breach of a promise, made in a sealed instrument, to pay a fixed amount of money. Covenant could be brought for a breach of a promise under seal (but until rather late in the history of the action only if the promise were not to pay a fixed sum of money).[37] These actions did not provide a remedy for the breach of an informal, executory agreement.[38] In the fifteenth century the common-law courts started to develop a form of action that would render such agreements enforceable. By "the middle of the sixteenth century the modern conception of contract [in the common law] had, in essence, been formulated."[39] Assumpsit provided a comprehensive remedy for executory parol agreements.

It was now necessary for the common-law courts to determine the limits of the new action. The problem was put in an early case. "Truly, if this action is maintained, one shall have trespass on the case for breach of any agreement in the world."[40] The courts found the limiting principle in the doctrine of consideration.[41] This doctrine came, as it was developed, to embody the concept of bargain. Many theories have been offered to explain why the common law adopted the principle of bargain while the continental legal systems were developing in the direction of a principle of agreement that would enable them to deal more simply and directly with promissory situations in which there is no element of bargain. Doubtless there is no single or simple explanation. However, at least four elements in the English picture may help to explain this divergent development.

Firstly, there is the fortuitous element of the inherited materials with which the system had to work. "The Elizabethan judges, though the choice was not consciously present to their minds, were impelled by every tradition of the common law to prefer the principle of bargain. Gratuitous promises were associated with the writ of covenant and were excluded from the province of Debt sur contract. During the early experiments with assumpsit the idea of reciprocity was constantly asserted."[42] It is thus understandable that the judges came to insist, through the doctrine of consideration, on an element of bargain in the transaction that they were asked to enforce.

Secondly, a case law, in the process of formulating the principle that executory parol agreements were enforceable, would have found it rather difficult to develop a formality, such as the notarial contract adopted in France, to provide guarantees against the dangers inherent in gratuitous promises. Such guarantees were already present in the actions of debt on a specialty and covenant, which could be brought to enforce gratuitious promises under seal. It may, therefore, well have been sound judicial statesmanship to leave the enforcement of gifts to these actions.

Thirdly, the development of assumpsit was doubtless basically due to pressures from important commercial interests and was carried on largely by the practicing legal profession. Such interests, and such advocates, did not seek a general sanction for all executory agreements, including charitable gifts, but only for business enterprise.[43]

Fourthly, the common law of contract was little influenced by the speculation of learned men, relatively remote from the day-to-day practice of the law as were many of the civilians and canonists who played such a large role in the development of the general principles of the law of contractual obligation in France. The common law of contracts developed concretely and pragmatically, not systematically and speculatively. The absence of general theory can be seen even as late as Blackstone (1723–1780), who disposes of the subject of contract in a few pages that form a kind of appendix to his treatment of the law of property.[44]

It is thus perhaps inherent in the method and manner of the development of the common law that the doctrine evolved to rationalize, and limit, the enforceability of parol executory agreements should not be "as wide as morality and as warm as conscience" but should rather be "commercialized into the price of a bargain."[45]

On the continent of Europe the process by which a law of contracts appropriate to the needs of the emerging commercial society was developed is significantly different. By the twelfth and thirteenth centuries speculative and systematic thought began to play a role of increasing importance in the development of the new law of contracts. The characteristics of the theory of formation and of the approach to the general problem of form today found in the French Civil Code result, in considerable measure, from the efforts of speculative and systematic thinkers in reworking the primitive contract law with which both they and the common law began.

The Church supported strongly the proposition that a simple, formless promise should be binding: *Pacta sunt servanda*. This attitude was to encourage the development of formless contracts even though the canonists were divided on the question whether formless civil obligations could be enforced by the Church in those fields in which it had civil jurisdiction.[46] By the thirteenth century canonists were writing that "[e]ven the 'nude pact' [of Roman law] should be enforced, at least by penitential discipline."[47] In the development of the canonists' thinking on these matters the notion of *causa,* which had played such a limited role in Roman law,[48] came to be used as a new *vestimentum* ("garment"), thus maintaining continuity with Romanist teaching by fitting the canonist doctrine of *pacta sunt servanda* into the framework of the *pacta vestita*[49] ("clothed pact") and providing a substitute for formal requirements by ensuring, through the requirement of a cause, that a serious intention to assume a legal obligation had existed.[50]

Perhaps the most important speculative and systematic influence on the development of contract law in Europe from the twelfth century on was the revived study of Justinian's *Corpus Juris Civilis*. Certain Roman law practices had, of course, been continued as custom in the period before the revival of Roman law. The revival of classical Roman law, however, increased immeasurably the Roman influence on the developing law of contracts.

This influence was to lie in two directions. Firstly, the study of the *Corpus Juris Civilis* stimulated men to rediscover or construct a general law concerning the validity of agreements. Secondly, the Roman law, as crystallized in Justinian's law books, tended both to confirm the notion already present in the old customary practices that something more than a formless expression of agreement must be required if an action is to be given, and to introduce the idea, through the learning about innominate or unnamed contracts,[51] that the number of recognized types of enforceable, purely consensual transactions was limited. The Roman law maxim, *"ex nudo pacto non oritur actio"*[52] was commented on, often in picturesque phrases,[53] and became a part of the civilian's doctrine of contract.[54]

The Roman learning relative to innominate contracts, and Roman maxims such as *"ex nudo pacto non oritur actio,"* could have formed the basis for a development in the civil law of contracts of a doctrine rather similar to the common-law doctrine of consideration. It would not have been difficult, by using the concept of *causa,* to have fastened the principle of bargain upon the civil law. Some such development might well have occurred if the civil law of contracts had developed judicially and pragmatically. That it did not occur is doubtless due in part to chance, but also, it would seem, in part to the speculative and systematic thought of jurists. Consider the tendencies discernible in the Italian literature of the fifteenth century. Firstly, the actionability of formless contracts concluded between merchants was generally accepted. Secondly, the theory was current that a *nudum pactum geminatum* ("a twin-born naked pact") was actionable: it was held that a nude pact produced a natural obligation and that the repetition of the nude pact made this original natural obligation enforceable. This theory was based on an extension of the *Constitutum*[55] of Roman law and a misunderstanding of the Roman law conception of the *naturalis obligatio.*[56] It was also connected with the explanation, which now came to be offered for the Roman law rules relative to nude pacts, that such pacts were not enforceable because of the need for protecting inexperienced persons from the consequences of unconsidered statements.[57] The repetition of the statement tended to provide a safeguard against inconsiderate action, the reason for not enforcing the transaction thus ceasing to exist.[58] Thirdly, some jurists held that an action *de dolo* would lie for damages caused by breach of an informal pact.[59] Fourthly, the canon-law doctrines were discussed by most civilists. But only at the very end of the century, and then only with a very few writers, was there any notion of the general applicability of these doctrines.[60]

By the sixteenth century the importance of speculative and systematic thought in shaping Continental thinking on contract law is clearer and greater. The natural-law philosophers took up such ideas as the principle *pacta sunt servanda,* supported originally by the Church, the merchants,[61] and certain civilists. The influence of natural law can be seen in the work of a jurist and legislator such as the German Ulrich Zasius (1461–1535). In his legal writings Zasius taught the Roman law rule that an action could not be based on a *nudum pactum.*[62] When, however, asked in 1520 to draft the city law of Freiburg, he provided for the enforceability of nude pacts.[63] But Zasius did not, even as a legislator, abandon the Roman teaching relative to innominate contracts.[64] The city law of Freiburg explicitly provided that an exchange is not binding without part performance.[65] The influence of natural-law theories is also seen in the writings of the German Matthäus Wesenbeck (1531–1586) and of the Frenchman Charles Dumoulin (1500–1566), who were probably the most influential supporters in the sixteenth century of the validity of informal contracts.[66] However, Wesenbeck, like Zasius, still made the actionability of innominate contracts, especially contracts of exchange, depend on part performance.[67]

The speculative and systematic thought embodied in the principle of the enforceability of formless contracts did not, therefore, operate at this period to break down completely the limited contractual categories of the Roman law.[68] Some of the writers appear to have failed to see that the actionability of nude pacts led logically to the binding effect of consensual innominate contracts. Others rationalized the result by seeing in an innominate transaction before part performance only preliminary, nonobligatory dealings.[69] Only a very few, among them the German Peter Gudelin (1550–1619), argued for the binding effect of innominate contracts before part performance.[70]

By the end of the sixteenth and the beginning of the seventeenth century the number and influence of the supporters among legal writers and philosophers of the validity of formless contracts increased markedly, even though the opposing view did not entirely disappear.[71] The writings of Grotius (1583–1645)[72] and Pufendorf (1632–1694), which based the binding effect of formless executory contracts on natural law, had great influence. The large majority of seventeenth-century writers continued, however, to treat innominate contracts as unenforceable in the absence of part performance.[73] The great French lawyer Domat (1625–1696) was one of the few who considered all formless executory contracts binding. "[A]ll contracts, whether they have a particular name or not, always have their effect, and oblige the parties to what is agreed on."[74] The legislation of this period fell by and large into the same pattern. It accepted in general the actionability of formless contracts but did not draw from this principle the conclusion that innominate contracts were enforceable without part performance.[75]

The eighteenth century saw the speculative and systematic thought of jurists and philosophers finally and fully carry the day. The enforceability of formless contracts was generally recognized and most legal writers supported the proposition that executory innominate contracts were also thereby made actionable.[76] And the position taken by the legal writers is reflected in the legislation of the period.[77]

Such are the general outlines of the long and complex process that gave France, along with Western Europe as a whole, the basis for a general law of contractual obligations largely freed from historical anachronisms and capable of being developed in functional terms. Consensual and formless contracts had been accepted by the legislator and justified by the theorist. The Roman law's closed contract system, which, through the learning about nominate contracts, innominate contracts, and nude pacts, in effect held contractual transactions within the limiting framework of recognized contractual types, had been supplanted by the new learning. Men were permitted to transact more freely in terms of their needs and desires. The ground was cleared for the great codifications of the nineteenth century. Starting with a theory of formation based on agreement, they could approach rationally the problem of the element of formality that should be required before the legal order will sanction a particular type of transaction.

The theory of contract formation and the approach to the problem of form thus prepared for the drafters of the French Civil Code fitted in remarkably well with their intellectual preconceptions and with the technique of a code. The theory of formation, based as it was on agreement, was rational, offered the generality that codification required, and raised directly and clearly the problem of form. This problem could in its turn be handled in a code through formalities, particularly various requirements of writing, that were understandable to the ordinary person and peculiarly appropriate for legislative adoption.

The common law, as has been pointed out above, never managed to develop a general approach to formation and formality that went beyond the requirements of the typical business transaction, envisaging an exchange of economic values, to deal helpfully with more marginal problems such as those presented by the commercial option, the so-called "unilateral contract," and the promise to give. Lord Mansfield, perhaps the most speculative of the great common-law judges, attempted such a further development of the doctrinal structure of the common law in Pillans v. Van Mierop.[78] He made two arguments: firstly, that the case, being commercial, was governed by the customs of merchants, which did not require consideration; secondly, that consideration, even where no business interest was involved, had a purely evidentiary function and consequently need not be shown where the agreement was in writing. But Mansfield's attempted innovations were soon repudiated.[79]

The more satisfactory treatment accorded problems of formation and form in the Civil Code, as compared with the common law, seems to be due in large measure to the role that speculative and systematic thought played in the evolution and ultimate codification of French law. At least until recent times, the common law has not benefited from any comparable efforts to think legal problems through systematically and to develop a rationalized body of legal solutions, rules, principles, and doctrines. Nor has the common law had the benefit of a thorough legislative reshaping in the course of which many inherited complexities and encumbrances could be discarded. In some areas of the law of contracts the common law may be better today just because this has not taken place; but it would seem that the common law pays a price in other areas—areas that can benefit from rationalized, speculatively developed doctrines and in which the greater freedom of action at any given point in time ordinarily possessed by a legislature, as compared with a court, can be of considerable importance in determining the shape the law will take. At least these are the conclusions suggested by a comparative study of the evolution of contract in the civil and common laws.

V

This brief investigation of the history and present-day functioning of legal concepts in two important areas of the French and the common law of contracts—the theory of formation and the problem of form—may be suggestive for the comparative study of contracts. They may also be significant for an understanding of fundamental differences between the common and the civil laws.

There are various areas of the law in which general and relatively rationalized doctrines appear to operate more effectively than doctrines whose fabric, though richer, is more pragmatic and less capable of generalized application. These are the areas in which a general policy is needed, a policy that can then be tailored to take into account particular difficulties by the use of more specific supplementary rules. The common law may have more difficulty than the civil law in developing and using such general policies as guides to legal reasoning. It has been suggested above that this is true with respect to formation and formality in the law of contracts. And it should be remembered in this connection that the basis for the relatively satisfactory approach to the problems of form and formality found today in French law was laid in a codification made one hundred and fifty years ago.

In other areas of the law, of course, more precise and concrete principles are needed. In these areas the advantage may lie with the common law, particularly when compared with a relatively old codification such as the French Civil Code. It is perhaps true that in such areas a codified system tends more than the common law to treat rules and principles as ultimate verities rather than as working hypotheses. Here the process through which the common law develops probably tends to operate, over the long run, to its advantage. In the common law rather more than the civil law "Every new case is an experiment. . . . The principles themselves are continually retested; for if the rules derived from a principle do not work well, the principle itself must ultimately be reexamined."[80]

NOTES

[1] The results actually reached by the French courts in dealing with these questions have not been entirely satisfactory. The general rule appears to be that the offer can be withdrawn at any time by a revocation communicated to the offeree (see note 4 *infra*) before acceptance and that the point at which the acceptance becomes effective is a question of fact. The legal writers have argued, advancing various theoretical justifications, that offers, at least if they set a definite time period, should be irrevocable. See, e.g., 2 Ripert and Boulanger, Traité Élémentaire de Droit Civil de Planiol §334, pp. 126–27 (4th ed. 1952) (withdrawing of offer constitutes a fault); 2 Colin and Capitant, Cours Élémentaire de Droit Civil Français §46, pp. 35–36 (10th ed. by Julliot de la Morandière, 1948) (discusses three theories: civil delict, precontract to hold offer open, unilaterally assumed obligation). The courts do not appear, as a general matter, to have accepted these theories. See, e.g., *Henry de Portes v. Albert Vuillier,* Cour de cassation, Chambre civile, February 3, 1919, Recueil Dalloz de Doctrine de Jurisprudence et de Législation [hereinafter D.]. 1923. I. 126. A few cases can, however, be cited in support of the proposition that, in certain situations, the offer is not fully revocable. See e.g., *Schmitt v. Mey,* Cour d'appel of Colmar, February 4, 1936, D. 1936. 187 (precontract theory); *Jahn v. Charry,* Cour d'appel of Bordeaux, January 17, 1870, D. 1871. II. 96 (withdrawing of offer effective to prevent a contract from arising, but considered a fault). It can be noted that the commission preparing a draft for a new Civil Code has proposed that "The offeror may revoke his offer if it has not yet been accepted. However, when the offer sets a period for acceptance or such a period results from the circumstances of the case, the offer cannot be revoked before this period has expired, except in the case where the offer has not yet come to the attention of the offeree." [1948–1949] Travaux de la Commission de Réforme du Code Civil 705 (1950).

The rule that the question when an acceptance is effective to form a contract concluded by correspondence is a question of fact now appears firmly established in the case law of the Cour de cassation. See, e.g., *Cave Coopérative de Novi v. Ricôme,* Cour de cassation, Chambre des requêtes, January 29, 1923, D. 1923. I. 176, Sirey, Recueil Général des Lois et des Arrêts [hereinafter S.] 1923. I. 168; cf. *Le Lloyd de France v. Faucheux,* Cour de cassation, Chambre des requêtes, March 21, 1932, D. 1933. I. 65 (note Sallé de la Marnierre), S. 1932. I. 278. There does not appear to be any judicial discussion of standards to be applied by the courts in determining this question of fact. It is not clear whether the result depends on the intention of the parties, the equities of the situation, or the reliance of the offeree. The commission preparing a draft for a new Civil Code has proposed the rule that "In the absence of a stipulation to the contrary, a contract is formed between persons not present at the same place at the time and place of the emission of the acceptance." [1948–1949] Travaux de la Commission de Réforme du Code Civil 706 (1950).

[2] Article 1119 provides that: "One cannot, in general, either obligate himself, or stipulate in his own name, except for himself."

Article 1121 allows one "to stipulate for the benefit of a third person, when this is the condition of a stipulation which one makes for himself or of a gift which one makes to another. The person who has made this stipulation cannot revoke it if the third party has declared that he desires to take advantage of it."

Ripert and Boulanger comment on the interpretation given Article 1121 as follows: "Literally interpreted, Article 1121 would . . . [prohibit the insurance contract for the benefit of a third person where the assured is liable for the premiums and the third party is entitled to the indemnity] as the party to the contract does not stipulate for himself, that is to say, is not himself owed an obligation under the contract.. . . . Article 1121 must be interpreted as though it reads 'One may stipulate for another when he *contracts* for himself.' The courts have accepted this solution, thus giving satisfaction to practical necessities. In particular, the courts sanctioned insurance contracts for the benefit of third parties long before this was expressly authorized by the Law of July 13, 1930." 2 Ripert and Boulanger, *op. cit. supra* note 1, §635, p. 226.

[3] Article 1142 provides that: "Every obligation to do or not to do is resolved into damages in the event that the obligor does not perform." A leading treatise comments on this article as follows: "Article 1142, in spite of its apparently very general formula, . . . [does not change the general rule that it is only in the case where specific execution is impossible that an obligee must be content with a substitute form of execution, money damages]. . . . Article 1142 merely expresses the result which is usual in obligations of this sort." 7 Planiol and Ripert, Traité Pratique de Droit Civil Français §780, p. 89 (2nd ed. 1954). The problem raised by Article 1142 is part of the general problem of specific performance in French law. Much of the difficulty arises from the absence in French law of any technique analogous to contempt procedures for enforcing judgments ordering performance. This lack, as well as the problem posed by Article 1142, has been remedied to a certain extent by the judicial development of the *astreinte,* the imposing of a cumulative penalty, under the guise of damages, to compel performance. See, for a discussion of the *astreinte, id.,* §§787–95 *quinquès,* pp. 97–118; for a consideration of the extent to which the *astreinte* is effective in practice, see Fréjaville, *La Valeur Pratique de l'Astreinte,* Juris-Classeur Périodique 1951. I. 910.

[4] The basic Code provision is Article 1108, which provides that "Four conditions are essential to the validity of a contract:

"The consent of the party who binds himself;

"His capacity to contract;

"A defined object which forms the subject matter of the obligation;

"A licit cause in the obligation."

Only one of these conditions, the first, is of importance for the topic under discussion in this paper. With regard to the first condition the language of the Code is misleading; both parties must consent to the transaction even if the agreement obligates only one of the parties. Cf. 2 Colin and Capitant, *op. cit. supra* note 1, at §40, p. 30. It is also clear that when consent to a transaction has been communicated to the other party, as, for example, by an offer, this consent remains effective, even though the party subsequently changes his mind, until his change of attitude has been communicated to the other party. Cf. 2 Ripert and Boulanger, *op. cit. supra* note 1, at §327, p. 125, §331, p. 126; compare also note 1 *supra*.

It should perhaps be noted that the fourth condition, the requirement of a licit cause, does not make the enforceability of the agreement turn on the presence of an element of bargain in the transaction. The doctrine of cause is much discussed and its implications much disputed in French legal writing. See, in general, Capitant, De la Cause des Obligations (3rd ed. 1927); Lorenzen, *Causa and Consideration in the Law of Contracts*, 28 Yale L. Jour. 621, 632–34 (1919). As it has been developed and applied by contemporary French law the doctrine is complex and serves a variety of purposes. It does not today, however, represent a requirement that the transaction contain an element of bargain. This can be clearly seen from the fact that the donor's liberal intention is considered the cause of a promise of a gift. Cf. 1 Maury, Essai Sur Le Rôle de la Notion de l'Équivalence en Droit Civil Français 39–72 (Thesis Toulouse, 1920). A promise to give in French law is never held unenforceable on the ground that it has no cause, but instead only on the ground that it was not made in the proper forms. See Civil Code, arts. 931, 932. "It does not follow [in French law] that, because the cause of an agreement does not have economic value, the agreement has no cause if it is possible to find in it an intention to make a sacrifice for one's tranquility, for one's respect, for the peace of one's conscience." 1 Larombière, Théorie et Pratique des Obligations 288 (2nd ed. 1885). "Every obligation, every promise or transfer which has on the part of the obligor a normal explanation in the mores of the community is valid." 2 Demogue, Traité des Obligations en Général 544 (1923). Cause, in this connection, becomes a description of what might be called the generalized motivation of the transaction; it does not require that the transaction, to be enforceable, contain an element of bargain or reciprocity.

[5] 1 Restatement of Contracts §19 (1932). The old common law also recognized the possibility of forming a contractual obligation by a writing under seal. This possibility has been removed by statute in most states of the United States. See 1 Williston and Thompson, A Treatise on the Law of Contracts §218, pp. 659–62 (rev. ed. 1936); Comment, *Present Status of the Sealed Obligation*, 34 Ill. L. Rev. 457 (1939).

[6] The Restatement states, though here it does not accurately reflect the law in all jurisdictions, that "A promise which the promisor should reasonably expect to induce action or forbearance of a definite and substantial character on the part of the promisee and which does induce such action or forbearance is binding if injustice can be avoided only by enforcement of the promise." §90; cf. *id.* §45. Some courts have indicated that this doctrine may be limited to the field of noncommercial transactions. See *James Baird Co. v. Gimbel Bros., Inc.*, 64 F. 2d 344, 346 (2d Cir. 1933); but see *Robert Gordon, Inc. v. Ingersoll-Rand Co.*, 117 F. 2d 654, 661 (7th Cir. 1941) ("The mere fact that the transaction is commercial in nature should not preclude the use of the promissory estoppel").

[7] The result, although indicated by the general approach of the Code to the problem of formation, was not always clear because of Articles 1174 ("Every obligation contracted under a potestative condition on the part of the person who obligates himself is void") and 1589 ("The promise of a sale is equivalent to a sale when there has been reciprocal agreement between the parties relative to the object and the price . . ."). Both of these articles were used in an attempt to fasten the principles of bargain upon the French law of contracts relating to nongratuitous transactions.

A promise subject to a *condition potestative* can be compared to what is called in the common law an illusory promise. Article 1174 thus gave a basis for arguing that an option contract was not binding because the party holding the option had not promised, as the case might be, to buy or sell. Some early cases accepted this line of reasoning. See, e.g., *Blanche Raymond v. Varlet,* Cour d'appel of Paris, Fifth Chamber, April 26, 1898, D. 1898. II. 526 (employment contract with employer having right to terminate "at the end of each month by notifying the employee eight days in advance"), *quashed,* Cour de cassation, Chambre civile, March 1, 1899, D. 1899. I. 360. It now appears established that Article 1174 merely states the platitude that, in a transaction in which neither side makes a binding promise, no enforceable obligation arises. Cf. 2 Demogue, *op. cit. supra* note 4, at §475, p. 22. However, from time to time, a lower court may even today misapply Article 1174 in the context of an option or other one-sided contract. See, e.g., *Vallernaude v. Vignal,* Tribunal de premier instance of Valence, December 19, 1929, S. 1930. II. 85.

The possible bearing of Article 1589 on the validity of the option contract requires explanation. Article 1589 treats a promise to sell as equivalent, under certain circumstances, to a sale. This gives a basis for arguing that the only promise of sale known to French law is one made in return for a promise to buy, for a completed sale always involves an element of reciprocity. This position was stated by Merlin, an early commentator on the Civil Code, as follows: "And it necessarily follows [from Article 1589 of the Civil Code] that the promise to buy is not obligatory if it is not accompanied by the promise to sell and that, reciprocally, the promise to sell is null if it is not accompanied by the promise to buy. . . ." 36 Merlin, Répertoire Universel et Raisonné de Jurisprudence, *Vente,* §VII, V, 85 (5th ed. 1828). Some early cases accepted this line of reasoning. See, e.g., *Gonguet v. Tardy,* Cour d'appel of Lyon, Second Chamber, June 27, 1832, D. 1833. II. 95, S. 1833. II. 285. The argument has, however, long since been rejected in French law. See, e.g., *La Ruche Roubaisienne v. Desquiens,* Cour d'appel of Douai, First Civil Chamber, November 2, 1898, 55 Jurisprudence de la Cour d'appel de Douai 257 (1898).

[8] Some courts may today be willing to apply the promissory estoppel theory of Section 90 of the Restatement of Contracts in these option situations. See note 6 *supra;* see also 1 Williston and Thompson, *op. cit. supra* note 5, at §61, p. 176; 1 Corbin, On Contracts §263, pp. 869–70 (1950).

For a general discussion of the common law treatment of the option, see *id.* §§259–74, pp. 855–925.

[9] An entirely different situation exists, of course, where the option is contained in a printed form and the full import of the transaction is not understood by one party. The problems presented by the use of standard forms might, however, be better handled through selective doctrines designed to distinguish between the fair and the unfair situation rather than by an approach through the general theory of formation.

[10] See 1 Williston and Thompson, *op. cit. supra* note 5, at §61, p. 179; 1 Corbin, *op. cit. supra* note 8, at §263, p. 868–69.

In a few states, statutes have modified the consideration requirement as applied to the option and firm offer problem. See N. Y. Personal Property Law §33 (5); Uniform Written Obligation Act (adopted Pa. 1927, Utah 1929, repealed Utah 1933). Section 2–205 of the Uniform Commercial Code would make options for a period not exceeding three months, given by a merchant for the sale or purchase of goods, binding if contained in a signed writing.

[11] For discussion of the unilateral contract of the common law, see Stoljar, *The False Distinction between Bilateral and Unilateral Contracts,* 64 Yale L.J. 515 (1955); Llewellyn, *On our Case-Law of Contract: Offer and Acceptance,* 48 Yale L. J. 1, 779, *passim* (1938, 1939); Pollock, *Book Review,* 28 L. Q. Rev. 100, 101 (1912); Wormser, *The True Conception of Unilateral Contracts,* 26 Yale L. J. 136 (1916); McGovney, *Irrevocable Offers,* 27 Harv. L. Rev. 644, 654–63 (1914).

[12] In the hypothetical case stated, it would seem, as a matter of strict theory, that the offer could be withdrawn at any time before the performance was completed. However, a court would presumably treat the situation as one in which the contract was concluded when the painter commenced the job. If this construction were not put on the situation, a quasi-contractual recovery would probably be available to the promisee for any benefit actually conferred on the promisor, but the arrangement could not be enforced as a contract. See 1 Williston and Thompson, *op. cit. supra* note 5, at §60AA, p. 172.

[13] See 1 Restatement of Contracts §31 (1932); 1 Williston and Thompson, *op. cit. supra* note 5, at §31A, pp. 76–77, §60, p. 166.

[14] See 1 Restatement of Contracts §45 (1932); 1 Williston and Thompson, *op. cit. supra* note 5, at §§60A–60B, pp. 167–75.

[15] For an excellent discussion of the problem of form, see Fuller, *Consideration and Form,* 41 Col. L. Rev. 799 (1941); 2 Ihering, Geist des Römischen Rechts §45, pp. 480–99 (7th ed. 1923). Professor Fuller distinguishes three possible functions of legal formalities: the evidentiary function, the cautionary function, and the channeling function. See *op. cit. supra,* 800–1. In the text of this paper, in order to simplify the comparative analysis, the channeling function is not taken into account.

[16] Under Article 109 of the Commercial Code, as now interpreted by the courts, the judge can admit oral testimony, when he considers such testimony desirable, to prove any transaction that is commercial in the technical sense unless the law expressly requires a writing. *Jaladon v. Rocher,* Cour de cassation, Chambre des requêtes, March 24, 1825, S. 1825–1827. I. 90; see 4 Fuzier-Hermann, Code Civil Annoté, comment 216 to art. 1341 (ed. Demogue, 1938).

[17] This watering-down of the formal requirement has taken two forms: a very broad conception of the *commencement de preuve par écrit* (Article 1347) and a willingness to find that it would have been morally impossible, under the circumstances of the case, for the party to have obtained a writing (Article 1348).

The scope of Article 1347 has been particularly expanded by the use of procedures, made more effective by a law of May 23, 1942, amending Articles 324 to 336 of the Code of Civil Procedure, by which the court, either on its own motion or upon the request of one of the parties, can question the parties on the subject matter in litigation. The answers given by a party in response to the questions put can represent an admission that will constitute a *commencement de preuve par écrit.* Moreover, if a party does not appear when summoned for such an interrogation, or, on appearance, does not answer the questions asked, the court can, pursuant to Article 336 of the Code of Civil Procedure, consider this conduct as "equivalent to a beginning of proof by writing under the conditions of

Article 1347 of the Civil Code." Hébraud, in a comment on the law of May 23, 1942 (D. 1943. Leg. 10), indicates that, as a consequence of this legislation, the formal requirement of Article 1341 may be virtually eliminated in practice. See *id.* at 11; see also Meurisse, *Le déclin de la preuve par écrit,* Gazette du Palais. 1951. II. Doctrine. 50; Manuel, Le Commencement de Preuve par Écrit (Thesis Lyon, 1937).

For an example of the application of the doctrine of moral impossibility under Article 1348 see *Ihasusta v. Bianchi,* Cour de cassation, Chambre civile, March 17, 1938, D. 1938. I. 115 (note Mimin); see also Lyon-Caen, note to *Boutenjeun v. Reynier,* Cour de cassation, Chambre des requêtes, March 27, 1907, S. 1907. I. 209, notes 1–4 (this system has "from the practical point of view, . . . a great advantage because it leads, in fact, to a system in which any method of proof is admissible. . .").

[18] Law Reform Committee, First Report 3, Cmd. No. 8809 (1953); see generally *Recent Statute,* 68 Harv. L. Rev. 383 (1954).

[19] Williston devotes forty pages to a discussion of the statute-of-frauds provision relating to the sale of goods. See 2 Williston and Thompson, *op. cit. supra* note 5, at §§505–24A, pp. 1474–513.

[20] Both the French and the common law must face the problem of classifying borderline transactions for the purposes of formal requirements. The common law approaches the question by an analysis based on consideration, imposing a formal requirement if no consideration is found in the transaction in question. The comparable analysis in French law is in terms of the concept of gift. French law reaches in borderline situations results somewhat more restrictive of the scope of formal requirements than does the common law. For example, a sufficiently strong moral obligation will cause a French court to refuse to classify a transaction as a gift when a common-law court, in a comparable situation, would fail to find consideration. Compare *Pagês v. Frères Saint-Jean-de-Dieu à Lyon,* Cour de cassation, Chambre des requêtes, May 5, 1868, D. 1869. I. 285 with *Mills v. Wyman,* 3 Pick. 207 (Mass. 1825); for the general problem of the moral obligation in French law, compare *Darier v. Dubois,* Cour d'appel of Paris, Eighth Chamber, November 5, 1925, D. 1925. 656 (promise of man to continue to support former mistress who later made a "rich marriage" held a promise of a gift) with *P. v. Docteur de L.,* Cour d'appel of Rennes, First Chamber, March 7, 1904, D. 1905. II. 305 (note Planiol), S. 1907. II. 214 (promise of man who lived twenty years with a woman to support her after the relationship was terminated held not a promise of a gift); see also 7 Planiol and Ripert, *op. cit. supra* note 3, at §982, pp. 316–18.

A charitable subscription is, it appears, treated in French law as a distinct form of transaction and consequently is not classified as a gift. Cf. *Bailly v. Ville de Nancy,* Cour de cassation, Chambre civile, February 5, 1923, D. 1923. I. 20. This treatment is to be contrasted with the approach in the American common law through consideration, an approach that has led to some rather curious analyses in the courts' attempts to work out an acceptable solution. See 1 Williston and Thompson, *op. cit. supra* note 5, at §116, pp. 403–9.

[21] Civil Code, Arts. 931 and 932.

[22] See 3 Ripert and Boulanger, Traité Élémentaire de Droit Civil de Planiol §3350, pp. 1067–68 (4th ed. 1951); cf. *Malapert v. Devaux et Pauly,* Cour de cassation, Chambre civile, July 11, 1888, D. 1889. I. 479, S. 1888. I. 409. In order to have a disguised donation, the donor must cast the gratuitous transaction in the guise of an onerous transaction. For example, a father will sign what is, on its face, a contract of sale with his son. If the intention of the parties was that the father's performance is to be uncompensated, the

father can be required to perform and the son need not make his performance. Similarly, if the parties recite in a document that the son has paid the father a sum of money in return for which the father obligates himself to make a certain performance, the father must perform even though the son has not, in fact, made such a payment.

The disguised donation can be compared with the doctrine of nominal consideration. In this connection it is interesting to consider the justification advanced for the disguised donation: "... [T]he will of the donor finds in the deception to which the donor believes it is necessary to have recourse the equivalent of the protection which the [code] requirement of form would have procured for it: The donor must so arrange the contract containing the gift as to give it the appearance of an onerous juridical act. The donor is thus clearly aware of the scope of his obligation." 3 Ripert and Boulanger, *op. cit. supra* §3351, p. 1068.

[23] The requirement of an express acceptance has been criticized. "... It is an element of the formalism of the act, designed to make the donation still more solemn and, as a consequence, still more difficult. The Parlement of Paris introduced this rule. ... There is no longer today any reason to preserve this exaggerated formalism. It is curious that the drafters of the Civil Code maintained the rule without any criticism having been made of it." Capitant, *Preface* to 1 Regnault, Les Ordonnances Civiles du Chancelier Daguesseau—Les Donations et L'Ordonnance de 1731 xiv (1929).

[24] *Morizot et Guérard v. Compagnie le Phénix et autres,* Cour de cassation, Chambre civile, October 18, 1909, D. 1910. I. 462, S. 1911. I. 489 (note Tissier).

[25] Article 1341 of the Civil Code requires a written instrument either executed in the presence of a notary or signed by the parties. Articles 1347 and 1348 introduce certain exceptions to this formal requirement, the most important of which is the provision that a so-called beginning of written proof will satisfy the formal requirement of Article 1341.

[26] For one aspect of the evolution of Article 1347, see note 17 *supra.*

[27] See 1 Williston and Thompson, *op. cit. supra* note 5, at §218, pp. 659–62.

[28] If A asks, in return for his promise to give B $10,000, that B promise to give (or that B give) A a pepper corn, B's promise (or performance) furnishes consideration to support A's promise.

[29] 17 Ind. 29, 79 Am. Dec. 453 (1861); see also *Fisher v. Union Trust Co.,* 138 Mich. 612, 101 N. W. 852 (1904) (promise of an indeterminate value, nominal consideration of one dollar held not to satisfy requirement of consideration).

[30] See Fuller, Basic Contract Law 318 (1947).

[31] Pirenne, Economic and Social History of Medieval Europe 53 (trans. Clegg, 1937).

[32] See Goldschmidt, Universalgeschichte des Handelsrechts 305 (1891).

[33] Mitchell, An Essay on the Early History of the Law Merchant 10–11 (1904).

[34] See *id.* at 12–16.

[35] See generally Fifoot, History and Sources of the Common Law 289–98 (1949).

[36] See *id.* at 330. The availability of certain special techniques, such as the penalty bond under seal, recognized by the common-law courts should not be overlooked. See Thorne, *Tudor Social Transformation and Legal Change,* 26 N.Y.U.L. Rev. 10, 19–22. (1951).

[37] It is interesting to note that a writing under seal was originally not always required for the action of covenant. See Fifoot, *op. cit. supra* note 35, at 219–20, 257–58. At first there was no great point made of the requirement of a deed or even a writing in covenant, which was then used chiefly between landlord and tenant and to enforce other agreements relative to land. It "... might have been adapted to the enforcement of con-

tractual promises in general, and it was almost a century [*i.e.,* almost the fourteenth century] before the common law definitely indicated that it would not take this important step." *Recommendation of the Law Revision Commission Relating to the Seal and Consideration* 15 (1936) in [1936] State of New York Second Annual Report of the Law Revision Commission 95. If the requirement of a seal had not grown up the common law would have had a general contractual action, based not on bargain but on a unilateral promise, at a very early date. See Fifoot, *op. cit. supra,* at 257.

[38] Some concessions were made by the common law in connection with sales, which became in effect a consensual contract with the seller having an action in debt and the buyer an action in detinue. But this change, due in part to mercantile pressure, was only "an artificial, if salutary, refinement upon existing principle." *Id.* at 330.

[39] *Id.* at 339. The evolution of assumpsit was slow and involved. Fifoot gives an excellent sketch of the development. See *id.* at 330–57.

[40] Y. B. 3 Hen. VI. 36, pl. 33.

[41] For an excellent discussion of the development of the doctrine of consideration see Fifoot, *op. cit. supra* note 35, at 395–443.

[42] See *id.* at 398.

[43] Cf. *id.* at 399.

[44] See Fuller, *op. cit. supra* note 30, at 303–4.

[45] Fifoot, *op. cit. supra* note 35, at 398.

[46] See Seuffert, Zur Geschichte der Obligatorischen Verträge 52 (1881).

[47] 2 Pollock and Maitland, The History of English Law 195 (2nd ed. 1898). The teaching of the later canonists has been summarized as follows: ". . . (1) The promise must be intentional; (2) it is subject to be taken back in consequence of a material change of circumstances; (3) it must have a reasonable cause, which may consist either in a material equivalent or moral considerations; (4) a liberal disposition is to be deemed sufficient cause in the case of gifts; (5) promises to moral persons, to political, learned or religious bodies are legally valid if they are made for the sake of their moral aims, e.g. for the honor of God, the advancement of learning, assistance of the poor, and the like." Vinogradoff, *Reason and Conscience in Sixteenth-Century Jurisprudence,* 24 Law Q. Rev. 373, 382 (1908).

[48] The law of contracts found in Justinian's Institutes and Digest recognized several categories of transactions. Four types of nominate or named contracts were enforced at this stage in the development of Roman law: *re,* a contract (of which there were four types: *mutum,* a loan for consumption, *commodatum,* a loan for use, *depositum,* a deposit, *pignus,* a pledge or a pawn) in which the obligation arose from the handing over of a thing: *verbis,* a contract (the well-known stipulation) in which the obligation depended on a form of words; *litteris,* a contract (which had become obsolete) in which the obligation depended on a special kind of writing; and *consensu,* a contract, of which only four special cases (sales, hire, partnership, and mandate) were recognized, in which the obligation rested on agreement alone. A large group of transactions not referable to one of the recognized named contracts formed a second group of contracts, the so-called innominate or unnamed contracts (including exchange and compromise). In all these contracts there is the common feature that something is done or given on one side that gives rise to a duty on the other. See Lee, The Elements of Roman Law §510, p. 335 (3rd ed. 1952). A third group of agreements, some of which came to be enforceable, were not classified as contracts but as pacts. An unenforceable pact was called a bare pact and could be

pleaded as a defense. See *id.* at §511, pp. 335–37. Pacts that were made actionable were called *pacta vestita,* clothed pacts.

The principal reference to *causa* found in the Justinian Code is in The Digest, 2. 14. 7. pr.–4. The passage has been commented on as follows: "Th[is] famous passage [especially D. 2. 14. 7. 4 which states that: 'If there is no additional ground (*causa*), in that case it is certain that no obligation can be created, [I mean] on the mere agreement; so that a bare agreement (*nudum pactum*) does not produce an obligation, it only produces an *exceptio.*'] on which the whole theory of *cause* was based, and which was taken to mean that every contract must have a *cause,* in reality says nothing of the kind. It distinguishes between agreements which have been recognized as nominate contracts, such as sale and hire, and agreements for which no special régime has been laid down. Then it goes on to say that in all these latter cases there will still be an action provided that there is also a *cause.* The text, which may well be due to the compilers, clearly deals with what later came to be known as innominate contracts, and *causa* here means what English lawyers call executed consideration. The contracts are of the type *do ut des, do ut facias, facio ut des,* or *facio ut facias.* Thus the passage goes on to say that if there is no *causa,* it is a case of *nudum pactum,* which will give rise to an exception but not to an action.

"*Causa* is here evidently made to play a part only in the theory of innominate contracts. It has nothing to do with the consensual contracts, which have always been recognized to present a serious difficulty, but it has also, for the purpose of this passage, nothing whatever to do with the real or verbal contracts either. In other words, all it says is that executed consideration is required where no régimes have been set up for particular contracts." Buckland and McNair, Roman Law and Common Law 229–30 (2nd ed. rev. by Lawson, 1952).

[49] See Chevrier, Essai sur l'Histoire de la Cause dans les Obligations 174–75 (1929).

[50] See *id.* at 15–16. See also the discussion at p. 123 *infra* and the quotation from the Summa of Angelus Carletus given in note 60 *infra.*

[51] See note 48 *supra.*

[52] See note 48 *supra.*

[53] Azo, in his famous Summa, written in the first quarter of the thirteenth century, discussed the clothing of naked pacts as follows:

"Moreover, a pact is clothed in six ways: by a thing, by words, by consent, by a writing, by having a connection with a contract and by the interposition of a thing. It must be observed that the pact is said to be clothed in these first four ways because it was never without these garments and began to have them upon its coming into existence. It is clothed in the last two ways after its birth. When we make a pact it is, in fact, born naked, as is proved by the continuation of the two sections . . . [D. 2. 14. 7. 4 and 5], but, once born, the pact looks around and opens its eyes to see whether it has been preceded or can be followed or whether there is at once some contract, the clothes of which it puts on so as to drive away the north wind and the fury of the storm and be able to give its help to its master in the action. The pact is made, in fact, immediately, that is, a little before the contract or a little after the contract or in the same contract—I do not distinguish whether the contract is *bonae fides* or *stricti iuris.* . . . A pact can [also] be clothed by the interposition of a thing, as in the innominate contracts, which do not at the beginning give any action but, in which, after the thing is interposed and delivered, the action belongs to him who clothed the contract by the interposition of the thing. . . ." Translated from the Latin text as given in Maitland, Select Passages from the Works of Bracton and Azo 143–44 (Selden Society, Vol.VIII, 1895).

[54] See Seuffert, *op. cit. supra* note 46, at 34–45.

[55] The Constitutum was a praetorian action based on an informal undertaking to pay an existing debt at a fixed time. At first the debt had to be of money, but this rule had disappeared by the time of Justinian. The Constitutum was void if there were no real debt, but a *naturalis obligatio* sometimes sufficed (see note 56 *infra*) to satisfy this requirement. See Buckland, A Manual of Roman Private Law 308–9 (2nd ed. 1939).

[56] See Seuffert, *op. cit. supra* note 46, at 76–77. In Roman law a nude pact usually created a natural obligation, although there were a few exceptions. See Buckland, A Textbook of Roman Law 553 (2nd ed. 1932). The effect of a natural obligation varied, however. The only rules common to all natural obligations were that no action lay and that a payment made to discharge such an obligation could not be recovered. See *id.* at 552. In particular, not all natural obligations could form the basis of a Constitutum. See Seuffert, *op. cit. supra,* at 19.

[57] See *id.* at 68, 76–77.

[58] See *id.* at 76–77, 80.

[59] See *id.* at 84–85.

[60] See *id.* at 85–86. It is interesting to note in this connection that the canonists were, in their turn, influenced by the teachings of the civilians. By the fifteenth century the canonists sought to reconcile their teachings with the Roman law principle, *ex nudo pacto non oritur actio,* by developing the doctrine of a *causa* clothing the naked pact. A pact was declared valid if it were adorned by an adequate *causa.* "The definition of *causa* was a more embarrassing task and encouraged ingenious speculation, but, by the general consensus of opinion, the doctrine required the plaintiff to prove only that the promise had been made with a serious purpose. Unless his design was manifestly unreasonable or improper, the promisor was bound. Nor need his aim be commercial: benevolence, piety or the discharge of a moral obligation sufficed." See Fifoot *op. cit. supra* note 35, at 306; see also note 47 *supra.* Fifoot quotes an interesting fifteenth-century example of such writing from the Summa Angelica of Angelus Carletus:

"The question is whether a man is bound by a naked pact or simple promise. The answer is that he is so bound by canon law and in conscience, under pain of mortal sin, provided that a cause is expressed, as if I promise you ten pounds because you have sold me such a thing or have lent me the money, and so forth. But if it be so naked that no cause is added, he is not bound even in conscience; and the reason is that he is taken to have made the promise in error. . . . But notice that, if a man say, I promise to give you a hundred pounds, then the liberality of the promise is presumed to be the cause of the gift, and so it is not without cause. So, too, if anything is promised to a pious foundation because he is taken to have bound himself for motives of piety. . . . No one is bound from whatever cause unless he has intended to bind himself. He is not required, under pain of mortal sin, to keep a naked pact, unless there exist a cause which requires him to be so bound by moral precept, as if I have promised my robe to my father, who is perishing with cold; for in such a case as this a man is bound, even if he never intended to be bound."

[61] Mitchell, *op. cit. supra* note 33, at 102.

[62] See Seuffert, *op. cit. supra* note 46, at 96–97.

[63] See *id.* at 99–102. Seuffert considers this the earliest German legislation providing for the actionability of nude pacts. See *id.* at 101.

[64] See note 48 *supra.*

[65] See Seuffert, *op. cit. supra* note 46, at 100.

[66] For Wesenbeck, see *id.* at 106–8; for Dumoulin, see Spies, De l'Observation des Simples Conventions en Droit Canonique (Thesis Nancy, 1928).

[67] See Seuffert, *op. cit. supra* note 46, at 107–8.

[68] See *id.* at 119–29.

[69] See *id.* at 143.

[70] See *id.* at 128–29.

[71] See *id.* at 118–19; see generally *id.* at 119–29.

[72] See especially De Jure Belli Ac Pacis Libri Tres, Book II, chapter XI (1625), where Grotius argues that every deliberately made promise is binding. For an English translation of this work see 2 Grotius, De Jure Belli Ac Pacis Libri Tres (trans. by Kelsey, 1925).

[73] See the quotations in Seuffert, *op. cit. supra* note 46, at 130–38. Spies considers that the general enforceability of formless executory contracts was accepted in French practice during the first half of the sixteenth century. See Spies, *op. cit. supra* note 66, at 217, 221. He connects this development in the practice with the Ordinance of Villers-Cotterets (1539), which ended the plaintiff's right to choose between civil and ecclesiastical courts in ordinary personal actions. See *id.* at 217–19. If the civil courts had not so changed the rules of law that they administered, certain formless executory contracts that were formerly enforced in the ecclesiastical courts would have been rendered unenforceable by the abolition of the ecclesiastical jurisdiction.

[74] Domat, Les Lois Civiles dans Leur Ordre Naturel (2d ed. 1695) Title I of Covenants, n. 150 (1st ed. 1694); for an English translation, see Domat, The Civil Law in its Natural Order (trans. by Strahan, ed. by Cushing, Vol. 1, 1850; Vol. 2, 1853).

[75] See Seuffert, *op. cit. supra* note 46, at 144–65, for examples of such legislation.

[76] See *id.* at 138–44.

[77] For example, the state law for Bavaria recognizes, with a clear reference to natural law, the actionability of formless contracts, including executory innominate contracts. See *id.* at 165–66.

[78] 3 Burrow 1663, 97 Eng. Rep. 1035 (K. B. 1765).

[79] The efforts of Lord Mansfield and the subsequent reaction are sketched in Fifoot, *op. cit. supra* note 35, at 406–11. See also Fifoot, Lord Mansfield 118–41 (1936). *Pillans v. Van Mierop* was overruled by the House of Lords in *Rann v. Hughes,* 7 Term R. 350, note, 101 Eng. Rep. 1014 (1778). "In *Rann v. Hughes* Lord Mansfield had held an administratrix liable upon a written promise, made in her personal capacity, to pay a debt due by the deceased to the plaintiff. [Footnote omitted.] The judgment was reversed in the Exchequer Chamber and the reversal sustained in the House of Lords. Butler, for the plaintiff, urged uncompromisingly the intrinsic validity of a written agreement. He dared to impugn the sanctity of the Deed. To affix a seal was notoriously a farce, and, if so trivial an act dispensed with consideration, why should it be required when the parties, by embodying their terms in a document, even if unsealed, had attested to their serious purpose? But two centuries of precedents were not to be 'melted down into common sense.' The general opinion of the judges, accepted by the Lord Chancellor, declared the antithesis of written and oral agreements to be heretical; and consideration remained a vital element in all contracts not under seal." Fifoot, *op. cit. supra* note 35, at 409.

[80] Smith, Jurisprudence 21 (1909).

8

The Code and the Family

MAX RHEINSTEIN

THE Code Napoleon, in the long period during which it has been in effect, has been amended in numerous parts, especially in the field of family law, and a vast gloss of *jurisprudence* has grown around its sections, both as they were worded originally and as they have been reformulated. The Code's family law has gone through a process of transformation, and this paper will trace certain aspects of this process. In that way we shall perhaps find out not only about developments in French family law, but also about the French family itself, the transformations of which are reflected in those of the law.

However, before we touch on these subjects it will be appropriate to say a few words on the Code's general attitude toward the family.

I

The makers of the Code have been blamed for having lacked a clear and consistent policy with respect to the family.[1] This charge appears to us to be founded on the misapprehension that a legislator, and quite particularly the maker of so great a legislative undertaking as a code, could ever be able consistently to follow just one single policy. Unless the lawgiver is a despotical dictator, his very task is that of combining and reconciling conflicting policies.

Conflicting policies had, indeed, to be reconciled by the makers

MAX RHEINSTEIN *is Max Pam Professor of Comparative Law at the University of Chicago Law School*

of the Code Napoleon. It was one of the foremost tasks of the Code to continue and consolidate the achievements of the Revolution, and one of the principal achievements was the liberation of the individual and the establishment of a direct and immediate relationship between the individual citizen and his nation. Those numerous and powerful groups that under the *Ancien Régime* had stood between the individual and the nation were either destroyed, like the manors, the guilds, and the provinces, or subdued, like the Church, or, like the municipalities, transformed into subdivisions of the national governments. Only one social group could not be treated in this fashion: the family. Its functions as the basic cell of society, particularly as the cradle of the nation's future generations, could neither be dispensed with nor transferred to any agency of the national government. Though the individual citizen was constituted as the bearer of the *"nation une et indivisible,"* he was to be, not an individual living in isolation, but one born into and living within a family.

One kind of family, it is true, had to be destroyed by the Revolution, viz. the aristocratic house. Its powers were broken not only by the dramatic repudiation of all the privileges of the nobility, but also by less spectacular measures within the range of private law, e.g. the compulsory partition of decedents' estates among the several children of a decedent, and the provisions of the Code by which entails of land and other restraints on the alienation of property were declared legally ineffective. How clearly the political implications of these measures were recognized is proved by the well-known letters in which Napoleon admonished his brother, the King of Naples, speedily to introduce in his realm the Code, so that existing entails would be destroyed and the old nobility reduced to powerlessness. "Then, when you have achieved this," Napoleon exhorted his brother, "open up the possibility of new entails to your most loyal supporters. There is no better way to insure the security of your dynasty."[2]

The houses of the old aristocracy thus had to go, but the family as such, the family of the bourgeoisie and the peasantry, was left untouched, or almost untouched. Under the Code it remained what it had been before, a closely knit group, in each household patriarchically lorded over by the husband-father. But family was not identical with household. Several "nuclear families" together formed that wider kinship group of brothers, sisters, aunts, uncles, nephews, and cousins that was strongly held together by the bonds of blood relationship. The vitality of this wider group of the "extended family" was well recognized in the law, not only in the rules on descent of property, but also in that peculiarly French institution the Family Council, to which the nation entrusted the protection of orphans and their property.[3]

Though the structure of the family was thus left almost untouched by the Revolution and the Code, a major transformation was nevertheless performed through the secularization of marriage. Under the *Ancien Régime* the State, at least on general principle, had nothing to do with marriage.[4] Marriage was a sacrament and as such belonged to the sphere of the Church. The mode of its conclusion, the requirements of its validity, and the impediments to marriage were regulated not by the law of the State but by the canon law of the Church. Jurisdiction in matrimonial causes also belonged to the Church, and the State's secular courts had nothing to do with such matters as nullity, jactitation, restitution of conjugal rights, or separation from bed and board. In the course of the Gallican movement the royal government attempted to obtain some influence on marriage regulation and a limited jurisdiction in matrimonial causes,[5] but it was not until the Revolution and the Code that the regulation of marriage and jurisdiction in matrimonial causes were taken over by the State under complete elimination of the Church from all influence in the sphere of the law.[6]

II

The effects of the secularization of marriage have been far-reaching, and one of them was the admission of the possibility of divorce.

The institution of divorce has had a checkered history in French law. Under the *Ancien Régime* the regulation of marriage was left to the Church, which, of course, meant the Church of Rome. Under the dogma of the Roman Catholic Church marriage is regarded as indissoluble. This sublime view elevates man's most animalic act to the dignity of a vessel of divine grace and thus to the sphere of man's deepest responsibility. However, the idea that marriage must be indissoluble came to be attacked from various quarters. For extreme cases dissolubility of marriage was admitted by the Protestant reformers.[7] More radically, its free dissolubility was postulated as a command of reason by the thinkers of the Enlightenment, among whom the French philosophers occupied the front ranks.[8] The postulate was heeded by such enlightened rulers as Frederick II of Prussia, by whose pronouncements divorce became possible not only on the grave marital misconduct of one of the parties, but also on the ground of deep and lasting incompatibility of temperament and on the mutual agreement of the parties to an "utterly childless marriage."[9]

The philosophical postulate was also taken up by the French Revolution, which, in its Constitution of 1791, proclaimed that marriage is a civil contract.[10] In detail divorce was then regulated by the law of 1792,[11] by which divorce was permitted both for cause and on mutual agreement of the parties. This famous law has long constituted the subject matter of heated controversy, and it has been denounced as an act calculated to destroy the very institution of marriage.[12] It must be remembered, however, that that Revolutionary law was considerably less radical than the laws of the Prussian, Danish, and other monarchs. The dissolution of a marriage by mutual agreement, in particular, was hedged in by cumbersome and time-consuming formalities, and the agreement required was constituted not so much as one between the immediate parties concerned as one between their families, in the sense of extended kinship groups. Even on the crest of the Revolutionary wave the number of divorces obtained by mutual agreement remained small.[13] Furthermore, as recent research, currently carried on at the University of Chicago Comparative Law Research Center, has shown, the law of 1792 was not so much intended to facilitate divorce as to spell out, and thus to restrict, the Revolutionary postulates the pronouncement of which, in a much more radical form, had resulted in the factual termination of quite a few marriages without any decree of court or other public record.

The law of 1792 did not remain in effect long. During the preparation of the Code divorce was discussed extensively and heatedly.[14] Under the compromise finally enacted the institution of divorce was maintained, but on a limited scale, *i.e.* as a punishment for grave marital misconduct.[15] In addition, divorce on mutual agreement was carried over into the Code,[16] as rumor has it on the active intervention of the First Consul, who is suspected of having already considered sacrificing Josephine to his ambition to be married to a princess of royal blood.[17]

With the resurgence of Catholicism and conservatism that set in with the restoration of the Bourbons, it is characteristic that the complete abolition of divorce was among the earliest acts of the government of Louis XVIII.[18] The liberal individualists had to wait some seventy years before they were again strong enough, in 1874,[19] to restore those articles of the Code that had been repealed in 1816. But even then they had to forgo the re-enactment of Article 233, by which divorce on mutual consent, narrowly restricted though it was, had been possible under the original text of the Code. Divorce was to be admissible only for cause. Adultery was to be treated differently according to whether committed by the wife or by the husband. If it were committed by the wife, the husband was to have an absolute right of divorce even for a single isolated act[20]; but the wife was to be entitled to a divorce only in the extreme case in which the husband not only maintained a permanent mistress but also introduced her into the marital household.[21] The bourgeois morals of the *fin de siècle* are as faithfully mirrored in these articles of the *Loi Nacquet* as in the novels of Emile Zola.

Cruelty was defined, in Article 232, as "acts of excess, corporal attack and grave injury (*excès, sévices et injures graves*), and it was that latter concept of *injures graves* that opened the door to a development which has profoundly changed the nature of divorce.

In this country, in England, and in most other countries of European civilization in which the institution of divorce exists at all, the dissolution of a marriage is, as a general rule, not obtainable unless one spouse has become guilty of some serious act of martial misconduct. Divorce is, so to speak, a privilege of an innocent spouse to repudiate, and thus to punish, a guilty partner. This idea stands in contrast to that other one under which divorce is regarded as an escape from a marriage that has become an insufferable or disagreeable burden to the parties, or to just one of them.[22] In Continental theory these two different conceptions of the function of divorce are contrasted with each other as the principle of guilt (*Verschuldensprinzip*) and the principle of objective disruption (*Zerrüttungsprinzip*), or, as one says in France, as *divorce-sanction* and *divorce-faillite*.[23] Under the former conception, divorce is to be a punitive sanction for misconduct; under the second, the winding up of a marriage gone bankrupt, possibly without any fault of either party.

In England and the United States the concept of *divorce-sanction* has until very recent times been the almost generally prevailing one. In France the law of 1792 and the original version of the Code had combined both approaches. When, after the total suppression of divorce in 1816, it was re-established by the law of 1884, it was conceived exclusively as *divorce-sanction*. Nothing but one party's grave and blameworthy misconduct was to entitle a court to pronounce a decree of divorce. The kind of misconduct that came to be resorted to the most frequently as a ground for divorce, viz. *injures graves,* is still characterized by its subjective element of guilt and blameworthiness, but in a short period emphasis more or less imperceptibly came to shift toward the objective side. *Divorce-faillite* was thus reintroduced into French law by the judiciary.[24] To a limited extent it was sanctioned by the legislature later on, when, by the Law of June 6, 1908, it became permissible for either party to apply as a matter of right for the transformation of a judicial separation into a divorce when at least three years have passed since the decree of separation.[25] However, the separation itself cannot be granted without proof of facts that would constitute a ground for divorce.[26] The novel feature is that at the expiration of the three years' period the divorce must be granted on the application of even that party who had been declared to be the guilty one in the decree of separation. This provision of Article 310 of the Code, as amended, is important in the rare cases in which, although the marriage is disrupted, the innocent party is unwilling to have it completely dissolved. Where, as seems to be the fact in the great majority of disrupted marriages in France as elsewhere, both parties are willing to have it dissolved,[27] Article 232 furnishes the easily available basis. Just as in this country and in other places, divorce by mutual agreement has been rendered available by the courts' ready connivance at collusion.

The steady rise of the French divorce rate has, of course, been widely publicized by viewers-with-alarm as indicating the need of restricting or altogether abolishing divorce. But even the Vichy government did not dare do more than slightly to amend Article 232 so as to indicate that a divorce on the ground of *injures graves* should not be granted in cases other than those of true seriousness.[28] The amendment, which was partially left in effect after the liberation,[29] seems not, however, to have had any appreciable effect. The latest phase in the Church's fight against divorce is constituted by the proposal to establish two different kinds of marriage, one to be concluded in secular form and susceptible to dissolution by divorce, and the other concluded by a religious ceremony and, when concluded according to the rites of the Roman Catholic Church, to be indissoluble as a sacrament.[30] This proposal, which follows the example of fascist Italy[31] and Salazar's Portugal,[32] does not appear to have much chance of being adopted. The laicist tradition is still too strong in France to allow such a return to ecclesiastical dominance over the institution of marriage. Indeed, in spite, or perhaps just in consequence, of the easy availability of divorce, marriage and the family are still strong in France.[33]

III

One of the most far-reaching transformations of life set in motion by the industrial revolution has been the emergence of the female half of the population from the seclusion of the home into the spheres of the productive process and of public life. Concomitantly with the transformation of woman's role and position in society, her legal status had to be changed, too. In 1804, in France as elsewhere, woman's position was in the home, and in the home she was subordinate to the husband. Not in all parts of France had the *ancien droit* gone to the full rigor of the common law of England and America, where marriage was regarded as extinguishing the wife's legal personality and merging it in that of the husband. In the south of France, the so-called *pays de droit écrit, i.e.* Roman law, a measure of legal capacity had been preserved for married women. In the north, however, where, in continuation of Frankish and other Teutonic traditions, various forms of community property had come to prevail, under practically all of which the husband was to be the sole manager not only of the community fund but also of the separate assets of the wife, the wife's capacity to transact legal business was to all practical effects extinguished. It was precisely the northern system of community of movables and acquests that was established by the Code as the common law of France, susceptible, it is true, of being contracted out by antenuptial settlement in favor of either some other form of community property, of the dotal system of Roman progeny, or of a regime of complete separation of assets. From the very beginning such settlements have been common among the propertied classes of France, but, just as in England, they have been concerned with the wife's financial security rather than her personal status. The husband's position as the head of the family was expressly declared by Article 1388 of the Code not to be susceptible to alteration by contract, and in Article 1124 married women, together with infants and persons of unsound mind, were expressly declared to be incapable of making contracts.

Though the system of the Code faithfully reflected the social facts of 1804, it could not be continued unchanged into the twentieth century, when women had come to new positions of personal independence. In France, it is true, the factual emancipation of woman has not gone to the full length that it has reached in the Scandinavian countries, Germany, or the United States, but it has gone far enough to require profound changes in the law. These changes have occurred with respect to the political and other public rights of women in general, both married and unmarried, and with respect to the position of women in marriage concerning the wife's relationship to the husband, the children, and the family property.

In the political sphere French women have, of course, obtained the rights to vote, to be elected to legislative bodies, and to be appointed to public office.[34]

In connection with the grant to women of political rights there should also be mentioned the severance of nationality from marriage status. Up to very recent times it was axiomatic that a family group should have one single nationality for all its members and that the nationality of the group should be determined by its head, the husband-father. Like a great many other countries, including the United States, France has found it proper to yield to feminist pressure and to loosen the connection between the nationality of a woman and that of her husband. Under the Nationality Code of October 19, 1945, a Frenchwoman does not necessarily lose her nationality by marrying a foreigner.[35] Characteristically, however, the unity of the French family is sought to be preserved by retaining the rule under which French nationality is acquired by the foreign woman who marries a Frenchman.[36] Some exceptions have been established, however, to this principle.

The principle of equal rights of husband and wife within marriage cannot be implemented as easily as it is pronounced. The family is a unit, and its basic relationship, that of marriage, is postulated to be indissoluble. How the affairs of the family are to be conducted must be determined in some way; but how can a determination be made if the two partners have an equal voice? This problem has arisen in every modern legal system. The way in which it has been met in France and in the United States presents a characteristic difference, perhaps the only one that can be said to express that difference of approach which was once regarded as distinguishing the civil law from the common law. In the United States we have refused to meet the problem consciously, at least in the sense of searching for a general answer. In a marriage husband and wife may easily have different ideas as to where the family shall live and in what style, which acquaintances should be invited and which not, how the vacations are to be spent, in what religion, if any, the children are to be brought up, to what schools they are to be sent, for what kind of life they are to be prepared, etc. Where the marriage functions well the parties will find a solution. One partner at any rate will move one way or another, and the other will agree or just give in, perhaps grudgingly. If however, a deadlock occurs as to a matter that cannot be left open, a break will develop that may result in the parties' appearance in court in a suit for separate maintenance, child custody, or divorce. If that happens, the court may have to decide who was right in the original quarrel and who was wrong. But why bother about such a problem before judicial decision becomes inevitable? And what general principle should one formulate in advance? Up to now American courts have avoided pronouncing such a general principle. Each case is treated on its own merits, although a certain tendency can be observed in matters touching on economic issues; for example, in determining the family's dwelling place there is a tendency to ascribe the final voice to the principal family breadwinner. Since in most instances this is still the husband, his voice usually prevails, and in such cases the courts are prone to refer to the ancient rule of the common law that declared the husband to be the head of the family. But where it is felt that the husband's decision does not sufficiently respect the interests and susceptibilities of the wife, her status of equality is eloquently emphasized.

To the French legal mind such a muddling-through method is unacceptable. A general rule has to be established even though it may be couched in terms of no or little meaning. It was stated in its present form by the law of September 22, 1942, after a somewhat different version had already been enacted by the law of February 18, 1938.[37] A comparison of the text of Article 213 of the Code as originally worded in 1804 and as it reads now signifies the social change that has taken place.

As originally worded Article 213 proclaimed: "The husband owes protection to his wife, and the wife owes obedience to her husband."

Now it reads: "The husband is the head of the family. He exercises this function in the common interest of the married couple (*du ménage*) and its children. The wife joins (*concourt*) with her husband in determining the moral and economic direction of the family, in providing for its maintenance, in raising the children, and preparing them for their establishment in life."

As to the choice of the marital home, which was once the exclusive domain of the husband, Article 215 now provides:

"The choice of the family home belongs to the husband; the wife is obliged to live with him and he is required to receive her. If the home chosen by the husband presents dangers of a physical or moral kind for the family, the wife can, as an exception, be authorized to have for herself and her children another home to be determined by the court."

The court may thus be invoked to settle such a dispute and, perhaps, others as well,[38] but its decision will hardly have any significance other than determining, for purposes of a later suit for maintenance or divorce, whether one or the other party's conduct amounts to *injures graves*.

As to problems concerning the children and their education, the

Code's system of the father's sole paternal power has been replaced, through the comprehensive reform law of July 23, 1942, by the new principle that the power over the children belongs to both father and mother; but the text immediately goes on to say that "during coverture [this power] is exercised by the father by virtue of his position as head of the family."[39] Its exercise belongs to the mother only in such exceptional situations as those of the husband's inability to exercise it because of absence or similar reasons, or of the husband's having been judicially deprived of his parental power because of grave abuse. Proceedings to have the father thus deprived of his power may, of course, be set in motion through the mother, who may also, it seems, challenge the husband's decision on the general ground that his power is alleged not to have been exercised "in the common interest of the married couple and its children."[40]

In the property field the possibility of adapting the law to the changed social and economic status of women has been provided to a considerable extent through the general power by marriage settlement to contract out the Code's scheme of community of movables and acquests.[41] This possibility has been limited, however, by the rule of Article 1395, which deprives any postnuptial attempt to make a new, or to change an existing, settlement, of all effect not only as against third parties but also *inter partes.* This rigid rule has not been changed. It is believed to be indispensable for the protection of third parties as long as there is not established in France a system of public registration of marriage settlements, such as exists in Germany[42] and Switzerland.[43] The introduction of so costly a system is generally regarded as impracticable. In consequence of the postnuptial unalterability of the *régime matrimonial,* no adaptation to changing conditions has been possible in any existing marriage.

Another even more important reason why marriage settlements have not been generally used to bring about full financial independence of the wife lies in the fact that the idea of community property seems to have taken deep roots in the conviction of the

French people. Marriage is widely regarded as a community not only of souls and bodies but also of property. "Parties not belonging to such special groups as Parisian intellectuals or big business, among whom it is customary to contract out the common-law system of community of movables and acquests, *i.e.* farmers, workers, white-collar people, or craftsmen . . . always join together in their thinking the ideas of marriage and of community property. Normally they regard as somehow lacking in completeness a marriage that does not result in the community of the economic gains made during coverture."[44]

Marriage settlements are still made in large numbers, but the overwhelming majority of them seem not to eliminate but only to modify the community property system. Under the scheme of the Code the assets owned by either party at the time of the marriage (only the immovables, but not the movables) remain outside the community fund. This differentiation seems no longer justified at a time in which movable assets have become the more important and more commonly owned kind of wealth. There has thus become very general that kind of marriage settlement by which all assets held before marriage are excluded from the community fund, which is thus transformed from a community of movables and acquests into one of acquests alone.[45] Together with the antenuptial immovables the antenuptial movables remain the separate property of either party, but, under the Code's general system, the wife's separate estate is managed by the husband, and she is excluded from all power to alienate, encumber, or otherwise dispose of it otherwise than by testamentary act.

What was required in consequence of the steadily increasing influx of women into gainful activities outside the household was the grant to married women of the power of management and disposition of the assets acquired by their own work. This power was granted them by the law of July 13, 1907, as now amended by law of February 18, 1938.[46] Property acquired by a married woman through her own activity outside the household or the husband's business is to constitute her "reserved fund," of which she has the exclusive right of enjoyment and power of disposition. If the parties live under one of the community property systems, the "reserved fund" of the wife is at the termination of the community added to the community fund and distributed with it among the parties concerned.[47] As a married woman may now own assets of which she can dispose freely, she can also bind herself by contracts. By her contracts she binds, however, not only herself but also the husband and the community fund, unless the debt has been contracted neither in the interest of the household nor in the course of her business or profession.[48] The husband has, of course, always been liable for the debts that the wife has incurred as his agent, and such agency is presumed with respect to all transactions that are normally left to the wife as the manager of the kitchen and the household.[49] The husband may deprive his wife of this power, but since the enactment of the law of September 22, 1942 it seems that he can no longer do so without cause.[50] The liability of the husband and the community for the wife's business or professional debts is excluded if the husband has declared his opposition to such activity of his wife.[51] What other effects the exercise of the husband's right of such opposition[52] can have under present circumstances is not clear, except insofar as it seems to be certain that the wife's disregard of the husband's opposition may constitute, as *injure grave,* a ground for divorce. Newly established by the law of February 18, 1938[53] has been the wife's power to have the husband's opposition set aside by the court when it is "not justified in the interest of the family." As the husband is liable for the "legitimate" debts of the wife, so, in the manner of an American family expense statute, she is now liable with her reserved fund for those of his debts that have been incurred in the interest of the household.[54] The solidarity of the spouses is strongly emphasized by these joint liabilities.

Other improvements of a married woman's property status have been brought about by provisions intended to enable her to transfer, encumber, or otherwise dispose of assets, not only of her own, but also of her husband and the community, where such disposition is necessary and the husband is either not in a position to act or refuses to act, against the best interest of the family.[55]

Altogether, the changes in the French law of marital property law have been modest. Even the most far-reaching, *i.e.* the establishment of the wife's free enjoyment and management of her reserved fund, seems to be limited in its effect by the cautious attitude of banks and business circles in general, which, before honoring a married woman's transaction, are wont either to require strict proof that the asset in question is part of her separate fund or, even more generally, will not act unless her act is countersigned by her husband.[56]

A more fundamental revision of the entire system of matrimonial property law has been under consideration for some time.[57] The prewar draft of a major reform law passed the Senate but failed of adoption in the Chamber of Deputies. Since the end of the war a Commission has been at work to draft an entirely new Civil Code, which is totally to replace the Code of 1804. In the discussions of this Commission the marital property law has been the subject matter of a major dispute.

In the last decades revisions of the law of marital property have been undertaken in a number of countries, and several of the revisions have resulted in the adoption of a system that appears highly attractive under modern conditions. Under this system of "acquest participation," the assets of husband and wife remain completely separate during the marriage, not only as to title but also as to management. Just as under the system obtaining in most of the jurisdictions of this country, the husband owns *his* property and the wife *hers,* and each of them freely manages and disposes of his respective assets. But when the marriage comes to an end by death or otherwise, a computation is made to find out whether the total mass of property has increased beyond the value of the parties' holdings at the beginning, and if it turns out that there has been an increase that can be regarded as due to the exertion of one party or the other, it is split between both. This system thus tries to combine the advantages of both separation of assets and community property.[58] Originating in local customs of various parts of Northern and Central Europe, this system has been adopted by recent legislation in Sweden,[59] Norway,[60] Denmark,[61] Iceland,[62] Finland,[63] Hungary,[64] Costa Rica,[65] Colombia,[66] and Uruguay.[67]

It was but natural that in the French draft of 1932 the system of acquest participation was proposed;[68] but it was not adopted, and the current discussions in the Civil Code Commission indicate that it is unlikely to be adopted as the law of the new Civil Code of France.[69] Two arguments militate against the abandonment of the system of community property. The first is based on the notion that in marriage the community of life necessarily includes the community of property. The second argument is that separation of marital assets is impractical in fact. Observation is said to indicate that among most married couples the assets of husband and wife are in fact intermingled with each other to such an extent that it is impossible to say what is his and what hers, and that the only practical way is that of simply treating them as theirs. This argument appears, indeed, to be based on sound observation. Except among the very wealthy, who have their property affairs managed by, or with the constant advice of, professional counselors, it will be rare that every piece of furniture, silverware, or other appurtenance is earmarked as his or hers. That it is not decisive for "real" ownership in whose name the bank account is kept or in whose name the car, the stocks and bonds, and even the real estate are registered, has long been recognized, and in this country as well. Who under such circumstances is to have what in the case of death, divorce, bankruptcy, or attachment? How do *we* handle these problems? It is not easy to find out, because published decisions are rare. Are there no litigated cases? Or do they only fail to reach appellate courts? Somehow the problems must be solved in practice, but how? Here is a challenging field for research. Perhaps light can be thrown on the situation from the experience of such countries as Norway, the U.S.S.R., or Germany, where furniture and household apparel are sufficiently valuable to justify litigation at the low cost at which justice is available there. To the French legal mind the lack of neatness that seems to be necessarily implied in the system of separation of assets appears so appalling as to block its adoption as the general law of the land.

IV

The increased emphasis on freedom of the individual as against the ties of the family group has been one of the great social trends which, in the wake of the industrial revolution, have changed the structure of the family wherever Western civilization has come to exert its influence. Another trend, closely connected with it, that has worked in the same direction has been the emancipation of the small family group from the bond of the large group of the kindred. In France the decline of the kinship group has not been nearly so complete as in the United States, where immigration from without as well as the constant flux of internal migration have left little room for intensive feelings of family solidarity between brothers and sisters, not to speak of cousins or more distant relatives.

In France the weakening of the kinship bond has found expression in the facilitation of the devices by which strangers to the blood can be made to participate in the succession to family property. The Code, in what it provided as well as in what it failed to provide, was inspired by a powerful feeling that family property ought to be kept within the blood line. Such a feeling is characteristic of landowners, both aristocrat and peasant, who have been settled on inherited land for generations. It also develops among merchants and other owners of urban wealth, who are anxious to stabilize the splendor, wealth, and influence of their houses.[70] The sons of the Revolution of 1789 did not wish to restore the power of the deposed aristocracy, but both the peasantry and the bourgeoisie were anxious to maintain beyond their own generation the stability and integrity of their family fortunes. The resurgence of the old aristocracy was, as we have seen, sought to be counteracted by the elimination of property settlements from the scope of legally effective transactions. This aim as well as ideas of abstract justice and other motives also helped to anchor in the Code the limitation of testamentary freedom by which an owner of property is prevented from leaving all his property to strangers of the blood.[71] The ambivalence of the lawmakers' motives is indicated, however, by the fact that in the event of intestate succession the Code allowed collateral kindred to succeed up to the 12th degree,[72] while it simultaneously excluded from intestate succession the surviving spouse. Though the widow was to receive one half of the community fund, and thus of the property acquired by the husband during the marriage and all his movables, she was excluded, as a stranger to the blood, from any share in his inherited lands, which were thus to be kept within the group of the kindred.[73] French law thus closely resembled the common law of England, which was somewhat more generous, however, to the surviving spouse by granting her or him an estate of dower or courtesy. By limiting these rights to life estates, care was still taken to prevent freehold land from passing from the blood line of the husband into that of the wife, and vice versa. In France even a life estate in a portion of the estate of the predeceasing spouse was not granted to the survivor until 1891,[74] and the right to inherit a fee interest did not accrue to the surviving spouse unless there were no blood relatives of the decedent within the twelfth degree of consanguinity. Even now, under the law of December 31, 1917, the surviving spouse is entitled to a portion in fee only in the absence of relatives within the sixth degree of consanguinity.[75] These modifications, modest though they are, indicate that the feeling of blood kinship has abated at least to a certain degree. The same phenomenon is indicated by the great extension of the scope of adoption, which under the original text of the Code was kept within the narrow limit of an institution that would allow a childless couple to perpetuate the family name by the adoption of an adult person.[76] Not until the need of caring for orphan children came to be acute in the wake of the First World War was the Code, in several steps, so amended as to give to adoption that new character of an institution of child welfare which it has assumed all over the region of Western civilization, conspicuously including the United States.[77]

V

The impact of industrialization, urbanization, and other phenomena of modern life has in other respects affected the family and consequently its law. Parental power, almost unrestrained under the Code of 1804, has come to be subject to forfeiture in the event of abuse.[78] Significantly, too, the once existing power of parents, and in certain cases even of grandparents, to veto the intended marriage of a son (or grandson of less than twenty-five years of age)[79] has been restricted to the age of twenty-one.[80] The status of illegitimate children has been changed by permitting, at least in some cases, claims for support against the father who has failed or refused to recognize his paternity,[81] as well as by increasing the portions that may be given to a recognized illegitimate child by gift or will of his father or mother.[82] The formalities required for the conclusion of marriage have been made less cumbersome and less expensive in order to make marriage more easily accessible to those who might otherwise prefer to live in the *union libre* of concubinage,[83] which, in France, the United States, and elsewhere has been, and still is, not uncommon among the lowest groups of the populace.

Although there has been neither a weakening of the French family nor a subversion of its basic structure, it has, as we can see, undergone changes in many respects, and, concomitantly with them, the law has changed in numerous points from the original text of the Code of 1804. How have these adaptations of the law been brought about?

Legislation has, of course, played a conspicuous role. But in those numerous situations in which the law was not authoritatively laid down by a clear provision of the Code, its adaptation has been brought about by the creative activity of the judiciary or simply by changing patterns of party transactions, especially through the invention by the *notaires*[84] of new form clauses in marriage settlements. It would be difficult exactly to compare the relative roles of legislative, judicial, and cautelary lawmaking in France and the United States. Intensive research would be necessary for the purpose. But prima facie one may venture to say that the role of judicial lawmaking in the field of family law has been no less in France than in the United States. If we were to extend our comparison beyond France, we should find that the creative role of the judiciary has been about equally considerable in other Continental countries and that in a good many of them it has been more considerable than in the home country of the common law, England, at least within the field of family law.

Both family law and the family have thus been transformed in numerous respects, in France and elsewhere. But the changes have more affected the functions of the family than its basic role in society. French law has kept abreast of these changes, and it has succeeded in doing so without breaking with sound and well-tested tradition. Today the family constitutes as much the basis of the social structure of France as it did when the rules of its legal regime were systematically formulated in Napoleon's Code.[85]

NOTES

[1] See Bonnecase, La philosophie du Code Napoléon appliquée au droit de famille 21 *et seq.* (2d ed. 1928).

[2] Letter of June 5, 1806, Correspondance de Napoléon 1er, Vol. 12, 432; see also Letter of August 14, 1806, *id.* at 167.

[3] Civil Code, Arts. 405–19.

[4] Cf. Lepointe, La famille dans l'ancien droit 254, 274 (4th ed. 1954); Basdevant, Des rapports de l'église et de l'état dans la législation du mariage du Concile de Trente au Code civil (1900).

[5] Martin, Le Gallicanisme et la réforme catholique. (1919). Planiol, Traité élémentaire

de droit civil; revu et complété par G. Ripert, Vol. 1, No. 736 (3d ed. 1946); Brissaud, Manuel d'histoire de droit privé 11 (1908).

6 Planiol, *op. cit. supra* note 5, at Nos. 738 *et seq.;* Conrad, Die Grundlegung der modernen Zivilehe durch die französische Revolution, Zeitschrift der Savigny Stiftung für Rechtsgeschichte Vol. 67 (Germanistische Abteilung), 336 (1950).

7 Cf. Martin Luther, Von Ehesachen (1520) in Weimarer Ausgabe, Vol. 30, Abt. 3, 205 (1910); Friedberg, Das Kirchenrecht 512 (5th ed. 1903).

8 See Voltaire, Dictionnaire philosophique (1764) sub tit. "Divorce"; J. Lescène des Maisons, Contract conjugal ou loix de mariage (1781); Diderot, Supplément au voyage de Bougainville (1772, published 1796); cf. 1 Taine, Les origines de la France contemporaine 372 (1876).

9 In Prussia the first step was taken by Frederick II in his Corpus Juris Fridericiani of 1749, which was promulgated as a statute in several parts of the monarchy. The final codification was contained in Part II, §§668 *et seq.* of the Prussian General Code (Allgemeines Landrecht für die Preussischen Staaten), which was prepared during the reign of Frederick II, but promulgated in 1791–94 by his successor, King Frederick William II.

On the practice of the Danish kings, since about 1790, of granting divorces on the ground of "incompatibility of temperament," see Borum, Personalstatuttet 472 (1927).

10 Tit. II, Art. 7; see Duguit, Monnier et Bonnard, Les constitutions et les principales lois politiques de la France depuis 1789, 6 (1932).

11 Law of September 20, 1792.

12 Cf. Bonnecase, *op. cit. supra* note 1, at 84; Olivier-Martin, La crise du mariage dans la législation intermédiaire (1901).

13 For statistics see Maleville, Du divorce et de la séparation de corps (1801); Olivier-Martin, *op. cit. supra* note 12, at 157; Glasson, Le mariage et le divorce 261 (1880).

14 For a full account see Fenet, Recueil complet des travaux préparatoires du Code civil, Vol. 1 (1836).

15 Adultery (Arts. 229, 230); cruelty and grievous injury (Art. 231); commission of a crime resulting in conviction to a degrading punishment (Art. 232).

16 Art. 233.

17 On Napoleon's divorce see the literature listed by Viollet, Histoire du droit civil français 489, n.4 (1905); cf. also Glasson, *op. cit. supra* note 13, at 264.

18 Law of May 8, 1816.

19 Law of July 27, 1884 (loi Nacquet).

20 Art. 229.

21 Art. 230.

22 Cf. Rheinstein, Trends in marriage and divorce laws of Western countries, 18 Law and Contemporary Problems 3 (1953).

23 See Carbonnier, Terre et ciel dans le droit français du mariage. Le droit privé français au milieu du 20e siècle, Etudes offertes à Georges Ripert (cited in the following notes as Etudes Ripert), Vol. 1, 325, 334 (1950).

24 See Cass. March 14, 1928, S. 1929. 192, D. H. 1928. 253 (affaire Ferrari); cf. Planiol, Note, Rev. Crit. 689 (1887); Hitier, Le développement de la jurisprudence en matière de divorce. Annales de l'enseignement supérieure de Grenoble 439 (1894).

25 Civil Code, Art. 310.

26 *Id.*, Art. 306.

27 Cf. Durckheim, Le divorce par consentement mutuel, I Revue bleue 553 (1906); M.

Marc Ancel, Justice of the Court of Cassation, estimates that some 75 to 80 per cent of all divorces granted in France are actually obtained by the mutual agreement of the parties. Travaux de la Commission de réforme du Code civil. Année 1947/48 (1950), at 604.

[28] Law of April 2, 1941.

[29] Ordinance of April 12, 1945; cf. Carbonnier, Commentaire, R. D. 1945, Lois 145.

[30] Savatier, Le droit, l'amour et la liberté 33 (1937); Mazeaud, Solution du problème du divorce, D. 1945, Chron. 11; same, Travaux de la Commission de reforme du Code civil, Année 1947/48, at 498.

[31] Lateran Treaty of February 11, 1929; Codice civile of 1942, Art. 82 *et seq.*

[32] Concordat of 1940.

[33] For a sociological analysis see Desforges, Le divorce en France (1947); Ceccaldi, The Family in France, 16 Marriage and Family Living 326 (1954).

[34] This development, which proceeded in several steps, has been terminated by Para. 3 of the Preamble to the Constitution of October 27, 1946, which proclaims: "In all respects the law guarantees to women equal rights with men."

[35] Art. 94.

[36] Art. 37.

[37] Cf. Rouast, La famille, Vol. 2 of Planiol et Ripert, Traité pratique de droit civil français, No. 374 *et. seq.* (2d ed. 1952).

[38] Cf. L. Aulagnon, L'intervention du juge à propos de l'exercice des droits des époux. Etudes Ripert 390.

[39] Art. 323, par. 1, second sentence.

[40] Arg. Art. 213 Civil Code as amended.

[41] Civil Code Art. 1387.

[42] German Civil Code §§1435, 1558–63.

[43] Swiss Civil Code, Arts. 248–51.

[44] Jousselin, Travaux de la semaine internationale du droit 96 (Paris 1937).

[45] Cf. P. Kayser, L'évolution de la communauté réduite aux acquets dans la pratique notariale. Etudes Ripert 478.

[46] Civil Code, Art. 224.

[47] *Id.,* Art. 226.

[48] *Id.,* Art. 225.

[49] *Id.,* Art. 220.

[50] Cf. Rouast, *op. cit. supra* note 37, at No. 393 bis.

[51] Civil Code, Art. 223, par. 2.

[52] *Id.,* Art. 223, par. 1.

[53] The present text of *id.,* Art. 223, para. 3, which has been established by the Law of September 22, 1942, is practically identical with that established by the Law of February 18, 1938.

[54] Civil code, Art. 225, par. 2.

[55] *Id.,* Arts. 217 and 219, as amended by the Law of September 22, 1942.

[56] Cf. Choteau, La reforme des régimes matrimoniaux. 1 Etudes Ripert 455, 458.

[57] Cf. *ibid.*

[58] Cf. I. Zaitay y E. Vaz Ferreira, Regímenes matrimoniales de participación, 1 Rev. de la Facultad de derecho y ciencias sociales (Montevideo) No. 3, 1 (1950); Travaux de la semaine internationale de droit: Le régime matrimonial de droit commun (1937); H. Dölle,

Rechtsvergleichende Bemerkungen zum Problem des künftigen gesetzlichen Güterstandes in Deutschland, 18 Zeitschrift f. ausl. u. intern. Privatrecht 608 (1953).

[59] Law of June 11, 1920. A similar system had already been adopted in 1907 in Switzerland, where, however, in the absence of an agreement to the contrary, the estate of the wife is managed by the husband. See Swiss Civil Code, Arts. 178, 194, 195, 214.

[60] Law of May 20, 1927.

[61] Law of March 18, 1925.

[62] Law of June 20, 1923.

[63] Law of June 13, 1929.

[64] Law XII of 1946; cf. I. Zaitay, Les régimes matrimoniaux du droit hongrois [1949] Rev. internationale de droit comparé, No. 3.

[65] Codigo civil of 1888, Arts. 76, 77.

[66] Law No. 28 of November 17, 1932.

[67] Law of September 18, 1946.

[68] Doc. parl., Sénat, 1932, annexe No. 594.

[69] Cf. Chateau, *op. cit. supra* note 44, at 469 *et seq.*

[70] See Rheinstein, Law of Decedents' Estates 25, 34 (2nd ed. 1955).

[71] Civil Code, Arts. 913 *et seq.*

[72] *Id.*, Art. 755.

[73] *Id.*, Art. 767.

[74] Law of March 9, 1891. Civil Code, Art. 767, has since been amended repeatedly.

[75] Civil Code, Art. 767, par. 1, in connection with Art. 755, as amended by the Law of December 31, 1917, Art. 17. If there are collaterals within the sixth degree in the paternal line, but not in the maternal, or vice versa, the surviving spouse is entitled to inherit the fee in one half of the estate; see Art. 767, par. 2, as amended by the law of December 3, 1930.

[76] Cf. Rouast, *op. cit. supra* note 37, at Nos. 1003 *et seq.*

[77] As to the present law, see Civil Code, Arts. 343 *et seq.*

[78] Savatier, Les personnes, Vol. 1 of Planiol et Ripert, Traité pratique de droit civil français, Nos. 384 *et seq.* (2d ed. 1952).

[79] So-called acts of respect; Civil Code, Art. 148 *et seq.*

[80] Law of June 21, 1907.

[81] Law of November 16, 1912.

[82] Law of March 3, 1896.

[83] See H. Capitant, L'évolution du droit de famille depuis le Code civil. Le droit français. Livre souvenir des Journées du droit civil français, Montréal 1, 5, 1936 (1936).

[84] See Kayser, 1 *op. cit. supra* note 45.

[85] Cf. H. Capitant, *supra* note 83, at 14: "It would be false to believe that the French family of today is in a state of disintegration. Among the peasantry, which constitutes the largest class of the population, among the bourgeoisie, and even among the workers, the family has maintained its strength. . . . The tie of affection between parents and children has remained extremely powerful in France. The traditions of family life have maintained themselves, the respect of the children for their parents has always been potent. The French family has preserved itself through love. It is very solid."

9

The Code and Property

CLAUDE LÉWY

APPARENTLY only a rather short title of the French Civil Code, Title II of the Second Book, deals with the law of property. It is the only one captioned *De La Propriété*. But this title includes only a definition of property and the provisions governing the right of accession. Actually, Title III and Title IV of the same Second Book also concern themselves with the law of property (usufructs and easements), and so do a number of articles or sections of the Third Book, captioned "Of the various ways of acquiring property."

Hence the subject is much too broad even to be fully summarized in the present paper, which must be limited to certain aspects believed to be of more interest to an English-speaking audience. This paper will treat successively:

First: Of the concept of property under the law of the Civil Code and how it was arrived at.

Secondly: Of the division of "things" that may be the object of the right of property.

Thirdly: Of the passing of title *inter vivos* to purchasers or grantees for consideration.

I

THE CONCEPT OF PROPERTY

At the dawn of the Revolution, when the *Etats Généraux* convened, the French law of property, particularly of real property, was extremely complicated.

CLAUDE LÉWY *is Professor on the Faculty of Law and Political Sciences of the French University of New York*

(1) The influence of the feudal system was still present. The lords owned very large estates. Formerly, the *seigneurs* who had held the same estates centuries before had granted certain rights of enjoyment to the tenants who cultivated the land as villeins. We need say nothing about that period, because the reader may be assumed to be familiar with the English feudal system. Since it was directly borrowed from the French system, after the Norman Conquest, you know the basic features. The differences are not in its earlier but in its later evolution. In France the result of the system was that, down to the eighteenth century and even after villeinage had practically disappeared, the ownership of land was split in two: on one hand, the lord—who kept the eminent domain and the rights flowing therefrom—and on the other hand the tenant, who had the *dominium utile.*

(2) Apart from the encumbrances of feudal ownership (which has tended to diminish through the centuries), the rights of ownership of the lords themselves and of the alodial owners (*propriétaires de francs alleux*) were limited, restrained, and shackled by important family rights, which sounded in property interest.

A certain portion of land could not be given away, either *inter vivos* or by will; estates in the nature of fee tail were generalized under the name of "substitutions fidei commissaires" borrowed from the Roman law; powers of pre-emption (*retraits lignagers et autres*) were vested in the family, even for conveyances for consideration. Generally, the power of alienation of the owner was limited by numerous restrictions.

(3) The right of ownership in land was also whittled away by the impact of economic factors; currency was rare at that time; banknotes did not yet exist. Consequently very often the grantor, instead of selling his land outright in consideration of a lump sum of money, transferred it under a perpetual lease and in consideration of a perpetual rent—like fee farm in England. This rent ran with the land as a lien and was considered a right *in rem*. Mortgages were also frequent and not recorded.

(4) Finally, the Church and religious institutions under its con-

trol owned vast estates, governed by special rules of ownership, since they were removed from the channels of commerce and known as *biens de mainmorte*. Such was the state of affairs in 1789.

The French Revolution proclaimed individual property to be a human right and a necessary concomitant of the right of liberty.

Consequently the feudal eminent domain was abolished; interests carved out of absolute property were strictly limited; powers of the family were reduced. Finally, the Church estates were nationalized. Since then, the tendency to avoid the reconstitution of huge *biens de mainmorte* has persisted, both for economic and for political reasons. According to the persistent prevailing view, the neutrality of the State cannot be real if the holdings of religious associations are too extensive. This is the reason why, since the Revolution, the capacity of associations to hold real estate and to take by gift or will has been and still is strictly limited.

In all these matters the Civil Code has crystallized and organized the spirit of the Revolution, despite the restoration of certain rights of the family, mainly as to forced heirship and some permissible substitutions.

For its framers, the right of property was the cornerstone of the social system. All rights, *in rem* as well as *in personam,* the manner of acquiring them and of losing them, the rules of inheritance, contracts, including prenuptial agreements—all these topics are organized in relation to the right of property, although this is often poor legal logic.

In any event, the right to individual property, under the law of the Code, was a return to the Roman conception of *dominium.* It is a perpetual, exclusive, quasi-absolute right of enjoyment, use, and disposition over any thing, land, or chattel capable of being owned, provided, however, that no use of it be made against the rules of law.

The first characteristic, perpetualness, is extremely noteworthy in connection with the Anglo-American law of property. It raises a question of vocabulary that goes much beyond a mere point of language, and the study of it is of great help in clarifying the French notion. *Propriété* is often translated by "ownership" and believed to be the same. Now, if it were not for this ingredient of perpetuity, *propriété* would indeed correspond fairly to ownership in English. But the possibility of limitation as to time is an essential feature of Anglo-American ownership. The tenant for life or for years has a right of ownership. A bailee has it. But it could never be said in French that a tenant is *propriétaire* for five years, or a bailee *propriétaire* during the bailment. The idea of limitation in time, which is not only consistent with, but a normal incident of the right of ownership, is completely repugnant to the French right of *propriété*.

It may well be that the concept according to which ownership can be divided into slices of time, each one retaining the same nature of dominion and differing from any other only by its duration and the actuality of the possession, is no more than a metaphoric illusion, as I am inclined to think. A man who has an interest limited as to time can dispose only of that interest. Clearly he cannot dispose of the thing itself, either legally or materially, prevented as he is by the action of waste or its modern equivalents. Now, if ownership is defined by the totality of the powers of use and disposal allowed by law, then the power of disposition and alienation over the thing is of the very essence of ownership. Consequently, eviscerated* of such power, so-called limited ownership is perhaps no ownership at all. But since we are comparing institutions as they are designated in fact, and not as we believe—maybe wrongly after all—that they should be, we are bound to find that *propriété* is not ownership.

* Naturally it will be otherwise in case of mere suspension of the power of alienation.

Is it, more simply, "property"? If "property" is applied to the right of ownership, we meet with the same difficulty. If it is applied to the thing owned, we can even find additional discrepancies. Suffice it to mention two:

Propriété in this second meaning designates in French almost exclusively a piece of real estate. A man would say, speaking of his farm or of his villa on the *Côte d'Azur: "J'ai une belle propriété."* He will almost never so refer to his jewels, his books, or his hat. When he says, *"Ils sont ma propriété personnelle,"* he means that they belong to him, and not at all that they are personal property.

"Fee simple absolute" will be even more misleading. In the first place, it conveys, at least ordinarily, only the idea of an interest in real property, whereas *propriété* may as often and as well be an interest in personal property. Secondly, a fee simple absolute involves the right of immediate possession, whereas *propriété* does not necessarily do so. A man may have *propriété* of a thing over which another has a right of possession (as lessee, bailee, pledgee, etc.). Only in the extreme case of a usufruct does the right of *propriété* appear so weakened as to become qualified, and designated as *nue propriété*—the situation then being comparable to a reversion or remainder in fee after a life estate.

To be sure, many of the differences are more historical than actual. But the fact remains that, in the mind of an American lawyer, the words "ownership," "property," or "fee" raise definitely different connotations from those of the word *propriété* in the mind of a French lawyer.

The difficulty is generally by-passed, but it is worth while knowing at least that it exists.

Using the Gordian-knot technique, this paper will from now on employ the French word to designate the French institution. So much for its traits of perpetuity and power of disposition. There is nothing about the details of use and enjoyment that differs strikingly from the corresponding features of Anglo-

American ownership. Therefore only the quality of absoluteness of the *propriété* remains to be examined.

In the definition given by the Code itself it was admitted that in use *propriété* could be limited by law or regulations. Consequently "absolute" never meant unlimited; rather, it meant that the limitations should be strictly construed. As a matter of fact, they have steadily increased. One of the most striking features of the administration of the Code during the last hundred and fifty years is the progressive socialization (either by statutory law or by case law) of the right of *propriété*.

Restrictions or limitations that were at first very exceptional have become almost the rule. The reasons for this evolution in every country of Western Europe (and also in the United States, although less noticeably) are well known, but remain outside the scope of this study.

The Code itself provided for certain limitations to the right of *propriété* that were prescribed by the normal enjoyment of the adjoining owners. Under the name of "legal" or "natural" easements it set up a rather elaborate system concerning boundary trees (Articles 671 to 673, amended by the law of August 20th, 1880), objectionable structures or works (wells, *fosses d'aisance,* chimneys, stables, etc.); the rights to light and air; party walls (Articles 678 to 680); ways of necessity *(servitude d'enclave:* Articles 682 to 685).

Furthermore, the case law developed for the protection of neighbors a set of limitations that, under the name of *abus de droit,* produces about the same results as the Anglo-American notion of "nuisance."

The restrictions named were designed for the protection of other private interests.

Another class of restrictions, resulting either from the original Code or from later statutes, is aimed at the protection of public interests: condemnation by eminent domain, provided for by Article 545 *(expropriation pour cause d'utilité publique),* simplified by statutes of 1935 and 1940, now administered by boards in lieu of the traditional juries of landowners, who usually gave high awards; restrictions of private buildings in the vicinity of national defense structures or camps; easements established in the interest of aircraft navigation, visibility on highways, electric power, etc.

More recent restrictions (each of which modified the regime of property in a given field) include the following:

In the field of fine arts: Certain works of art may not be exported. Certain monuments, like castles or manors, are classified as historical monuments. This means that, although they are privately owned, their owners are prohibited from making any alteration without approval of the Administration, which in turn takes charge of the repairs and of the maintenance. Zoning ordinances have about the same impact as they have in the United States, although apparently they are less frequent.

In the field of production: Many statutes provide for production control, as a counterpart to price control, so that the owner is no longer free to grow corn or vines or beets as he sees fit.

According to a statute of May 23, 1943, the *propriétaire* who allows his land to lie fallow can be compelled to rent it. A statute of 1941 provides that the owners of very small plots can be forced to surrender them in exchange for others in order to curb the excessive splitting of real property. Many statutes had provided and still provide for ceiling prices, especially for rents. Permanent dispositions known as *propriété commerciale* and *statut du fermage* give to the tenant of commercial space, or to the farmer, a right of renewal of his lease. Compensation is to be paid to him by the landlord who refuses to renew, and the rights of property are consequently curtailed.

An ordinance of February 1945 provides for the formation of a committee of workers in any enterprise employing more than fifty persons, and grants to this committee certain powers, if not of control, at least of inspection, consultation, and advice. Finally, the public utility companies—the purveyors of gas and electricity, the coal companies, the great banks, the railroads—were nationalized, with compensation to the shareholders.

In this connection, a simple observation seems appropriate: The danger of excessive concentration of economic power has been noticed everywhere in the free world, and especially in the United States, for more than fifty years. Now, one way of controlling this danger is to maintain free competition. This is the aim of the American antitrust laws. But sometimes, and for certain branches of production, a country is not big enough to maintain a multiplicity of competitors within a certain branch: for instance, though it may make sense to have various aviation companies competing in the New York-Miami flight, it would make no sense and it would be utterly impossible to have more than one company on the Paris-Nice flight. Mr. Lilienthal recently asserted that even in the United States there are some sectors of production in which Big Business, to be efficient, should be really big. Hence there are instances in which, because of the size of a country, there is room for only a single big enterprise, and competition is consequently technically impossible, as it is for the railroads of France. In that event monopoly is no longer a moot question: it is a fact. At this level the services to be rendered are nation-wide public services, essential to the very life of the nation. The old notion of absolute *propriété individuelle* is no longer the possible instrument of administration for these national interests. The individual owner of a shop may open or close his shop as he pleases. Who will argue that the public utility company may do the same? But if it has to obey, to a large extent, the commands of the administration, if it has, as a counterpart, to be largely subsidized, if the salaries of its employees are fixed through compulsory collective bargaining, if the rates of its services are dictated to it, what remains of its property rights? There remains only an arrangement to have management fairly compensated and a fair return given to the investors—the administration having become more and more, by the way, the main investor directly or through loans and advances. At this point nationalization against compensation is less than a condemnation: it is the mere legalization of a de facto situation.

II

DIVISION OF THINGS

We come now to the division of things—using the word in its Blackstonian sense—that can be the object of the right of *propriété*.

Before the Civil Code, French law, though it kept Roman terminology most of the time, had classified things not according to their physical mobility or immobility, but mainly according to their productiveness and, if we may say so, their solidity. Property capable of bearing fruits or rents for its owner, and at the same time sturdy and durable, was classified as *héritages,* which was not exactly the English "hereditament." Its conservation in the family was specially protected by law. The rights of husbands and guardians over the *héritages* of wives and wards were cautiously limited, and their descent obeyed special rules of succession.

Below this first-class category of property was a second class comprehending both the movables or goods and the "chattels" or *cateux.* Chattels were structures of small value, like barns, pens, stables, and trees that were not fruit trees. Movables and chattels, which constituted the second-class category of property, were less protected by law. Their alienation was easier; the powers of guardians and husbands were broader. Especially for the movables or goods there was no right to follow the *res.* Finally, upon the death of the owner, both goods and chattels formed a separate estate and obeyed special rules of succession, inspired not by the family origin or interest like the *héritages,* but by the presumed affection of the deceased toward his nearest relatives, regardless of their lineage.

The similarity between the former Anglo-American system of administration and descent does not need to be pointed out. Observe only that, even now in New York, the administrator is called "administrator of goods and chattels"—which nowadays appears to be merely repetitious; it comes from the old French division and terminology, more than five hundred years old.

The Civil Code dropped the word "chattel" except in its original meaning of "cattle" (*capitalia-catalla:* heads of cattle) in Articles 1800 to 1831. It divided property into immovables and movables, according to the Roman law. Roughly, this corresponds to the Anglo-American division of real and personal property. However, the Code considers as "immovables by destination" a certain number of rights whereby the thing on which they bear is immovable, whereas these rights are generally deemed personal property under Anglo-American law. Also the treatment of fixtures is not exactly the same. But these differences are of secondary importance, and no substantial error is committed when *immeubles* is translated by "real property" and *meubles* by "personal property."

IMMOVABLES. Under the present Civil Code system the immovables or real property include three classes of things:

(1) *Immovables by nature,* which are the land and the buildings annexed to the land.

(2) *Immovables by destination.* These are really chattels, which are deemed immovables and treated accordingly by a fiction of law. For the fiction to operate, it is necessary for these chattels to have been brought upon the land by the *propriétaire* himself. Chattels brought in by a tenant always remain chattels. In addition they should have a link with the land. The link may be a physical annexation, which shows the intent of the owner to make it permanent (*Choses attachées au Fonds à perpétuelle demeure,* Article 525). Resemblance to fixtures annexed by the owner in fee under American law is evident. But the link may be merely functional. For instance, the cattle on a farm, or the machinery in a plant, are immovables by destination. (Article 524).

(3) *Immovables by the object to which they apply.* By that the Code means certain categories of rights bearing on immovables, like usufruct, mortgages, or right of action concerning real estate, as the action to foreclose a mortgage or the action of ejectment.

MOVABLES, OR PERSONAL PROPERTY. Following the Roman law, the Code classifies as personal property (1) what are called corporeal movables, *i.e.* chattels, and (2) what are called incorporeal movables.

This second group itself includes rights *in rem* in movables (for instance pledges), intellectual rights (copyrights or patents), and rights of action *in personam,* or *choses* in action. Certainly, from an analytical point of view the classification of mere rights as either movables and immovables or corporeal and incorporeal is inaccurate. This division has been criticized by legal writers on both sides of the Atlantic and of the Channel. It has been observed that rights as such are always incorporeal; they are neither real nor personal property. The only right that it is normal to identify with the property to which it applies (either movable or immovable) is the right of absolute ownership.

In any event the Civil Code abolished all distinctions between real and personal property as to administration and descent, accomplishing the same reform as England in 1925 and New York in 1930. Furthermore, as between grantor and grantee and seller and buyer, no difference was retained as to the manner of passing title. For both real and personal property, mere consent is sufficient. Conveyances of land are treated exactly like sales of goods.

However, in other respects, the distinction was retained.

(1) As to subsequent purchasers, donees, mortgagees, or lienors, conveyances of real property are void if not recorded. On the other hand, no recording is necessary for acquiring as against the world title to personal property.

(2) The old idea that personal property was of less value *(res movilis res vilis)* was retained in matrimonial property status. This happened because the Code was enacted just before the economic revolution of the nineteenth century and just before the development of the stock market; and this is most unfortunate. Shocking results are to be found in the legal matrimonial regime touching community property. If the future spouses do not enter a special prenuptial agreement before a *notaire,* the system of their property is governed by provisions of the Civil Code known as "legal community." Now, pursuant to these provisions, real property, either owned by one spouse before the marriage took place, or acquired by him during the marriage through inheritance or by gift, remains the individual property of this spouse, whereas, under the same circumstances, personal property becomes community property. The consequence is this: If W., the wife, inherits a house worth $10,000, she keeps it, for instance, on a divorce or on the husband's death; but if H., the husband, has inherited one million dollars' worth of stock from his uncle, the million

"falls" into the community, and the wife acquires an inchoate right of half a million dollars.

(3) There is no such thing as a chattel mortgage—except in limited cases: boats, planes, cars, and certain incorporeal rights dealing with commerce.

(4) The *propriété* of real estate may be gained by possession of long duration (ten or twenty years: *usucapion*). The title to personal property—except in the event of theft or loss—results immediately from possession.

(5) In the conflict of laws, personal and real property matters are generally governed by different laws. For instance, as in the United States, the descent of land on the death of the owner intestate is governed by the *lex rei sitae,* whereas the devolution of personal property is governed by the law of the domicile of the *de-cujus* at the time of his death.

III

PASSING OF TITLE

Under the Roman law the transfer of "property" by agreement took place only when accompanied by delivery. Title did not pass by mere consent for the lands, nor for the goods: *traditionibus usucapionibus dominia rerum, non nudis pactis transferuntur* (*Code de Justinien* 2, 3; *De Pactis* 20). The rule was the same under the former Germanic law. It is consequently quite natural that, in conveyance of land, we find in French law, during the centuries preceding the Code, a formalist system of delivery. However, the system did not remain static during these centuries. Through a slow evolution it had come to a point at which actually very little remained to be done to achieve the apparent revolution of the Code. This evolution can be divided—though we must allow for the inaccuracy inevitable in extreme simplification—into three periods:

First Period: Actual Delivery by Real Investiture

The grantee went in person on the land itself, and there and then he performed certain acts of dominion; these evidenced the seisin. The grantor, who had brought the grantee on the land, declared that he gave up all his rights over it; he retired and abandoned the land; this was the disseisin. The whole ceremony took place in the presence of witnesses. Of course, we are not alluding to the different ceremony of homage between lord and vassal.

Second Period: Symbolical Delivery

Later on it was enough for the grantee to receive only a bit of grass, a branch of a tree, a stone of a house, a key, etc., even if both grantor and grantee were far away from the land itself.

Third Period: Delivery per Cartam in the South and Pretended Delivery in the North

Finally it was admitted that title passed by the mere delivery of the contract itself. This stage was reached a little earlier in the south and a little later in the north. In the north a clause was inserted in the contract setting forth that the formalities of disseisin-seisin had taken place. This eventually became a complete fiction; it was a mere recital like the one-dollar consideration. But it was attested to by a *notaire,* and it created an irrebuttable presumption that the formalities had been carried out. This is how the delivery of a piece of paper got the same effect as actual delivery.

Consequently, as far as the larger part of France was concerned, a uniform system was arrived at. And from this system ensued the simple rule of the Civil Code, which we shall meet in a few moments, that title passes by consent alone. Loisel stated: "One has no sooner sold a thing than one has nothing left." And his commentator Laurier added: "Thus, among us (meaning the French) as soon as the sale is made, dominion over the thing sold is transferred without delivery contrary to the provision of law 20 *de Pactis.*" Thus almost the only innovation of the Civil Code consisted in doing away with the insertion in deeds of a clause that had become a mere recital and in no longer demanding the drawing up of a notarial act.

The new rule is expressed in Articles 1582 and 1583 of the Civil Code.

Article 1582

"A sale is a convention by which one party binds himself to deliver a thing and the other to pay for it. It may be made by notarial act or in the form of private agreement." "La vente est une convention par laquelle l'un s'oblige à livrer une chose et l'autre à la payer. Elle peut être faite par acte authentique ou sous-seing privé."

As we can see, there is no distinction at all between the sale of goods or chattels and conveyances of land.

Article 1583

"It is completed between the parties, and title passes automatically to the buyer (or vendee) in his relation to the seller (or vendor) at the very moment when there is a meeting of the minds upon the thing sold, and the price (or consideration) to be paid for it; and this is so although no delivery has taken place, or the price been paid."

"Elle est parfaite entre les parties et la propriété est acquise de droit à l'acheteur à l'égard du vendeur, dès qu'on est convenu de la chose et du prix, quoique la chose n'ait pas encore été livrée, ni le prix payé."

Consequently, as between the parties, title passes at the making of the contract and by mere virtue of the meeting of the minds. And this is so for real property as well as for personal property, no distinction at all existing between the sale of goods and the sale of real estate. It may appear unusual to those accustomed to the distinction between the contract of sale and the conveyance. But after all, the rule is exactly the same as the one provided for in the Personal Property Law of New York under Section 100, where the goods are specific or ascertained and in a deliverable state at the time the contract for sale is entered into. Regarding real property, it should be noted also that by the effect of equitable title and the action of specific performance given under Anglo-American law to the vendee, his legal situation is almost the same as that of the French buyer of real estate. It is also noteworthy that the French rule making the passing of title an immediate and automatic result of the contract renders unnecessary in this particular instance the remedy of specific performance, which is generally, although not absolutely, unknown in French law. It is needless to repeat that this passing of title concerns only the rights of the immediate parties. As against other persons, and especially subsequent purchasers or encumbrancers, there is a system of recording *(transcription sur le registre des hypothèques)* provided for mainly by statutes enacted after the Code, but fitting into its general system.

The present writer fully realizes how fragmentary and incomplete is the picture of the French law of property that he has been able to convey. He hopes, however, that it has been possible for the reader to see how, by statutory amendments and case law, the living growth of the Civil Code has kept its original and essential love of liberty through the slow process of adjusting the regime of property to new circumstances. There may be said of the Code, after its continuous flow through a hundred and fifty years of French history—First Empire, Restoration, Second Republic, Second Empire, Third Republic, World War I, the disaster of the occupation, the grandeur of the liberation, the struggles of the Fourth Republic—what Jaurès said of the River:

"C'est en coulant vers la mer, que le fleuve reste fidèle à sa source."

10

The Code and Unfair Competition

WALTER J. DERENBERG

THE late Edward S. Rogers, one of the unforgotten leaders of the bar in the field of trade-mark law and unfair competition, once observed[1] that this branch of the law was interesting because it had been "moving swiftly during the past twenty years" and that it "showed the adaptability of the common law to meet changing conditions." He then added:[2]

"I shall never forget the first conference I had with a French lawyer. He got down a book and said, 'The case that you have stated comes within section so-and-so of the Code, or section so-and-so.' Then he looked at the Code. He said, 'No, it doesn't come within either of these sections. I am sorry, Monsieur, but nothing can be done. There is no law.'

"Under the common law system, however, in effect the parties and the court sit down and figure out what ought to be done, and then do it. The fact that there is no precedent makes no difference at all."

The impression was thus created that there is more inherent flexibility in the common law than in laws based on a civil code. Though this statement may be true of some aspects of private law, it hardly applies to that branch of the law that we now embrace within the definition of the law of unfair competition. On the contrary even a brief glance at the history of the law of unfair competition will reveal two significant facts: It will show, in the first place, that the entire vast body of the French law of unfair competition *(concurrence déloyale)* is not derived from any special legislation, but finds its origin in two of the most generally worded articles of

WALTER J. DERENBERG *is Professor of Law at New York University School of Law*

the *Code Civil* (Articles 1382 and 1383), which announce a general principle of tort law, applicable in all cases where, either intentionally or negligently, damage is inflicted on another person or his property. In the second place, it will be immediately discovered that the branch of law entitled *concurrence déloyale* was fully accepted and developed by the French courts—and by the courts of most other European countries—before the first mention of the term "unfair competition" appears in American jurisprudence toward the beginning of the twentieth century.

I

HISTORICAL BACKGROUND

The beginnings of the law of unfair competition in France almost coincide with the end of the French Revolution. A famous statute of March 1791 not only abolished all guilds and merchant corporations, but also broadly enunciated the principle that "every person shall be free to engage in such business or to exercise such profession, art or trade, as he shall see fit." As pointed out in a leading law review article,[3] the primary purpose of this legislation was to put an end to guild domination and governmental interference with production. This act thus became, in a sense, the Magna Carta of French business by encouraging free competition in all branches of trade. No provision of the Napoleonic Code interfered with this newly created freedom, and no express mention is found in it of any legal rules against unfair competition. Articles 1382 and 1383 of the *Code Civil,* which have served as the sole and entire basis of the French general law of unfair competition up to the present time, read as follows:

> Art. 1382. Any person who causes injury to another by any act whatsoever is obligated to compensate such other person for the injury sustained.
>
> Art. 1383. A person is responsible in damages not only for those acts which he has actually committed but also for any damage caused by his negligence or imprudence.

Within the frame of these two provisions a body of private law of unfair competition was soon developed by the courts covering so vast a field that it almost defies definition. By the middle of the nineteenth century not one but more than half a dozen outstanding treatises were published in France dealing specifically with the law of unfair competition.[4] By that time the two cornerstones of the Continental theory were firmly fixed. One of these was the concept of *propriété industrielle,* which not only comprised all industrial property rights based on special legislation, such as patents, trade-marks, designs, etc., but also reflected the much broader concept of protecting the entire relationship between a merchant and his clientele. The other collateral concept was a clear realization that the newly gained privilege of economic freedom and free competition should be held limited to those competitive efforts that are the result of a person's own labor and merit and should not be extended to give undeserved sanction to any commercial benefits derived from usurpation of the fruits of a competitor's labor.

It was this early recognition of the basic principle not to abuse competitive freedom by borrowing from or otherwise taking advantage of the success of a commercial competitor that led the French courts, without any other statutory basis than Articles 1382 and 1383, to enjoin as acts of *concurrence déloyale* practically all those methods and practices of unfair competition that today in the United States would fall within the administrative jurisdiction of the Federal Trade Commission,[5] but against which only limited protection is given even today by our equity courts in the course of private litigation. In other words the principles of the law of unfair competition according to the French doctrine are the ever-present general private-law foundation, implementing all the special legislation regarding designs, trade-marks, patents, and copyright that has been enacted from time to time since the coming into effect of the *Code Civil*[6] in 1804—legislation that has added new and more drastic remedies, both civil and criminal, to those previously available. It would therefore be generally correct to say that, as far as

Continental theory is concerned, the principles of the law of unfair competition were recognized and enforced even before separate statutory provisions were created for trade-mark infringement, patent infringement, and similar types of trespass.

In thus developing the law relating to *concurrence déloyale* during the nineteenth century, the French courts focused their attention on the concept of *achalandage,* which perhaps does not have an exact counterpart in the English language, for it goes somewhat beyond the meaning of "good will" and embraces—to quote one of the early definitions—"the sum of all relations created between a business man and his customers" *(cet achalandage qui résulte de la loyauté du fabricant dans ses relations avec le public constitue une valeur aussi digne de protection que la propriété matérielle).*[7] Within this concept of protection of *achalandage* the French courts gave early protection, not only in cases of trade-mark infringement and passing-off, but also, according to an early authority,[8] to all other acts intended either to produce confusion by imitation of the exterior characteristics of an establishment, or acts that, without producing confusion, are intended to divert the clientele of a competitor, such as, for instance, commercial disparagement of a competitor's products. Soon included also were instances of commercial bribery, betrayal of trade secrets, and similar practices.

By the end of the nineteenth century the scope of *concurrence déloyale* had assumed such proportions that the more modern French textbook writers no longer even attempt to treat of all varieties of unfair conduct. Thus Pouillet, generally considered the outstanding French authority on the subject, begins the discussion of unfair competition in the sixth edition of his work, *"Traité des Marques de Fabrique et de la Concurrence Déloyale"* (1912), with the following reservations:[9]

"We have neither the intention nor the hope of indicating all the forms of unfair competition. We can only point out the most important ones and those most frequently encountered; we feel certain in any event that our courts, as guardians of commercial fairness, will always be able, even in the absence of specific rules, to recognize and punish any acts that are contrary to the principles of fair competition."

He suggests the following definition of *concurrence déloyale:*[10]

"An act committed in bad faith with a view toward producing confusion between the products of two manufacturers or of two merchants, or which, without producing confusion, casts discredit upon a rival establishment."

Allart, in his much quoted treatise on the law of unfair competition, had the following to say:[11]

"There does not exist a law on unfair competition; the legislator, in fact, cannot codify a matter whose elements present an extreme diversity without a sufficient bond to unite them."

Thus it happened that, merely as a result of judge-made law and without any other statutory basis than the general provisions of Articles 1382 and 1383, the possibility of a civil action for unfair competition generally exists in France in situations involving any interference with a competitor's clientele, regardless of what form such interference may assume, and is available even where the more specific laws for the protection of patents, designs, trade-marks, or works of art may not provide adequate sanctions.

How different and how much slower and more cautious has been the gradual acceptance of the doctrine of *concurrence déloyale* in the United States! Instead of serving as a source from which more specific protection against infringement of exclusive rights could be derived, it was considered, when it was first mentioned sixty years ago, nothing but an extension of trade-mark law governing certain instances of passing-off that involved, not technical trade-marks, but rather trade names, corporate names, firm names, and the like. Such cases were referred to in the older treatises as involving "rights analogous to those of trade-marks."[12] In a famous article written in 1890[13] Grafton Dulany Cushing started his study with this observation:

"The law of a class of cases analogous to trade-marks is still in the process of evolution, and it may be useful to consider the principles which should govern the decision of cases of this sort."

And even this class of cases, not yet referred to as unfair competition, appeared to be limited in those days to different forms of the old passing-off action. The cases known as "analogous to trade-marks" were held to differ from trade-mark cases proper only in that no technical exclusive right could be recognized where a plaintiff used trade names, trade signs, and similar emblems incapable, according to common-law doctrine, of exclusive appropriation.

The author acknowledges that the French courts of that time had already developed the doctrine of *concurrence déloyale,* which, as he puts it, covered "all manoeuvres that cause prejudice to the name of a property, to the renown of a merchandise, or in lessening the custom due to rivals in business."[14] After reviewing some of the leading French cases, he reaches this conclusion:[15]

"In France commercial morality is high, and the rules as to unfair rivalry in trade are strict. In this country our commercial honesty is proverbially low, and it remains to be seen whether our courts will check the tendency of our business relations towards a lower standard."

Mr. Cushing's hope that our courts would soon apply equally high standards of commercial honesty was partially realized during the following three decades. Though unfair competition was still regarded as principally confined to different forms of passing-off, the concept of unfair competition as a separate branch of the law first became noticeable about 1901. At that time W. K. Townsend, in *Two Centuries' Growth of American Law,*[16] wrote:

"Not yet fully adopted by all the courts, still to be developed in its application to particular circumstances and conditions, this broad principle of business integrity and common justice is the product and the triumph of the development of the law of trade-marks in the last half century, and the bulwark which makes possible and protects the world-wide business reputations common and growing more common in this new country."

For a long time unfair competition continued to be considered as no more than a branch of trade-mark law. Even in 1909 we find statements to the effect that the law of unfair competition had been until then "practically unknown in the jurisprudence of English-speaking nations."[17] A real turning point was not reached until about the time of the publication of the first edition of Nims' *Law of Unfair Competition and Trade-Marks*,[18] which, for the first time, included a treatment of certain miscellaneous forms of unfair competition including disparagement of a competitor, interference with a competitor's business, and similar acts. But it was not until the United States Supreme Court's famous decision in the case of Hanover Milling Co. v. Metcalf[19] that the theory was for the first time expressed that the law of unfair competition was a genus rather than a species, and that the law of trade-marks was but a part of the broader field known as unfair competition. The Court said:[20]

> "In fact, the common law of trade-marks is but a part of the broader law of unfair competition."

Nevertheless, as late as 1924 a federal court said:[21]

> "The law of unfair competition is the natural evolution of the law of trade-marks out of which it has grown."

The real genesis of the law of unfair competition in the United States was, or at least might have been, the Supreme Court's famous decision in the International News case,[22] in which for the first time a determined effort was made to strip the doctrine of some of its historical limitations and particularly of the thought that there could be no unfair competition in the absence of "passing-off." Here, for the first time, in an approach similar to that of the French courts, is found a hint that the principle of denying protection to him "who reaps where he has not sown" may form a part of the law of unfair competition.[23] Perhaps the most interesting feature of the majority opinion in the International News case was the realization that a distinction should be recognized between the obligations of businessmen toward the public on the one hand, and the perhaps broader duties and standards to be applied and enforced between businessmen themselves. The Supreme Court said in this connection:[24]

"The fault in the reasoning lies in applying as a test the right of the complainant as against the public, instead of considering the rights of complainant and defendant, competitors in business, as between themselves. * * * Stripped of all disguises, the process amounts to an unauthorized interference with the normal operation of complainant's legitimate business precisely at the point where the profit is to be reaped, in order to divert a material portion of the profit from those who have earned it to those who have not; with special advantage to defendant in the competition because of the fact that it is not burdened with any part of the expense of gathering the news. The transaction speaks for itself, and a court of equity ought not to hesitate long in characterizing it as unfair competition in business."

The liberal doctrine of this case has not been unanimously followed in subsequent years. On the contrary, it is too well known to be elaborated on here that our courts have refused to apply the doctrine to a multitude of other types of unfair competition and have—with some few notable exceptions[25]—ruled that the International News decision should be considered limited to the particular facts there involved.[26] It is true that from time to time we find pronouncements such as this:[27]

"Yet there is no part of the law which is more plastic than unfair competition and what was not reckoned an actionable wrong 25 years ago may have become such today."

or this:[28]

". . . In earlier times, the right of identity most frequently was violated by downright misrepresentations by word ('passing off' cases), or by conduct (wrongful appropriation of trade-marks); much as the early violations of the right of reputation was by words slanderous, *per se*. But in the march of commerce, skulduggery seems to have kept abreast of science in inventiveness, so that new and more subtle means were found to violate the right of identity by introducing confusion into the public mind; much as sly innuendoes were substituted for cruder words wherewith to ape and destroy reputations. On the whole these subtleties have found small favor with the courts, and it is now at least well established that any act or conduct which confuses or tends to confuse the public mind in relation to the identity of the plaintiff or his products is a violation of the plaintiff's right . . ."

True it is also that the Supreme Court, in the only two subsequent cases in which the meaning of the term "unfair competition" was before it in a different context,[29] again took occasion to emphasize the broader meaning that the term had acquired over the course of years. In the case of Schechter Poultry Corp. et al. v. United States, particularly, the Court said:[30]

" 'Unfair Competition,' as known to the common law, is a limited concept. Primarily, and strictly, it relates to the palming off of one's goods as those of a rival trader. In recent years, its scope has been extended. It has been held to apply to misappropriation as well as misrepresentation, to the selling of another's goods as one's own,—to misappropriation of what equitably belongs to a competitor. Unfairness in competition has been predicated of acts which lie outside the ordinary course of business and are tainted by fraud, or coercion, or conduct otherwise prohibited by law."

But it is still indisputable today that the law of unfair competition has not been given the place in our country's legal system that it occupies in most European countries as the broad basis for civil relief against all kinds of interference with a person's reputation, clientele, and business in general.

II

ILLUSTRATIVE TYPES OF UNFAIR COMPETITION

But more than that: The development of our law of unfair competition has been hampered not only as a result of this rather slow process of emancipation from the narrow concepts of passing-off and trade-mark infringement, but it has also been greatly retarded by judicial retention of some historical concepts of equity law that should no longer have a place in protecting a modern society against unfair trade practices. Here again the European courts, unhampered by these historical maxims, encountered much less difficulty in awarding effective legal protection. As partial illustrations of these additional difficulties we shall briefly review three forms of unfair trade conduct that have been part of Continental law of unfair competition almost from the beginning, though they have had—and still have—very slow and inadequate recognition in the United States: commercial disparagement, deceptive advertising, and misappropriation in the form of slavish imitation of otherwise unprotected articles of manufacture.

COMMERCIAL DISPARAGEMENT AND "TRADE LIBEL"

Nowhere is the difference in philosophy and approach between the French doctrine and our own law more strikingly illustrated than in the multitude of situations involving the right of a competitor to refer to the merchandise of another in a disparaging way for the sole purpose of promoting his own business. When we use the word "disparagingly" we are already unduly limiting the problem, since it equally arises—at least under the Continental doctrine—in situations involving a mere comparison of the products for the purpose of gaining a competitive advantage; in other words, it embraces all kinds of so-called "comparative advertising." Concretely speaking: May a competitor advertise: "This antenna" (with a sketch of one television antenna) "OUT-PERFORMS" (with sketches of four other types of antennas and, under each of the other four types) "this antenna"?[31] How would other countries look on an advertisement such as "BUFFERIN works twice as fast as aspirin"? Would such a comparison be permissible on the ground that the word "Aspirin" in a particular country may have lost its trade-mark significance[32] and may have become a generic term, so that there are numerous "Aspirin" tablets on the market, and would it make any difference whether the advertiser is prepared to prove the alleged truth of the statement?

One glance at the voluminous French literature and that of other European countries reveals that, in striking contrast to our own law, commercial disparagement, including most forms of comparative advertising, has long been regarded as falling within the general law of unfair competition and not as, in the United States, a subdivision of the law of libel and slander. (In common-law doctrine these practices are significantly referred to as "slander of title.") In France all forms of *dénigrement* have been classified from the very beginning as one of the types of conduct falling within the general definition of *concurrence déloyale* and were held actionable on no other basis than the general provisions of Articles 1382 and 1383 of the *Code Civil*. In other words, they immediately fell within the previously mentioned concept of outlawing any competitive conduct not based on a person's own skill, labor, and effort but borrowing from or criticizing or attacking a competitor for the purpose of impairing or ruining his business. It is but another form of infringement on a competitor's *achalandage,* as previously defined. As a result a merchant under the French doctrine may make grossly extravagant claims for his own product without being civilly liable therefor as long as he does not refer to a competitor or his product at the same time.[33] On the other hand, even statements that do not expressly mention a competitor or his product, but do so by implication, may be actionable. To illustrate: As early as 1884 an English newspaper published in Paris, the *Morning News,*[34] inserted in some issues tables comparing the number of copies sold by it with those sold by another newspaper published in Paris in the English language, emphasizing the smaller number sold by the latter. This was held to be unfair competition, and the plaintiff was even awarded damages. The court said:

"The act by the director of the Morning News of using the name of Galignani's Messenger, whether in the said tables or in the different articles, for the purpose of disparaging the journal which bears this name constitutes an abuse and an act of unfair competition, injurious to the plaintiff, which it is proper to bring to an end."

This seems particularly interesting in the light of the widely prevailing recent custom among leading magazines and newspapers in the United States of publishing comparative figures on the amount of advertising published by each or on their general circulation.

Shortly thereafter, in 1896, the Mutual Life Insurance Company, a United States corporation, was found guilty of unfair competition as the result of its circularizing certain prospectuses comparing and criticizing the activities of competitive organizations. The court broadly stated:[35]

"The privilege which belongs to every merchant to praise his products in terms, the propriety of which, as a general principle, it is not for the tribunals to determine, does not confer on him the right to attack a competitor or to disparage or to depreciate the articles which he exploits, even by the way of simple comparison, with the aim of diverting the clientele to his own profit. * * * The tribunals are not required in principle to ascertain whether the criticisms formulated by a merchant against his competitor are well founded."

In 1904, the firm of Jules Mumm & Co., world famous champagne producers, was found guilty of unfair competition on similar grounds, the court observing:[36]

"Although it is lawful for every merchant in his circulars to praise the products of his establishment or the establishment itself, on the other hand he is absolutely prohibited from disparaging therein those of his competitors, especially in designating them by name and in terms susceptible of injuring them.

"These acts constitute a grave wrong *(faute grave)* and an act of unfair competition which has caused the house of Leon Chandon [plaintiff] considerable injury."

Hundreds of similar cases could be added, but these few extracts will suffice to indicate the extent to which the French civil courts have gone since the enactment of the *Code Civil* in protecting a businessman's good will and reputation even against comparative advertising.[37] It is, of course, essential that the comparison or disparagement must occur in public; mere private utterances do not give rise to a cause of action.[38] On the other hand—and this cannot be overemphasized—it is well settled in French jurisprudence that here, as elsewhere in cases of unfair competition, the alleged truth of the statement is not necessarily a defense. *Dénigrement,* which is found "in any case in which a merchant, not satisfied with praising his own products, depreciates by advertisements or prospectuses those of his rivals,"[39] is equally actionable whether the statements made are true or not. Thus it is stated in one of the early French textbooks:[40]

> "Any allegation which directly tends to depreciate the products of a competitor must be treated like a fraudulent transaction, even though the statement may be true."

Before comparing this specific type of unfair trading with the cumbersome and imperfect protection available in the United States, it may not be amiss to glance quickly at the laws of some other European countries that have developed the law of unfair competition into an independent branch of their entire legal systems. In Germany there has never been any serious question, since the enactment of the Unfair Competition Act of 1909, that disparagement and, indeed, all forms of comparative advertising fall within the so-called "general clause" of Section 1, outlawing any competitive conduct considered against *bonos mores.* In one of the most recent and thorough studies ever made of this aspect of the German law,[41] the conclusion is reached that any comparative reference to a named competitor is treated as unfair competition by the German Supreme Court except in the following three cases: (a) comparison and reference in self-defense as a countermeasure against attack; (b) comparison made on specific request for purposes of enlightenment (*Auskunft auf Verlangen*); and

(c) cases of so-called necessary comparison (*notwendiger Vergleich*), *i.e.* situations in which a comparison is necessary for the purpose of demonstrating scientific progress rather than for the purpose of enticing a competitor's customers. Save in these three exceptional cases the present German rule is stated to be:

> "It is generally prohibited to refer in any form whatsoever in one's own advertising to a competitor."

The German Supreme Court said:[42]

> "Competitors, even though their commercial accomplishments may in fact be of less value, do not have to tolerate it if they are referred to in competitors' advertisements as means toward increasing the advertiser's own standing in the public eye."

In all cases of such comparative advertising injunctive relief and damages may be obtained.

Similarly broad is the Dutch law. It may be recalled that Articles 1401 and 1402 of the Dutch Civil Code are exact counterparts of the corresponding provisions of Articles 1382 and 1383 of the French *Code Civil,* and, as in France, the Dutch law of unfair competition is derived exclusively from these general provisions. Disparagement and comparative advertising are quite generally held to be actionable in Holland. The Dutch Supreme Court has so held at least since 1938.[43] In a litigation before the Appellate Court of Amsterdam in 1940 the defendant had advertised:

> "Diucalc preparations are better than Diuri Tinum."

This was held to be unfair competition, regardless of whether the statement was true or not.[44] The Court said:

> "The misleading of the public is not an essential element to make this type of advertisement unlawful."

In still another of many significant cases the District Court of Rotterdam was asked in 1929 to enjoin use of the phrase "Spiran better than Aspirin."[45] This was held to be unfair competition regardless of the truth of the statement. The court there said:

"Trade ethics do not allow that the manufacturer of a new product introduce his product by merely stating that it is better than that of a competitor, who has spent much time and effort and money to make his mark known. In this way the competitor's mark is used as a ladder to climb into the favor of the public, which is contrary to the carefulness that must be observed in the trade."

In Belgium, the courts have gone at least as far as those of France and Holland. Thus it is stated in one of the leading Belgian texts on unfair competition:[46]

"Any reference to a competitor's product is unfair competition whether it be true or not. The courts and Belgian jurisprudence have always defended business men against abuses in advertising by condemning any reference to a competitor for the purpose of damaging him or his business; more particularly, it is not permissible to discredit the products of a competitor by comparing them with one's own or those of other competitors. Such comparisons serve only as an effort to take away the competitor's clientele or profit for one's own benefit."

Similar principles, although not so far-reaching with regard to comparative advertising, have long prevailed in Switzerland. As early as 1897[47] the Swiss Supreme Court protected the Singer Sewing Machine Company of New York against a dealer in competing sewing machines who alleged that the statements made by him in adversely criticizing the plaintiff's machines, as compared with the ones sold by him, were true. The Swiss Supreme Court significantly said:

"On the other hand we cannot hold that the mere fact that the disparaging statements are true makes the disparagement always lawful. There are circumstances under which even the dissemination of true facts may be regarded as unfair competition. For instance, if a business man makes it a practice to refer to his competitor's past, if certain irregularities that in fact occurred are maliciously exploited, furthermore in all cases where true facts are stated in such a way that the rival's reputation as a business man is unjustly discredited, an action for unfair competition lies."

So widespread is the recognition today of all forms of disparagement as a form of unfair competition that it has even found its way into some international conventions. Thus Article 10 *bis* of the Paris Convention, as revised in London in 1934, now condemns as acts of unfair competition "false allegations in the course of trade of a nature to discredit the establishment, the goods or the services of a competitor." It will be noted, however, that this section applies only to *false* statements. The Inter-American Convention, as signed at Washington in 1929, after its general clause condemning all forms of unfair competition (Article 20), specifically includes

"any other act or deed contrary to good faith in industrial, commercial or agricultural matters . . ."

How different, slow, and generally unsatisfactory has been our own domestic law in this regard, and how many historical and technical obstacles had to be surmounted until at least some courts were ready to accept commercial disparagement not as a subdivision of libel and slander but as a form of unfair competition that should be suppressed with the aid of the effective equitable remedy of an injunction! There is no need here to reiterate the numerous reasons why our courts have been so reluctant to give equitable relief in cases of this kind. All these have been thoroughly analyzed and criticized in the famous article by Roscoe Pound[48] and in the writings of Harry B. Nims.[49] Suffice it to say that no Continental lawyer, versed in the general doctrine of *concurrence déloyale,* would ever condone, or even understand, the New York Court of Appeals' well-known decision in the Marlin Firearms case,[50] which has never been expressly overruled up to the present time. In the Marlin case, it will be recalled, an injunction was sought against a magazine whose publisher had maliciously published disparaging statements about the plaintiff's merchandise. It was held that equitable relief was unavailable for a number of historical reasons, all based on libel and slander law. Inability to prove "special damage," the Constitutional guarantee of freedom of speech and of the press, the right to a jury trial, etc. were among the many reasons that led the court reluctantly to refuse any speedy relief and to relegate the plaintiff to an entirely inadequate action at law for damages. There was no indication that the defendant's conduct might come within the concept of unfair competition, which itself had not been fully recognized at the time of this decision (1902); instead, the disparaging statements were referred to as "slander of title," which required proof of "special damage" and for which no equitable remedy would lie.[51]

It was not until 1928 that a lower New York court[52] first indicated that, notwithstanding the Marlin case, a systematic effort by a competitor resulting in a campaign of false disparagement of the plaintiff's product should be considered a form of unfair competition in order to get away from the unfortunate doctrine of the Marlin case, which, in Dean Pound's words, "puts anyone's business at the mercy of any insolvent malicious defamer, who has sufficient imagination to lay out a skillful campaign of extortion."[53] Said the court:[54]

> "The courts have been increasingly inclined to protect business interests even when such interests do not come within strict definitions of property. The judgment here, in enjoining false and fraudulent disparagement, protects the intangible, but real, relationship existing between a merchant and his usual customers—his 'goodwill.' "

Another New York State court of first instance[55] stated even more bluntly that cases of commercial disparagement involve more than the mere publishing of a libel and may, in fact, constitute unfair competition. The court said:

> "The mailing or sending of false, untrue, and dishonest statements to the

customers of an established firm, for the purpose of injuring the firm in its business and deceiving the public and plaintiff's customers, is a form of unfair trade competition which can be as injurious as the establishment of a competitor in the neighborhood using the same or a similar name and circularizing the firm's customers for the purpose of confusing them and obtaining their patronage."[56]

It will be seen that in these fairly isolated cases an approach is made to classifying such competitive conduct as one type of unfair competition in the sense in which it has become an acknowledged part thereof in countries that have followed the lead of the French courts. However, how far we still lag becomes again obvious when it is considered that relief has been granted only in cases involving flagrantly false or unfair statements, and not in cases involving mere comparative advertising of the type discussed in connection with the European cases. On the contrary, what very little authority there can be found in this country with regard to the problem points in the other direction. Consider, for instance, the fairly recent case of National Refining Co. v. Benzo Gas Motor Fuel Co. (1927),[57] in which the court, in an unusually comprehensive opinion, distinguished three different types of commercial disparagement as follows: (1) disparagement including libelous words in reference to the person of the vendor or producer; (2) disparagement referring merely to the quality of the goods or products of another; and (3) disparagement in which "the alleged libelous statements amount to no more than assertions by one tradesman that his goods are superior to those of his rival." It was held that in cases such as type (2) no recovery may be had in the absence of proof of special damage, and that in cases falling within category (3)—the category with which we are here concerned—*no* recovery can be had although the statements may be false and malicious and even though "special damage" may be alleged. This is certainly a far cry from protecting and promoting commercial honesty and fairness in trade.

No wonder, then, that those groups in the United States that condemn comparative advertising, but have come to realize the inadequacy of legal protection in this field, have resorted to self-help and are trying through organizations such as the National Better Business Bureau and others to enforce higher standards of advertising. It is an interesting fact, for instance, that, according to an agreement among the leading newspaper publishers, no advertisements will be accepted in which a product is advertised in terms of a comparison with a named competitor's product, since such conduct is considered unethical, even though not actionable under our law. Significant, too, were the many code provisions during the administration of the National Industrial Recovery Act, which almost uniformly condemned comparative advertising as an unfair practice.[58] Even the Federal Trade Commission, although created solely for the protection of the public, has found it necessary to include commercial disparagement among the trade practices that the Commission may prosecute as unfair acts and practices under Section 5 of the Federal Trade Commission Act.[59] But even that is a long way from adoption of a general rule affording the equivalent of the speedy private remedies that are available under most Continental laws in cases of this kind. Such reliance not on one's own merits but on the alleged inadequacies of somebody else's product has never yet been condemned by our courts as it has been in Europe, even though the basis for this Continental approach—it may be re-emphasized—is entirely judge-made and derived exclusively from a liberal and constantly progressive judicial interpretation of Articles 1382 and 1383 of the French Code and of similar provisions in other European countries.

FALSE ADVERTISING AND FALSE DESIGNATIONS OF ORIGIN

There are undoubtedly more French trade names and designations of origin of world-wide celebrity than of any other country. This is particularly true, of course, of the names of wines, porcelains, cheeses, women's fashions, and many others. Hence the lead that French jurisprudence and legislation have taken toward protection of such designations and names, even though they may not qualify for registration as trade-marks. In France and in those countries that have followed its lead, there never was much question that misuses of such words as *Cognac, Limoges, Roquefort,* and innumerable others should be actionable not only on behalf of the government, but also on behalf of those whose private interests in the honest use of these names were impaired. Nor was there any doubt that the general provisions of Articles 1382 and 1383 of the *Code Civil* provided a sufficient basis for such protection, although special legislation was enacted by an act of July 28, 1824,[60] which makes a misuse of a manufacturer's name or place of manufacture a misdemeanor. With the enactment of the Trade-Mark Act of June 23, 1857,[61] even broader statutory provision was introduced in France, going beyond the Act of 1824 by extending the provisions of that Act not only to names and places of manufacture but to all those indications of origin, be they registrable as trade-marks or not, that have acquired distinctiveness in trade. What is particularly interesting for our purposes is not, however, that false advertising of this type, particularly with reference to famous designations of origin, may be the basis of a civil action, but the early recognition of the necessity of making such private action available to every member of the business community whose interests might be adversely affected by such improper use.

In other words, French jurisprudence considers the celebrity of a well-known designation of origin as a sort of community right in which all those located there may participate. In that sense, the concept of *propriété d'un nom de lieu* is recognized. Thus it is said in one of the early textbooks:[62]

> *"Telle localité est renommée pour ses draps, telle autre pour sa coutellerie etc; cette bonne réputation est la propriété de la ville ou de la contrée qui a su l'acquérir, elle est la propriété de tous les fabricants établis dans cette contrée ou dans cette ville."*

("This locality is famous for its sheets and that other for its cutlery; this great reputation belongs to the business community or the region that has been able to acquire it. It is the property of all manufacturers established in this particular community or city.") This concept of community participation in the celebrity of the name was expressed even during the debate of the Act of July 28, 1824:[63]

"Il est des villes de fabrique dont les produits ont une réputation qu'on peut appeler collective, et c'est encore une propriété."

("It is the places of manufacture of the products that have a reputation which may be designated as collective and in a sense as property.") In view of this broad property concept there was never any doubt, therefore, that most instances of the use of false designations of origin were actionable at the suit of anyone whose interests were adversely affected. It is interesting to note that, according to French practice, the right to institute a private action in such instances may be enjoyed not only by those who live directly within the boundaries of the locality, but even by those who live within a reasonable distance of it, as long as an "internal connection" exists between the well-known designation of origin and the actual place of manufacture.[64] A private right of action lies not only in cases involving false designations of origin, but also against most other forms of fraudulent or deceptive advertising as well. Thus, a competitor was entitled to sue where the value of bankrupt stock offered by two merchants was deceptively advertised.[65] Similarly, announcements to the public of liquidation sales and similar sales not in fact intended and carried out as such have been held to be unfair competition, actionable at the suit of any competitor in the town who may be damaged by them.[66]

The laws of most other European countries provide not only for criminal sanctions but also for private suits based on unfair competition in cases of this kind. Thus the German Unfair Competition Act of 1909 broadly provides that in all cases falling within the general unfair competition clause of Section 1 (cases against *bonos mores*) or within the specific prohibitions of Article 3 regarding false designations of origin, deceptive descriptions, etc., "a private suit for an injunction may be brought by any merchant who manufactures or does business in merchandise or services of the same or similar nature." In addition, private groups such as trade associations in the particular industry involved are entitled to sue for an injunction. In certain circumstances (defined in Section 13 of the German Act of 1909) the court may even award damages in its discretion in cases of this kind.[67] Similarly, the highest Swiss court has held that a private action for unfair competition may be instituted even by a person whose personal interests are only indirectly affected.[68]

In the United States certain historical concepts and technicalities had first to be surmounted until we have gradually tended toward the same principle that has long formed the cornerstone of the law of unfair competition in many European countries. In considering this vital problem our courts found themselves confronted with the age-old equity maxim that equity concerns itself only with "property rights" and that deception of the public and only indirect damage to a competitor or a group of competitors were insufficient bases for a private action in the absence of an established "property right." It proved somewhat difficult for our courts to recognize the type of community property right in the name of a famous locality in connection with products produced or manufactured there. Thus, a federal court held in 1890 that a deceptive use of the name "Rosendale" by someone not located there could not be enjoined by a competitor so located.[69] Since no "property right" of the plaintiff was infringed, he was held to have no right to act as "vicarious avenger of the public" or of those who actually did business at Rosendale. Particularly interesting is the following observation of the court:

"No man can maintain a private action for a public nuisance, though he is injured by it, unless his injury is of a special character different from that which is sustained by the public generally. This is a sound rule of the common law. It is intended to prevent vexatious litigation."

Fortunately this narrow doctrine did not remain the law even with regard to false designation of origin. One year after the Rosendale case, a federal court said with regard to a deceptive use of "Karlsbader Wasser":[70]

"The fact that many have a common interest in the same subject-matter ought not to deprive one of the many from being protected against an injury to the whole."

In more recent years an association of Grand Rapids furniture dealers were afforded effective relief against a defendant who made a deceptive use of the word "Grand Rapids" in connection with his furniture store in Chicago,[71] but still more recently it was held that a large group of California manufacturers had no standing to sue two New York concerns for alleged misuse of the name "California" in connection with men's shirts and similar articles.[72]

With regard to the use of false descriptions other than designations of origin, our courts have expressed in the past even greater reluctance to permit class actions or *qui tam* actions on behalf of one or a group of injured competitors. Here there comes to mind the celebrated Aluminum Washboard case,[73] which has never been expressly overruled by any subsequent court decision (although, as will be pointed out immediately, it should be considered in effect overruled by Section 43 of the Trade-Mark Act of 1946). In that famous case the defendant had used the word "aluminum" for washboards that did not actually contain that metal. Plaintiff company, at that time the only manufacturer in the country actually to use aluminum, brought suit on the theory that its trade would be greatly damaged by the defendant's misuse of the word "aluminum," even though the defendant was not guilty of passing-off but used his own name. In denying plaintiff all relief for fear that otherwise a "Pandora box of litigation" would be opened, the court accused the plaintiff of having lost sight of "the thoroughly well established principle that the private right of action in such cases is not based upon fraud or imposition upon the public but is maintained solely for the protection of the property of the plaintiff." The court then said:[74]

> "It is doubtless morally wrong and improper to impose upon the public by the sale of spurious goods, but this does not give a private right of action, unless the property rights of plaintiff are invaded. There are many wrongs which can only be righted through public prosecution and for which the legislature and not the courts must provide a remedy."

Not until forty-six years later was the court's hint that this was a matter for the legislature rather than the courts accepted in what is now Section 43 of the Trade-Mark Act of 1946.[75] Prior to 1946 the doctrine of the Aluminum Washboard case remained the law, even though Judge Learned Hand had made a courageous effort in the Mosler Safe case [76] to bring misrepresentations of the "Aluminum Washboard" type within broad general principles of unfair competition. Judge Hand's decision was reversed by the Supreme Court[77] for lack of a showing that the plaintiff was in fact the *only* competitor who might have suffered damage as a result of the defendant's fraud. There was no suggestion that, quite apart from the question of damages, the plaintiffs in those cases, as direct competitors, should have a right to secure at least injunctive relief for their own business as well as for the benefit of all those who might be similarly situated. In the meantime both the International Paris Convention of 1883 and the Inter-American Convention of 1929 had included broad provisions against any deceptive use in international trade of false designations of origin and other false descriptions. Thus Article 10 of the Paris Convention provides for Convention protection in all cases in which a product may "falsely bear as indication of origin the name of a specified locality or country . . ." and Article 21(b) and (c) of the Inter-American Convention pledge protection against unfair competition not only in case of use of false designations of geographical origin but also in any other case involving "the use of false descriptions of goods by words, symbols or other means tending to deceive the public in the country where the acts occur with respect to the nature, quality or utility of the goods."

Since it was one of the purposes of the new Trade-Mark Act of 1946 "to carry out the provisions of certain international conventions," it was deemed necessary to implement the just-quoted Convention provisions by domestic federal legislation. For this purpose Section 43 was enacted, which now creates a civil action on behalf of any person located in a falsely indicated locality or damaged by any other false description or representation. Thus we have now, by statutory federal enactment, over a century after such class actions were first recognized in Europe, an extension of the private law of unfair competition that is no longer based on an anxious search for an alleged "property right" on the plaintiff's part, but is designed as an effective and expedient weapon against unfair deceptive practices by business competitors. It seems strange indeed that until midway in 1954 no reported case could be found in which an action for unfair competition was based on this section.[78] But then, in July 1954, the Court of Appeals for the Third Circuit handed down its decision in L'Aiglon Apparel, Inc. v. Lana Lobell, Inc.,[79] in which, for the first time, the far-reaching scope of Section 43 is indicated. Here the court in effect declared the Aluminum Washboard case overruled by legislation. It said:[80]

"It seems to us that Congress has defined a statutory civil wrong of false representation of goods in commerce and has given a broad class of suitors injured or likely to be injured by such wrong the right to relief in the federal courts. This statutory tort is defined in language which differentiates it in some particulars from similar wrongs which have developed and have become defined in the judge-made law of unfair competition. Perhaps this statutory tort bears closest resemblance to the already noted tort of false advertising to the detriment of a competitor, as formulated by the American Law Institute out of materials of the evolving common law of unfair competition. See Torts

Restatement, Section 761, supra. But however similar to or different from pre-existing law, here is a provision of a federal statute which, with clarity and precision adequate for judicial administration, creates and defines rights and duties and provides for their vindication in the federal courts."

The importance of this judicial precedent cannot be overestimated. No longer will it be necessary to wait until the Federal Trade Commission may, in the exercise of its administrative jurisdiction under Section 5 of the Federal Trade Commission Act, issue a cease and desist order against false designations of origin or other misrepresentations, perhaps after several years have passed. A private remedy has now become available to get speedy injunctive relief in cases of this kind. A most important step was thus taken to liberate the law of unfair competition from the traditional limitations of the old equity action for passing-off.

MISAPPROPRIATION, FREE RIDE, AND "SLAVISH IMITATION"

It would seem to be almost a foregone conclusion that in those countries which, like France, frown on any unfair exploitation of a competitor's reputation or work in the promotion of one's own efforts, most forms of "taking a free ride" or "slavish imitation" would also fall within the condemnation of the courts, even though there be no direct evidence of substitution or passing-off. But since it was France that first pronounced the principle of free competition as one of the early results of its Revolution, it might have been expected that free competition should have been held to prevail with regard to the copying of all those designs and functional features of articles that are not separately protected by special legislation. It would not have been surprising, then, if French jurisprudence had reached the conclusion that the general provisions of Articles 1382 and 1383 of the *Code Civil* could not be resorted to even for the purpose of avoiding a likelihood of deception of the public wherever this likelihood results from the copying of otherwise unprotected external features of an article of manufacture. Thus it was said in one of the leading decisions by the *Cour de cassation:*[81]

"Attendu qu'à bon droit l'arrêt décide, que le principe de la liberté du commerce et de l'Industrie s'oppose à ce que la fabrication et la vente des pièces détachées que ne protège plus aucun brevet, soient considerées comme des actes de concurrence illicite ou déloyale. . . ."

Similarly, two leading French jurists, Fernand-Jacq and Demousseaux, in a report to the Budapest Congress of the International Association for the Protection of Industrial Property in 1930, said:[82]

"Depuis la proclamation des droits de l'Homme et du Citoyen, tout au moins, et, déjà même avant, les législations de tous les pays civilisés admettent, comme base fondamentale de l'activité humaine, la liberté du commerce et de l'industrie; les restrictions apportées par certaines dispositions des codes et des lois speciales sont motivées par les abus, qui, sous le couvert de cette liberté de principe, permettraient de porter atteinte à la morale naturelle, c'est-à-dire aux usages loyaux, qui doivent présider aux tractions commerciales et industrielles."

However, we must not lose sight of the fact that in France, as well as in most other European countries, there is far greater specific protection for models, designs, and works of art than is available in the United States. In connection with industrial designs, for instance, and works of the applied arts, the Act of July 14, 1909 created special protection without any elaborate system of pre-examination for all those ornamental designs that are duly recorded. The provisions of this Act established a private right for all inventions "as to form" (*droit commun des inventions de la forme*).[83] The deposit of a design creates a presumption of ownership. In addition to this type of design protection, those technical features of an article that may be capable of patent protection under the French Patent Law of July 5, 1844[84] may find additional protection under that Act. Moreover, since the French Copyright Law is governed by the over-all principle of the "unity of art" *(unité de l'art),* the same artistic features may also gain additional protection under the French Copyright Act of 1793.[85] According to the leading French treatise on protection of works of applied art,[86] toy models fall within the design statute, and so do textile designs, even to their color nuances and effects. The creations of high fashion *(haute couture)* are usually classified as works of art, and even hats, artificial flowers, embroideries, and others may enjoy statutory protection in France either under the copyright or the design statute. Jewelry, silverware, ceramics, and similar objects of the applied arts are likewise held capable of copyright protection. It should also be remembered that an act of infringement *(contrefaçon)* under any of these statutes not only gives rise to a civil action, but may be a criminal offense at the same time. It is therefore particularly significant to note that, despite this very large scope of special statutory protection, it is still recognized that an action based on the general provisions of Articles 1382 and 1383 of the *Code Civil* may lie as a supplementary remedy in some instances of *imitation servile* that do not fall within any of the accepted statutory categories. Thus, to industrial designs of the type of the German "small patents" *(Gebrauchsmuster)* the French law does not give separate statutory protection. In other words, a great many of these so-called *modèles de fabrique* have remained outside both the patent and the copyright law as well as the design statute. The result has been that, as a general rule, the courts have granted protection against slavish imitation of such designs on the basis of Article 1382 of the *Code.*[87] "Slavish imitation," said the Appellate Court of Paris as early as 1854,[88] "demonstrates that the imitator did nothing but take advantage of the results of the skill and labor of somebody else."

On the whole it can be said with some assurance that original models and designs of any kind are broadly protected in France by a series of statutes with a minimum of formality requirements and that in those cases in which such statutory protection is unavailable the imitation either concerns such trifling or obvious aspects as are not worthy of protection even under the most liberal standards or are in fact protected, if they are found worthy of protection, under the over-all provisions of Articles 1382 and 1383 of the *Code*. In this way the courts and the numerous private organizations that were created in France for the protection of artistic designs in various industries have been fairly successful in their own country in enjoining design piracy in all branches of industry, despite the fact that, particularly in recent years, the French courts and jurisprudence have taken as their starting point the rule that slavish imitation of those relatively few designs that are incapable of separate statutory protection does not—without more—constitute an actionable wrong.[89] At the same time it is held that where the imitation is accompanied by other circumstances resulting in the possibility of deception and intended for that purpose, the general sanctions of the *Code Civil* may, in a proper case, be called on to implement both the criminal and civil provisions of the design statute and other kindred legislation.

Before examining our own law with regard to this problem, we might take a quick look again at the law of a few other leading European countries. Let us begin with Germany.[90] After many turbulent years of controversy it is now generally recognized that so-called *"sklavischer Nachbau"* (slavish imitation) without more is not deemed unfair competition under the general clause of Article 1 of the Act of 1909; in other words, it is not considered as such to be against *bonos mores*. It is equally well settled, however, that while not illegal *per se,* it may become so in any situation in which an imitator of nonfunctional features fails adequately to protect the public against confusion that may result from the identical appearance of the two products. In this regard the mere use of the competitor's name on the imitated product would almost certainly be held to be insufficient in any case in which the over-all appearance of the products involved—in their nontechnical aspects—is so closely similar that ultimate confusion appears unavoidable. In a much quoted decision of the German Supreme Court (in 1928) involving imitation of a new type of hat hook, the following general guide was laid down:[91]

"Articles coming within the protection of the Patent or Small Patent *(Gebrauchsmuster)* statutes will not receive supplemental protection under unfair competition once the patent or small patent has expired or has become invalid. The same is not true, however, for mere ornamental designs since the same reasons of public policy do not apply here; but even with regard to designs, protection in unfair competition may occasionally be available where the product involved is a commercially mass-produced article which the public does not associate with one particular source of manufacture."

But in 1940 the German Supreme Court modified this rule by broadening the applicability of the unfair competition statute as follows:[92]

"It is true that slavish imitation of an article not protected or no longer protected by patent is not itself an act of unfair competition even though objectively some likelihood of confusion may exist. In order to find unfair competition, there must be additional factors which render the imitation *contra bonos mores.* Such factor is found above all wherever there is an intent to mislead the public as a result of a deliberate leading of the public into error with regard to the origin of the imitator's product."

The latest word in this regard was spoken by the new West German Supreme Court in a comprehensive decision of March 12, 1954.[93] The case involved, *inter alia,* slavish imitation of certain external parts of a machine on which a small patent (*Gebrauchsmuster*) had expired. Here the Court, in elaborating on the previously mentioned decision of the predecessor court, said:

"Slavish imitation may be a violation of Section 1 of the unfair competition statute in case of a uniquely designed product of above-average distinction wherever the imitator markets the imitated product without being concerned at all about the possibility of confusion or without taking all steps which may be necessary to prevent confusion."

In evaluating the present policy of the German courts we must again bear in mind that the vast majority of designs, both industrial and ornamental, are effectively protected by special statutes that provide both criminal and civil sanctions.[94] In addition Section 25 of the German Trade-Mark Act of May 5, 1936 provides a statutory cause of action against any form of infringement of the "getup" *(Ausstattungsschutz)* of a person's merchandise. This provision, though it does not cover ornamental designs of articles of the applied arts or of machines, does apply to all packages, containers, bottles, envelopes, etc. that have become known in the trade as someone's distinctive emblems. As a result there appears to be little more need for supplementary protection against slavish imitation under the German law of unfair competition than under the French law.

The law in Italy and Switzerland—to mention only two more countries—is similar.[95] Switzerland, too, has liberal provision with regard to the protection and registration of ornamental designs (the Act of March 30, 1900), although, with the exception of technical models in the watch industry, the Swiss law does not know the "small patent" of the German law. According to the Swiss Supreme Court any design that may have a peculiar aesthetic effect on the onlooker may qualify as an original design. As a result the mere arrangement of lines may qualify for such protection.[96] Technical elements that may approach the German concept of *Gebrauchsmuster* are protected in Switzerland by a very liberal interpretation of the requirements of invention under the Swiss Patent Statute.[97] Moreover, watch models and lace designs are regulated and protected by special statute. In addition to the design and patent law the Swiss Copyright Act also affords a considerable measure of copyright protection to artistic designs.

However, like French and German jurisprudence, the High Swiss Court has recognized that, although slavish imitation as such may not be unlawful, it may well become so if accompanied by a purpose to capitalize on a competitor's reputation and to exploit the commercial success of his merchandise. It would appear that Swiss jurisprudence in permitting supplementary reliance on Article 1 of the Swiss Statute against acts of unfair competition[98] goes even farther than the German courts, because the general clause of Article 1 of the Swiss Statute does not refer to acts against public *bonos mores,* but even more broadly reads:

> "Unfair competition under this act is any misuse of commercial competition by deceptive or any other means which run afoul of the principles of bona fides *(treu und Glauben)* between competitors."

As a result the Swiss Court, in a leading decision of September 1931,[99] reached the conclusion that Article 1 of the Unfair Competition Act may be invoked even in cases of slavish imitation of otherwise unprotected products wherever the method used by the imitator in introducing his product to the public runs afoul of the basic requirements of honesty and good faith in trade; there is no indication in the Swiss decision that the imitator's liability in such cases can be avoided merely by the use of his name.

In Italy, too,[100] the courts now recognize the principle of free imitation of any product or features of a product not protected by special statute; but a distinction is made, based on Article 10 *bis* of the Paris Convention as revised in London 1934, between what our own courts would call "functional" and "nonfunctional" features. Slavish copying of the latter is generally considered an act of unfair competition under Italian law. Thus it was stated in Wax & Vitale v. Martino (July 1936):[101]

> "A nonpatented product may lawfully be imitated with regard to its internal elements which are indispensable for its reproduction; however, its external features may not be slavishly imitated."

How has slavish imitation and the making of "Chinese copies" fared under our own law of unfair competition? Has the broad policy of the International News case[102] been carried out in this important field, so that industrial designers in the United States can rely on effective protection against unfair competition even in the absence of special legislation? The answer, as is only too well known today, is clearly No. There is no need or room here to review in detail the hitherto unhappy plight of the industrial designer in the United States. Suffice it to mention that at this moment the prevailing philosophy in the United States is expressed in these words of Mr. Justice Brandeis in the Shredded Wheat case:[103]

> "Sharing in the goodwill of an article unprotected by patent or trade-mark is the exercise of a right possessed by all—and in the free exercise of which the consuming public is deeply interested."

Although the doctrine of the International News case has been followed in relatively few enlightened lower court decisions,[104] it was soon declared to be inapplicable in the absence of special legislation in the case of textile designs,[105] and, since then, in almost all situations involving ornamental or industrial designs that fall outside the protection of the patent or design patent statutes. The gradual elimination of design piracy of all types from the law of unfair competition has been traced and illustrated elsewhere[106] and will not be repeated here, but the result of a long line of recent cases has been to leave industrial designers and those who pay for their services virtually without any legal protection whatsoever.[107]

This gap in the law of unfair competition (in the absence of proof of a secondary meaning that can almost never be established, even though, as in the General Time case, millions of dollars' worth of clocks with the design may have been sold) is even more disconcerting if it is considered that, as a result of false historical analogies, design patents in our country are subjected to the same tests as mechanical patents, including the same rigid test of "invention." We know that fewer than ten per cent of all design patents, although issued only after thorough pre-examination, are held valid by the courts and that it has become almost axiomatic immediately to discard any allegation of unfair competition with the convenient excuse that, contrary to Continental practice, such protection may, as a practical matter, be afforded only in cases of obvious passing-off, which apparently can be readily avoided in the United States by the mere device of adding the defendant's name to the product.[108]

It may be of some comfort, to be sure, to learn from the Supreme Court's widely discussed recent decision in Mazer v. Stein[109] that, under the Rules of the Copyright Office as revised in 1949,[110] the "artistic features" of certain works of the applied arts (*i.e.,* jewelry, glassware, etc.) may now be registered in the Copyright Office, and that a work of art, such as a sculpture, does not lose its protection under the Copyright Act by subsequent embodiment as a lamp base in an article of commercial mass production. Under this form of relief the Copyright Office will now register the artistic features of wallpaper, textiles, etc., provided they are separately identifiable as such, but the vast majority of models and works of the applied arts, as such, will remain outside such protection. Moreover, there appears to be a consensus in this country that neither the present design patent statute nor the Copyright Act provides a workable measure of protection for artistic designs (the Copyright Act, where applicable, may even result in overprotection by providing a 56-year period of protection for a model or design that may actually require such protection for only an initial period of, say, three to five years). What is more interesting for the immediate purpose of this study is the now acknowledged self-imposed restraint of our equity courts in applying and enforcing the same basic principles of fair competition that are observed in many foreign countries simply on the basis of such general statutory provisions as Articles 1382 and 1383 of the French *Code Civil.* Though some forward-looking decisions have characterized unfair competition as embracing any conduct that "shocks judicial sensibilities,"[111] others in more recent years have gone so far as to say:

> "While plagiarism in any form is to be deplored and certainly not condoned or encouraged, we are concerned here not with one's sense of fairness, but with the law."[112]

And though it may be true that our fear of creating or extending monopolies, recently referred to by Judge Jerome Frank as "monopoly-phobia,"[113] may warrant legislative and judicial reluctance unduly to expand an author's or inventor's rights, we should recognize at the same time that fundamental principles of fairness and business ethics should not be readily sacrificed but should be considered an inherent part of the general law of unfair competition.[114] As was said by the late Judge Shientag in a design piracy case,[115] "Even in the present state of the law the piracy of styles is not entirely without the pale of the Seventh Commandment."

CONCLUSION

Having attempted to consult the experience of some European countries in connection with an evaluation of our own problems of unfair trade, we have seen that from the very start this branch of the law was permitted to develop in Europe as an independent body of general law to which special remedies, both civil and criminal, were added for the protection of trade-marks, designs, and other artistic or industrial productions in implementation of the patent and copyright laws, whereas in the United States the doctrine of unfair competition had a slow start indeed, having been originally applied only in so-called "cases analogous to trade-mark infringement."[116] But quite apart from that, our brief review of some of the major types of conduct that form so important a part in the Continental theory of unfair competition has emphasized the fact that our equity courts deemed themselves hampered by the existence of certain historic maxims that for a long time have served, and to some extent serve even today, as stumbling blocks to the formulation of a more effective body of private law against all forms of unfair trade. This, it has been shown, was true of such practices as, for instance, disparagement of a competitor, false and deceptive advertising, and misappropriation as well as slavish imitation. And even where in the past our courts dared condemn—even before the International News case—instances of outright misappropriation in the absence of passing-off, there has recently appeared a retrogressive trend.

Suffice it to refer to the memorable Fonotipia case,[117] in which an equity court granted relief against the making of a phonograph record from another record, although the record itself, under the then and now prevailing Copyright Act, was not capable of copyright protection and although no elements of passing-off were present. The court there said:[118]

> "The jurisdiction of a court of equity has always been invoked to prevent the continuance of acts of injury to property and to personal rights generally, where the law had not provided a specific legal remedy, and it would seem that the appropriation of what has come to be recognized as property rights or incorporeal interests in material objects, out of which pecuniary profits can fairly be secured, may properly, in certain kinds of cases, be protected by legislation; but such intangible or abstract property rights would seem to have claims upon the protection of equity, where the ground for legislation is uncertain or difficult of determination, and where the principles of equity plainly apply."

This would undoubtedly be the type of reasoning that a French, German, or Swiss court would have applied in a case of this kind. However, only four years ago the Court of Appeals for the Second Circuit[119] held that the making of a photographic copy of a work the text of which was in the public domain, but which embodied some especially beautiful typographical work, was not actionable because the special typography used to embellish and distinguish the book was not capable of separate legal protection. In effect overruling the Fonotipia case, the court concluded:

> "We do not mean that the defendant could under no circumstances be guilty of 'unfair competition' in his use of the 'work'; but it would have to be by some conduct other than copying it. Since he confined himself to that and gave notice that it was his product, the Copyright Act protected him. This reasoning applies as well to any rights which may be supposed to flow from the doctrine of International News Service v. Associated Press, 248 U.S. 215, 39 S.Ct. 68, 63 L.Ed. 211, although, as we have several times declared, that

decision is to be strictly confined to the facts then at bar. So far as Fonotipia Limited v. Bradley, C.C., 171 F. 951 may be thought to conflict with what we are holding, it is overruled."[120]

There is still another important factor to be taken into account in reviewing the present status of our law of unfair competition in the light of foreign experiences. The famous Supreme Court decision in Erie v. Tompkins,[121] no matter how beneficial its results may have been in other fields of the law, has served greatly to retard the development of the law of unfair competition in this country, at least in areas such as Illinois, in which the doctrine of unfair competition had never found much recognition outside and beyond the traditional action for passing-off. As recently as 1923 the Appellate Court of Illinois, in refusing to apply the rule of the International News case, had said:[122]

"The 'palming off' rule is expressed in a positive, concrete form which will not admit of 'broadening' or 'widening' by any proper judicial process. It is rigid and inelastic. . . . According to the view we have taken, the Supreme Court of the United States holds that the 'palming off' rule is not the only ground of equitable relief in unfair competition, and the Supreme Court of this State holds it is the only rule of decision."

Thus another severe blow was dealt the doctrine of unfair competition, particularly in jurisdictions such as Illinois, which are unwilling even to recognize the existence of this branch of the law outside the narrow limits of passing-off.[123]

Where then should we turn for a possible solution of our difficulties? At least four possibilities suggest themselves. The most interesting, but certainly the most roundabout, is the theory first advanced by the late Edward S. Rogers in 1949,[124] and earlier in his preface to *The New Trade-Mark Manual,*[125] that the answer lies in Section 44 of the Trade-Mark Act of 1946 and more particularly in Section 44(i). The latter provision unobtrusively states that all benefits to which foreigners may be entitled in the United States under the international conventions to which we have adhered should be equally available to United States citizens. Thus, it is argued, a federal law of unfair competition has been created that will make a wide category of unfair trade practices actionable in the federal courts on the ground that they should be considered part and parcel of our own substantive law. This has been the origin of the now famous Stauffer doctrine,[126] named after a case in which the Court of Appeals for the Ninth Circuit expressly adopted this theory, thereby eliminating in effect the Erie v. Tompkins doctrine[127] with regard to all those many types of unfair competition that have found condemnation in either the revised Paris Convention of 1883 or the Inter-American Convention of 1929. However, it seems that, thus far at least, other appellate federal tribunals have been disinclined to expand our domestic unfair competition law in this ingenious but rather roundabout fashion. The Court of Appeals for the Second Circuit has expressly refused to follow the doctrine, at least in its procedural aspects,[128] and more recently the Court of Appeals for the Third Circuit likewise expressed its disapproval of the doctrine.[129] Unless the United States Supreme Court should eventually express itself in favor of the Stauffer doctrine, we must conclude that it is at least very doubtful whether the Trade-Mark Act of 1946 has succeeded in either creating or enlarging a federal law of unfair competition outside the previously discussed Section 43, which now gives a federal cause of action in cases involving false designations of origin or false descriptions.[130]

Nor has the second possible solution, offered by Professor Bunn of the Wisconsin Law School,[131] which considers Section 5 of the Federal Trade Commission Act as a possible basis for a private federal law of unfair competition, found any general acceptance or support. It was Professor Bunn's suggestion that the general clause of Section 5, broadly authorizing the Federal Trade Commission to "prosecute unfair acts and practices," might be considered a source of federal unfair competition law even for purposes of private litigation.

A third solution might be the enactment of uniform state legislation supplemented by a federal act under the commerce clause of the Constitution—legislation that would specifically outlaw all those practices enumerated as types of unfair competition in the international conventions and would in addition embody the kind of general clause against unfair trade practices that is found in Article 10 *bis* of the Paris Convention and Article 20 of the Inter-American Convention. It is particularly interesting to note in this regard that at least one of the forty-eight states has written into its statutory law a general clause against unfair competition. Section 3369 of the Civil Code of California provides in part:

"Any person performing or proposing to perform an act of unfair competition within this State may be enjoined in any court of competent jurisdiction. . . . unfair competition shall mean and include unfair or fraudulent business practice and unfair, untrue or misleading advertising."[132]

Fourthly, and finally, however, it might well be asked whether, in the light of the European experience, our courts, both state and federal, might not be in a position to establish a workable and effective body of private law against all types of unfair conduct in business without the help of any new legislation, but merely in the exercise of sound discretion and established rules of fair play. Though it is undoubtedly true, as stated by Mr. Justice Brandeis in his famous decision in the International News case, that the "noblest of human productions,—knowledge, truths ascertained, conceptions, and ideas—become, after voluntary communications to others, free as the air to common use,"[133] it is equally true that there are ways and means, even in a free competitive economy, which, being generally considered unfair and unethical and, in the European sense, *contra bonos mores,* should at the same time be considered illegal. As was said by the Supreme Court of California as far back as 1895:[134]

". . . the fact that the question comes to us in an entirely new guise, and that the schemer has concocted a kind of deception heretofore unheard of in legal jurisprudence, is no reason why equity is either unable or unwilling to deal with him."

Or, as stated even more plainly by the Court of Appeals for the Seventh Circuit in National Telegraph News Co. v. Western Union:[135]

"Property, even as distinguished from property in intellectual production, is not, in its modern sense, confined to that which may be touched by the hand, or seen by the eye. . . . It is needless to say, that to every ingredient of property thus made up—the intangible as well as the tangible, that which is discernible to mind only, as well as that susceptible to physical touch—equity extends appropriate protection. Otherwise courts of equity would be unequal to their supposed great purposes; and every day as business life grows more complicated, such inadequacy would be increasingly felt. . . . Are we to fail our plain duty for mere lack of precedent? We choose, rather, to make precedent."

In concluding his study on unfair competition in 1940,[136] Professor Chaffee said:

"A court may find it very helpful to consult the experience of Germany and Austria in their more enlightened days, and of France and Switzerland. Their problems of unfair trade are much the same as ours. If in a novel situation we find that their courts have given private relief without any resulting harm, this encourages us to be bold."

If this paper has demonstrated that in many situations of this kind, the courts in foreign countries have given private relief without any resulting harm, then—according to Professor Chaffee—we may be encouraged "to be bold." "Foreign experience," Professor Chaffee continued, "is like a map of the territory we are still exploring." Perhaps continued exploration along the lines we have outlined may not only eventually result in a much needed expansion of our own law of unfair competition, but at the same time also furnish a more enduring basis for effective international protection of industrial and artistic property.

NOTES

Key to periodical abbreviations:

Annales. Annales de la Propriété Industrielle, Artistique et Littéraire, Paris

Annuaire. Annuaire de l'Association Internationale pour la Protection de la Propriété Industrielle (A.I.P.P.I.), Paris

BGE. Entscheidungen des schweizerischen Bundesgerichtes

GRUR. Gewerblicher Rechtsschutz und Urheberrecht

MuW. Markenschutz und Wettbewerb, Monatsschrift fur Marken- , Patent- und Wettbewerbsrecht, Berlin

Propriété Industrielle (PI) Revue. Revue mensuelle du Bureau international pour la protection de la propriété industrielle, Berne

Rivista. Rivista della proprieta intellettuale ed industriale, Mailand.

1 New York Law Review, June 1940, pp. 317–41.

2 *Id.* at 341.

3 Deák, Contracts and Combinations in Restraint of Trade in French Law—A Comparative Study, 21 Iowa L. Rev. 397 (1936).

4 Calmels, *Des noms et marques de fabrique et de commerce et de la concurrence déloyale* (Paris 1858); Gastambide, *Traité théorique et pratique des contrefaçons en tous genres* (Paris 1837); Rendu (A.) et Delorme, *Traité pratique de droit industriel* (Paris 1855) and *Traité pratique des marques de fabrique et de commerce et de la concurrence déloyale* (Paris 1858); Mayer, *De la concurrence déloyale et de la contrefaçon en matière de noms et de marques* (Paris 1879). The outstanding treatises of more recent origin include Allart (Henri), *Traité théorique et pratique de la concurrence déloyale* (Paris 1892), and Pouillet, *Traité des marques de fabrique et de la concurrence déloyale* (6th ed. Paris 1912).

5 For a list of types of unfair methods and practices condemned by the Federal Trade Commission, see *Annual Report* 113–18 (1952).

6 For a complete history of this development since 1804, see Roubier, *Le Droit de la propriété industrielle* 494 *et seq.* (Paris 1952).

7 Waelbroeck, *Cours de droit industriel* (Brussels 1863–1867), "Cours de code Napoléon," *t.* IX, *n.*440.

8 Fuzier-Herman, *Répertoire Général Alphabétique du Droit Français, t.* 13, p. 63.

9 Pouillet, *op. cit. supra* note 4, at 716: "Nous n'avons, ni le prêtention, ni l'espérance d'indiquer toutes les formes de la concurrence déloyale; nous signalerons les principales, les plus ordinairement usitées; nous sommes sûr d'ailleurs que les tribunaux, gardiens de la loyauté commerciale, sauront toujours, même en l'absence des règles précises, reconnaître et punir les actes qui y sont contraires."

10 This statement is also quoted in a pioneering article by Dr. Otto Mayer, "Die concurrence déloyale," in Goldschmidt, *Zeitschrift für Handelsrecht,* Vol. II, New Series (Stuttgart 1881), 363, at 394: "La concurrence déloyale c'est l'acte pratiqué de mauvaise foi à l'effet de produire une confusion entre les produits de deux fabricants, ou de deux commerçants, ou qui, sans produire de confusion, jette le discrédit sur un établissement rival."

11 Allart, *op. cit. supra* note 4 at v.

12 Cf. Browne, *A Treatise on the Law of Trade-Marks,* Ch. XII, 524 *et seq.* (2d ed. Boston 1885).

13 On Certain Cases Analogous to Trade-Marks, 4 Harv. L. Rev. 321 (1891).

[14] *Id.* at 328.

[15] *Id.* at 332.

[16] New York, 1901.

[17] For a comprehensive review of the historical development see Derenberg, *Trade-Mark Protection and Unfair Trading* 40 *et seq.* (Albany 1936).

[18] New York, 1909.

[19] 240 U.S. 403 (1916).

[20] *Id.* at 413.

[21] Coty, Inc. v. Parfums de Grande Luxe, 298 Fed. 865 (2d Cir. 1924). For a full discussion of the development of the doctrine of unfair competition in the United States during the last seventy-five years, see Haines, Effort to Define Unfair Competition, 29 Yale L.J. 1 (1919–1920).

[22] International News Service v. Associated Press, 248 U.S. 215 (1918).

[23] Cf. Callmann, He Who Reaps Where He Has Not Sown: Unjust Enrichment in the Law of Unfair Competition, 55 Harv. L. Rev. 595 (1942).

[24] 248 U.S. 215, 239–40.

[25] See, for instance, Metropolitan Opera Ass'n., Inc. et al. v. Wagner-Nichols Recorder Corp. et al., 101 N.Y.S.2d 483 (Sup. Ct. N.Y. 1950).

[26] Cf. Callmann, *Unfair Competition and Trade-Marks,* Ch. 15, 875 *et seq.* (2d ed. 1950).

[27] Ely-Norris Safe Co. v. Mosler Safe Co., 7 F.2d 603 (2d Cir. 1925), at 604.

[28] Premier-Pabst Corp. v. The Elm City Brewing Corp., 9 F. Supp. 754, 758 (D. Conn. 1934).

[29] Federal Trade Commission v. R. R. Keppel & Bros., Inc., 291 U.S. 304 (1934); Schecter Poultry Corp. v. United States, 295 U.S. 495 (1935).

[30] 295 U.S. 495, at 531–32.

[31] Davis Electronics Co. et al. v. Channel Master Corp., 116 F. Supp. 919 (S.D. N.Y. 1953).

[32] Bayer & Co., Inc. v. United Drug Co., 272 Fed. 505 (S.D. N.Y. 1921).

[33] Pouillet, *op. cit. supra* note 4, at 959.

[34] Galignani's Messenger v. Morning News, Trib. comm. Seine, May 21, 1884, *Annales* 1885, p. 119.

[35] Compagnie d'assurances générales v. Mutual Life, Baudry et Beziat d'Audibert, Paris, June 23, 1896, *Annales* 1897, pp. 30–32.

[36] François v. Jules Mumm et Cie., Trib. comm. Reims, September 9, 1904, *Annales* 1910, pp. 175, 177.

[37] For a multitude of similar cases, see Pouillet, *op. cit. supra* note 4, Sec. 1176, at 961 *et seq.*

[38] Pouillet, *op. cit. supra* note 4, at 966.

[39] A. Rendu, *op. cit. supra* note 4, at n.507: ". . . dans le cas où un fabricant non content d'exalter ses produits, déprécierait par des annonces ou prospectus ceux de ses rivaux."

[40] Mayer, *op. cit. supra* note 4, at n.35: "Toute allégation qui directement dans la forme tend à déprécier les produits d'une maison rivale, pourra être relevée comme un procéde frauduleux, quelle que soit la vérité."

[41] Droste, "Das Verbot der bezugnehmenden Werbung und die Ausnahmefälle," 53 GRUR 140 (April 1951).

[42] "Hellegold," GRUR 1931 S. 1301.

[43] Hoffman la Roche & Co./Nederlandsche Maatschappij, Dec. 21, 1938, N.J. n.601.

[44] Appellate Court of Amsterdam, January 31, 1940, N.J. 1940, p. 809.

[45] Jan. 25, 1929, N.J. 1929, p. 1077. Many more illustrations can be found in a comprehensive study by Prof. M. H. Bregstein, "Comparative Advertising as Unfair Competition," published in four installments in *Weekblad voor Privaatrecht, Notarisambt en Registratie,* July 11, 18, 25, and Aug. 1, 1953. With regard to the British law on comparative advertising, cf. the articles on "Slander of Goods," 78 *Solicitors' Journal* 607 (1934) and 82 Sol. J. 536 (1938).

[46] Fredericq, *La concurrence déloyale* 58–59 (Gent 1935).

[47] Schweizerisches Bundesgericht, November 23, 1895, GRUR 1897, p. 110.

[48] Equitable Relief Against Defamation and Injuries to Personality, 29 Harv. L. Rev. 640 (1916).

[49] Nims, *Unfair Competition and Trade-Marks,* Ch. XVII, 830 (4th ed.). Cf. also the most recent valuable study, The Law of Commercial Disparagement: Business Defamation's Impotent Ally, 63 Yale L. J. 65 (1953), and Notes, West, Recent Trends in Trade Disparagement Doctrines in Relation to Unfair Competition, 13 Geo. Wash. L. Rev. 468 (1945), and Trade Disparagement and the "Special Damage" Quagmire, 18 Chi. L. Rev. 114 (1950).

[50] Marlin Firearms Co. v. Shields, 171 N.Y. 384, 64 N.E. 163, 59 L.R.A. 310 (1902). On the contrary, in the recent case of Eversharp, Inc. v. Pal Blade Co., 182 F.2d 779 (2d Cir. 1950) the Court of Appeals for the Second Circuit held that since the New York Court of Appeals in the more recent case of Advance Music Corp. v. American Tobacco Co., 70 N.E. 2d 401 (1946), in which the requirement for special damages was somewhat modified, had not once mentioned the Marlin case, the latter still remained the law in New York, so that the publication of untrue, disparaging statements should not be restrained by injunction.

[51] Dean Prosser in his textbook on *Torts* (1941) observes at p. 1036: "Because of the unfortunate association with 'slander' a supposed analogy to defamation has hung over the tort like a fog, concealing its real character, and has had great influence upon its development, the plaintiff's title of property seems to have been regarded as somehow personified and so defamed." The inadequacy of the present state of the law with regard to commercial disparagement in all its aspects is most convincingly set forth in the Note by West, *supra* note 49.

[52] H. E. Allen Mfg. Co., Inc. v. Smith, 224 App. Div. 187, 229 N.Y.S. 692 (4th Dep't 1928).

[53] Pound, Equitable Relief against Defamation and Injuries to Personality, 29 Harv. L. Rev. 640, 668 (1916).

[54] 224 App. Div. 187, at 192.

[55] Old Investors' & Traders' Corp. v. Jenkins et al., 232 N.Y.S. 245 (N.Y. Sup. Ct. 1928).

[56] The decision in Dehydro, Inc. v. Tretolite Co., 53 F.2d 273 (N.D. Okla. 1931) is to the same effect: "Where the gravamen of the action is to enjoin unfair competition, the question of libel and slander is only incidental to the action, and such an action is not one to enjoin a libel or slander."

[57] 20 F.2d 763 (8th Cir. 1927).

[58] See 63 Yale L. J. 65, *supra* note 49, at 66 *et seq*. For illustrations see Lee, *Business Ethics* 87 (1926); Taeusch, *Policy and Ethics in Business* 445 (1931). For a thorough review of the entire subject see Wolff, "Unfair Competition by Truthful Disparagement," 47 Yale L. J. 1304 (1938).

[59] The *1952 Annual Report* of the Federal Trade Commission includes, among "Types of Unfair Methods and Practices," the following: "7. Making false and disparaging state-

ments respecting competitors' products and business, in some cases under the guise of ostensibly disinterested and specially informed sources or through purported scientific, but in fact, misleading, demonstrations or tests."

[60] Law of July 28, August 4, 1824, *relative aux altérations ou suppositions de noms dans les produits fabriqués.*

[61] Law of June 23, 1857, *sur les marques de fabrique et de commerce,* modified by the Law of May 3, 1890.

[62] Gastambide, *op. cit. supra* note 4, at n.60.

[63] Dalloz, *Jurisprudence générale. Répertoire et Supplement,,* V° Industrie et commerce, n.350.

[64] Pouillet, *op. cit. supra,* note 4 at 446.

[65] Trib. comm. de Rouen, June 4, 1877, Lévy, Jacob et Legrande v. Francfort et Kahn, *Annales,* 1877, p. 258.

[66] Lévy v. Saintin et Flisseau, Sirey, *Recueil Général des Lois et de Arrêts,* 1892, II, p. 202.

[67] Reimer, *Wettbewerbs-und Warenzeichenrecht* 836 *et seq.* (1954).

[68] Migos A. G. v. Tanner, BGE 58 II, p. 430 (1932).

[69] New York Cement Co. v. Coplay Cement Co., 44 Fed. 288 (C.C. E.D. Pa. 1890) and 45 Fed. 212 (C.C. E.D. Pa. 1891).

[70] City of Carlsbad v. Tibbetts, 51 Fed. 852, 856 (Mass. 1892).

[71] Grand Rapids Furniture Co. v. Grand Rapids Furniture Co., 127 F.2d 245 (7th Cir. 1942).

[72] California Apparel Creators et al. v. Wieder of California, Inc. et al., 162 F.2d 892 (S.D. N.Y. 1946). Cf. 174 ALR 496 (1946).

[73] American Washboard Co. v. Saginaw Mfg. Co., 103 Fed. 281 (6th Cir. 1900); cf. Handler, False and Misleading Advertising, 39 Yale L. J. 22 (1929), and Callmann, False Advertising as a Competitive Tort, 48 Col. L. Rev. 876 (1948).

[74] *Id.* at 285.

[75] A previous legislative attempt to remedy the situation was made in Section 3 of the Supplementary Trade-Mark Act of March 19, 1920. The section proved entirely ineffective because it was restricted to "willful" misrepresentations and limited to false designations of origin.

[76] See *supra* note 27.

[77] Mosler Safe Co. v. Ely-Norris Safe Co., 273 U.S. 132 (1927).

[78] The only two cases in which the section was referred to until then, Samson Crane Co. v. Union National Sales, Inc., et al., 87 F.Supp. 218 (D. Mass. 1949), a labor dispute, and Carpenter v. Erie R. Co., 178 F.2d 921 (2d Cir. 1949), misrepresentation regarding medical services, bear no similarity to the type of case to which the section applies.

[79] 214 F.2d 649 (3d Cir. 1954).

[80] *Id.* at 651.

[81] April 27, 1937, Sté Monotype v. Sté la Monographe, P.I. *Revue* 1937, s. 203: "Whereas it is with good reason that the court decided that the principle of freedom of commerce and industry is opposed to considering the manufacture and sale of articles unprotected by patent as acts of illegal or unfair competition. . ."

[82] *Annuaire* 1930, s. 425: "Since at least the proclamation of the rights of man and the citizen, and even before, the governments of all civilized countries admit, as a fundamental basis of human activity, the freedom of commerce and industry; the restrictions

brought to bear by certain provisions of the codes and special laws are directed solely against abuses, which, under the guise of that principle, would run counter to good business morals, i.e., principles of fair competition which must control commercial and industrial transactions."

83 Triboulet-Arsandaux, *La Protection des œuvres françaises d'art Appliqué*, s. 43. (1936).

84 Law of July 5, 1844, *sur les brevets d'invention.*

85 Laws of July 19 and 24, 1793, modified by the Law of March 11, 1902, *loi sur la propriété artistique et littéraire, étendue à l'art industriel.*

86 Triboulet-Arsandaux, *op. cit. supra* note 83, at 37.

87 This is also the view expressed by Prof. Roubier in his recent admirable textbook, *Le Droit de la Propriété Industrielle* 495 (Paris 1952). Roubier cites numerous recent cases to the effect that the reproduction and imitation of industrial designs may constitute an act of unfair competition, even though the designs as such are in the public domain. If they are so offered to the public as to create a possibility of confusion in any manner, a cause of action in unfair competition under Article 1382 of the French Code will lie.

88 Calmels, *op. cit. supra* note 4, at n.40.

89 Fernand-Jacq and Demousseaux, *Annuaire* 1930, s. 423.

90 For a list of the voluminous German literature on this point, see Henssler, *Urheberschutz in der Angewandten Kunst und Architektur* 116 *et seq.* (Stuttgart-Köln 1950).

91 Huthaken-Entscheidung January 31, 1928, GRUR 1928, s. 289.

92 May 18, 1940, MuW 1940, s. 147.

93 March 12, 1954, GRUR 1954 (July-August), p. 337.

94 Gebrauchsmustergesetz, June 1, 1891; cf. two recent commentaries, Furler, *Das Internationale Musterrecht* (Berlin 1951) and same, *Das Geschmacksmustergesetz* (Berlin 1950).

95 One of the most complete recent studies of the problem is the excellent dissertation by Blum, *Schutz der Immaterialgüter vor sklavischer Nachahmung auf technischem Gebiet* (University of Zurich); cf. also, Troller, *Der Schweizerische Gewerbliche Rechtsschutz* 89 *et seq.* (Basle 1948).

96 BGE 29/2/365.

97 BGE 23/1865, 38/2/714.

98 Bundesgesetz über den unlauteren Wettbewerb of September 30, 1943.

99 S. Buser Frères & Co. v. Thommen's Uhrenfabriken A.G., BGE 57, II, 457.

100 Blum, *op. cit. supra* note 95, at 63 *et seq.*

101 Rivista 1936, s. 31.

102 See *supra* note 22.

103 Kellogg Co. v. National Biscuit Co., 305 U.S. 111, 122 (1933).

104 Metropolitan Opera Ass'n. v. Wagner-Nichols Recorder Corp., *supra* note 25, and, most recently, Haeger Potteries v. Gilner Potteries, 123 F.Supp. 261 (S.D. Calif. C.D. 1954).

105 Cheney Bros. v. Doris Silk Corp., 35 F.2d 279 (2d Cir. 1929), *cert. den.* 281 U.S. 728 (1930).

106 Gotshal and Lief, *The Pirates Will Get You!* (New York 1945); Derenberg, Copyright No-Man's Land: Fringe Rights in Literary and Artistic Property, *1953 Copyright Problems Analyzed* (Commerce Clearing House Inc. 1953), reprinted 35 *J. Pat. Off. Soc.* 627, 690, 770 (1953).

107 Chas. D. Briddell, Inc. v. Alglobe Trading Corp., 194 F.2d 416 (2d Cir. 1952);

Pagliero v. Wallace China Co., Ltd., 198 F.2d 339 (9th Cir. 1952), General Time Instruments Corp. v. The United States Time Corp., 165 F.2d 853 (2d Cir. 1948), and many others.

[108] Chas. D. Briddell, Inc. v. Alglobe Trading Corp., *supra* note 107.

[109] 74 S.Ct. 460 (March 8, 1954).

[110] 37 CRF, 1949, Sec. 202.8, "Works of Art" [Class GO (a)].

[111] In Margarete Steiff v. Bing, 215 F. 204 (S.D. N.Y. 1914), Judge Hough said: " 'Unfair competition' consists in selling goods by means which shock judicial sensibilities; and the Second Circuit has long been very sensitive."

[112] Stein v. Benederet, 109 F.Supp. 364 (E.D. Mich. 1952), at 366.

[113] In Eastern Wine Corp. v. Winslow-Warren, Ltd., Inc., 137 F.2d 955 (2d Cir. 1943), *cert. den.* 64 S.Ct. 65 (1943), Judge Frank said at 958: "There are some persons, infected with monopoly-phobia, who shudder in the presence of any monopoly. But the common law has never suffered from such a neurosis. There has seldom been a society in which there have not been some monopolies, i.e., special privileges."

[114] In denying protection against unfair competition in cases of this type our courts have often quoted Judge Learned Hand's statement in one of the early Shredded Wheat cases, involving the imitation of the shape of the product: "Under the guise of protecting against unfair competition, we must be jealous not to create perpetual monopolies." Shredded Wheat Co. v. Humphrey Cornell Co., 250 Fed. 960, 964 (2d Cir. 1918). It would seem regrettable, however, if the philosophy expressed in this statement were extended to such a point that it actually becomes a windfall for unfair competitors.

[115] Margolis v. National Bellas Hess Co., Inc., 249 N.Y.S. 175 (N.Y. S.Ct. 1931).

[116] See *supra* notes 12 and 13.

[117] Fonotipia Limited et al. v. Bradley, Victor Talking Machine Co. v. same, 171 Fed. 951 (E.D. N.Y. 1909).

[118] *Id.* at 962.

[119] G. Ricordi & Co. v. Haendler, 194 F.2d 914 (2d Cir. 1952).

[120] *Id.* at 916. A ray of hope for a return to the International News doctrine, even by the Court of Appeals of the Second Circuit, may, however, be found in Judge Clark's recent opinion in Hartford Charga-Plate Associates, Inc. v. Youth Centre-Cinderella Stores, Inc., 215 F.2d 668 (2d Cir. 1954). Although plaintiff was not held entitled to relief, the court there said, with regard to the International News case and its own previous decision in the Ricordi case (*supra* note 119): "In fact, as freely conceded, defendant was at liberty to duplicate and use a system like plaintiff's; the only attempted ban was by way of servitude upon a use otherwise freely possible of plaintiff's plates in defendant's addresser. We do not think the precedent will therefore bear the burden thus laid upon it, even if we do not follow the repeated trend in this court, noted as lately as G. Ricordi & Co. v. Haendler, 2 Cir., 194 F.2d 916, 92 USPQ 340, to confine that decision strictly to the facts then at bar."

[121] 304 U.S. 64 (1938).

[122] Stevens-Davis Co. v. Mather & Co., 230 Ill. App. 45 (1st Dist. 1923), at 65. Cf., with regard to this case, Rissman, The Law of Unfair Competition in Illinois, 1950 U. of Ill. L. Forum 675 (1950).

[123] This has been strikingly pointed out in a leading law review article by Sergei S. Zlinkoff, Erie v. Tomkins: In Relation to the Law of Trade-Marks and Unfair Competition, 42 Col. L. Rev. 952 (1942), as well as in a challenging paper by the late Mr. Rogers on

Unfair Competition, 35 T.M.Rep. 126 (1945). Mr. Rogers wrote: "But then came Erie Railway v. Tompkins, 304 U.S. 64, and there was chaos. There were 48 different sovereignties the decisions of whose courts were the law. The body of federal decisions which had been 50 years evolving was not binding either on the state or federal courts. No one knows what the law is. Theoretically, what the federal courts are required to apply is the law of the state where they might sit. And it was frequently found that there were no applicable state decisions, or that the decisions of the states comprising the same circuit were not uniform. It may take fifty years to get a body of decisional law in the State of Illinois comparable to the one already developed in the Circuit Court of Appeals for the Seventh Circuit." Mr. Rogers went so far as to prepare a model unfair trade act, which is printed as an appendix to his article, at 133.

[124] The Lanham Act and the Social Function of Trade-Marks, 14 Law & Contemp. Probs. 173 (1949).

[125] Robert, 1947.

[126] Stauffer v. Exley, 184 F.2d 962 (9th Cir. 1950).

[127] *Supra* note 121.

[128] American Automobile Ass'n v. Spiegel, 205 F.2d 771 (2d Cir. 1953), *cert. den.* 74 Sup. Ct. 138 (1953).

[129] L'Aiglon Apparel, Inc. v. Lana Lobell, Inc., *supra* note 79.

[130] See *supra* p. 201 *et seq.*

[131] The National Law of Unfair Competition, 62 Harv. L. Rev. 987 (1949).

[132] Partly because of this broad statutory provision, a California district court recently granted extremely liberal and effective protection against slavish copying of pottery and ceramic products not protected by design patent or copyright. In Haeger Potteries v. Gilner Potteries, 123 F. Supp. 261 the court said (at 268): "Even though each feature composing the article be open to public use, if the ensemble created by the imitator produces an object which misleads the public to the prior user's detriment, there arises under California law a cause of action for unfair competition."

[133] *Supra* note 22, at 250.

[134] Weinstock, Lubin & Co. v. Marks, 109 Cal. 529, 42 Pac. 142, 145 (1895).

[135] 119 Fed. 294, at 299.

[136] Unfair Competition, 53 Harv. L. Rev. 1289 (1940).

II

The Code in a Socialist State

NIKOLA STJEPANOVIC

I

TOWARD the end of and immediately after the Second World War Yugoslavia was subjected to sociopolitical, economic, and legal changes that have made that country a completely different State from that between the two wars. The changes were revolutionary: they have made Yugoslavia into a *republic* instead of the prewar monarchy, into a federal State instead of the earlier centralized State, and into a socialist State. Although the continuity between old and present-day Yugoslavia has been preserved so far as territory, national entity, and international status are concerned, such continuity has clearly not been maintained with regard to the sociopolitical and legal systems. As far as the latter are concerned, indeed, it is not going too far to say that a new State has come into being as a result of the revolution that occurred simultaneously with the liberation of the country from the Germans in 1945. Not only have the form of government and the organization of the State been modified, but the very sources of State authority have also been changed.

The revolutionary postwar change in both the legal and the political sphere was signalized, even before the enactment of the Constitution of 1946, by the decree of the Presidium of the AVNOJ[1] (Provisional Revolutionary Government) of February

---

NIKOLA STJEPANOVIC *is Professor of Law at the University of Belgrade and a member of the Advisory Council of the New York University Institute of Comparative Law*

3, 1945, which, after the adoption of the Constitution, was confirmed and somewhat amended by the law of October 23, 1946.[2] By that decree, as confirmed by the 1946 law referred to, the laws and other statutory provisions in force prior to April 6, 1941 (the day Yugoslavia became involved in the war) were abrogated, and the enactments imposed by the Germans and their supporters during the occupation of the country were proclaimed nonexistent. Domestic legal continuity was thus expressly interrupted, so far as the statute law was concerned. Individual decisions of the courts and administrative agencies, based on the abrogated laws, remained in force as a rule, but they could be revised under certain defined conditions and within certain prescribed delays. The postwar revolution, illegal in terms of the old law, endeavored then to become legal by creating its own positive law, intended to legalize, confirm, and further develop its actions.

It is of interest to observe here that the old law was not entirely excluded from application in new Yugoslavia. The old law as an entity ceased to be valid; it ceased to be binding on the organs of the State and on individual citizens; but the decree of February 3, 1945 as well as the law of October 23, 1946 permitted the use of the old law in two ways. First, the presidia, both federal and state,[3] could by their acts proclaim as binding certain defined statutory rules and other provisions of the old law, with whatever modifications were required. Secondly, the organs of the State—and especially the courts and administrative agencies—could apply under the 1946 law, in the execution of their functions, the pre-1941 statutes dealing with the particular subject (1) if and in so far as there were no new statutory provisions (2) if the pre-1941 statutory provisions in question were not contrary to the Constitution of the Federal People's Republic of Yugoslavia, or to the laws and other legislative provisions adopted by the competent organs of the new State, and (3) if they were not contrary to the fundamental principles of the constitutional organization of the Federal People's Republic of Yugoslavia and its various states (republics). The provisions of the 1946 law just discussed, it should be noted, apply only to acts having statutory effect.

The provisions of the law of October 23, 1946 show two things. First of all, they show that even the impetus of a revolution cannot completely wipe out a pre-existing legal system, provided that the leaders of the revolution are not devoid of common sense and have a sound understanding of political realities and that the theory and the ideology with which they have been inspired have not made them pure dogmatists. Secondly—and this is of special interest for this paper—the 1946 law gave the organs whose duty it is to administer the laws, especially the courts, a considerable role to play in the creation of law in those fields in which the legislator of the new State had not yet intervened. In Yugoslavia this covered particularly the field of private law—*i.e.* the field of the law concerned with the right of ownership of the individual citizen operating in the so-called "private sector" (contracts and other sources of obligations, torts, property relations, inheritance). This matter was not only not codified at the time, but to this day it has not been regulated at all or has been regulated only to a very insignificant degree under the new law. Thus many of the statutory provisions of the abolished civil codes in force in prewar Yugoslavia—for example, the Austrian General Civil Code (1811) and the Serbian Civil Code of 1844—are even today being applied in the private-law relations between Yugoslavian citizens. These codes were drafted under the direct influence of the Code Napoleon. The courts and especially the highest courts in Yugoslavia have in this field a position not dissimilar to that of the courts in the common-law world.

Legalization of the revolution has, however, also led to revolutionizing of the law. The following illustrative laws have been enacted: on the expropriation of enemy property and sequestration of the property of absent persons; on the confiscation of the property of collaborators during the occupation and of persons who have gone abroad and have failed to return or to register with

Yugoslav diplomatic representatives (1945, 1946);[4] and on the confiscation of war profits (1945, 1946).[5] All business enterprises in the country were classified according to whether they were such as to be of direct interest to the nation as a whole, to a particular state, or only of local interest. Those deemed to interest the nation or a state were nationalized—in so far as they did not become the property of the State, under the already mentioned laws relating to confiscation and war profits—by laws of December 1946 and April 1948.[6] The acts of nationalization have included not only the immovable and the movable property of the enterprises concerned, but also the rights that belonged to these enterprises or served their purposes (patents, licenses, mining rights, trade-marks, etc.). In addition there were enacted the law relating to the final liquidation of agricultural debts (1945)[7] and several laws relating to agrarian reform and colonization[8] (1945, 1946, 1948),[9] which made agricultural producers, and especially small and medium landholders, free from debt and abolished large agricultural holdings in so far as such land tenures had continued to exist in old Yugoslavia—which, it should be noted, was primarily a country of small and medium landholdings anyway. These laws fixed the maximum agricultural holdings of private persons in the following manner: nonagricultural owners, 3 to 5 hectares;[10] agricultural owners, 20 to 35 hectares. A law enacted in 1953 reduced the maximum permitted agricultural owners to 10 hectares. Land owned over and above these maximum figures is confiscated, together with buildings and inventory. Out of the land fund accumulated by means of these confiscations land is given partly to families of poor peasants and families of those who are landless, or it is used to create state agricultural farms. The law relating to the revision of permits to operate retail businesses and catering establishments (1948) reduced these private economic activities to an insignificant amount (only a very small percentage of the activity that had existed prior to the adoption of the law), for in place of the earlier private enterprises of this kind, which were refused permits after the adoption of this law, retail businesses and catering establishments operated by towns and municipalities were created. Thus, by the end of 1948 only small and medium agricultural holdings and small businesses remained in private hands.

II

The new economic, social, and legal system in Yugoslavia has been developed within the framework of the Constitution of January 1946, which recognized three economic sectors—namely, the State, co-operative, and private sectors, with the State sector predominant—and on the basis of the new situation brought into being by the above-mentioned laws relating to confiscation and nationalization. Two specific periods can be noted in this development.

1. *The first period,* preceded by a transitory stage in 1945–46, began in 1946–47 and lasted until 1950–51. This is the period of so-called State or administrative socialism. Collective ownership, especially ownership of the means of production, was legally defined and was in practice treated in this particular period as State ownership. It is well known that, according to socialist theory and practice, ownership, especially ownership of the means of production, determines in the final analysis the substance and the forms of the social and political organization of society. Hence in this particular period we had an all-embracing, powerful, very active and very lively intervention by the State apparatus in economic and social relations, and we had it in all its manifold forms of intervention, such as regulation, control, and supervision, and especially by direct activity by the State administration in all spheres of social and economic life. The State economic enterprises in this period were part of the State machinery. They were managed by higher organs of the State administration, such as directorates and ministries, which interfered directly in all aspects of their work. Planning in the economic field was centralized, all-embracing,

and detailed. It was developed from above by prescribing to every enterprise what, how, and how much it should produce and to whom it should sell its products. The planning was detailed not only in respect of the production, but also in respect of the distribution of the commodities produced. The market was closed. The commodities for which prices were not fixed were very rare. Since compulsory deliveries at fixed prices existed for all basic agricultural products and since this was a rule that applied not only to State and co-operative agricultural enterprises but also to private agricultural producers, every single agricultural enterprise was given the exact total and specific figures of what it must produce and how much it was obliged to deliver to the State. The State administration determined, by means of coupons, points, permits, and allocations, not only what quantities of raw materials should be acquired by each factory and what quantities of goods should be acquired by each commercial enterprise, but also what kinds and what quantities of basic consumer goods (shoes, clothes, fuel, food) should be acquired by individual citizens. A similar degree and intensity of State intervention was introduced in this period in other fields as well: e.g. education, culture, protection of national health, and social welfare.

This period (1947–51)—in addition to an almost indescribable multitude of subordinate legislation (rules and regulations, orders, bylaws, and directives)—was also characterized by certain major legislative documents enacted by the highest organ of federal authority, the Federal People's Assembly *(Skupstina)*. Some of them are called "codes"; others are actually codes or part codes. In this connection we should note: the basic law relating to State economic enterprises (1946);[11] the law relating to the planning of the national economy and to the planning organs (1947); the law relating to the five-year plan for the development of the national economy during the period 1947–51;[12] the law relating to State officials (1946);[13] the Criminal Code, General Part (December 1947); and, before and after its enactment, several separate laws covering specific criminal offenses or groups of criminal offenses, such as criminal offenses relating to speculation and sabotage, criminal offenses against the people and the State, criminal offenses against the joint national and co-operative property and against the property of social organizations, criminal offenses against official duties, etc. To criminal offenses against the honor, body, lives, and property of private citizens the courts applied, in this same period, the legal provisions of the old law on the basis of the already discussed law of October 1946. During this period a law relating to criminal procedure was likewise enacted (in 1948). This last law is a code, although it is not so called.

It should be mentioned separately that during this period codification was carried into effect in a branch of the law that in the western states of Europe generally falls within the orbit of the civil code: namely, family law. The basic law relating to marriage (May 1946),[14] the basic law governing the relations between parents and children (December 1947),[15] the basic law relating to guardianship (April 1947),[16] and the law relating to adoption (April 1947)[17] are formally and, in point of time, separate laws. Nevertheless, taken together they constitute a logical and harmonious statutory entity and may be called the family code of Yugoslavia. This codification has created a unified system of family relations, as compared with the several different systems in force in old Yugoslavia in this field. The codification has introduced the secularization of marriage and of the family by applying the principle of separation between Church and State recognized by the Constitution; Church marriage continues to be permitted, but only *after* the civil marriage, which takes place before the competent organs of the State and which alone has legal effect. Church marriage is the exclusive concern of the citizen; it is without legal consequences. The new family code has consistently and constitutionally carried into effect the principle of equality of rights between men and women in all fields of social and economic life; specifically, there are no longer any limitations in the business

...ity of married women, which did exist in some of the sepa- ...nal areas of old Yugoslavia. Although the codifica- ... is not revolutionary if considered from the point ... progressive Western legal systems, it nevertheless becomes revolutionary when considered in the light of the legal system in old Yugoslavia.

Many other laws were enacted in this same period, but they are of no special interest and need not be noted here.

Worth mentioning, however, are the preparations for the enactment of a code of civil procedure and a law of succession that were made in this period. Activity in these fields has remained to this day in the stage of drafting by technical commissions and public discussions among jurists and has not yet reached the stage of legislative enactment. The courts in these matters apply the legal provisions of old Yugoslavia in accordance with the law of October 23, 1946, already referred to, relating to the invalidity of legal provisions.

2. *The second period,* the beginning of which is marked by the enactment of the law relating to the management by workers' collectives of State economic enterprises (June 1950),[18] can appropriately be called the period of the "second revolution" in Yugoslavia—a revolution brought about, however, by legal means and legal procedures. It was therefore a revolution in substance and not in form. This law and other laws and statutory regulations enacted in the economic field, as well as several constitutional laws and especially the law of January 13, 1953,[19] which dealt with the reorganization of the State machinery, have so changed the socioeconomic and political organization of Yugoslavia that it would not be an exaggeration if one said that Yugoslavia today differs completely from the State of the first postwar period.

What do these changes, brought into being gradually from the middle of 1950 to the end of 1953, consist of?

(1) First of all, *the economic system has been changed.* From a rigidly closed domestic market Yugoslavia has entered the open

market. Administratively controlled distribution has given way to the free exchange of commodities. Prices as a rule are no longer controlled: they are fixed in accordance with supply and demand. Compulsory deliveries no longer exist; their counterpart, compulsory cultivation—that is to say, compulsory production of agricultural commodities—is also a thing of the past; production is now regulated according to estimates freely made by the producers, both collective and individual; the producer is also free to negotiate contracts and free to sell all his commodities on the open market. This system now operates both with respect to industrial products and with respect to products of the various branches of craftsmanship and agricultural products; it replaces the earlier planned distribution of products. The all-embracing and elaborate planning of the economy has also been done away with. Planning now consists of laying down the over-all lines for the development of the economy. Nor is planning done any longer by means of direct administrative measures or projects determined by different layers of superimposed authorities. It is now effected indirectly by means of various economic and financial measures: *i.e.* by allocation of credit and control of investments, amortization, and rate of interest on basic assets, rate of interest on credits granted, etc.

(2) It is especially important to point out here the *changed economic and legal status of economic enterprises* that operate in the so-called "social," *i.e.* socialist, sector (earlier called State sector). The economic enterprise ("economic organization") is the organization used for the purpose of conducting a specific economic activity. It possesses economic independence and is a legal subject; it possesses the capacity of a juridical person and has the possibility of independent participation in legal transactions and in the economic exchange of commodities. It is no longer part of the State administration, but a self-managed economic and legal entity. The enterprise is managed by its workers' collective, either directly (if it is small) or indirectly through its elected organs—the workers'

council and executive board, which it elects fc
it can recall before the expiration of the one-
enterprise, acting independently through its org
plan of production, its plan of activity, the price.
ties, the prices of its services, its internal organizat.
the framework of existing legislation, its rules re… wage scales. The wages of members of the workers' collectives depend in the final analysis on the economic success of the enterprise. Competition exists and is growing between the various social enterprises that operate in industry (there are no private enterprises in industry) as well as between the various private and social enterprises that operate in the various branches of craftsmanship and in agriculture. Competition takes place with respect to assortment, quality, and prices of products and services. The enterprise can freely expand its business organization throughout the territory of Yugoslavia. However, each separate part of a given enterprise possesses certain independent rights in the conduct of its business and (under conditions clearly defined) can secede from its parent organization. Each economic enterprise is part of the local community within which it conducts its business operations as a "basic association of producers." The organs of the State, as representatives of the community, no longer have any administrative or operative jurisdiction with respect to the management of the given enterprise. Within the framework of the Constitution and within the limits of the law they can enact legal provisions relating to business operations of economic enterprises and concerning their obligations to the community. The organs of the State, and in particular the relevant administrative agencies, exercise supervision and control to ensure legality of operations and observance of the obligations assumed by the economic enterprise. In short, into the system of collectivized economy a kind of collective liberalism has now been introduced, instead of the earlier purely bureaucratic management.

Neither the workers' collective nor the enterprise as a legal person is the owner of the "basic assets" (machines, tools, buildings, etc.) and of the "working means" (raw material, prospects, money, etc.) that constitute the material components of the enterprise. The workers' collective, acting on behalf of the community, only manages the enterprise. Its income is divided between the cost of production and the profit. The cost includes the obligation of the enterprise to pay interest on the "basic assets" and rent for the land, as well as amortization of the basic assets and interest on the "working means," and this it has to pay regardless of the level of production and sales. A tax on turnover, included as part of the sales price, is paid by the enterprise when the products are sold or the services rendered. The enterprise is under an obligation to maintain its basic assets at their full value and to make good every reduction in their value, except the reduction that occurs as a result of amortization. Under these conditions it is in the interest of the working collective to increase its production and sales, as well as to exploit as much as possible the "basic assets" on which it pays interest regardless of the quantities produced. Since the exchange of "basic assets" themselves is in principle freely permitted, the enterprise is permitted to sell or lease the "basic assets" that it cannot adequately exploit. This legal capacity has a limitation: "basic assets" in the field of social ownership cannot as a rule be sold to private persons, though the Federal Secretary of State responsible for national economic affairs can prescribe exceptions. The profit of the enterprise—shown in the provisional statements of account and in the final accounts, controlled and audited most often by the competent agencies of local government (district, town), more rarely by agencies of the various states, and very rarely by federal agencies—is divided between the federal government (which takes it in the form of taxation in respect of profits), the communities (district, city, municipal councils), and the enterprise. The enterprise can dispose independently of the ultimate profit thus realized; it can employ a portion of the profit, within the limits permitted by the law, to increase the earnings of its workers.

(3) A *constitutional reform carried out at* the beginning of 1953 abolished the Presidium as the collective "Chief of State" and intermediary between the government and the National Assembly; it also abolished the Ministerial Council as the highest executive organ and the various ministries or departments. Since this reform the federal executive organs have been the President of the Republic and the Federal Executive Council. These are elected by the Federal People's Assembly from its own midst. Both organs are responsible to the Federal Assembly, which can replace them before the expiration of their terms (four years). The constitutional reform emphasized the principle of unity of power and stressed the active role of the representative bodies. The constitutional reform has also brought into being a certain division of State functions by attributing all the political and executive functions to the executive councils (to the federal council and executive councils of the states), while the direct practical executive functions have been vested in the organs of the State administration (State secretariats, independent administrations, administrative bodies, etc.).

The great innovation in the political organization of present-day Yugoslavia is the Council of Producers. This is a newly established chamber in the representative organs at all levels of governmental authority (people's committees in towns and districts, the assemblies of the various states, and the federal assembly). The representatives in the Council of Producers are elected by the producers (workmen and employees) in industry, crafts, and agriculture, trade, transport, and communications, within the framework of two economic groups: Group I (town economy, *i.e.* all groups except agricultural), and Group II (agriculture). Each group of producers is represented in the Council of Producers in proportion to its participation in the total production of the respective territorial-political unit (town, district, the states, the federal government). The Council of Producers together with the house of general political representatives elects, in all representative organs of the country, all the executive organs of the State and considers and decides with equal rights all questions that concern changes in the Constitution, planning, economy, budget, finances, working relations, and social security. The Council of Producers reflects the tendency to emphasize the primary role of the working class and is intended to enable those who actually create values and provide surplus products (*i.e.* direct producers) to take part effectively in the distribution of and control over the use of national income and in the management of the national economy.

If we wanted to describe in the briefest possible way the changes of the last four or five years in Yugoslavia, we would say that they consist of decentralization (horizontal and vertical), destatism, debureaucratization, and the widest possible democratization of economic, political, and social life.

In this spirit two further codes were enacted: the Criminal Code of March 1951, which came into force on July 1, 1951, and the Code of Criminal Procedure of September 10, 1953, which came into force on January 1, 1954. The Criminal Code, in addition to its general part, which contains the provisions relating to criminal responsibility and punishment (common to all criminal offenses), also contains a specific part that deals with specific offenses classified under sixteen groups: criminal offenses against the people and the State, criminal offenses against humanity and international law, against freedom and rights of citizens, against honor and reputation, against personal dignity and morals, against marriage and the family, against the national economy, against social and private property, and others. The Code of Criminal Procedure includes many provisions contained in the earlier code in this particular field, but it also embodies considerable innovations, especially touching the status of the accused and procedure—innovations that tend to enlarge his rights in criminal proceedings against him. It introduces new procedures under which investigative functions are transferred to the courts, and certain other innovations. By the enactment of these codes, the codification of the criminal law, both substantive and procedural, has been completed in Yugoslavia. Of course this does not mean that the enactment of new provisions modifying and amending the existing specific groups of criminal offenses is excluded. Indeed, at this very moment the problem of so-called economic offenses and that of the criminal responsibility of legal persons arise in a fairly acute form. The independent economic and legal activity of economic enterprises and their interest in the increase of profits, combined with an inadequately developed social consciousness, may well tempt their organs to commit certain illegal, criminal acts.

III

One of the fundamental *legal* questions of present-day Yugoslavia is the codification of the law that relates to property, and more particularly the law that relates to the economy, as well as certain other areas involving the completion and adjustment of the legal system. This problem occupies the minds of statesmen and politicians as well as theoreticians and practical jurists. It is a matter to which the Federal Executive Council and the Federal People's Assembly have devoted attention; it is expressly mentioned in the constitutional law of January 13, 1953 (Article 15). This same problem was emphasized by the First Congress of Jurists of Yugoslavia, held at the beginning of October 1954 in Belgrade. Some 2,000 delegates from all over the country were assembled, representing all branches of Yugoslavian legal activity. The Congress discussed the question at length, and its concluding resolution contains a special paragraph on codification. It declares that the codification of the law relating to property and in particular the law relating to the economy—based on social ownership, planned orientation of economic development, and self-management of economic organizations (enterprises, co-operatives)—is of the greatest significance. It adds that a theoretical elaboration of the codification problem is a vital condition for the construction of the socialist legal system of Yugoslavia.

Yugoslav jurists, in their studies and public discussions, point out that the creation of an adequate socialist system cannot successfully be fulfilled on the basis of the doctrine of "social explosion"; that is, by constant change and constant reorganization. Although it is necessary, they say, to reject "social statics" as an aim *per se* or as a law of human society, it would also be a mistake to proclaim "social dynamics" as the prime goal and as a law of socialism. It is necessary to complete, build on, and adjust the Yugoslav legal system, which is still unfinished and undeveloped, and which still has a good many discordant elements: "the old," which survives in part, albeit with modifications, mixes with "the new," which tends to affirm and develop itself. Yet, even when the legal system *is* technically completed, it will still "be in process of becoming"; that is to say, out of it and within it changes by constant betterment and constant internal adjustment will always take place, so that there will finally be created a system that will be no longer a system of positive law, "but an aggregate of adjusted moral principles and rules, a system which will find its support predominantly in the conscience of developed and free socialist citizens and in the automatic reaction of society against the acts of individuals who might want, not to destroy the whole system, because that will then no longer be possible, but only to violate certain rules of social behavior."[20] But even before this it is necessary to pass through certain phases of stabilization—certain processes of "strengthening based on fundamental achievements," so that the basic foundations, forms, and institutions of the new social arrangement can be better perfected and accepted on a broader scale.

What are the basic problems of codification of the laws relating to property and in particular the laws relating to the economy in Yugoslavia—the problems that have now become especially acute?

History shows us that codifications appear in developed legal systems, so that, in order for codification to be successful, it is necessary for law to have reached a certain degree of development. On the other hand, codification also means the end of a period and the beginning of a new one in the development of the given society. Therefore the first question that arises is the sociopolitical conditions of codification. This question has recently arisen in Yugoslavia and, as we have already seen, it has been answered in the affirmative. In this connection it should be noted that complete unanimity does not exist on this point. Both at the Congress of Jurists and elsewhere there was and still is a current of opinion that maintains that the required sociopolitical and even legal conditions for codification do not yet exist. The majority is nevertheless of the view that there are in Yugoslavia today both the need and the required conditions for successful codification of the law relating to property and of the law relating to the economy.

Many of the technical problems raised by such codification still have to be settled; for example, it is necessary (1) to clarify legal concepts—to define the precise legal content of the new institutions, concepts, and principles, as well as the content of the old institutions that are applied under the new conditions; (2) to create a unified system of legal concepts that correspond as fully as possible with existing social realities; and (3) to solve the question of classification of the matters involved, as well as to ascertain whether the codification shall be effected by means of a single legislative act or by several acts. In connection with this issue, it is important also to consider how deeply the projected code would interfere with social relations and how far its provisions should be the creation of theory and political doctrine, how far the creation of practice and everyday life.

IV

Two fundamental legal concepts must be clarified here—two new and basic institutions whose legal content and nature must be established as exactly as possible. They are *social ownership* and the *right of management* of the property held by social (socialist) legal persons, and especially by economic organizations, *i.e.* enterprises.

In the statutory provisions now in force, *i.e.* in the regulations that have the force of law, passed at the end of 1953 and the beginning of 1954 by the Federal Executive Council and confirmed by the Federal Assembly, as well as in the law relating to real estate transfers of June 1954,[21] the question of the system of social ownership is not yet solved in its entirety; not all relations regarding social ownership are completely settled, although they are extensively regulated. Therefore the theoreticians and the law-makers, when it comes to the codification, will have not only to classify the materials involved, to formulate and systematize the legal rules, but also to act creatively and perhaps even reformatively.

From the discussions now taking place in Yugoslavia, and especially from those conducted at the Congress of Jurists on the basis of the statutory provisions in force, and in consideration of what existing theory and current ideological and political thinking hold could be done, we can come to the following conclusions regarding the legalities of social ownership in Yugoslavia:

According to some (Gerskovic[22] and others), social ownership is primarily an institution of constitutional law. It reflects the fact of nationalization of the means of production and the fact of social management of the general national (*i.e.* nationalized) property. A single organ of society that can perform the role of the general legal possessor of social ownership does not exist and is not even needed. Different social organs have different rights in managing the various portions of social ownership. Social ownership consists of objects which in their entirety belong to society, while the right of use, enjoyment, disposition, and exclusion of others—that is to say, everything that constitutes the content of ownership—refers only to specific pieces or objects of social ownership. The social organs—enterprises, establishments, the relevant governmental organs of the various territorial-political units—are the possessors only of certain rights that stem from social ownership, and these organs, by basing themselves on the right of management, exercise clearly defined rights on behalf of society, including the real right to specific portions of social property. The enterprise as a legal person is not the owner of the property that it manages; all the acquisitions that it makes in the course of legal transactions are made in the name and for the account of society. Individual workers can only acquire the fruits of their work in the form of their right to earnings (wages), which constitutes the legal form of this acquisition. There is, therefore, a division of the functions performed in the enjoyment of the right of social ownership—a division that manifests itself in the various forms inherent in the exercise of the right of management that various social organs possess. In addition to its aspects based on constitutional law (public law), it should be noted that social ownership also has aspects based on civil law. They become evident in legal transactions connected with the transfer of objects from private ownership to social ownership and *vice versa,* as well as in actions for restitution brought against private persons and in similar actions brought by private persons claiming the return of objects from social ownership. In all these cases the social legal person—which appears either as the subject of the legal transaction or as defendant or plaintiff—acts only as the representative of society and not as the owner. For this reason there is, according to the view under discussion, no need at all to have one single possessor of social ownership. It is, however, necessary to determine precisely which social legal persons can sue individual citizens or be sued by citizens for claims involving property rights.

According to others (Rastovčan, etc.), social ownership in Yugoslavia today is not the same as State ownership in capitalist countries, nor is it identical with State ownership in the Soviet Union. They consider, however, that it would be wrong to disrupt the entity of social acquisition, and therefore it would also be wrong to dismember social ownership, which must theoretically be given one single possessor. And this possessor, according to this school of thought, is the national community of the Federal

People's Republic of Yugoslavia considered as a State. For, they argue, "for society there is no other legal term but State, at least as long as the State exists"[23] (*i.e.* while it does not whither away). The element that does not exist in any other State, and that gives Yugoslav economic law its true socialist character is the right of management. *According to this conception, the right of management is the central institution of Yugoslav economic law, and it puts even the very right of social ownership in second place.* The right of management is a very broad right enjoyed by the limited political-territorial units (people's republics, districts, towns, and municipalities) and by direct producers. It is their own right guaranteed by the Constitution. This right restricts social ownership in the hands of the joint representative, the Federal People's Republic of Yugoslavia, as ownership is practically and *de facto* restricted even according to Anglo-American conceptions, if in regard to one and the same object there are other real rights and titles.

A third group (Gams and others) begins from the *economic* substance of ownership—from acquisition as the process "which amalgamates the concrete, the useful value, 'usefulness,' of a commodity with our own needs."[24] In the final analysis, they argue, the object is acquired by the one who uses it in the way in which he uses it, regardless of the question how this relation is legally to be regulated and expressed. Consequently ownership exists only where there exists such real acquisition. According to this opinion there is no room for discussion of whether ownership withers away or not, or whether it has a subject or not. In Yugoslav positive law all legal relations are formulated as subjective law, and this is therefore done in regard to ownership, too. That is why ownership must have its subject. And who is it? "To say that it is society as a whole may be correct from the sociological point of view but legally that is not enough. In the present phase of the development of productive forces, when a commodity economy necessarily still exists . . . it is impossible for society as a whole to acquire the objects of socialist ownership."[25] For, they say, the commodity economy under a more profound analysis reveals itself as a reflex of the divergent interests of individuals and of the limited social collectives as against society as a whole. From the point of view of law the subject of socialist ownership is a legal expression and an organ representing society. The broadest representative of society is the State; in the particular case it is the Federal People's Republic of Yugoslavia which is the broadest subject of social, *i.e.* socialist, ownership. The representatives of this school of thought add that other subjects of social ownership are the various people's republics, the limited political-territorial communities, and the economic organizations. *Accordingly, social ownership is divided like any other and earlier forms of collective ownership. There is therefore more than one subject of such ownership.* The State community, *i.e.* the Federal People's Republic of Yugoslavia, is the supreme ranking subject "because it co-ordinates the authorizations and the interests of the lower ranking subjects"[26] (the limited communities). However, according to this conception the socialist type of social ownership is divided, not only according to its subjects, but also according to the nature of the powers vested in them. Contrary to private ownership, which by itself vests complete authorization to deal with objects in accordance with the free and inexorable will of the owner, the acquisition of objects of social ownership is effected according to a certain order and arrangement, according to a certain plan. The plan is an integral part of the socialist type of social ownership; today in Yugoslavia it consists in the first place of economic and financial instruments by means of which the realization and the distribution of the national income are anticipated. And since the plan, by its nature, belongs to the area of public law, the content of social ownership, too, appears primarily as an institution of public law, because it gives the subjects of that ownership certain financial authorizations pertaining to public law, by means of which they acquire, in various degrees and within various frameworks, the objects of social ownership.

V

The foregoing analysis has dealt with the legal system established in a specific socialist state—namely, postwar Yugoslavia—and with the growing movement for codification in that country. The codification of the law pertaining to property and the economy that is being prepared by Yugoslav lawmakers in close co-operation with theoreticians and professional practitioners will, no doubt, introduce a great deal of innovation both into Yugoslav law and into social relations in general. But it will not be able to by-pass certain categories, institutions, and instruments of law that are the product of social creative activity, which constitute the general achievement of human civilization and cultural heritage, and among which the French Civil Code has its esteemed place.[27]

NOTES

1 Anti-Fascist Council for National Liberation of Yugoslavia.

2 Official Gazette, Federal People's Republic of Yugoslavia, No. 86, October 25, 1946.

3 Yugoslavia is today a federation of six state units called "republics."

4 Official Gazette, F.P.R.Y., No. 2 (1945) and No. 63 (1946).

5 *Id.*, No. 36 (1945) and No. 52 (1946).

6 *Id.*, No. 98 (1946) and No. 35 (1948).

7 *Id.*, No. 89 (1945).

8 Under the law referred to, landless peasants from poorer regions were given land in other portions of the country, which they were to "colonize."

9 Official Gazette, F.P.R.Y., No. 64 (1945), No. 24 (1946), and No. 105 (1948).

10 One hectare equals 2.471 acres.

11 Official Gazette, F.P.R.Y., No. 62 (1946).

12 *Id.*, No. 36 (1947).

13 *Id.*, No. 44 (1946).

14 *Id.*, No. 29 (1946).

15 *Id.*, No. 104 (1947).

16 *Id.*, No. 30 (1947).

17 *Ibid.*

18 *Id.*, No. 46 (1950).

19 *Id.*, No. 3 (1953).

20 Djordjevic, "*O nekim aktuelnim pitanjima dalje izgradnje naseg pravnog sistema*" ("Some present questions concerning the further creations of a Yugoslav legal system"), in *Nova Administracija*, Beograd, No. 3 (1954), 197, 199.

21 Yugoslavia has not nationalized all land and buildings. As has been mentioned, how-

ever, a part of the arable land and many building sites, as well as individual buildings, especially in towns, have become social property. Most land and buildings are, nonetheless, still privately owned.

[22] Gerskovic, *O osnovnim institutima imovinskog prava (Fundamental devices of property law)* (1954).

[23] Rastovcan, *O problemima kodifikacije s narocitim osvrtom na kodifikaciju privrednih propisa (Codification issues with special reference to the codification of economic laws),* 5 (1954).

[24] Gams, *Neka pitanja u vezi sa kodifikacijom prava svojine (Some questions pertaining to the codification of property law),* 2 (1954).

[25] *Id.* at 3.

[26] *Id.* at 4.

[27] The following short Bibliography will be of interest to those desiring to pursue further researches into recent Yugoslav law:

J. B. Tito, Radnicko upravljanje u privredi (Workers' Management of State Economic Enterprises), Beograd, 1950.

E. Kardelj, Osnovi drustvenog i politickog uredjenja Jugoslavije (Fundamentals of the [new] social and political system of Yugoslavia), Beograd, 1953.

Dr. J. Djordjevic (Professor of Law, University of Belgrade), Some principles of socialist democracy in Yugoslavia, "The New Yugoslav Law," Beograd, No. 3–4 (1952), pp. 10–19.

———, O nekim aktuelnim pitanjima dalje izgradnje naseg pravnog sistema (Some present questions concerning the further creation of a Yugoslav legal system), "Nova administracija," Beograd, No. 3 (1954), pp. 197–213.

Dr. L. Gerskovic (Secretary for Legislation and Organization in the Federal Executive Council), Sistem—osnovni principi propisa o privrednom sistemu (Fundamental principles of legal prescriptions pertaining to the economic system), "Ekonomska politika," Beograd 1954, February 4, 11, 18, 25; March 4, 11, 18, 25.

———,O osnovnim institutima imovinskog prava (Fundamental devices of property law), Report (mimeographed) at the First Congress of Yugoslav jurists, Beograd, October 3–6, 1954; 13 pp.

Dr. B. Blagojevic (Professor of Law, University of Belgrade), Uticaj francuskog Gradjanskog zakonika na srbijanski Gradjanski zakonik (Influence of the French Civil Code on the Serbian Civil Code (1844), "Pravna Misao," Beograd (1939), No. XI–XII, pp. 477–93; (1940), No. I–II, pp. 43–84.

Dr. P. Rastovčan (Professor of Law, University of Zagreb), O problemima kodifikacije s narocitim osvrtom na kodifikaciju privrednih propisa (Codification issues with special reference to the codification of economic laws), Report (mimeographed) at the First Congress of Yugoslav jurists, Beograd, October 1954; 9 pp.

Dr. A. Finžgar (Professor of Law, University of Ljubljana), Drustvena svojina kao osnova naseg pravnog sistema (Social property as the base of the Yugoslav legal system), Report (mimeographed) at the First Congress of Yugoslav jurists, Beograd, October 1954; 47 pp.

Dr. A. Lazarevic (Associate Professor of Law, University of Skoplje), O problemima kodifikacije s narocitim osvrtom na privredne propise (Codification issues with special reference to the codification of economic laws), Report (mimeographed) at the First Congress of Yugoslav jurists, Beograd, October 1954; 21 pp.

Dr. A. Gams (Associate Professor of Law, University of Belgrade), Neka pitanja u vezi sa kodifikacijom prava svojine (Some questions pertaining to the codification of property law), Report (mimeographed) at the First Congress of the Yugoslav jurists, Beograd, October 1954; 9 pp.

Dr. L. Lukic (Associate Professor of Law, University of Belgrade), O nekim problemima kodifikacije (Some issues of codification), "Arhiv za pravne i drustvene nauke," Beograd, 1954, No. 2, pp. 121–44.

N. Smailagic, Odnos revolucije i prava (Revolution and the Law), "Pregled," Sarajevo (1954), No. 3, pp. 187–97.

Dr. N. Stjepanovic (Professor of Law, University of Belgrade), Les reformes constitutionnelles et administratives en Yougoslavie 1950–1953, Revue International des Sciences Administratives, Bruxelles (1954), No. 1, pp. 119–42.

12

The Code and Public Law

BERNARD SCHWARTZ

ONE CALLED on to discuss the influence of the Code Napoleon on the field of public law cannot help recalling a famous passage from *The Memoirs of Sherlock Holmes.* In a case involving the disappearance of a champion race horse Holmes was asked by the horse's owner: " 'Is there any point to which you would wish to draw my attention?'

" 'To the curious incident of the dog in the night-time.'

" 'The dog did nothing in the night-time.'

" 'That was the curious incident,' remarked Sherlock Holmes."

The jurist who asks about the influence of the Napoleonic Code on public law will be answered, as Holmes was, that the Code has had no influence. It is, however, the absence of influence that has been the significant thing. For it has enabled the public law of France to evolve in a manner unlike that in which its private law, wholly dependent on the Code, has been developed. And this difference has, in turn, made the methods and techniques of French public law more akin to those employed in the common law than is generally supposed.

JUDGE-MADE LAW

The common lawyer who seeks to pursue research in a civil-law system, such as that in France, soon finds that he must work along lines to which he is wholly unaccustomed. The concepts and tech-

---

BERNARD SCHWARTZ *is Professor of Law and Director of the Institute of Comparative Law at New York University* niques that have served him so well in his own law are all too often handicaps to accurate understanding. He is now in a system in which the case law is of secondary significance; in which the legislative *ought* is, at least in theory, of more importance than the *is* of the decided case. For he is in a realm where the Code reigns supreme. "Franco-German doctrine rests upon the absolute sovereignty of the written law."[1] Legal principles are deduced from the law laid down by the legislator. The role of the judge is limited to interpretation and to filling in the lacunae in the Code. The inductive method, which is second nature to the Anglo-American, leads only to misconceptions.

The Code Napoleon was, however, promulgated at a time when legal thought was concerned primarily with the field of private law. Public law, in the modern sense, had only begun to develop. Codification was hence largely a codification of the rules of private law. The result was that when the need arose for a system of public law and, above all, with the diffusion of the democratic ideal, for a system of legal principles to govern the relations of the State with the citizen, such a system had to be developed without the aid of a detailed set of authoritative principles laid down in a code. If such a system were to be developed at all, in the absence of legislative intervention, it had to be done by the judges, along the lines that are so familiar to the common lawyer. In this field the judicial role was not limited to filling in the gaps in the Code. The judge was confronted with a *tabula rasa,* much as were the creators of the common law.

The normal reluctance of the judge in a civil-law system to make law, in the Anglo-American sense, has had to give way in the face of the need for defined rules in the field of public law. The need for such rules has been at least as pressing in countries governed by the civil law as it has been in the common-law world. "How to fit ancient liberties, which have gained a new preciousness, into solution of those exigent and intricate economic problems that have been too long avoided rather than faced, is the special task of Administrative Law," wrote Justice Frankfurter in 1941.[2] An adequate system of administrative law fulfills the task referred to by ensuring that governmental functions shall be exercised "on proper legal principles"[3]—"according to the rules of reason and justice,"[4] and not at the mere caprice of the magistrate. It affords a remedy to the citizen who has been adversely affected by improper governmental action.

As has been indicated, the development of a system of public and administrative law to attain these ends has, in France as in the common-law world, been largely the handiwork of the judge. In this respect the *droit administratif,* unlike most other branches of French law, bears a close resemblance to the kind of law prevalent in the Anglo-American system. The French administrative lawyer, like his confrere in the common-law world, is accustomed to derive the basic principles of his system inductively from the decided cases. Since these principles have not been clearly expressed by the legislature, they have had to be worked out by "the gradual process of judicial inclusion and exclusion,"[5] much as they have in Anglo-American law. The judge, having to seek a correct solution in the infinite variety of cases presented to him, and finding no clear guide in a code enunciating the fundamentals of administrative law, has had to establish these himself.[6] It is this necessity that gives to the common lawyer seeking a comparative understanding of the *droit administratif* a facility of comprehension that is his in almost no other branch of a civil-law system. French administrative law, like that of the system in which he has been grounded, is judge-made law.

AUTONOMOUS PUBLIC LAW

The fact that the Code Napoleon has not had any direct influence on the field of public law has, however, meant that there is a fundamental difference between the approach of the common lawyer and that of the civil lawyer to questions of public law.

"Since the work of Dicey, the contrast between Continental systems, which distinguish between administrative law and private law and have a separate system of law Courts for each, and the Anglo-American system, which professes to know only one type of law, is familiar to Anglo-American lawyers."[7] In the common-law world, as is well known, there has been no sharp dichotomy between public law and private law.[8] Questions of public law have, with us, been determined by the ordinary law courts and on the basis of principles worked out by analogy from those developed by them in private-law cases. "In short, the principles of private law have with us been by the action of the courts and Parliament so extended as to determine the position of the Crown and of its servants; thus the constitution is the result of the ordinary law of the land."[9]

The situation in a civil-law country, such as France, is entirely different. Its legal system is grounded on a division between public law and private law. "A cardinal distinction of great antiquity," declares the leading contemporary treatise on French private law, "must be made between the rules of *public law* that govern the activities of the State or of persons acting in the public interest and the rules of *private law* that govern the relations of individuals acting in their personal interest."[10] Since the Revolution, indeed, a clear-cut separation between public law and private law has been the dominant feature of legal doctrine in France. As it has been expressed by an outstanding French jurist, such doctrine "establishes an absolute separation, a sort of impassable wall, between public law and private law, maintains that principles valid where the relations of private individuals are concerned cease to be valid when they are applied to the relations between the government and its employees or between the government and private citizens. The starting point is the notion that private law is a body of rules applicable to persons who are equal, but that these rules are no longer applicable where questions of public law are to be decided, because such questions arise between persons who are not equals, one of whom, the State or some public agency, is in a superior position, a position of authority over the other."[11]

What have been the practical effects of the fact that, in France, public law and private law form, as it were, in de Tocqueville's phrase,[12] two separate worlds? It has resulted in a development of public law wholly unlike that which has occurred in the Anglo-American system. The dichotomy in the French legal system has meant complete autonomy for public law, which has been able to evolve independently of the law governing the relations of private individuals. Public law in France has been administered by a series of administrative courts, wholly separate from the ordinary law courts, which, since the Revolution, have been barred from exercising jurisdiction in other than private-law cases. And the law fashioned by the French administrative courts has been worked out by them free from the direct influence of the principles of private law.

This independence has been clear ever since the decision in 1873 of the celebrated Blanco case.[13] That case, which remains still the most famous in the jurisprudence of French public law, dealt with the question of public tort liability. In the course of its decision the court made the following statement, since repeated in innumerable cases. "The liability which falls upon the State for damages caused to private individuals by the acts of persons employed by it in the public service cannot be governed by the principles laid down in the Civil Code for the regulation of the relations of private individuals. Such liability . . . has its own special rules, which vary according to the needs of the administrative service and the necessity of reconciling the rights of the State with private rights."[14]

The Blanco decision had the effect of emancipating French public law from the restrictions imposed by private-law concepts. Its holding eliminated the notion of fault, on which the private law of torts in France was grounded, from the law of public liability.[15] But its implications are much broader, and it is these that are of significance for our present purposes. For the Blanco case is the basis of the autonomy of public law, which, as has been indicated, sharply differentiates the French from the Anglo-American legal system. There is no reason why what is true, under the Blanco decision, of the law of State responsibility is not also true of public law in general. And, in fact, the administrative courts in France have regarded the Blanco case as a mandate to them to develop their public law as a body of law distinct from the ordinary private law, proceeding on wholly different principles. French public law, as a consequence, has come to be based on the existence of a special law for cases involving the administration, as well as of special courts to decide such cases.[16] In the French system "the relation of the government and its officials towards private citizens must be regulated by a body of rules which are in reality laws, but which may differ considerably from the laws which govern the relation of one private person to another. This distinction between ordinary law and administrative law is one which since 1800 has been fully recognized in France, and forms an essential part of French public law."[17]

PRIMACY OF PRIVATE LAW

To the common lawyer the civil-law treatment of public law as wholly apart from the law applicable in cases arising out of disputes between private individuals "rests on ideas foreign to the fundamental assertions of our English common law, and especially to what we have termed the rule of law."[18] Anglo-American jurists have always felt that the absence of a separate body of public law, in the Continental sense, has constituted the great strength of our jurisprudence. It is this absence that has enabled control over the legality of executive action in the common-law world to be maintained by the same institutions that administer the ordinary law of the land, and on the same basic principles of justice. Basic in our system has been a rejection of the French conception of autonomy of public law. With us, cases involving State action have been placed in the same position as those involving the action of ordinary citizens. Public-law cases, like those in the field of private law, are decided by the law courts, and our judges have refused to accept the notion that wholly different rules must be applied in their decision.

If anything, indeed, the outstanding feature of the Anglo-American legal system has been, at least until recently, the primacy of private, as compared with public, law. The subordinate position of public law in the common-law world has been a natural result of our refusal to oust the ordinary courts of jurisdiction in other than private-law cases.[19] Judges whose principal concern was administering justice between private citizens were to be expected to decide cases involving agents of the State in accordance with the principles already developed by them in the fields of law that they were accustomed to dealing with. It should not be forgotten that the need for Anglo-American courts to resolve questions of public law, in the modern sense, is comparatively recent. Only in the contemporary State has the lack of an adequately developed system of administrative law become especially evident. And when our courts were finally confronted, because of the tremendous expansion of the role of the State during the past century, with the necessity of deciding an ever-growing number of public-law cases, they had at hand to aid them the fully developed system of the common law.

At the time when the common law was being developed by the King's courts at Westminster the role of the State was, as is well known, nothing like what it has become in the present-day world. Government was then but one of many competing power structures and, at times, not even the strongest of them, at that. In the modern State, on the other hand, "there is not a moment of his existence where . . . man does not find himself in contact with government and its agents."[20] Government tends more and more to become the all-dominant factor in society by taking over or controlling the functions heretofore performed by private institutions. As it does so it comes into ever-increasing contact with the individual life. "It is in this ceaseless contact of the individual with the State that the danger of arbitrariness has especially arisen."[21] It was not surprising that our judges, in developing a system of public law to help minimize this danger, proceeded whenever they could by analogy with the principles of the common law that had been constructed so meticulously by their predecessors in the resolution of centuries of private-law disputes. The result has been that, in the Anglo-American system, the State has been subject, not only to the same judges as the individual, but also to the same law.

In both respects, as has already been mentioned, the situation in the common-law world is wholly unlike that which prevails in Continental legal systems such as that in France. Nor, from the French jurist's point of view, is the difference in this respect necessarily unfavorable to his system. "In reality," asserts a leading treatise on French administrative law, "for France, the system is, on the whole, satisfactory. It is wise not to submit cases involving the knowledge of administrative law and the necessities of administrative life to the law courts. The law courts do not possess such knowledge. They would be inclined either to exaggerate the prerogatives of the administration or to neglect them through ignorance or partisanship."[22]

The development of public law in the common-law world shows that there is some truth in the above analysis. Anglo-American judges have both neglected the rightful claims of administration, through ignorance and an inordinate bias in favor of private law, and, more recently, have been coming to exaggerate the prerogatives of administration, influenced by excessive deference to claims of administrative *expertise*. In many respects the latter tendency is the more important one, for it can lead to the practical ineffectiveness of our system of judicial control of administrative action.

The primacy of private law that has been, at least until recently, the outstanding feature of the common-law world has been characterized, as we have already seen, by the refusal of Anglo-American courts to treat cases involving questions of public law any differently from those involving only disputes between ordinary individuals. "In Blackstone's system," as Dean Pound succinctly expresses it, "public law is a part of the private law of persons. Officials are persons and the law applicable to them is the law applicable to everyone else."[23] The result is that, as far as possible, public law cases have been decided by our courts in accordance with the same principles that have been developed by them in the field of private law.

Reliance on private-law concepts to deal with cases involving questions of public law has been, in the view of most common lawyers, one of the fundamental bases of the rule of law. And it cannot be denied that, even today, there is still much to be said for this point of view. The primacy of private law in the Anglo-American world has, until now at any rate, prevented the acceptance in our system of the notion that the administration of justice must be dualist—that different rules are to be applied to State action, that different consequences are to follow where the acts of governmental officials are involved, that such cases are to be removed from the cognizance of the ordinary law courts. It has enabled us successfully to reject the consequences flowing from these ideas: that the official is to be placed on a higher plane than the individual, that immunity must be given to government officials *qua* officials.

At the same time it should be recognized that the primacy of private law in our system has also had undesirable consequences. It has been, at least in part, the reason why common-law jurisprudence has been so long delayed in fashioning an adequate system of administrative law to govern the relations between the State and the citizen. "In this country and in England," wrote a pioneer American administrative lawyer in 1893, "where no serious attempt has been made to classify the law in accordance with the relations which it governs, the term administrative law is almost meaningless. While we speak with perfect propriety of administration as indicative of a function of government, and of the administrative as an executive organization, there is hardly an American or English lawyer who would recognize the existence of a branch of law called administrative law."[24] At a time when public law was considered a part of the everyday law for the ordinary courts,[25] it is hardly surprising that Anglo-American jurists could declaim, with Dicey, that "In England, and in countries which, like the United States, derive their civilisation from English sources, . . . administrative law and the very principles on which it rests are in truth unknown."[26]

The failure to take cognizance of administrative law as a recognized rubric of Anglo-American law did not, however, prevent administrative law from developing in the common-law world. What that failure did do was to make an orderly development of the system more difficult. In this respect the situation in the common-law world can be compared to that which prevails in a country like France. *Droit administratif* has been recognized as an important branch of French law almost from its beginnings in the post-Revolutionary era. And almost from the beginning French jurists have turned their attention to the subject, with the result that important doctrinal writings on administrative law have been common in France for over a century. As early as the 1870's there began to appear the classics of modern French administrative law. With them came a synthesis and systematization of the *droit administratif* far beyond anything attempted in the common-law world. With the aid of constant classification and analysis by doctrinal writers French administrative law has been able to develop in an orderly fashion.

Anglo-American administrative law, on the other hand, has been characterized largely by the planlessness of its development. "Thus far our Administrative Law has largely 'growed' like Topsy."[27] Nor has there been any real attempt at systematization and synthesis by doctrinal writers, in the French sense. Indeed, perhaps the most salient thing about the field of administrative law in the common-law world has been that detailed textbooks devoted to it have been almost nonexistent. This lack is most striking, especially when one compares it with the situation in other branches of Anglo-American law. If one seeks to solve a problem, no matter how piddling, arising in a field of private law, one can turn to a plethora of texts to aid one. But let one's case refer to the relations of the administration and the citizen, and there is an almost complete dearth of doctrinal writing. As was recently stated in a work seeking to explain the fundamentals of the American system to a civil-law audience, "an over-all account of administrative law does not yet exist in contemporary American literature."[28]

The lack of adequate doctrinal writings on Anglo-American administrative law has been a direct result of the common lawyer's almost exclusive concentration on private law. And, as has been pointed out above, that lack itself has been, in large part, responsible for the failure of our administrative law to evolve in a more orderly and systematic manner. It should be noted that the relationship between the lack of writings and the lag in developing an adequate system of administrative law is a direct causal one. "This is no accident. Wherever courts have power to form the law, there writers of texts will also have influence."[29] A system of law, such as that in the Anglo-American world, based primarily on case law and the inductive method, is bound to be profoundly influenced by the writers of textbooks and commentaries. The courts themselves, whose precedents make up the bulk of the law, are concerned mainly with rendering decisions in the cases coming before them, and not with reducing the pre-existing case law into a synthesized system. That is the role of the doctrinal writers. "Courts are affected, as Parliament never is, by the ideas and theories of writers on law. A Court, when called upon to decide cases which present some legal difficulty, is often engaged—unconsciously it may be—in the search for principles. If an author of ingenuity has reduced some branch of the law to a consistent scheme of logically coherent rules, he supplies exactly the principles of which a Court is in need. Hence the development of English law has depended, more than many students perceive, on the writings of the authors who have produced the best textbooks."[30]

PRIVATE-LAW DOCTRINES

Even more important than its effect on the dearth of doctrinal writings that has been, in part, responsible for the common-law world's delay in developing a systematized system of administrative law, has been the primacy of our private law's consequences on the techniques and concepts of our public law. As we have already seen, when the Anglo-American courts began to be confronted with cases involving questions of public law, in the modern sense of that term, they had available the fully developed system of the common law to aid them in their resolution. It was not unnatural for them to decide, wherever possible, in accordance with the concepts and techniques that had served them so well in the private-law cases with which they were accustomed to deal. The result has been the penetration of public law in the common-law world by the spirit and methods of private law. Our system has been distinguished, in Dean Pound's phrase, by its attempt to reduce the whole law to private law.[31]

Anglo-American courts have tended to conceive of the State as just a collective person and then to resolve cases involving the State by analogy with the private law of persons. The common-law system of public law, as Frank J. Goodnow pointed out half a century ago, is characterized by the use of the ordinary judicial machinery and by the application of the ordinary rules of law to the officers of the State. "Thus the government may be regarded as a juristic person when it enters into contracts or violates the rights of individuals, and as such juristic person may be treated as the subject of private rather than public law. If the government is so regarded, the ordinary means of enforcing contracts and redressing wrongs which are applicable to private persons may be adopted in the case of the government. Again the administration may be put in the position of an ordinary suitor, and may be obliged to apply to the courts before it may enforce the law. Such is the case where the law provides for what has been spoken of as judicial process in the execution of the state will. Finally, the officers of the government may be treated as private persons without regard to their official capacity, and their acts done under color of office but not in accordance with the law may then be treated like the acts of private persons and subject to the control of the ordinary courts. If, without jurisdiction, such officers have injured private individuals, they may be made responsible to such individuals in damages."[32]

Our courts have held these consequences to be basic public-law principles. What Anglo-American judges have, however, all too often failed to realize is that private-law principles are frequently ill fitted to the field of public law. Their deficiency in this respect led them to impose on the nascent public law of the common-law world a number of doctrines and conceptions, drawn from the different branches of private law, that were out of place in the new field. And the fact that our public law has since been saddled with these incongruous private-law principles has hindered its effective development. Much of the progress in Anglo-American public law has, in fact, consisted in the elimination or modification of these intrusive private-law doctrines.[33]

ADMINISTRATIVE PROCEDURE CODE

The French system has avoided these difficulties by making its public law wholly autonomous. And this autonomy, in turn, has been possible because, as has been pointed out, public law in France has developed uncontrolled by the private-law principles laid down in the Code Napoleon. Indeed, it is the field of public law alone in France that has not been dominated by the concept of codification. "*Droit administratif* has not been put into a strait-jacket of codification as has private law. This circumstance has had most fortunate effects, permitting constant adaptation to new necessities of life."[34]

Few who are familiar with the subject will deny that both the French and the Anglo-American law have been right in rejecting the concept of codification in the field of administrative law. "The rules of administrative law, taken as a whole, are much too numerous and above all too changeable to lend themselves to codification."[35] It is impossible, as a practical matter, to codify the rules of administrative law, and this is true even in countries where codification of the private law has long been the accepted order of the day. At the same time it should not be thought that less ambitious legislative attempts at systematization in this field are wholly out of place. Administrative agencies are peculiarly sensitive to provisions of statute (whose creatures they are), however general their terms—far more than to the statements of courts.[36] There is a great deal that the legislature can accomplish in administrative law, even though it cannot achieve the ultimate goal of the codifier in such a field. "Without impairing government, a legislative statement of principles will go far toward dispelling the cloud that hovers over the administrative process. It will guide administrators and protect the citizen far more than the judicial review of particular administrative cases, which is available only to those few who can afford it. What is needed is not a detailed code but a set of principles and a statement of legislative policy. The prescribed pattern need not be, and should not be, a rigid mold. There should be ample room for necessary changes and full allowance for different needs of different agencies."[37]

American administrative lawyers have come to see that what has just been said is particularly relevant in the field of administrative procedure. As Dean Pound has aptly expressed it, "there are certain fundamentals of just procedure which are the same for every type of tribunal and every type of proceeding."[38] In this country these procedural fundamentals have been given a constitutional base in the due-process clauses of our federal and state constitutions. In recent years, however, it has come to be seen that the minimal requirements prescribed by due process have not been enough. "The conviction developed, particularly within the legal profession, that this power was not sufficiently safeguarded and sometimes was put to arbitrary and biased use."[39] The resolution of the difficulty has been sought in the imposition by the legislature of proper procedural safeguards. It was the minority members of the Attorney General's Committee on Administrative Procedure who first urged that this be done by the enactment by the Congress of a so-called Code of Standards of Fair Administrative Procedure. According to them, "An adequate pattern of procedure is imperatively needed to serve as a guide to and check upon administrative officials in the exercise of their discretionary powers. . . . No more satisfactory way can be found of minimizing abuses, or the fear of abuses, than by legislative statement of standards of administrative procedure to chart the course of action, to insure publicity of process, to give the citizen every reasonable opportunity to present his case, and to insure that public officials act under circumstances calculated to produce a fair and prompt result."[40] As is well known, the recommendation of the minority of the Attorney General's Committee bore fruit in 1946 with the passage of the Federal Administrative Procedure Act (APA).[41]

It should be obvious to anyone at all familiar with the great European codes (from the Code Napoleon down to more recent enactments) that the Federal Act of 1946 is nothing like a complete and rounded code of administrative law, or even of agency procedure. Nor, it should be noted, is the Procedure Act a revolutionary law that drastically changes pre-existing administrative procedures. What the APA does is to take the essentials of the best pre-1946 agency practices, together with some of the recommendations of the Attorney General's Committee, and give them statutory form. And it does so (and here is its most significant aspect) by making them applicable to the entire federal administrative process.

In specifying the procedures that the federal administration must follow, the Procedure Act does not lay down detailed procedural rules. Despite the title suggested by the minority of the Attorney General's Committee, it is not really even a code of administrative procedure. It contains only twelve sections, none of them long by modern statutory standards. Nor do its provisions supersede the procedural rules promulgated by the different federal agencies. Instead they lay down what the Supreme Court has well termed the "fundamentals of fair play,"[42] the basic procedural principles that are to govern the different types of administrative action. The APA, in other words, establishes a procedural framework within which the federal agencies must operate. All of them must come up to the procedural level prescribed by the 1946 statute, even though the details of their procedures are still primarily for them to determine.

To a comparative observer the American Administrative Procedure Act is a law of fundamental significance. Though the act may not yet have wholly achieved the intent of its draftsmen in practice, this limitation does not mean that it has not been of great value in regularizing federal administrative law. Certainly, to quote a leading American jurist's recent conclusions on this point, "Seams have appeared and, as in the case of the Federal Rules of Civil Procedure after a similar trial period, it may sooner or later require a revision, but even with its defects it has gone far to achieve the goal asserted by Mr. Justice Brandeis, 'In the development of our liberty, insistence upon procedural regularity has been a large factor.' "[43]

The value of the Federal Act of 1946 has, however, been doubted by some non-American jurists. "The introduction of statutory procedures for administrative agencies . . . ," asserts one such writer, "judged by the experience in the United States with the Administrative Procedure Act, 1946, has little to commend it."[44] To one familiar with the provisions of the American act it is difficult to see the basis for so extreme a criticism. From the point of view of individuals adversely affected by administrative action the 1946 act would seem, on the contrary, to mark a substantial step forward in the direction of ensuring adequate procedural safeguards in their dealings with the administration.

It may well be that the criticism quoted is based on the view that the provisions of the federal act, though motivated by a laudable purpose, must, as a practical matter, prove ineffective. This is, indeed, a key point in the consideration of any law. A statute is not self-executing. The legislative *ought* must run the gauntlet of judicial interpretation before it attains the practical status of an *is*. This is true in all legal systems; but it is especially true in this country where the courts play so prominent a constitutional role. The APA, like other legislation, would lose much of its efficacy if its terms were to be read by the courts in a decimating spirit.

Our courts have clearly indicated, however, that they will give the Procedure Act the full remedial effect that the legislature intended it to have. The leading case is Wong Yang Sung v. McGrath,[45] a 1950 decision of the Supreme Court. In that case the Court set aside an order for the deportation of an alien who had not been afforded a hearing before an independent examiner, such as that required under the 1946 act. A case like this, in which an administrative decision is quashed because of the administration's failure to observe the essentials of fair procedure prescribed by the APA, furnishes a pragmatic answer to those who deride the value of that law. Certainly it would be difficult for Wong Yang Sung, saved from deportation only by the American act, to agree with the assertion already quoted that an act like it "has little to commend it."

American developments in the field of administrative procedure are, despite such criticisms, particularly pertinent in other countries. The APA represents the first legislative attempt in the common-law world to ameliorate the defects that have arisen in the administrative process. It is not contended, of course, that a detailed code of administrative procedure is desirable or even feasible. One must ever bear in mind the warning of Lord Shaw against the overcrystallization of the principles of natural justice.[46] The recognition of that fact does not, however, deny the need for a rigid insistence on the "fundamentals of fair play"[47] in administrative action. The Federal Administrative Procedure Act points the way to a legislative formulation of these fundamentals.

In the field of administrative law it is thus the common-law, rather than the civil-law, world that is now moving (albeit not very far as yet) in the direction pointed by the great codification of a hundred and fifty years ago. It is in the United States particularly that the law of administrative procedure has become sufficiently mature to permit some legislative systematization and standardization. In a country like France that law is not nearly so well developed, though there are recent indications that the French system may well in this respect soon duplicate the American experience.[48]

Developments in administrative law bear out the thesis that it is in the field of public law that the American system has its greatest comparative contribution to make. It is precisely in those fields in which the codification technique has not proved fruitful that the methods of the common-law world have been shown to be the most useful. As already noted, the absence of any administrative code has led the French courts concerned with administrative law themselves to develop techniques and methods exactly analogous to those employed by Anglo-American judges. And in the field of administrative procedure it is the common-law system (and particularly the American one) that has evolved a law adequately to protect the private individual at the agency level. And it is the American legislator who has now intervened to introduce greater uniformity of procedure and standardization of administrative practice.[49] In its action in this respect the federal Congress is the first legislature to follow in the footsteps of the draftsmen of the Code Napoleon in the field of public law. It may well be that it will never be possible to have a real code in that field. But that likelihood does not mean that the legislator must adopt a completely hands-off policy and leave the development of administrative law and procedure exclusively to the agencies and the courts. The experience of the federal APA shows, on the contrary, that the legislature too has a vital role to play.

NOTES

1 Alibert, Le Contrôle Juridictionnel de l'Administration 15 (1926).

2 Frankfurter, Foreword, 41 Col. 585, 586 (1941).

3 Pioneer Laundry and Dry Cleaners, Ltd. v. Minister of National Revenue, [1940] A.C. 127, 136.

4 Sharp v. Wakefield, [1891] A.C. 173, 179.

5 Davidson v. City of New Orleans, 96 U.S. 97, 104 (1877).

6 Waline, Traité Élémentaire de Droit Administratif 21 (6th ed. 1951).

7 Friedmann, Legal Theory 382 (3d ed. 1953).

8 See Garner v. Teamsters Union, 346 U.S. 485, 495 (1953).

9 Dicey, Law of the Constitution 203 (9th ed. 1939).

10 1 Ripert, Traité Élémentaire de Droit Civil de Planiol 12 (5th ed. 1950).

11 Duguit, Manuel de Droit Constitutionnel 42 (1923).

12 Quoted, in Dicey, *op. cit. supra* note 9, at 331.

13 February 8, 1873. Tribunal des Conflits.

14 This is the form given in Waline, *op. cit. supra* note 6, at 576; it differs slightly from the original decision.

15 For a fuller discussion, see Schwartz, French Administrative Law and the Common-Law World 289 *et. seq.* (1954).

16 Laubadèrè, Traité Élémentaire de Droit Administratif 25 (1953).

17 Dicey, *op. cit. supra* note 9, at 339.

18 *Id.* at 329.

19 The French law courts, it should be noted, were ousted of such jurisdiction in 1790. See Schwartz, *op. cit. supra* note 15, at 6.

20 Duguit, *op. cit. supra* note 11, at 39.

21 *Id.* at 40.

22 Rolland, Précis de Droit Administratif 277 (10th ed. 1951).

23 Pound, Administrative Law 8 (1942).

24 1 Goodnow, Comparative Administrative Law 6 (1893).

25 Compare Pound, *op. cit. supra* note 23, at 10.

[26] Dicey, *op. cit. supra* note 9, at 330.

[27] Frankfurter, *loc. cit. supra* note 2.

[28] Schwartz, Le Droit Administratif Américain; Notions Générales 231 (1952).

[29] Dicey, *op. cit. supra* note 9, at 375.

[30] Dicey, Law and Public Opinion in England 365 (1926).

[31] Pound, *op. cit. supra* note 23, at 13.

[32] Goodnow, The Principles of the Administrative Law of the United States 378 (1905).

[33] Among the doctrines imported from private law that have, at least to many observers, hampered the proper development of American administrative law are: the maxim against the delegation of legislative power (derived from the law of agency); the doctrine of *ultra vires* (imported from the law of corporations); the rule of strict personal tort liability of public officers (based on the treatment of administrative wrongful acts as private torts); and the concept of government employment as only a privilege (based on the treatment of the State employer as an ordinary private employer).

[34] Waline, *op. cit. supra* note 6, at 20.

[35] *Ibid.*

[36] Report of the Attorney General's Committee on Administrative Procedure 215 (1941).

[37] *Ibid.*

[38] Pound, *op. cit. supra* note 23, at 75.

[39] Wong Yang Sung v. McGrath, 339 U.S. 33, 37 (1950).

[40] *Loc. cit. supra* note 36.

[41] 60 Stat. 237 (1946), 5 U.S.C. § 1001.

[42] Federal Communications Commission v. Pottsville Broadcasting Co., 309 U.S. 134, 143 (1940).

[43] Vanderbilt, The Doctrine of the Separation of Powers and Its Present-Day Significance 94 (1953).

[44] Northey, Curial Review of the Determinations of Administrative Tribunals, 28 New Zealand L. J. 135, 136 (1952).

[45] 339 U.S. 33 (1950).

[46] Local Government Board v. Arlidge, [1915] A.C. 120, 138.

[47] *Loc. cit. supra* note 42.

[48] See Schwartz, *op. cit. supra* note 15, at 208–11.

[49] Wong Yang Sung v. McGrath, 339 U.S. 33, 41 (1950).

13

Codification in Anglo-American Law

ROSCOE POUND

IN the nineteenth century there was but one way of beginning an exposition of any subject. One must begin with its history. As juristically a son of the nineteenth century, I must preface a historical sketch. But I need not go back farther than the seventeenth century. In the sixteenth century the reception of Roman law on the Continent had made some impression on English legal thinking.[1] In the next century French influence was strong under the Stuarts. Then the contemporary proposals for codification in France[2] had an echo on the other side of the channel.

BACON'S PROJECT. A proposal to codify the common law was made by Bacon, then Attorney General, in 1614. It was entitled "A proposition to His Majesty by Sir Francis Bacon, Knight, His Majesty's Attorney General, and one of his Privy Council, Touching the Compiling and Amendment of the Laws of England."[3] His plan, as he stated it, contemplated (1) an institutional part, to be made up of (a) a Book of Institutes, (b) a Treatise on Maxims, and (c) Terms of the Law (*i.e.* an authoritative law dictionary); (2) a new edition of the Year Books, abridging the reports of the cases, leaving out repetitions and queries, and collecting antinomies, which were then to be settled by the opinions of the judges in the Exchequer Chamber or in Parliament; (3) a compilation of statute law, cutting out what was obsolete, repealing what was

ROSCOE POUND *is Dean Emeritus of the Harvard Law School*

dormant and "snaring," mitigating the old severe penalties that had come down from the Middle Ages, and reducing "concurrent statutes to one clear, uniform law." Pursuant to this proposal, among four bills proposed by Bacon at the instance of the Crown in 1614 the second was "An Act giving authority to certain commissioners to review the state of penal laws to the end that such as are obsolete and snaring may be repealed and such as are fit to continue and concern one matter may be reduced respectively to one clear uniform law."[4] This bill contemplated a compilation of penal legislation. The project submitted to the king contemplated codification on the lines of Justinian's Institutes, Digest, and Code. Owing to political controversies the Parliament in which Bacon's bills were introduced was dissolved. Bacon thereupon persuaded the king to take the matter up by royal commission. Accordingly, in 1620 a report was made of what had been done "by direction from the King and the lords of the council upon the advice of the now Lord Chancellor." Bacon was then Chancellor. Seven lawyers, including Sir Edward Coke, Noy (afterwards Attorney General to Charles I), and Finch, who were the commissioners appointed by the king, reported that they had found almost six hundred statutes fit to be repealed. But owing to political controversies nothing more was done.[5] It was well that Bacon's ambitious project came to nought. The time was not ripe for putting the law developed in the King's courts in the Middle Ages in legislative form. Coke's Institutes became books of authority. But his working over and analogical development of Magna Carta, the legislation of Edward I, the later statutes, and the Year Books were needed before the law could be fixed in form for the seventeenth century.

THE ANGLO-INDIAN CODES.[6] A next essay at codifying was brought about by the conditions of administering English law in India. The first of the Anglo-Indian codes was a penal code drawn up by a commission of which Lord Macaulay was a member. It was presented to the Governor General in 1837, but did not become law till 1860. Holland said of it that it was the most scientific piece of legislation in the English language.[7] Lord Bryce, after a full inquiry in India, reported that in 1889 it was regarded by practicing lawyers there as eminently satisfactory.[8] A code of civil procedure was enacted in 1859, and a code of penal procedure in 1861. Meanwhile, as far back as 1840, agitation began in India for a code of substantive law, and a commission was appointed, of which Sir John Romilly and Lord Chief Justice Jervis were members, which in 1855 reported that such a code was required by conditions there. Accordingly a commission was set up, of which Sir John Romilly, Sir William Erle, and Sir John Shaw Willes were among the members, which in 1863 reported a Succession Act, codifying the law of succession except for Hindus, Mohammedans, and Buddhists. A further installment, known as the Contract Act, was reported in 1866 and adopted. Since that time the greater part of the English law in force in India has been codified.[9] Except for the Penal Code the statutes are not well done. They follow too much the Field draft code.[10]

The New York Codes.[11] Agitation for codification in New York was in part a phase of the legislative reform movement of the fore part of the nineteenth century,[12] and it was influenced by the wide attention given to the writings of Bentham.[13] In part it grew out of the hostility toward English institutions and English law in the period after the American Revolution and the favor toward things French that went along with Jeffersonian democracy. Both were well marked in New York. The French Civil Code had fascinated many, as it had almost everyone abroad. Lay discussions of American law in the first part of the nineteenth century abound in demands for an American code.[14] Very likely the connection of Livingston with the code in Louisiana was also an influence. But the prime mover was David Dudley Field.[15] He had urged a general code before the New York constitutional convention in 1846. Largely as a result of his agitation the constitution in 1847 provided for commissioners to reform legal procedure and codify the law.[16] The commission to reform procedure was appointed in 1847 and reported the first installment of the Code of Civil Procedure, which was enacted in April of that year and put in effect in July.[17] The rest of the code was reported from time to time in four different reports until in 1850 complete codes of civil and criminal procedure were submitted to the legislature.[18] The history of the Code of Civil Procedure is well known.[19] Either substantially as reported by Field's commission or in the form of codes based on his draft, it came to be in force in about thirty jurisdictions. After the adoption of the Code of Civil Procedure the enthusiasm for law reform in New York waned, and in 1850 the legislature repealed the act appointing a commission to reform procedure and codify the law.[20] One reason seems to have been that the commission on codifying the substantive law, which was headed by Chancellor Walworth, had proceeded with a deliberation not satisfactory to the public.

Field thereupon renewed his agitation for codification of the common law, and in 1857 the legislature provided for a new commission "to reduce to a written and systematic code the whole body of the law of this state, or so much and such parts thereof as shall seem to them practical and expedient."[21] The commissioners were David Dudley Field, William Curtis Noyes, and Alexander W. Bradford; obviously too small a commission for such a purpose. Noyes undertook the penal code and Field the political and civil codes. In preparing the civil code Field was assisted by Thomas G. Shearman and Austin Abbott, both well known as text writers. This commission put forth the first draft of a civil code in 1862.[22] The draft of the penal code, which had been assigned to Noyes, was presented in 1864.[23] The political code was reported by Field in 1860.[24]

In 1865, after Field had been at work on these codes for eighteen years, the full text of the five codes—namely, the code of civil procedure, the code of criminal procedure, the penal code, the civil code, and the political code—were submitted in the ninth and last report of the commission. For the eighteen years in which Field devoted a large part of his time to these codes, he received no compensation except for the first two years.

The original code of civil procedure adopted in New York was Field's first draft. His final draft was not adopted, but a different one, prepared on a different plan, although founded on Field's code, was adopted between 1876 and 1880.[25] This code, prepared by Throop, went into great detail. Whereas there were 392 sections in Field's original code, in Throop's version these were extended to 3356, and further additions in 1890 and 1897 made the whole number of sections 3441. A great deal of the deservedly severe criticism that has been directed against the New York Code of Civil Procedure applies rather to this attempt to regulate by precise rule every action of the judge from the time he enters the courtroom than to the original Field draft. The Civil Practice Act of 1920 reduced the 3341 sections to 1540 (still too much detail), and further simplification has been going on.

In 1881 the Code of Criminal Procedure was enacted,[26] but the other codes failed of adoption in New York. As was said above, some thirty jurisdictions adopted the code of civil procedure. Sixteen jurisdictions adopted the penal code and the code of criminal procedure. California,[27] Montana,[28] and North and South Dakota[29] adopted all five of Field's codes; California and North and South Dakota have in addition a code of probate law. But it should be said in this connection that the civil code has accomplished little in the four jurisdictions that adopted it. The courts, especially in California, have frequently ignored the civil code, deciding questions as matters of common law, seldom referring to the code or, if they did refer to it, assuming that it was merely declaratory.[30] This attitude of the courts, however, was not the sole cause of the comparative failure of Field's civil code. It must be admitted that the code was by no means well drawn.[31]

THE MOVEMENT FOR CODIFICATION IN MASSACHUSETTS. Along with the movement for codification in New York there was for a time a like movement in Massachusetts. In 1825 the Massachusetts legislature provided for the appointment of commissioners "to take into consideration the practicality and expediency of reducing to a written and systematic code the common law of Massachusetts or any part thereof, and report to the next legislature, subjoining to their report a plan or plans of the best method in which such reduction can be accomplished."[32] The commission appointed consisted of Joseph Story, Theron Metcalf, Simon Greenleaf, Charles E. Forces, and Luther S. Cushing. It reported in December 1836, on the whole distinctly in favor of codification. Its report, reprinted in 1882[33] in connection with one of Bentham's letters to the people of the United States with respect to codification, is one of the classical authorities on the subject. This movement for codification in Massachusetts was during the full tide of the legislative reform movement. Interest in the subject seems to have waned quickly. Judge Story's books soon supplied the need that had been behind the agitation for codification.[34]

THE CIVIL CODE OF GEORGIA (1860). In Georgia in 1858[35] an act of the legislature provided for the election of three commissioners to "prepare for the people of Georgia a Code, which should, as near as practicable, embrace, in condensed form, the laws of Georgia, whether derived from the common law, the Constitution, the Statutes of the State, the Decisions of the Supreme Court or the Statutes of England in force in this State." Three commissioners accordingly were elected. They prepared a code divided into four parts: first part, the political and public organization of the state; second part, the civil code; third part, the code of practice; fourth part, penal laws. For the most part this was simply a compilation and revision of the statute law of the state. But the part known as the civil code, consisting of 1586 sections, is made up of extracts from the ordinary textbooks of the common law in use in this country at that time.

Two examples will suffice to illustrate this code. A typical provision is §1697:[36] "Marriage is encouraged by the law, and every effort to restrain or discourage marriage by contract, condition, limitation or otherwise is invalid and void. Prohibiting marriage to a particular person or persons, or before a certain reasonable age, or other prudential provision looking only to the interest of the person to be benefited, and not in general restraint of marriage will be allowed and held valid." This is taken slightly altered from Story's Equity Jurisprudence.[37] Another is §2739: "A consideration is essential to a contract which the law will enforce. An executory contract without such consideration is called *nudum pactum,* or a naked promise. In some cases a consideration is presumed, and an averment to the contrary will not be received. Such are generally contracts under seal, and negotiable instruments alleging a consideration on their face, in the hands of innocent holders without notice, who have received the same before dishonored." This is taken abridged and somewhat altered from a well-known text writer of that day.[38] It will be seen at once that this is not a code in any modern sense. The best that can be said for it is that it furnished an authoritative textbook of the common law at a time when there were few extensive libraries in the state and few law books at hand in many rural courthouses and many questions remained unanswered in the local reports.

It should be added that the code was prepared in about a year, was reported in 1860, and was adopted that year to take effect in 1862.[39] It goes without saying that codification of the common law by three commissioners in one year is a wholly impossible undertaking. The code has had little effect. For the most part the courts treat it as declaratory of the common law. It means what the common law as found by the court means.

LORD WESTBURY'S PLAN.[40] In 1860 Lord Westbury, then Sir Richard Bethell and Attorney General, announced in Parliament a plan of the government that he represented for a revision and compilation of the statute law of England. In 1863, when he had become Lord Chancellor, in a speech in the House of Lords he proposed that in addition to the revision of the statute law then in progress a digest should be made of the reported cases with a view to an ultimate combination of statutes and cases alike in a digest and finally in a code of the whole English law. In 1866 a royal commission was set up, the members of which were, among others, Lord Cranworth, Lord Westbury, Lord Cairns, Vice-Chancellor Wood (afterward Lord Hatherley), Sir Roundell Palmer (afterward Lord Selborne) and Mr. Thring (afterward Lord Thring and Parliamentary Counsel), which was to "inquire into the expediency of a digest of law, and the best means of accomplishing that object and of otherwise exhibiting in a compendious and accessible form the law as embodied in judicial decisions." The first report of this commission in 1867 endorsed the idea of codification and recommended that the commission be authorized to superintend the preparation of a proposed digest as an example of what might be done. Accordingly some drafts were prepared that finally took the form of textbooks on branches of the common law.[41] Nothing else came of the project. The movement for reorganization of the courts and reform of procedure, which culminated in the Judicature Act (1873), turned the energies of law reformers in a different direction.

The Project in Victoria (1879–1888).[42] In Victoria in 1879 a bill was introduced "to declare, consolidate and amend the general substantive law relating to certain duties of the people." It covered the greater part of the substantive law except as to property. It got no further than a second reading. In 1880 the bill was revised and completed and passed by the Legislative Council, but was not considered by the legislative assembly. In 1881 a part covering obligations was introduced in the Legislative Council but was not proceeded with. But Parliament made an appropriation for the expense of revision, and a "Draft Code of the General Substantive Law of Victoria" was prepared. In 1882 this draft was turned over to a committee of eight barristers for revision.[43] It was in complete form in 1885 and was submitted to the Legislative Council.[44] It was not enacted, but was reintroduced in 1888.[45] The draft, containing in all 3244 sections, was the work of W. E. Hearn, a well-known contemporary writer on economics, jurisprudence, and politics.

Conditions That Have Led to Codification. A number of common features can be found in the conditions that have led to the important codes. In Justinian's time (1) juristic development of the law had come substantially to an end; the possibilities of further juristic development of the traditional element were exhausted. (2) The authoritative legal materials were unwieldy in bulk, and finding out what was the law involved great labor. (3) The body of the law was full of more or less obsolete rules that depended only on history and fitted in ill with the more modern parts of the system. For example, there were legal title and equitable title; there were two orders of succession, legal heir and equitable heir. (4) Many important questions debated by jurists for centuries remained unsettled. (5) A period of legislation had been in progress for some hundreds of years, and the growing point of the law had shifted completely to legislation. Legislation had long been the ordinary form of lawmaking. (6) What was perhaps no less significant, there was general agreement as to the end or purpose of social control and as to the basic principles or starting points for legal reasoning on such subjects as the acquisition and control of material things, the scope and effect of agreements, and the ground of imposing liability to answer for or repair injuries.

When the French Civil Code was adopted, (1) juristic doctrinal development of the purely Roman materials and of the French customary (Germanic) law had substantially come to an end. Pothier had for the time being exhausted the possibilities of purely juristic development of the traditional materials. (2) The law was very unwieldy in bulk and uncertain in form: (a) the modern Roman law; (b) French exposition and commentary; (c) French customary law and exposition and commentary; (d) French legislation; (e) French *usus fori,* which had grown up to a certain extent. (3) The law was full of more or less obsolete rules of a historical sort, some Roman and some Germanic. (4) Many important questions that had been debated on the basis of the Roman texts since the revived study of the Roman law in the twelfth century still remained open. (5) A period of legislation had been in progress for one hundred years—since the ordinances of Louis XIV in which he began to make royal legislation the ordinary agency of growth of the law. The growing point of French law had definitely shifted to legislation. (6) The idea of the end or purpose of the legal order as harmonious maintaining of the social *status quo,* which obtained in antiquity and was taken over by the Middle Ages, had been supplanted by one that began to affect the content and application of the law in the sixteenth century, had been given its final statement at the end of the eighteenth century, and became fully accepted and made to shape the legal system for the nineteenth century. The juristic world was agreed on fundamental starting points, and the French Civil Code could announce them authoritatively in a world prepared to receive them.

One more point must be added. When the French Civil Code was enacted there was imperative need of a unified law. The old provinces had each to a great extent its own law. The customary law (the Germanic element) differed much in detail with each locality. The abolition of the old provinces by the Revolution and the thorough political unification of France demanded a legal unification. There had to be one law of France.

In the same way when the German *Bürgerliches Gesetzbuch* was adopted (first draft 1887, final draft 1896, took effect 1900), (1) the German jurists of the historical school had so completely worked out the possibilities of purely juristic development of the Roman texts that a new start, a new basis for further juristic development, was imperative. (2) The law was unwieldy in bulk and uncertain in form. It was made up of: (a) the *Corpus Iuris Civile,* (b) the academic development of the *Corpus Iuris* from the twelfth to the sixteenth century, (c) the *usus modernus,* that is, German juristic exposition of the modern Roman law on the basis of the practice of the courts; (d) Germanic law (customary) and juristic exposition of it; (e) local codes and legislation; (f) *usus fori,* the settled course of decision on certain points. (3) Many historical rules and traditional doctrines were wholly out of touch with the world of today, e.g. the contract theory of agency. (4) Many fundamental questions, e.g. the will theory or the declaration theory of a legal transaction, remained open and controverted. (5) The growing point of law had definitely shifted to legislation, and an efficient organ of legislative lawmaking was at hand in the empire. (6) Although the stage of legal development that has been called the socialization of law had begun to be manifest about 1890, it had not so disturbed juristic agreement as to the end of law and the fundamental idea of property, contracts, and liability to repair injuries, as to make laying down of fundamental starting points for legal reasoning impossible. It was not so easy to make generally acceptable pronouncements of universal starting points for legal reasoning in 1896 as it was in 1804. But it had not become impossible. Moreover, here again there was an imperative need of a unification. Each of the old states had its own legislation and more or less its own law. The modern Roman law, which was called *gemeines Recht* (the common law of Germany), was a bond more or less feebly uniting these diverse bodies of law just as our Anglo-American common law more or less holds together forty-eight diverse bodies of state law.

A like condition was behind codification in Switzerland.

Two classes of countries have adopted codes: (1) those with well-developed systems that had exhausted the possibilities of juristic development through the traditional element and so needed a new basis for further juristic development—Justinian's empire, Revolutionary France, Austria at the end of the eighteenth century, and the German Empire after 1871 are in this class; (2) those that had their whole modern legal development ahead of them and needed an immediate basis for development. Japan (1896, took effect 1900) is a conspicuous example. China (1930) may be added. In this category we might put also Soviet Russia

(1922), were it not that Soviet law grew to be no more than pretentious window dressing, as is well shown by Gsovski.[46] The Latin-American republics are also in this class. They started from adaptations of the French Civil Code as we started from the seventeenth-century English law.

Another point is significant. For each original code there was a strong organ of legislation that could insure adequate preliminary study and resist the pressure of those not competent to the work. Justinian, Napoleon, the German Empire, Japan engaged the best legal talent that could be had. So also did the Republic of China. Also the German Empire gave the commission ample time.

If historical experience is to be relied on, then, codes are demanded where (1) the traditional element of the law for the time being has substantially exhausted its possibilities, so that a new basis is required for a juristic new start; or, instead, a basis is required on which to build a body of law for a country with no juristic past. (2) Where there is a juristic past, the law has become unwieldy, full of archaisms, and uncertain. (3) The growing point of the law has shifted to legislation, and an efficient organ of legislation has developed. (4) There is need of one law in a political society whose several subdivisions have developed divergent local laws. The fourth is not essential, as Justinian's legislation shows, but it played a great part in bringing about the French, German, and Swiss codes.

Gradual Codification.[47] Perhaps the pioneer bit of partial codification in the formative era of American law is the New York Real Property Law of 1828,[48] revised in 1896.[49] It was a better piece of work than judicial construction and application have made it appear. The English land law of the end of the eighteenth century was far from suitable to pioneer agricultural America or to the developing commercial America of the Atlantic seaboard. The New York statute was necessarily a reforming act, largely making over the law rather than restating it in legislative form. American law was not far enough along in its development in the first third of the nineteenth century to make such an act achieve its purposes. Moreover, common-law lawyers are not at their best in developing legislative texts. They seem bound to treat them as declaratory or else ignore them. But codification of particular branches of the common law, as distinguished from reforming legislation, is a phenomenon of the last decades of the nineteenth century and of the present century. After the adoption of the Judicature Act the need of putting commercial law in England into a more certain form led to three statutes in which portions of the law were codified. These are the Bills of Exchange Act of 1882,[50] codifying the law of negotiable instruments, the Partnership Act of 1890,[51] and the Sale of Goods Act of 1893.[52] This sort of codification—legislative restatement of particular fields of the law—has been going forward in Great Britain, for example, in the English Law of Property Act, 1922, a reforming codification,[53] and the administration of Estates Act, 1925.[54]

Agitation in the United States for uniform commercial law, demanded more and more by increasing economic unification of the country and only feebly maintained by the now abandoned doctrine that the federal courts, where they had jurisdiction because of diversity of citizenship of the parties, would apply what they held to be the common law instead of the law administered by the state courts, was stimulated by the example of the English Bills of Exchange Act. As a result, at the instance of the American Bar Association an annual Conference of Commissioners on Uniform State Laws was organized. It is composed of commissioners appointed by the governors of the several states and meets in connection with the annual meetings of the American Bar Association. It had its inception in a special committee of that Association on Uniform State Laws appointed in 1889.[55] In 1895 the commissioners appointed a committee to draw a draft of an act codifying the law of negotiable instruments to be submitted at the annual meeting in 1896. The draft, drawn in a year, was agreed on and, with some changes of detail in some of the states, has been adopted in fifty-six jurisdictions. In 1901 the commissioners authorized draft of a law to make uniform the law of sales. This was drawn up much more carefully. The first draft was prepared by Professor Williston in 1902 and 1903, was printed in 1903, and was distributed to teachers of law, text writers, and practicing lawyers with a request for criticism. In the light of criticisms submitted, a revised draft was drawn up and presented to the commissioners in 1904. This was gone over section by section at the conference in 1904. A second revised draft was presented and considered in 1906, and then a final draft in 1906, which was adopted by the commissioners. The draft was enacted by some thirty-five jurisdictions. It was the first thoroughgoing bit of common-law codification in the United States. None of the drafts prior to this had been drawn with the thoroughness and care that characterized this act. The important codifying acts drafted by the Commissioners on Uniform State Laws are: the Negotiable Instruments Law (1896), Sales Act (1906), Warehouse Receipts Act (1906), Stock Transfer Act (1909), Bills of Lading Act (1909), Partnership Act (1914), and Conditional Sales Act (1918).[56]

A Uniform Commercial Code, Codifying the Law of Contracts, Commercial Paper, Banking, Warehouse Receipts, Bills of Lading and Other Documents of Title, and Securities, had its inception in 1942 in negotiations between the American Law Institute and the National Conference of Commissioners on Uniform State Laws for co-operation of the two organizations in the production of a model Code of Commercial Law.[57] After eight years of thorough consideration of repeated drafts of separate parts and four drafts of the whole, the final draft was adopted and published in 1950. It has thus far been adopted in but one jurisdiction.[58]

"Private Codification," *i.e.* private texts, in code form, not prepared under public authority, and private texts that put the law in form for codification. Following the example of the books that represented drafts prepared for the commissioners under Lord Westbury's plan,[59] it became not uncommon in England at one time to put textbooks of the law in the form of codes. In addition to the books noted in another connection,[60] Dicey, Rules for the Selection of the Parties to an Action (1870), Dicey, Law of Domicile as a Branch of the Law of England stated in the form of rules (1879), Dicey, Digest of the Law of England with reference to the Conflict of Laws (1896), Bower, Code of Actionable Defamation with a Continuous Commentary (1908), and Bower, The Law of Actionable Misrepresentation Stated in the Form of a Code, followed by a Commentary (1911) may be referred to. We have a book of this sort in the United States in Wigmore, Pocket Code of Evidence (3d ed. 1942).

In this connection the work of the American Law Institute in "restating" the law is specially significant. That organization had its inception in a report submitted to a meeting of representative judges, lawyers, and law teachers at Washington on February 23, 1923. The meeting adopted articles of incorporation, and the Institute was incorporated in the District of Columbia.[61] In thirty years of fruitful activity it has put forth a series of thoroughly prepared restatements of the common law on many subjects, such as (to name some only) Conflict of Laws, Contracts, Torts, Trusts, Agency, Property, Restitution, and Judgments; a model Code of Criminal Procedure, one of Evidence; and as set forth above, in co-operation with the National Conference of Commissioners on Uniform State Laws, a Draft Uniform Commercial Code.

These private restatements, which are being widely followed by the courts, might well pave the way for codification.[62] But there is some advantage in these restatements over a general code. As they have no legislative binding authority, they are helpful guides to the courts rather than strictly binding. In the present state of our common law, when so much that has come down to us shaped to the conditions of pioneer, rural, agricultural communities is undergoing painful adaptations to the conditions of crowded, urban, industrial communities, and the rapid development of mechanical contrivances on every hand has infinitely multiplied conditions of peril to life and limb beyond all previous experience, possibility of free judicial development of principles worked out by experience must be given much weight.

Possibilities of a Civil Code in Common-Law Jurisdictions

1. *Purposes of codification.* Three different ideas of a code have been urged. The first, which may be called the Benthamite idea, is really the idea of the eighteenth-century law-of-nature school. It regards a code as a complete legislative statement of the whole body of the law in the form of rules, prescribing definite legal consequences for definite states or situations of fact, so as to put it authoritatively in one self-sufficing form.

A second view, at the other extreme, was urged particularly by Sir Thomas Erskine Holland, professor at Oxford and a leading authority on analytical jurisprudence, and by Sir James Stephen, writer of standard works on evidence and on criminal law, afterwards a Justice of the King's Bench. According to this idea, orderly arrangement, convenience of ascertainment, and convenient accessibility to the public at large are the chief purposes; so that the preparation of a code involves (a) republication in systematic form of the whole mass of existing law of every kind, and (b) separate codification of statute law and common law, adhering as closely as possible to the language, concepts, and methods of the old law.[63]

A third view, the one taken on the whole by the framers of the French Civil Code and by those who at the end of the last century framed the German Civil Code, is that the purpose must be primarily to provide so far as possible a complete legislative statement of principles so as to furnish a legislative basis for juristic and judicial development by reasoning along modern lines; laying down rules sparingly and for the analogies they furnish, except in the law of property and of inheritance, where precise rules are called for.

Bentham[64] and Austin[65] following him conceived that it would be possible not only to make the law certain and accessible but also to remove all ground for dispute as to the meaning of terms or interpretations of the code provisions. In other words, they conceived that the function of the court could be limited to the application to concrete cases of rules so clearly formulated that nothing more than genuine interpretation would be necessary except for unforeseeable situations of fact. The notion that something of this sort can be done has been widespread, but is refuted by all juristic and judicial experience. In Frederick the Great's Code the lawmaker's intention was to formulate with such careful minuteness that no possible doubt could arise in the future. Hence it was provided that the judges were not to have any power of interpretation, but were to consult a royal commission on any points they found doubtful and were to be absolutely bound by the answer of the commission.[66] This stereotyping of the law was in accordance with the doctrine of the law-of-nature jurists who believed that a perfect and complete system could be worked out by pure reason, for which no change would ever become necessary. Thus rational propositions could be laid down once for all so as to be available for every possible combination of circumstances. It need not be said that the attempt to realize such an ideal proved impossible. After a time the royal commission was abolished, and the duty of judges to interpret and develop by analogy had to be recognized.[67]

Conceding that the first idea is not practicable, the second plan seems not worthwhile. Sir James Stephen's idea was that it would furnish a prelude to an eventual code in which the results of the development of the imperative element and of the traditional element were to be combined, as was proposed by Lord Westbury. Justinian's codification shows us that a parallel compilation of the legislature-made law and digest of judge-made law are likely to come into conflict not merely by overlapping of precepts, but also because the presupposition of a precept in the one may not be that of a precept on the same point in the other. In this respect the codifier of Anglo-American law will encounter a difficulty in the distinction of our substantive law into law and equity. It would be much greater if he started with a compilation of statutes and a digest of decided cases. He would have much more to do than be sure to choose between all conflicting precepts and fix the limits of all overlapping precepts. He would need to be sure that precepts presupposing divergent starting points for reasoning were not laid out in his code side by side.

Those who drew up the French Civil Code made the first attempt to put the third idea into operation. In that code, on the whole, the attempt was made not to lay down minute rules on every conceivable point but to formulate broad principles. Of course this attempt can be carried too far. On certain points and in certain fields of the law definite detailed rules are expedient or even necessary. But in general the lawmaker, whether legislative or judicial, must not be overambitious to lay down universal rules. Property and succession require many rules. Civil wrongs admit of relatively few. Sometimes in the law of property, as in the case of what the civilians call "specification," a rule is necessary; yet no rule has been found wholly satisfactory since Roman jurists argued about it in antiquity. In the German Code and the codes since 1900 this idea has usually been carried out consistently. The aim has been to formulate the principles worked out by juristic or judicial or legislative experience, to develop them analytically, and to set forth as clearly as possible a body of principles representing the highest development of the law in modern times, rather than a complete body of rules, though at the same time to lay down carefully formulated rules where, as in property and succession, rules are required.

2. *Objections to codification.* Many Anglo-American lawyers have insisted that codification of the common law would be, if not impossible, at least highly unfortunate. Almost everything written in English in opposition to codification has its basis directly or indirectly in Savigny's tract on the Vocation of Our Age for Legislation and Jurisprudence.[68] Savigny's objections to codification were answered by Austin.[69] But the weight of Austin's arguments is

somewhat impaired by his acceptance of Bentham's idea of a code.

Savigny's objections resolve themselves to three. First, he argues that the growth of the law is likely to be impeded or diverted into unnatural directions. Experience, however, shows that this is not necessarily true. It seems clear that on the whole the French Civil Code was followed by a juristic new start that made for development of the law not only in France but in no small measure everywhere. No doubt an ill drawn or hastily drawn code might afford so poor a basis for further juristic or judicial development as to impair the progress of a system of law. There is no reason to suppose, however, that the carefully drawn codes of the present century have had any such effect.

Savigny's second objection is that a code made by one generation is likely to project directly or indirectly the intellectual and moral notions that existed at that time into days when such notions have become anachronisms. There is undoubted truth in this objection, and the result might well follow from a code made on the basis of such a digest as was contemplated by Holland and by Sir James Stephen. But it must be observed that development of the law through juristic working over of the traditional element of a system of law is open to the same objection. Anglo-American law today can show more than one example of projection into the present of the ideas and modes of thought of the past. The law of the last century was full of such instances.

One example may be seen in the Connecticut voting trust cases.[70] In these cases the court assumed a medieval trade or craft guild corporation. It thought of a modern American industrial or business corporation as a partnership in which there is an intimate relation between the partners. Compare the way the Roman jurists argued about a partnership on the analogy of the consortium of coheirs.[71] In the argument of the Connecticut case there is a like case of arguing about a modern business company as if it were a medieval craft fraternity. Moreover, if a code can arrest the progress of the law by projecting into the law ideas and modes of thought of the past, the traditional law can affect the interpretation and application of a code in the same way. Legislation has a difficult task in emancipating a legal system from the ideas around which it has grown up.

Savigny's third objection is based on defects of codes in the past. They may be summed up in two: (a) The codifiers but too often had only superficial knowledge of the law they tried to codify. Partly this superficiality was due to the eighteenth-century notion of a law of nature, which made men think they could make a wholly new body of law by pure reason without regard to the juristic or judicial experience of the past. Partly it has been due to the attempt of one person or of a small number of persons to codify the whole law. The developed law of a modern state is too complex to be so thoroughly mastered in all its parts by one man or by a few men as to enable that one man or those few men to draw up a code.[72] (b) In most cases codes in the past have been drawn too hurriedly. The Georgia Code and the Negotiable Instruments Law in the United States[73] are examples of the defects that necessarily result from undue haste. Field's Civil Code is an example of the defects sure to result from the attempt of one man to cover the whole field. The German Code, which set the pace for twentieth-century codes, shows what can be accomplished by a sufficiently large commission taking sufficient time for its work and utilizing full criticism from every side.

To the points that Savigny made against the codes of the past, Austin added two others worthy of notice. (1) He objected to them because they made no adequate provision for the incorporation from time to time of judicial interpretation.[74] He insisted that there should be some provision whereby periodically the results of judicial interpretation and application of the code should be incorporated therein and in that way the traditional element that grows up around a code be made part of it. But this insistence goes on Bentham's idea of a code as a complete body of rules. If new rules result from judicial decision or rules in the text are given new or modified shape by interpretation and application, the code as a complete statement of the law in detail should be amended by legislation. Undoubtedly repealing or supplanting legislation should be inserted in an appropriate place. Also amending legislation should replace texts amended. But the real problem is as to judicial interpretation and application of principles such as the pronouncements of the French Civil Code with respect to the liberties of an owner, to the lawmaking force of a contract, and to the effect of culpable causation of injury. Here it is an advantage that working over of jüdicial development of principles—of starting points for reasoning—be left to juristic writing rather than be crystallized by legislative enactment before the process has become complete. (2) Austin objected especially to the French Civil Code because it was not complete and was intended to be eked out by the pre-existing law.[75] This is based largely on his idea that a code can be made substantially self-sufficing. It is impossible to draw up a code in such a way that all reference to the pre-existing law to throw light upon it will be obviated. It is true that so far as possible this necessity of looking into the law before the code should be done away with, since otherwise a tendency will arise to treat the code as only declaratory. Herein is one of the chief defects of Field's Code. It assumed at every point pretty thorough knowledge of the common law, and was not in itself so clear and sound as to be of much real help toward ascertaining the pre-existing law. On the other hand, the attempt to foreclose all judicial or juristic working over of the material of the code, in view of the experience of the past, must be pronounced futile. The most serious objection to a code in a common-law jurisdiction is that we have no well-developed technique of building the law on legislative texts.[76]

Advisability of Codifying Anglo-American Law.[77] If we apply to common-law jurisdictions what experience has shown as to the conditions that lead to codes, it would seem that, especially in the United States, we are approaching a condition in which codification is not unlikely to be resorted to.

(1) It can hardly be questioned that our case law, especially in America, has not been rising to new situations as it did in the formative era of the fore part of the last century. Practically it broke down on the important subjects of employers' liability and workmen's compensation. There was clear failure in holding promoters to their duties. Development was too slow in the law of public service agencies and conspicuously too slow in labor law. In these and many others, legislation and administrative commissions and boards have replaced common law and adjudication. Even in legal procedure it took legislation in England, Canada, and Australia to provide a modern system, and American courts have been hesitant or unwilling generally to exercise their common-law rule-making power. There is much to suggest that the traditional element of our law has for some time exhausted its possibilities of bringing our legal system abreast of the demand on it made in the crowded machine-conducted, danger-ridden society of today.

(2) The defects of form in the Anglo-American law of today are obvious. They may be summed up as five.

(a) Want of certainty. This is very marked in jurisdictions in which questions passed upon in other jurisdictions remain open. There is no assurance that the solution adopted elsewhere will be followed. Moreover, it often happens that different solutions have been reached in other jurisdictions, so that on many questions there are a number of competing rules of equal authority from which to choose, with respect to which the law is still open in some of our most important states.[78] All sorts of trivial questions receive elaborate answers in the books while great and fundamental questions may remain in a provoking state of uncertainty in a particular state because lawyers advise clients to settle rather than pursue a doubtful litigation. Statutory changes are piecemeal and haphazard, and the law has to be settled in each jurisdiction by an elaborate system of judicial opinions that detracts much from thorough judicial consideration of individual cases.

(b) Waste of labor entailed by the unwieldy form of the law. As Chief Justice Sharswood put the matter, the difficulty is not so much to know the law as to know where to find it. Undoubtedly in the long run it is a good thing for the science of law to leave rules and principles to be worked out, in the language of Mr. Justice Miller, by a process of judicial inclusion and exclusion. But the process is hard on the community and the law and takes time away from thorough consideration of cases. Our appellate courts have often to put in so much time in finding the law that they cannot always give adequate consideration to the case itself. In a case decided by the Supreme Court of Pennsylvania on October 8, 1954[79] twenty-five cases were cited in the two opinions reported, and ten of them were elaborately discussed. In 1885 a committee of the American Bar Association found that in one volume of New York Reports, in 79 decisions reported, the judges cited 449 cases, or between five and six to each, of which 303 were from New York, 56 from England, and the rest from 16 different states. But the 449 cases cited by the court were taken from 5300 cited in the briefs of counsel. In other words, a conscientious court was expected to look at 5300 reported cases in order to decide 79 cases.[80] From personal experience I can testify that the labor is very heavy. The judges in important appellate courts today must have law secretaries to enable them to reduce this task to reasonable proportions.

(c) Lack of knowledge of the law on the part of those who amend it. It must be admitted that the fault in our sometimes crude legislation on matters of private law is not all with the legislators. It is sometimes an almost impossible task in jurisdictions where many controverted questions, sometimes fundamental, are still open, to ascertain what the law is that is to be changed or amended or abrogated.

(d) Irrationality due to partial survival of obsolete precepts. In Illinois in 1910 the Supreme Court had to decide that contingent remainders could still be barred by merger.[81] After that, real property lawyers in Chicago trembled for a decade. What other supposedly obsolete common-law rules must they reckon with? No one knew. A much vexed question today is as to the immunity of charitable nonprofit hospitals. Twenty-one jurisdictions now reject the doctrine. It is adhered to still in twenty-five, but in only eight is there complete immunity. In two recent cases courts have overruled older decisions adopting the doctrine.[82] Other courts recently have refused to give it up.[83] In jurisdictions that have not passed on the question, and even in some in which it has been reviewed recently, who can be sure what is the law? But what is most vexatious today is the question how far particular rules of the old common law, quite out of line with such far-reaching legislative reforms as Lord Campbell's Act, the Married Women's Acts, or the Federal Tort Claims Act, but not expressly repealed, are still in force.[84] Anomalous rules and rules based on history only, wholly out of touch with the legal system as a whole, embarrass many fields of the law. Our analytical methods have been identifying these anomalies. But we do not get rid of them. Moreover, irrationality of form continually begets irrationality of substance, as is brought out particularly in case of fictions.[85]

(e) Confusion. Courts are frequently led into mistakes between the two parallel lines of statute law and case law dealing with the same subjects, the one potentially with the whole, the other unsystematically here and there.[86] No court has authority and no legislature as a rule undertakes to reduce any subject to systematic and orderly statement.[87]

(3) Passing to the third point that we have seen in connection with the enactment of codes, we come to a matter that is likely longest to retard effective codification in the United States. Where significant codes have been enacted the growing point of the legal system had shifted to legislation, and an efficient organ of legislation on matters of law had developed. Undoubtedly with us the growing point has largely shifted to legislation. But we have not developed an efficient organ of lawmaking for the ordinary civil

side of the law.[88] In England, if the government takes up a proposal for legislation it has the machinery for pushing it through Parliament. Also through the institution of parliamentary counsel England has got rid of some of the causes of crudity in legislation as to private law. But, as Ilbert put it, Parliament is "not interested in lawyer's law." In the United States both houses of Congress now have competent legislative counsel, and so do some states. This, however, does not suffice to do more than insure the form of statutes. It seldom involves grasp of the legal difficulties at the root of a question. Moreover, there is nothing with us comparable to the taking up of a measure of detailed law reform by the Cabinet in England and thus giving it the right of way in a crowded session.

(4) On the other hand, the fourth point, the need for one law, is of more importance with us today than any of the others. It is suggestive that with the economic unification of the country the conflict of laws is becoming one of the most important everyday subjects in the average American practice. The demand for one law was behind the growth of the common law. Before the Conquest there was no one law of England. Local customary law differed greatly. As one of the demands in Magna Carta was for one measure of corn and one measure of ale for all England,[89] so another demand of the time was for one measure of law. Such a demand may some day lead to codification in the United States. The growth of businesses extending beyond state lines has already led to the draft Uniform Commercial Code.

Attempt to reshape the law by judicial overruling of leading cases is no substitute for well-drawn, comprehensive legislation. The English have an advantage in that down to the nineteenth century, and indeed till the second half of that century, relatively few cases were decided by the House of Lords. Hence old cases decided by tribunals not of ultimate authority may be questioned, whereas with us the ultimate reviewing court is likely to have fixed a century ago or more the law one should like to see changed or given up. Patchwork overruling along with patchwork legislative tinkering often does at least as much harm to the legal system as it does good. Our situation calls for a ministry of justice or a code, and a code will need a ministry of justice also.

In the medieval universities the Roman law as codified by Justinian was taught as the universal law of Christendom conceived of as the empire of which Justinian was the lawgiver. The academic idea of the Roman law as universal gave way in the sixteenth century. The idea of the end of law that had been received from the classical jurists began to go at the same time and was completely gone when the newer idea on which the French Civil Code proceeds was given final formulation at the end of the eighteenth century. Today the French are doing wisely in revising the Code instead of writing a new one. It is not possible today to declare the broad statements of fundamental principles, the unrestricted right of exclusion, liberty of using, of enjoying, and destroying, and power of disposing of property, nor the full freedom of contract or power of making law for oneself by contract, nor binding force of agreement, nor liability to repair injury caused by fault, as announced by the French Civil Code. These, and the rules framed in their spirit, were so suited to the conditions of the nineteenth century that the Code could serve as a model for the greater part of the world. No one today can formulate with assurance the idea of the end of law that will underlie the law of property, the law of contracts, and the law of torts in the twenty-first century. The French are revising, not recodifying. Very likely the time is not ripe for a complete code of Anglo-American law.

NOTES

[1] Maitland, English Law and the Renaissance (1901).

[2] 1 Planiol, Traité élémentaire de droit civil, Nos. 54–59 (12th ed. 1932).

[3] 2 Spedding, Letters and Life of Bacon 61–71 (1872); Bacon, Law Tracts 1–14, 15–22 (1741).

[4] 5 Spedding, *op. cit. supra* note 3, at 41 (1869).

[5] 7 *Id.*, at 181 (1874).

[6] Stokes, Anglo-Indian Codes (2 vols. 1887–1888) and Supplement (1889), also Second Supplement (1891); Acharyya, Codification in British India (1912).

[7] Essays in the Form of the Law 50 (1870).

[8] Essays in Jurisprudence and Legal History 109 (Am. ed., 1900).

[9] The statutes that make up the Anglo-Indian Codes are: the Penal Code (1860); the Succession Act (1865); the Contract Act (1872)—including quasi contract (restitution), sales, suretyship, bailments, agency, and partnership; the Negotiable Instruments Act (1881); the Transfer of Property Act (1882); the Trust Act (1882); the Easements Act (1882); the Specific Relief Act (1877); the Code of Criminal Procedure (1882); the Evidence Act (1872); the Limitation Act (1877).

[10] See Pollock, The Law of Fraud in British India 20 (1894).

[11] Fowler, Codification in the State of New York (2d ed. 1884); David Dudley Field Centenary Essays (Reppy ed. 1949).

[12] Dicey, Lectures on the Relation Between Law and Public Opinion in England 62–65 (1905).

[13] *Id.* at 133 *et seq.* Dillon, Laws and Jurisprudence of England and America 339–42 (1894); Letter of Jeremy Bentham in Field (editor) Codification of the Common Law; Letter of Jeremy Bentham and Report of Judges Story, Metcalf, and others (1882).

[14] See, e.g., Walker, Introduction to American Law 58–61, 648–49 (1837).

[15] Field, H. M., Life of David Dudley Field (1898); Obituary in 17 Am. Bar Assn. Rep. 517 (1894); Browne, David Dudley Field 3 Green Bag 49 (1891); Hall, Reminiscences of David Dudley Field 6 Green Bag 204 (1894); Fiero, David Dudley Field and His Work 18 Rep. N.Y. State Bar Assn. 177 (1895); David Dudley Field Centenary Essays (Reppy ed. 1949).

[16] Const. N.Y., 1846, Art. 6, § 24.

[17] An Act to Simplify and Abridge the Practice, Pleadings, and Proceedings of the Courts of this State, passed April 12, 1848. Laws of New York, 1848, ch. 379, pp. 497–565.

[18] Reports, 1st to 4th of Commissioners on Practice and Pleadings (1848–1849) in one volume—1–3 Code of Civil Procedure, 4 Code of Criminal Procedure.

[19] Hepburn, Historical Development of Code Pleading (1901).

[20] Laws of New York, 1850, ch. 281, p. 618.

[21] 1 *id.*, 1857, ch. 266, p. 552.

[22] New York, Draft of Civil Code: Prepared by Commissioners of Code (1862).

[23] *Id.*, Draft of Penal Code (1864); *id.*, Penal Code, reported by Commissioners of Code (1865).

[24] *Id.*, Political Code, reported by Commissioners of Code (1860).

[25] Throop, Code of Civil Procedure, 2 pts. in 1 vol. (1880); Revised Code of Civil Procedure amended 1877–1880, 2 pts. in 1 vol. (1881).

[26] 2 Laws of New York, 1881, pp. 1–235.

[27] Haymond and Burch, Civil Code 1872 (2 vols. 1874); *id.*, Code of Civil Procedure 1872 (2 vols. 1874); *id.*, Penal Code 1872 (2 vols. 1874). The California Civil Code was adopted for the Canal Zone, Act of Congress of February 27, 1933, 47 St. 1124.

[28] Laws of Montana, 1891, 278, Montana Codes and Statutes (1895).

[29] Dakota, Revised Codes (1877). The preface gives an account of the taking over of the four codes from the New York drafts.

[30] See Pomeroy, The True Method of Interpreting the Civil Code, 3 West Coast Reporter, 585, 691, 777; 4 *id.* 1, 49, 109, 145 (1884).

[31] E.g., the part entitled "maxims of jurisprudence," in imitation of the title of Justinian's Digest, "On Divers Maxims of the Old Law" (Dig. 50, 147). This by no means includes all the common-law maxims that have proved useful, and includes some of doubtful value. One ("No one should suffer for the act of another") could be positively mischievous. Compare also: "Where one of two innocent persons must suffer by the act of a third, he by whose negligence it happened must be sufferer."

[32] Resolves of the General Court of the Commonwealth of Massachusetts, 1835, 312; *id.* 1836, 401.

[33] Massachusetts: Commissioners appointed to consider and report upon the practicability and expediency of reducing to a Written and Systematic Code the Common Law of Massachusetts. Report (1837). Reprinted in Field (editor), Codification of the Common Law: Letter of Jeremy Bentham, and Report of Judges Story, Metcalf, and others (1882).

[34] See Pound, The Place of Judge Story in the Making of American Law, 48 Am. L. Rev. 676 (1914).

[35] Georgia, Public Laws, 1858, No. 94, pp. 95, 302.

[36] The sections are numbered through the four parts.

[37] I Story, Commentaries on Equity Jurisprudence §§ 274 *et seq.* (1836).

[38] It is pieced out from chs. 1–2 of Addison on Contracts (1847).

[39] Georgia, Public Laws, 1860, No. 10, p. 24.

[40] Holland, Essays in the Form of the Law 54–55 (1870); Nash, Life of Lord Westbury 56–65 (1888).

[41] See preface to Goddard, Treatise on the Law of Easements (1871); to Stephen, Digest of the Law of Evidence (1876); and to Stephen, Digest of the Criminal Law (1877).

[42] Hearn, Theory of Legal Duties and Rights 378–82 (1883).

[43] See an analysis of the introductory part, *id.*, Appendix, 385–93.

[44] The General Code, 1885: Being A Bill to Declare, Consolidate and Amend the Substantive General Law, Prepared and Brought into the Legislative Council of Victoria by the Hon. W. E. Hearn (1885).

[45] [Hearn] The General Code (printed by authority, the Government Printer, 1888).

[46] Gsovski, Soviet Civil Law (1949). See my review, 50 Mich. L. Rev. 95 (1951).

[47] Chalmers, An Experiment in Codification 2 L. Q. Rev. 125 (1888).

[48] 1 Revised Stat. N.Y. 717–63 (1829).

[49] 1 Laws of New York, 1896, ch. 547, pp. 559–624.

[50] An Act to Codify the Law Relating to Bills of Exchange, Cheques, and Promissory Notes, 45 & 46 Vict., ch. 61 (1882).

[51] An Act to Declare and Amend the Law of Partnership, 53 & 54 Vict., ch. 39 (1890).

[52] An Act for Codifying the Law Relating to the Sale of Goods, 56 & 57 Vict., ch. 71 (1894)—approved February 20, 1894, but § 64 provides that it is to be cited as "The Sale of Goods Act, 1893."

[53] 12 & 13 Geo. 5, ch. 71 (1922). See also the Settled Land Act, 1925, the Trustee Act, 1925, and the Law of Property Act, 1925, consolidating statutes that unify the preceding statute law.

[54] An Act to Consolidate Enactments Relating to the Administration of Estates of Deceased Persons, 15 Geo. 5, ch. 23 (1925). This has been said to be "something on the nature of a code," Clauson, J., in In re Cockell [1931] 1 Ch. 389, 391.

[55] See 14 Am. Bar Assn. Rep. 365 (1891).

[56] Terry, Uniform State Laws in the United States (1920); Williston, The Uniform

Partnership Act With Some Remarks on Other Uniform Commercial Laws 63 U. of Pa. L. Rev. 196 (1915); Vold, Some Reasons Why the Code States Should Adopt the Uniform Sales Act 5 Calif. L. Rev. 400, 491 (1917).

57 67 Am. Bar Assn. Rep. 132 (1942); 19 Proceedings, American Law Institute 57 (1942).

58 1 Laws of Pennsylvania, 1953, p. 3.

59 *Supra* note 40.

60 *Supra* note 41.

61 1 Proceedings, American Law Institute (1923).

62 Franklin, The Historic Function of the American Law Institute: Restatement as Transitional to Codification 47 Harv. L. Rev. 1367 (1934); Cardozo, The American Law Institute, in Law and Literature 121–41 (1931); Goodhart, Law Reform in the United States, Journal of the Society of Public Teachers of Law 19–27 (1934); Clark, The Restatement of the Law of Contracts, 42 Yale L. J. 643 (1933).

63 Holland, Essays in the Form of the Law 12–23 (1876); Stephen, Digest of the Criminal Law, Introduction (Am. ed. 1878).

64 Papers on Codification, 4 Works, 453–530 (Bowring ed. 1843); Codification Proposal Addressed by Jeremy Bentham to All Nations Professing Liberal Opinions, *id.*, 537–64; Commentary on Humphrey's Real Property Code, 5 Works, 390–416 (Bowring ed. 1843).

65 2 Jurisprudence 660 *et seq.* (5th ed. 1885).

66 Allgemeines Landrecht für die preussischen Staaten, Introduction (1794).

67 Landé, Das allgemeine Landrecht für die preussischen Staaten in seiner jetzigen Gestalt 11 (3d ed. 1896).

68 Vom Beruf unsrer Zeit für Gesetzgebung und Rechtswissenschaft (1814, 3d ed. 1840, reprinted 1892), translated by Hayward as The Vocation of Our Age for Legislation and Jurisprudence (1831).

69 2 Austin, Jurisprudence (5th ed. 1885) lect. 39 and Notes on Codification, 1021–39.

70 Shepaug Voting Trust Cases, 60 Conn. 553, 579 (1890).

71 As between partners there was the *beneficium competentiae* in an action *pro socio*, 2 Buckland, Text Book of Roman Law (2d ed. 1932).

72 The work of Huber on the Swiss Code must give one pause here. But before he began his work in 1892 he had the French Civil Code and the first draft of the German Civil Code (1887) before him and the final draft of the German Civil Code (1896) was available before the Swiss Code of Obligations (1901) and Civil Code (1907). See the historical introduction in Shick, Translation of the Swiss Civil Code.

73 Brannan, Some Necessary Amendments of the Negotiable Instruments Law, 26 Harv. L. Rev. 493 (1913); Chafee, Shortcomings and Successes of the Negotiable Instruments Law, reprinted from preface and discussions in the 4th edition of Brannan, Negotiable Instruments Law Annotated (1926), reprinted in Chafee, Reissued Notes on Bills and Notes 51–56 (1943).

74 2 Jurisprudence 675 (5th ed. 1885).

75 *Id.*, 672–73.

76 Pound, Courts and Legislation 21 Harv. L. Rev. 383 (1908).

77 Amos, Systematic View of the Science of Jurisprudence 471–90 (1872); 2 Austin, Jurisprudence, lect. 39 (5th ed. 1885); Notes on Codification, *id.*, 1021–39; Bentham, Note on the "Unwritten Law," 6 Works 529 (Bowring ed. 1843); 1 Birkenhead, Points of View

150–90 (1922); Carss, The Codification of Laws, 40 Canadian Law Times, 14, 126, 216, 292, 379, 451 (1920); Carter, Law: Its Origin, Growth and Function, lects. 11–12 (1907); Clark, Practical Jurisprudence 380–94 (1883); Clarke, The Science of Law and Lawmaking (1898)—the whole book is an argument against codification; Dillon, Laws and Jurisprudence of England and America 178–87 (1894); Goadby, Introduction to the Study of Law, ch. 1 (2d ed. 1914); Goudy, Mackay and Campbell, Addresses on Codification of Law (1893); Gregory, Bentham and the Codifiers 13 Harv. L. Rev. 344 (1900); 1 Lord Halsbury, Laws of England, Introduction (1st ed. 1907); Hart, The Way to Justice, ch. 4 (1941); Hearn, Theory of Legal Rights and Duties ch. 19 (1883); Holland, Essays in the Form of the Law 65–100 (1870); Isaacs, The Aftermath of Codification 45 Rep. Am. Bar Assn. 524 (1920); Matthews, Thoughts on Codification of the Common Law (2d ed. 1881); Pollock, First Book of Jurisprudence 367–70 (6th ed. 1929), Essay on Codification [preface to 4th ed. of his Digest of the Law of Partnership (1888)]; Lord Robson, Codification of the Law 43 The Law Journal 286 (1908); Seagle, The Quest for Law 277–98 (1941); Salmond, Jurisprudence § 53 (9th ed. 1937); Sharswood, Lectures Introductory to the Study of Law, lect. 9 (1870); Smith, Compendium of Mercantile Law, Introduction (1835); Terry, Leading Principles of Anglo-American Law §§ 609–12 (1884); Walker, Introduction to American Law §§ 52–53 (1st ed. 1837); Williston, Modern Tendencies in the Law, ch. 2 (1929); *id.*, Written and Unwritten Law, 17 Am. Bar Assn. Journ. 39 (1931).

See also Pound, Codification, in 1 Cyclopedia of American Government, 302–6 (1914); Lobingier, Codification, in 3 Encyclopaedia of the Social Sciences, 600–13 (1930).

[78] See, e.g., Rose v. Socony Vacuum Corp., 54 R.I. 411 (1931), in which the Rhode Island Court refused to follow Rylands v. Fletcher, L.R. 3 H.L. 330 (1868); Berry v. Shell Petroleum Co., 140 Kan. 94, 141 Kan. 6 (1934), following Rylands v. Fletcher and Helms v. Eastern Kansas Oil Co., 102 Kan. 164. In Rhode Island pollution of plaintiff's well and the brook on his land by oil escaping from defendant's refinery was held not actionable without showing negligence, whereas in Kansas there was held absolute liability. Another jurisdiction where the case had not arisen might hold either way. The Restatements have endeavored to locate and settle such disputed questions. But no court is bound to follow them. The phrase "a split of authority" is a commonplace in the books.

[79] Finnegan v. Monongahela Connecting R. Co., 108 A. 2d 321.

[80] Report of Special Committee on Delay and Uncertainty in Judicial Administration 8 Am. Bar Assn. Rep. 323, 329–30 (1885). The number of cases cited has grown since, despite judicial attempts at limitation. See Williston, Life and Law 303–8 (1940).

[81] See Note, 10 Ill. L. Rev. 355 (1915).

[82] Pierce v. Yakima Valley Memorial Assn. 260 P. 2d 765 (Wash. 1953); Noel v. Menninger Foundation, 267 P. 2d 934 (Kan. 1954) overruling five prior cases.

[83] Averbach v. Y.M.C.A., 250 Ky. 39 (1933).

[84] Certainly Lord Campbell's Act (the Wrongful Death Act) has been enforced long enough to have become thoroughly incorporated into the law. Recovery for wrongful causing of death is not something confined to Anglo-American legislation. It was worked out by the Civilians from Roman texts and is provided for in the modern codes. Yet the Supreme Court of the United States in 1907 thought of it as introducing a sort of temporary local innovation, not to be thought of as being as much a part of the general law as was the old doctrine that had been superseded. Chambers v. Baltimore & Ohio R. Co., 207 U.S. 142, 149 (1907). In the same spirit the Supreme Court of Missouri laid down that,

while every physical interference with the person of another short of killing is presumptively wrongful, because it gave rise to no action at common law it must be shown to have been wrongful by the complaining party. Nichols v. Winfrey, 79 Mo. 544 (1883). In like manner the majority of courts hold that a widow cannot recover for loss of consortium of her husband because the common law did not permit such an action and no statute expressly gives such a right. Ash v. S.S. Mullen, Inc., 261 P. 2d 118 (Wash. 1953). Hitaffer v. Argonne Co., 87 App. D.C. 57, 183 F. 2d 811 (D.C. Cir. 1950), allowing that recovery has the weight of authority against it. This treats the Married Women's Acts as not part of the general law. They are to be held as to their effect to have to do with remedies only and to be limited to what they specify. Again, the Federal Tort Claims Act doing away with immunity of the government for wrongs done by its servants or agents, something now universal outside of the United States and coming to be adopted by the several states, is treated as an alien element in the law calling for cautious holding down to detailed provisions and by multiplied judicial exceptions. Dalehite v. United States 346 U.S. 15 (1953); Feres v. U.S., 340 U.S. 135 (1950).

85 For striking examples of how fictions confuse the law, see Sceva v. True, 53 N.H. 637 (1873); Louisiana v. New Orleans, 109 U.S. 285 (1883); Sinclair v. Brougham [1914] A.C. 398.

86 E.g., in New Jersey for nearly ten years after the Uniform Fraudulent Conveyance Act the courts went on following the old-time decisions that the statute superseded. McLaughlin, Application of the Uniform Fraudulent Conveyance Act 46 Harv. L. Rev. 404, 408–9 (1933).

87 See Sir Frederick Pollock's satire, Essays in Jurisprudence and Ethics 61–62 (1882).

88 See Cardozo, A Ministry of Justice, 35 Harv. L. Rev. 113 (1921).

89 Magna Carta, ch. 35.

14

Codification in a New State

BENJAMIN AKZIN

I

IT IS the purpose of this paper to indicate some of the problems arising in a new state that, along with other activities incidental to its consolidation and development, is engaged in a wholesale program of revamping and integrating the legal structure inherited from previous regimes. In the course of this process codification and procedures akin to codification usually occupy an important place, and it is the complications appearing in this connection that will be reviewed here more particularly. The country against the background of which they will be studied is Israel. Inevitably the specific context in which problems arise and solutions are sought is peculiar to the state under study, and so is much of the factual material. Hence neither the phenomena observed nor any lessons that might be derived from them are literally translatable into the experience of any other state. On the other hand, as long as this reservation is kept in mind many of the problems, considerations, or even solutions might be applicable *mutatis mutandis* to other countries, whether new or of older vintage. In this sense the following might be regarded as a case study in codification problems, albeit on a miniature scale.[1]

As it happens, the minute size of the country involved—a mere 8,000 square miles—does not make its case a simple one. On the contrary, extreme complexity of the social and legal background

BENJAMIN AKZIN *is Herbert Samuel Professor of Constitutional Law and Political Science at Hebrew University of Jerusalem*

against which its efforts at codification are undertaken is its outstanding characteristic. Another characteristic of the country is that it is replete with paradoxes. Only so much of the complexities and paradoxes involved will be mentioned here as is necessary to understand what follows.

Culturally, Israel represents a Western-type democratic and urban society in the midst of a rather patriarchal and rural Middle East. Ethnically, it is a society largely Jewish established in a territory that, at least in recent centuries, has been predominantly Arab. Demographically, it is composed of several strata of inhabitants greatly differing from one another in religion, linguistic background, *mores,* and—correspondingly—inherited legal institutions. Most of Israel's present population are comparatively new arrivals, and their cultural integration is far from complete. From the point of view of dominant social values, it is a welfare state placed in a region in which social consciousness is perhaps as low as anywhere on earth. By no means unimportant is the country's character as central site of holiness for Christianity and Judaism and as an object of deep veneration to Islam and two smaller denominations—Bahaj and Druze;[2] which helps to explain why large groups and political entities outside the State regard with jealous interest everything that occurs within its borders. And lastly, it is well to remember that the search for a better legal structure that will be described in the following pages, just as all other efforts at social and economic consolidation, is taking place while the state of war between Israel and its neighboring states continues unabated.

A similar degree of complexity characterizes the country's legal structure. Again, only the barest elements of that structure will be mentioned here. Independent since May 15, 1948, Israel is a unicameral parliamentary republic.[3] The principal layers that compose the authoritative legal materials now in effect are as follows:

1. Statutory enactments of the State of Israel and regulations made pursuant to these enactments.[4]

2. Quasi-statutory enactments of the period of British rule, 1918–1947, and regulations made pursuant to these enactments.[5]

3. Ottoman law, such as was in force in Palestine on November 1, 1914. As a result of a series of enactments in the nineteenth and early twentieth centuries, this material was overwhelmingly statutory in form; a large part of it was codified. As for the historical origins of its contents, the provisions of that law are taken partly from Moslem religious law, partly from Turkish and Arab customs, partly from later local developments, and partly represent translations or adaptations from Western sources, chiefly French and German codes.[6]

4. "The substance of the common law, and the doctrines of equity in force in England."[7]

5. (As far as Jews are concerned) Jewish (rabbinic) law, in matters of marriage, divorce, and personal status. Developed from the Old Testament by centuries of theoretical writings and actual adjudication, the main body of that law has been set out in a succession of texts, most important of which are the Mishna (3rd century), the Babylonian Talmud (5th century), the Code of Maimonides (13th century), and the Shulkhan Arukh (16th century).[8]

6. (As far as Moslems are concerned) Moslem religious law *(sharyia)*, in matters of marriage, divorce, and personal status. Developed from the Koran and early Islamic traditions, it has been laid down by scholars and judges of the succeeding generations, and has never been properly codified.[9]

7. (As far as certain Christian denominations are concerned, viz.—Roman Catholics, Greek Orthodox, Armenians, Syrian Catholics, Chaldean Uniates, Greek Catholics, Syrian Orthodox, and Maronites) Christian church law, in matters of marriage, divorce, and personal status. For Roman Catholics and the denominations affiliated with the Roman Catholic Church this law has been elaborated in great detail and, moreover, has been the subject of a comprehensive modern codification, with the code, the *codex iuris canonici*, in effect since 1918. The church law of the Eastern de-

nominations, though equally based on Holy Writ, apostolic tradition, and the decisions of the early synods, has not been properly codified.[10]

8. (As far as the Bedouin tribes in the southern part of the country, the Negev, are concerned): "tribal custom, so far as it is not repugnant to natural justice or morality" (Palestine Order-in-Council, 1922, Art. 45).

The formal source of validity of the three religious layers, as far as the State is concerned, lies in the delegation of authority to religious tribunals as expressed principally in Sections 51–55 of the Palestine Order-in-Council, 1922, as amended. It is clearly understood that, where the religious law of the community conflicts with secular law, the latter prevails, a relationship guaranteed in practice in two ways: (a) by the control that the civil courts exercise over the religious tribunals by various means, chiefly through the execution of the decisions of religious tribunals by the execution offices attached to the civil courts, and (b) by the power of the Supreme Court to issue orders akin to orders of certiorari and prohibition. As between the second, third, and fourth layers the order of precedence is laid down by Section 46 of the 1922 Palestine Order-in-Council, with mandatory enactments coming first, Ottoman laws second, and common law and equity brought in as a subsidiary source only. Uppermost, from the point of view of validity, are Israeli enactments, not only because of the maxim of *lex posterior,* but also because of an explicit statutory provision at the time of the "reception" by the new State of the older layers of law.[11] But this enumeration will not give a true picture of the situation unless one bears in mind the practice of the civil courts, when applying and interpreting all these variegated materials, of following the general spirit of the common law and of equity and, more particularly, the rules of interpretation derived from the common law, including the tendency toward a narrow construction of statutes, rigorous adherence to *stare decisis,* and frequent recourse to older law.[12] In the light of this practice, common law and equity play a far greater part in the legal structure of Israel than might be guessed on the basis of the statutory and quasi-statutory material only.

II

The first complex of questions that had to be faced in Israel in connection with our subject is the fundamental complex that can be summarized under the general heading, To codify or not to codify.

To a large extent the various attitudes taken in this connection are determined by the meaning given to the terms "code" and "codification." The point involved is more than a mere exercise in semantics, for the meaning in which these terms are used determines the functions that the codes will fulfill on the legal scene, and it is the sympathy or antipathy with which the various factors involved view the proposed functions that will make them more or less receptive to codification. For this reason it will be best to recapitulate, at the risk of being redundant, some elementary issues. It will be good to recall, in the first place, the two underlying respects in which all statutory law differs from nonstatutory law: viz., (a) that in statutory law it is a nonjudicial—in our day mostly a representative—agency that lays down and formulates the rule; and (b) that the rule is laid down *ab initio* for an indefinite number of future situations rather than in the context of a specific case, and is only secondarily applicable (depending on the strictness with which *stare decisis* is used) to future situations. As a further step in this development, codification is a form of statutory law in which a broad range of interconnected subjects is treated systematically and simultaneously in one document, as against their more or less fragmentized treatment in a series of isolated or sporadically enacted documents.

But this purely procedural aspect, for all its practical importance, does not, of course, exhaust the significance of codification. As this term is invariably understood in civil-law jurisdictions, it denotes a process after the completion of which there is, generally speaking, neither need nor justification for referring, for the purpose of ascertaining the law, to precode sources except in so far as the code itself may sanction such references. This does not mean that no recourse can be had to judicial decisions, but such decisions will be decisions arrived at under the code rather than prior to its enactment, and, whatever the extent of binding force or persuasive value that is ascribed to them in a given jurisdiction, they will be regarded as a secondary source at best, rather than as a primary source, for ascertaining the law. In theory, this view is shared in Anglo-American law as well,[13] but in practice the traditional approach of the common lawyer frequently overrides the theoretically acknowledged limits: quite often do judge and counsel in a common-law jurisdiction handle the rule of a code as it was their wont to handle a proposition contained in a fragmentary statute; viz., as an added layer in the aggregate of positive law, to be construed, and rather narrowly construed at that, together with all other layers available, save in so far as some prior sources may have been explicitly repealed. At most the code will be regarded as complete in itself vis-à-vis older *statutes,* thus excluding reference to them. But as for the exclusion of older *judicial decisions,* such an operation represents, evidently, too much of a break with inherited habits of legal reasoning for many jurists steeped in the common law.[14]

It is in the light of this background of the problem that the basic difficulties surrounding the question of codification in Israel must be understood. The advantages of codification have been stated often and are particularly obvious in a country with so complex a legal structure as Israel; there is therefore no need to reiterate them in this paper. On the other hand, it will be useful to describe and analyze the chief factors that militate against codification or, to say the least, work to slow down its impetus and to reduce its intrinsic importance.

One factor of this kind is the attitude of members of the legislature and the cabinet. Their attitude has to do with the most elementary meaning of codification: the substitution of a systematic exposition of the law for fragmentary and *ad hoc* legislation. Indeed, it is a simpler task, at first sight, to enact rules piecemeal, if and as a specific problem urgently calls for a solution or for reformulation, and without undergoing the gigantic task of working out at once a major area of jural relations. This is especially true of many a modern parliament, and certainly of the Knesset in Israel. Even though the term "legislature" still figures pre-eminently in the designation of modern parliaments, the emphasis in their activities, especially in so-called "parliamentary" regimes, has shifted so definitely to nonlegislative tasks that there is no longer the leisure or, at any rate, the patience to undertake a very broad and very complicated piece of legislation, such as is involved in the enactment of a code; and this is the more true because the problems involved are, in the main, removed from the points around which parties form and in which parliamentary life is centered.

The task could still be undertaken if the legislature were content with a more or less formal role, such as that played by the German Reichstag, the Italian Parliament, the Swiss Federal Parliament, the Dutch legislature, and the legislatures of several American states in connection with the codes enacted by them. But the Knesset is jealous of its legislative functions. Neither in plenary session nor in committee do its members like to pass legislation without careful scrutiny of contents or even of actual wording.[15] On the other hand, the Knesset is more interested in measures that respond to an urgent need or have obvious political or social connotations than in long-range and nonpolitical measures. As a result it has happened that when fairly comprehensive technical bills were submitted to the Knesset, even though far shorter than full-fledged codes usually are, the committees concerned never got around to dealing with them. *A fortiori* this attitude is bound to discourage the introduction of complete codes.

To a lesser extent, but still perceptibly present, the same attitude can be detected in the responsible heads of the executive. As far as Israel is concerned there is discernible a veritable zeal for gradual codification (in the sense of a systematic exposition of statutory law, whatever their attitute as regards the relationship between the *lex scripta* and the *lex non scripta)* on the part of the officials of the Ministry of Justice entrusted with the preparation of long-range legislation,[16] and to a certain extent this attitude also characterizes the present holders of the offices of Minister of Justice and of Attorney-General.[17] But there it stops. Under Israeli practice every government bill is submitted to the Cabinet for approval before introduction in the Knesset, and the cabinet operates in an atmosphere not unlike that of the Knesset itself. Attention is focused, here no less than there, on urgent matters and on political issues. Hence there is a disinclination to take up comprehensive long-range bills of a highly technical sort, matched by an equal disinclination to pass on such bills to the Knesset without the usual scrutiny.

And yet it would be an error to believe that these phenomena are due entirely, or even principally, to the mere convenience, whim, or faulty working methods of legislature and cabinet. We shall not stray far afield if we assume that basically it is the greater dynamism and the speedier tempo of change of modern life that exercise an influence away from long-range and comprehensive legislation and toward immediate and piecemeal lawmaking. This is particularly characteristic of the extremely dynamic State of Israel, but it may be of interest to investigate whether the same situation does not also obtain in other states, especially other new states.

It has been said often since Savigny that codification, or at any rate successful codification, is predicated on a certain stage of "ripeness" of a country's laws. One wonders whether this is necessarily true: codification, especially in the sense of a wholesale reception of foreign legal material, can be, on the contrary, the result of a grossly inadequate state of the country's laws—as on the eve of recent codifications in Japan, Egypt, and Turkey. Far more apposite than the requirement of a "ripe" legal structure is another condition: a suitable climate of society, its willingness and self-denying ability to conform to an all-embracing body of rules the ultimate import of which cannot be easily gauged in advance; a condition that requires the added readiness either to undertake the laborious preparation of an original code or to "receive," ready-made and in a spirit of humility, a foreign product. Where this condition is not fully present—and this seems to be the fact in Israel—the path of codification is far from smooth.

A second major factor is the specific professional attitude of the members of the legal profession, resulting from their training and mental habits, and perhaps not uninfluenced by professional interests. It is here that the struggle between the common-law and the civil-law approaches is most discernible in Israel. The legal profession in Israel is about evenly divided between those who received their legal training in various Continental law schools and those whose legal training was influenced predominantly by the common law.[18] But, in fact, exposure to British-controlled courts under the Mandate and the need to pass a bar examination in, and to apply in practice, a large body of law modeled on British law and interpreted in accordance with common-law canons, have exercised a profound influence on "Continental" jurists as well; so that today we find a great many of them, including many of the most eminent members of bench and bar, who have become genuine and even enthusiastic converts to the common-law approach. All in all, therefore, it is the common-law school that is far more influential in Israel than the civil-law school.

The result is the familiar lack of complete acceptance, typical of the common-law jurist, of statutory law generally and of code law in particular. Statutes are to him an added layer, to be read together with the prestatute material, to be interpreted in the light of that material, and to be narrowly construed wherever they depart from the earlier rule. Both because the common-law method predisposes one to casuistic solutions and against broad principles, and because common-law jurists would like to hold down to a minimum the intervention of statutes in the domain of the common law, they tend to prefer fragmentary legislation to more comprehensive statutes. And when confronted with statutes of the latter kind that might be commonly called or even officially entitled "codes," they still apply and interpret them in the same manner in which they would apply legislation of the former kind: as another piece stitched on to the pre-existing legal structure. One might even say that where, in the classical common-law countries, England and the United States, a change of attitude can be denoted and codification finds numerous advocates,[19] the Israeli common-law jurist, with the enthusiasm of the neophyte, is even more devoted to a technique that he so recently acquired, and is therefore even less disposed to see its sway seriously interfered with by a fully implemented system of code law, with all its implications.

A further element in the situation is that statutes generally, and codes more particularly, by stating broad principles obviously intended to govern future situations rather than proceeding by way of reasonings that can be held to constitute *obiter dicta* or restricted to a narrow specific set of facts and therefore not binding in future cases, seriously narrow down the scope of the "fluidity" or "elasticity" with which courts can vary their decisions by way of "interpretation" and "distinction." However resourceful civil-law courts have been in developing new law under codes—with the French law of torts as the most renowned example—there is still a far stricter limit to their freedom of action in this respect where codes and statutes furnish the primary source of their jurisdictional powers than where codes do not exist, or are not regarded as excluding the application of prior sources, or where they are regarded as ancillary to judicial precedents. In addition, there is a basic difference between a situation where the extracode material applied is largely the *jurisprudence des tribunaux,* is postcode and flows from the authority of the code, and a situation obtaining where this material is largely antecode material in the light of which the code itself is read and interpreted. All in all, *stare decisis,* with the opportunity that this doctrine gives to the judge to "distinguish" on however minute grounds, is far less of a restraint on a judge in a specific case, precisely because it is meant to be less of a restraint, than is a section of a code or of a broadly interpreted statute intentionally designed to apply to sets of facts, however varying in detail, as long as they fall under the common denominator.

Here again one may note the contrast between the older common-law countries—England and the United States—in which there is a growing tendency toward true codification and toward the broad construction of statutes, and Israel. Many Israeli jurists, having, as it were, newly discovered the unrivaled opportunities for refined casuistic reasoning and the relative freedom of argumentation that the common-law approach affords to both judge and counsel, are rather enamored of it and are reluctant to go back to the relative narrowness of argument open to counsel and to the narrow scope of discretion left to the judge in a code-governed civil-law system. It is more work, but it is also more fun, to be a common-law jurist. And one wonders whether the higher social prestige that judges enjoy in common-law jurisdictions is not a faithful mirror of the fact that they are expected to fulfill a more creative function in the body politic than their civil-law brethren. And as for those jurists in Israel who are themselves products of the common-law school, once placed in this arena where the approach familiar to them has to compete against civil-law influences they often assume—whether out of habit or because of a sense of loyalty—the role of defenders of the common law against civil-law encroachments in various forms, including the encroachment by codification in the Continental sense of the word.

But here, too, it would be far too superficial to put down the reluctance to codify as due mainly to personal inclination. Serious objective considerations are involved, indeed, in this struggle. There is, first of all, the weighing of the advantage of greater "predictability" of the law under a code system[20] against the advantage of greater "elasticity," and therefore the greater opportunity given to the judge to insure substantive justice in the specific circumstances of a given case under the common law. There is, further, the weighing of the advantages of the more complete observance of the legislator's monopoly of lawmaking under the code system, against the advantage of a somewhat freer hand given to the judge to devise, as a presumably nonpolitical well-trained expert, timely refinements and adjustments in the law of the land. And arising from the latter there is, finally, the advantage that the will of the legislator will be obeyed by the courts in every single case until he, the legislator, speaking for the sovereign people, will deign to change the rule, as against the advantage that, where the application of that rule would go against the court's sense of justice and where its modification by legislative procedure would come too late, the court itself, by a judiciously "narrow" interpretation of the rule, may perhaps exclude a given case and other similar cases. One might say that two major problems are involved in the struggle over codification: on the one hand, the social values of stability and predictability versus elasticity; on the other, the relative importance, in the legal domain, of the essentially political modern legislator and the presumably nonpolitical expert, the judge.

As a result of the foregoing considerations the attitude of important segments of the legal profession in Israel is such as to make them prefer casuistically worded statutes to statutes setting out broads rules, fragmentary statutes to comprehensive codes, and codes of a largely declaratory character that permit going back to precode sources, to exhaustive codes that nullify all previous law from any source whatsoever. Where the legislature is slow to codify principally for pragmatic reasons, the legal profession, as we have seen, has a certain "ideological" bias against codification.[21]

In the special field of the law of persons one more factor exercises a restraining influence on codification. It has been noted that this field is largely governed by religious law and administered by autonomous ecclesiastical tribunals (though subject to the control of the civil courts). Codification by the authority of the State represents, therefore, in this field more than mere restatement or even legislation *de novo*. It connotes the direct and complete substitution of State-made law for rules that owe their intrinsic authority to the respective religious systems and are merely "recognized" or "received" by the State. Whereas in the West this process of secularization of the law has gone very far and is now regarded as normal even in many a Catholic country, in the Orient this process has no such uniform record of progress. In Israel, traditionally the "Holy Land," sensitivity in this sphere is particularly intense. Though large sections of the population and most members of the legal profession wish for a modern secular law, attempts to dislocate religious law are regarded in the light of a serious interference with religious beliefs, social *mores,* and vested rights by no fewer than three influential groups: orthodox Jews, Moslems, and Christians. What renders the situation even more delicate is the fact that each of these groups within the country has the support of still more influential and extremely vocal groups outside it.

Despite these restraining factors, the same pressures that increasingly force statutory law and codification on other countries exercise their influence in Israel as well. These factors are the complexity of legal sources, the need to ensure greater predictability and certainty of the law, and the innate search of the human mind for system and congruity. In democratic states a further factor has to be added: the basic assumption of the pre-eminence of the people's representatives over the trained élite. Therefore, while the considerations described above slow down the process of codification in Israel, its continued progress seems to be fairly certain. The principal questions that still remain open have to do with the kind of codes that will emerge, with the technique of their preparation, and with the relative importance of the codes in the legal structure of the State.

III

It is this latter question—the relative importance of the codes—that we shall take up now. Objectively stated, the question may be formulated as concerning the relationship of a code to precode sources in the absence of explicit repeal or reception. But unless this relationship is to be laid down by the legislature—a rather unlikely and hardly desirable contingency—it will be the courts that will determine it by the manner in which they will or will not take cognizance of those other sources in their decisions rendered under the code. In the last analysis, were the courts in Israel to accept the philosophy of a codified law with all its implications, even the form and technique of judicial decisions would have to be changed from that used in common-law countries to that practiced in civil-law systems.

Since the proposed codes now in various stages of preparation have not yet become valid law, it would be premature to scan the decisions of Israeli courts for indications of their future attitude on that score. All that can be said is that to date, when dealing with matters governed by some fairly comprehensive mandatory enactments that might be regarded as partial codes,[22] the Israeli courts have evidenced no tendency to modify the style and technique of their decisions from those of a court of common law or equity.

In one case only did the Supreme Court of Israel veer toward the view that a codelike enactment is relatively exhaustive and need not be read in conjunction with extraneous sources. It was a case involving the Interpretation Ordinance of 1945,[23] and the Court stated there:

" . . . we have to presume that the Interpretation Ordinance, 1929, and thereafter the Ordinance of 1945, contain the provisions according to which we must interpret the laws of this country. . . .

" . . . The Interpretation Ordinance, by its very nature, must be interpreted on the basis of its own contents. Such a statute, by its very essence, stands on its own feet and does not require interpretation in the light of other interpretation statutes. An interpretation statute which requires interpretation in the light of foreign interpretation statutes or in the light of legal history will not be worthy of its name." [24]

It then went on to cite with approval the opinion of Lord Herschell, L. C., in Bank of England v. Vagliano Brothers,[25] one of the classical statements in Anglo-American law as to the manner in which courts ought to apply codes. According to that statement a judge, in examining the language of a code, is "to ask what is its natural meaning, uninfluenced by any considerations derived from the previous state of the law, and not to start with inquiring how the law previously stood, and then, assuming that it was probably intended to leave it unaltered, to see if the words of the enactment will bear interpretation in conformity with this view"; and Lord Herschell further admonishes that "an appeal to earlier decisions can only be justified on some special ground." Having done this, the Israeli court continues:

"There is no need to explain at length that his words apply *mutatis mutandis* to our problem as well. The Interpretation Ordinance too will be perfectly useless if, instead of examining its wording and searching for its plain meaning, we shall open an inquiry in the history of the rule in question in this and in other countries and, as a result of this inquiry, will give to an explicit section a meaning different from its plain meaning." [26]

The Court does not, it should be noted, entirely forgo resort to earlier and extraneous sources: it only recommends their avoidance in the absence of special grounds. It should also be considered that, while Lord Herschell's opinion bore directly on the relation of a code to a rule of law previously in effect in the same jurisdiction, and while the Israeli Court includes in its reasoning resort to "legal history"—a broad expression which might apply to anything at all—the actual argument before the Court concerned resort to analogous *foreign* (*i.e.* English) statutory material rather than to previously valid law of the land. Therefore the court's conclusion does not necessarily extend to a case in which the principal issue concerns interpretation of a codelike provision in the light of a prior statute or of a common-law principle that had been in effect in the same jurisdiction. Furthermore, whereas the English case cited involved a codified provision of substantive law, the matter before the Court concerned a statute of interpretation, and the Court, if it so desires, can easily "distinguish" that case from any case in which the codelike enactment deals with a different subject matter. Finally, it will have been noted that, even while laying stress on the self-sufficiency of the Ordinance, the Court did not withstand the temptation to cite a decision of the British House of Lords, so that in the final analysis one could maintain that it is a common-law rule of interpretation that governs the interpretation of codes in Israel after all.

Nevertheless the opinion indicates a tendency toward ascribing to a codelike enactment a certain quality of completeness and exclusiveness, and this tendency makes the opinion interesting despite its uniqueness. It is only to be regretted that the opinion was written in connection with the Interpretation Ordinance, a rather brief and sketchy document that by no stretch of imagination can be said to exhaust the subject matter. The "presumption" that its provisions suffice for the interpretation of the country's laws is untenable, for the Ordinance in question is neither complete nor systematic and therefore falls short of the most elementary requirement of even a partial code. No attempt was made in other decisions of the Supreme Court to adhere to the above view, and numerous are the cases, both before and after the decision cited, in which common-law canons of construction are applied to the interpretation of Israeli and mandatory legislation.

The decision is unique also for another reason: Where the Interpretation Ordinance does not state anything regarding the relevancy of extraneous sources to its own interpretation, some other codelike enactments of the mandatory period explicitly posit such relevancy. Thus, Criminal Code Ordinance, 1936, Section 4:

> This Code shall be interpreted in accordance with the principles of legal interpretation obtaining in England, and expressions used in it shall be presumed, so far as is consistent with their context and except as may be otherwise expressly provided, to be used with the meaning attaching to them in English law and shall be construed in accordance therewith.

Similarly, Civil Wrongs Ordinance, 1944, Section 2 (1):

> The Interpretation Ordinance shall apply to this Ordinance, and subject thereto, it shall be interpreted in accordance with the principles of legal interpretation obtaining in England, and expressions used in it shall be presumed, so far as is consistent with their context, and except as may be otherwise expressly provided, to be used with the meaning attaching to them in English law and shall be construed in accordance therewith.

Now, both of these ordinances are far more complete in relation to their subject matter than the Interpretation Ordinance and are therefore far more susceptible of being regarded as "codes." Nonetheless their interpretation in the light of an extraneous source is expressly provided for. It is true that only English law is mentioned here, and that it is mentioned for purposes of interpretation only. But this one reference suffices to open the door to the introduction of other sources as well, and to their application as material law to boot, whenever English principles of interpretation permit this. In connection with the Civil Wrongs Ordinance it is interesting to note that the Interpretation Ordinance is referred to, but is obviously regarded as insufficient. But even where no express provision as to interpretation has been made in comprehensive mandatory enactments, the courts of the Mandate, and to an even greater extent the courts of Israel, have been reading and interpreting these documents in the light of Ottoman law, prior mandatory enactments, and the rules of the common law and equity, apparently in reliance on Section 46 of the Palestine Order-in-Council. Copious references to judicial precedents based on those sources are made by the courts in current cases in the familiar manner of English and American judges, and these precedents are treated, in accordance with common-law doctrine, as an authoritative formulation of the law in effect.

The question before draftsmen and legislators in Israel is to what extent they should follow established usage and regard future codes as merely another layer of the law of the land, superimposed on the earlier layers but allowing for their continued validity, and to what extent they should regard the future codes as self-sufficient repositories of the law of the land, until such time as the courts, acting under the codes, may develop additional refinements; if the latter attitude is taken, it would follow that reference to precode material in general and to older precedents in particular would be discouraged. It is impossible to know what the legislator will do in this respect. As to the draftsmen, we have available to us the two major projects of codification in Israel that, though not yet introduced as bills in the Knesset, have already undergone several changes and can be regarded as finished products: the project of a law of succession[27] and the project of a law of evidence.[28]

The Project of the Law of Succession contains, in Section 149, a repeal clause that specifically repeals several previous enactments. There is no general provision that the projected code will be the only valid source in respect to the subject matter. A provision tentatively inserted in Section 151 of an earlier, 1952 version of the Project, repealing "any other law repugnant to this law," is omitted from the later 1953 version, and the "Comment" accompanying Section 151 of the 1952 version vividly illustrates the scruples that the authors of the Project had when proposing to do away with older law. In some cases abrogation of earlier law appeared undesirable, as the authors of the Comment correctly stated, when the respective provisions governed certain situations outside the province of succession, and in those other situations it would not do to produce a vacuum. As far as the province of succession is concerned, one might assume that earlier law, where it conflicted with the code, would not apply, under the principle of *lex posterior,* even if this were not stated in the code. But the real difficulty arises, not in cases of clear conflict, but in cases where the construction of the code is in doubt. Should it be construed narrowly in such cases, so as not to conflict with earlier law, and should earlier law therefore continue in effect to that extent, or should the code be construed broadly so as to exclude earlier law? On this point the Project remains silent, nor do the comments and notes on both versions afford clear guidance. And nothing at all is said in the text that would resemble the doctrine of the Workers' Group case, in the sense that the Project should be regarded as the exclusive and complete repository of all law pertaining to the subject, and that no earlier law, whether conflicting or not, need be considered at all. Several passages in the introduction and the comments to the Project indicate that the idea of such exclusiveness and comprehensiveness of the projected code was present in the minds of the draftsmen, but they did not go so far as to give expression to it in the text itself.

The foregoing is correct with one very important exception. Ottoman law, mandatory enactments, and the law of the various religious communities might perhaps continue to apply to some extent,[29] but not so the common law. The 1952 version of the Project went somewhat farther in this respect than the present 1953 version. Section 151 (c) (1) of the 1952 version stated that "in matters of succession, Article 46 of the Palestine Order-in-Council 1922–1947, shall not apply." That article, it will be remembered, directs the civil courts to apply Ottoman law and mandatory enactments as well as common law and equity. But the 1953 version excludes only English law, and excludes it only for purposes of interpretation. (Section 151: "This Law shall be interpreted without reference to English Law.") Nothing is said about the applicability or nonapplicability of English law, to the extent to which it was formerly in effect in Palestine, for purposes other than interpretation, and nothing is said about the applicability or nonapplicability of other prior sources, either for purposes of interpretation of the code or as supplementing the code in relation to questions on which the code does not carry conflicting provisions. Where so much vagueness is present in the text, the ultimate decision as to the continuing importance of precode material will lie with the courts.[30]

Nor does the second major codification effort—the Project of a Law of Evidence—contain a full answer to the questions involved. The first two versions of that code, proposed respectively by the majority and the minority of a committee of experts appointed by the Department of Justice, do not go into the question at all, save for a remark in the Comment to the minority recommendation which indicates that the continued validity of certain extracode materials was taken for granted by the authors of that recommendation.[31] The latest version, prepared by the Ministry of Justice in 1952, merely states, in Section 110, that "the laws set forth in the first column of the appendix to this law shall be repealed to the extent set forth in the second column," and that one specific Ottoman law "shall no longer apply." In the Comment to that section, the authors give the impression of going much further. They state that "this Law will replace the common law of evidence as applied in Israel under Article 46 of the Palestine Order-in-Council of 1922. However, various provisions dealing with the law of evidence are scattered over a number of ordinances, rules and laws. They also will be repealed upon this Law's coming into effect." It is doubtful, though, whether their prediction as to the common law of evidence will be upheld by the courts of Israel, since neither the text nor the appendix to the Project rules out the applicability of Article 46 of the Order-in-Council and therefore of the law derived therefrom. On the face of it, Section 110 of the Project merely invalidates such prior laws as are enumerated in the appendix. It is quite conceivable therefore that judges, if confronted with this text, will hold that other prior law is applicable save where it conflicts with the code. This interpretation is strengthened by the language of Section 111 ("Whenever another law permits or requires the making of any statement under oath, such statement shall be made after caution . . .").

But whatever position is proposed by the draftsmen and adopted by the legislator, in the final analysis the problem will not be solved one way or another until the courts indicate by the technique and trend of their future decisions whether they are willing to accept to the full the logical implications of codification or whether, like their brethren in England and the United States, they will stop short of these implications.

IV

The next complex of questions concerns the contents of the proposed codes. Should they represent in the main a restatement of the law of the land, with revisions here and there so as to assure greater congruity of details, a measure of integration and some modernization, but principally retaining the character of a compilation? Or should they furnish an occasion for thoroughgoing changes and far-reaching innovations?

As far as Israel is concerned, the answer to this question seemed obvious from the beginning. Those who doubted the need for radical changes in the law of the land were also skeptical of the very idea of codification. They were found mainly among the extreme protagonists of British legal institutions, and to them contents of the law and its specific form—the form of a noncodified and often nonstatutory common law—were inextricably bound together. When the decision was taken to take up gradual codification, this spelled also the spirit in which the codification would be undertaken—a spirit of far-reaching change.

This, however, does not give us any indication regarding the specific direction of the change, the social purposes that should determine it, and the material sources whence solutions and formulations should be drawn. As to sources, all three imaginable possibilities and their various combinations were thought of. In the best traditions of Savigny and the historical school, serious efforts were made and are still being made to go back to Jewish sources and to develop a legal structure based on the specific *Volksgeist* of Israel. In practice this means drawing on the rich resources of Jewish religious law, also known as talmudic or rabbinic law. These efforts are enthusiastically supported by the religious-minded part of the Jewish population, since the development of rabbinic law, even in its purely secular phases such as agency, procedure, contracts, and torts, proceeded by way of *responsa,* rule-making and actual decisions by scholars whose authority derived from religious sources. Historic Jewish law is therefore, except for some isolated matters, sanctioned and hallowed by religion. But the appeal of rabbinic law is not limited to religious circles only. To some less religious or nonreligious elements, too, building on the basis of rabbinic law appears as the right solution, since it is in that and in no other legal system that the legal genius, the juristic *Volksgeist,* of the Jewish people is to be found. The protagonists of Jewish law, therefore, advocate a system of codes following as closely as possible the institutions of Jewish law. At the extreme wing of this group are those who deny altogether the need for secular codification in most fields in which there exists a developed system of rabbinic law *(i.e.* broadly speaking, in private law) and see such an activity as needed only in those spheres (criminal law, public law, conflicts, corporations, procedure) in which no such detailed and developed system has been prepared by rabbinical authorities. However, this extreme view is neither very representative nor very influential.

A second school of thought goes to the other extreme and wishes to do what a number of modern nations have done: adopt wholesale some good modern code of some other country. Presumably because in Anglo-American law codes are never regarded as embodying the whole law, and their adoption without the accompanying reception of the unwritten assumptions and principles of Anglo-American law would falsify the original, not even the greatest devotees of the common law have suggested the reception of any of the codes adopted in any common-law jurisdiction. Another reason for this omission may well lie in the fact that most significant common-law codes are American, whereas most Israeli common-law adherents follow the British version. Now and then, though, one finds the thought expressed that the wholesale reception of the best modern Continental codes, a procedure adopted by so many nations in Latin America, Eastern Europe, and the Orient, might prove the simplest solution for Israel as well.

A third school prefers to seek perfection, and proposes to do so in the most difficult manner of all: by way of writing codes *de novo,* on the basis of a comparative and critical survey of all possible sources, including existing local law, English and American law, the Continental legal tradition, and Jewish law, borrowing freely from all of them wherever possible and devising original solutions whenever necessary.

A sincere effort was made by the Ministry of Justice to go the first way and thus work out a law that would express the "national spirit" in Savigny's sense, and at the same time remain true to forms that have received religious sanction. However, by now most influential participants in the work of codification seem to have reached the conclusion that modern society requires a legal structure more directly influenced by the great Western legal systems. There is still every inclination to introduce selected elements, and especially nomenclature, from Jewish sources whenever practicable, but there is no longer any serious thought of making these sources the general framework for the future Israeli codes (except in those fields where it is desired that the religious law should continue to govern social relations; but then no one proposes codification by a secular authority in those fields). Still less attractive to most Israeli jurists is the idea of the "reception" of any French, Italian, Swiss, or other modern code of foreign nations. The opposition to this idea is a double one. It stems on one hand from the advocates of the common law, and on the other from a certain intellectual pride that does not take kindly to the idea that the ancient Jewish people, so steeped in a rich juristic tradition of its own, should give up any claim to original thinking and should simply copy the legal institutions of another nation. It is not that these modern codes were examined with a view to their adoption and found wanting, but that there is no disposition to examine them with a view to wholesale adoption.

There remains therefore only the third way of laboriously comparing texts and solutions, picking and choosing, and occasionally adding altogether new elements. It is a difficult road, and yet it is the road along which the preparatory work of codification is now firmly proceeding in Israel. Within this method there is plenty of room for choice of material, and British statutes, American codes, Jewish and Continental texts vie for pride of place and for acceptance as points of departure. Because of greater familiarity of Israeli jurists with British materials, these enjoy an initial advantage. But of late, partly because of the better channels of contact between Israeli jurists and American centers of learning, American texts are rapidly gaining in influence.

As will be readily conceded, the work of codification cannot proceed without reference to social purposes and values. If anything, there is room for surprise that the influence of these factors—in our days of deep ideological cleavages and fierce partisan loyalties —is not stronger than it is. It seems, however, that except where major postulates of public law are concerned the problems aroused by lawmaking and codification are of a technical sort rather than motivated by ideology, and are relatively little affected by struggles such as those between socialists and adherents of private enterprise, between devout believers and freethinkers, between partisans of a "strong State" and liberals, between authoritarians and democrats, between Jews and Arabs, or between representatives of competing economic interest groups. On those infrequent occasions when legal questions without obvious political implications have come before the Knesset, it was observed that most parliamentarians treated them with utter lack of interest, leaving the debate almost entirely to the few lawyers among them. And it was also observed that the debate between the lawyer-parliamentarians in these cases, contrary to the usual rigid demarcation line existing between parties in the Israeli legislature, tended to upset party lines, so that it assumed the character of a debate between legal technicians differing on the basis of their respective legal training and technical experience, rather than one between different politically motivated points of view. These observations, it is true, have been made *apropos* of fragmentary legal legislation, but there is no reason to doubt that something similar will hold true of the work of codification. In the present preparatory stage of codification, technicians are left to fight out among themselves any controversies that need fighting out. And it stands to reason that if and when the legislative stage is actually reached, it will again be the few lawyers in the legislature that will pay more than a cursory interest to the draft codes.

Nonetheless there are points, even aside from fundamental public-law problems, in which social values and purposes play a noticeable role. In a hotly conducted debate, during which the matter was treated as a moral and social rather than a legal problem, the Knesset adopted on February 16, 1954, a law abolishing the death sentence for murder[32] (except in cases of murder covered by the Law for the Punishment of Nazis and Nazi Collaborators).[33] Presumably the framers of a revised penal code, which is now in the first stages of preparation, will accept this value judgment as a guide in their work.[34] In another case laws were adopted, against the strenuous opposition of Arab members of the Knesset, establishing a minimum age of marriage, prohibiting polygamy, and enacting the principle of equal rights for women.[35] Here, again, the draftsmen of various proposed codes have before them a clear expression of the dominant social attitudes and will proceed accordingly. But these are exceptional points, likely to attract public and parliamentary attention. Other less "sensational" issues have to be faced, on which parties, newspapers, and Parliament have remained mute, but in respect of which the technicians involved in codification will nevertheless have to adopt a position based on social value judgments. Thus, in the work now beginning on a code of land law the basic question must be faced whether mobility of transfers in land should be furthered in pursuit of the principle of liberty of contract, or whether it should be restricted in the interest of social stability or of some socially desirable form of land tenure. Or in connection with the well-advanced work on a proposed code of succession, a basic problem that had to be solved was: To what extent should the principle of free testamentary disposition be allowed to interfere with stability and security of the family or *vice versa,* and at what point should the claims of the community take precedence over those of distant relatives in case of intestacy? And in connection with the proposed criminal code and various other enactments there is the often-debated issue whether the law should provide a minimum as well as a maximum penalty or indicate a maximum penalty only.

V

As would be expected, a series of questions had to be faced in connection with the method and techniques of codification. Arising out of the conditions described above, gradualness was chosen from the first as the prevailing method. At no time was there an over-all, general conception that was to govern all codification efforts. According to the more or less satisfactory state of the law in any area and on the degree of urgency or of interest in having the rules governing that area systematically set out anew, steps have been taken to codify those various areas. As a result we can speak at most of a process of partial codification, and the demarcation line between a code and a mere lengthy statute is not quite clear. It is perhaps not altogether accidental that none of the existing projects of what might be described as partial codes has been given by their draftsmen the Hebrew title corresponding to *code,* and that all of them are neutrally described as *laws.*[36] This title and the fact that the proposed enactments are partial may well signify more than a simple reluctance to undertake too thorough a revision of the existing law: they may signify an equal reluctance to discontinue the use as valid law of older sources and to abandon familiar techniques of adjudication. However that may be, the documents in various stages of preparation that are sufficiently comprehensive to merit tentative classification as codes are the Military Justice Bill,[37] the Project of a Succession Law and the Project of a Law of Evidence, both mentioned before, and the projects of a law of domestic relations, of a penal code, of land law, and of a companies' law—all in various stages of preparation in the Ministry of Justice.

A characteristic feature of governmental activity in Israel is the unusually wide scope of activities reserved to committees and, correspondingly, the relatively narrow scope of activities entrusted to individuals. On a number of occasions the task of legislative draftsmanship, too, was entrusted at first to specially set up committees, designated by the Ministry of Justice but composed wholly or partly of judges, law professors, and practicing attorneys. Experience has shown that this procedure is not uniformly satisfactory, and, except in one instance in which the technique of preparation is laid down by statute, the actual drafting is being increasingly entrusted by the Ministry to an individual, though the successive versions of his draft are submitted to an advisory body or are sent around to a group of individuals with requests for comments. In most cases the actual draftsman is an official of the Ministry of Justice, in which two separate units, the legislative section and the legal planning section, deal respectively with fragmentary and immediate legislation and with long-range legislation of a sort akin to codification. The over-all supervision of the two drafting activities of the two units is in the hands of the Attorney-General, who on occasion has personally appeared in the role of chief draftsman. As for the composition of the groups of advisers and commentators, these vary in accordance with the particular type of document. Judges are almost invariably invited to participate in these groups, and rather often government lawyers from various ministries, members of the faculty of the country's only university law school, and members of the bar are consulted on these occasions. In a few instances in which law professors were concerned, the Ministry, instead of turning to individual professors, addressed the request for comment to the law faculty as a body and left it to the faculty to submit the material to those of its members most likely to contribute relevant comments. Whether the comment comes from a group acting collectively or from individuals, they are merely referred to the actual authors of the draft, the sections of the Ministry of Justice or of the other ministries concerned responsible for the preparation of the document, and, in the final analysis, to the Attorney-General. It is he who, in his capacity as a legal adviser to the government, decides, alone or in consultation with the Minister of Justice and/or with other ministers, in what form the project is to be presented to the Cabinet prior to its formal introduction as a parliamentary bill.[38]

As has been pointed out, the procedure followed in preparing codification, or legislation generally, is decided on rather informally on an administrative level. The one exception is the technique followed in connection with the publication of a revised text of laws antedating the independence of Israel.[39] The only law published hitherto under this procedure is the Interpretation Ordinance.[40]

A peculiar aspect of the country's legislative and regulatory output, which figures in the work of codification as well, is the special care given to linguistic and stylistic problems. This aspect, which presumably does not loom large in countries with a well-developed modern language and an accepted legal phraseology and style, might or might not have parallels in other countries in which the national language, not hitherto used to the full extent, has to be rapidly adapted to novel usages. In Israel, at any rate, the aspect is considered particularly important. Pride in a rich Hebrew terminology, found throughout two and a half millennia of a literature at once sacred and juristic, from the Old Testament onward, causes many participants in the drafting process to take a passionate interest in the choice of words and style. The struggle around a "national" terminology is perhaps fiercer than the struggle around "national" contents of the country's laws. Linguistic purists plead for the use of legal terms taken from ancient Hebrew literary monuments, even if their use in the original context was somewhat different from the meaning to be given them now. Linguistic modernists of various schools of thought prefer to coin new and, until their social acceptance, inevitably artificial terms, though in keeping with Hebrew grammar and phonetics. Still others are not averse to translating literally or simply transliterating foreign-language terms where they denote legal institutions borrowed from the cultural orbit of the language involved. A special section in the Ministry of Justice, the section of Legal Drafting, is responsible for the style of projected legislation, a task which it approaches from the point of view of a linguist and literary stylist no less than from that of a jurist seeking meaningful legal terminology. The same interest in style, to be chosen for linguistic and literary reasons rather than in the interest of a legal congruity, is found all along the line: among the groups of advisers and commentators to whom the draft is sent, among government lawyers, in the Attorney-General, among several Cabinet members, among members of the Knesset, and generally in the literate sections of the public.[41] Particularly in the last two stages of legislation—consideration in the Cabinet and in the Knesset—where most participants are likely to be nonlawyers, changes of language are often introduced in accordance with the literary and linguistic predilections of the participants and without much thought for the effect of these changes on the eventual construction of the texts.

In one case, in connection with the Project of the Law of Succession, at one point in the drafting stage a rather unusual procedure was resorted to. It should be realized that this law raises rather delicate questions. Since Turkish times the area of family relations has been governed predominantly by the religious laws of the respective denominations and administered by autonomous ecclesiastical tribunals. Any change in this respect is bound therefore to arouse deep-lying sentiments in various sections of the population. In these circumstances, and in order to test sentiment in informed circles, the Ministry of Justice suggested to the University Law School that a public conference be arranged in which the Project could be submitted to critical scrutiny. The conference was held under the joint chairmanship of the Attorney-General and the Dean of the Law School. Government lawyers, law school professors, clergymen, and attorneys took part in the proceedings. A large number of attorneys and law students attended the session, which, indeed, aroused considerable interest in the immediately interested circles. Two members of the Knesset also participated in the debate; characteristically, perhaps, both were women interested particularly in the status of women under the projected law. A somewhat similar conference was arranged by the Law School, at the initiative of the Bar Association, on the subject of legislative draftsmanship. Again, the Attorney-General, government lawyers, practicing attorneys and law school teachers, and also philologists took part in the proceedings; and it is noteworthy that the linguistic and literary aspects of the problem focused the attention of the session no less than the impact of language on legal meaning and construction. In both instances, however, the newspapers of the country, though generally very alert to matters of social, religious, and literary import, paid but scant attention to the proceedings, a phenomenon possibly akin to the relative lack of interest of the nonlegal members of the Knesset when "legal" bills are under discussion.

Finally, a special feature of the Israeli codification effort is the extent to which the Israeli government draws on the accumulated experience of foreign scholars, especially of American scholars. In 1951, before starting on the work of codification, Dr. Uri Yadin, an assistant attorney-general and head of the Section of Legal Planning, undertook a study of American methods of legislative draftsmanship and of codification, in the course of which he consulted a number of legal scholars as well as specialists engaged in federal and state legislative drafting. The contacts thus established were continued and strengthened by the formation, under the joint auspices of Harvard Law School and the Israeli Ministry of Justice, of a center for "Cooperative Research for Israel's Legal Development." In this center a small staff working at Harvard conducts research on topics designated by the Israeli Ministry of Justice; Israeli jurists engaged in codification projects visit the center for varying periods of time, in order to pursue their work amidst the rich resources of the Harvard Law Library; and in addition the center acts as liaison agency with American specialists outside of Harvard, forwarding to them material for comments, arranging conferences, etc. This venture is interesting as a unique kind of "technical assistance," mobilizing in an organized and systematic way rich foreign resources for the benefit of the legal development of a far-off country. It may well have another result: because of the intimate and continuing contact between Israeli codifiers and American lawyers, American federal and state law may come to exercise on the future law of Israel a far greater influence than it would otherwise have had.

VI

Though codification is generally thought of as a phenomenon of private, criminal, and procedural law rather than of public law in the narrow sense of the term (*i.e.* constitutional law, administrative law, and, to the extent to which it is regarded as municipal law susceptible of formulation and codification by a single state, international law), some attention might be paid to developments in this latter area that can be said to be analogous to codification.

In this connection one may first of all wonder whether the modern trend toward very lengthy and detailed constitutions, such as the latest constitutions of France, Italy, India, several Latin American republics, and some states of the union within the United States, does not represent a kind of attempt to "codify" constitutional law, in the sense of bringing together the entire relevant material in one systematic and comprehensive document.

It is precisely in this area that codification in Israel has registered the least advance. Not only does Israel lack a comprehensive constitution, but it lacks any formal constitutional document altogether; moreover, there is no discernible present-day trend to have one enacted. At first it was taken for granted that the writing of a formal constitution would form the main and immediate business of the first legislative assembly to issue the new state from popular elections. Expression was given to this expectation in the nation's Declaration of Independence[42] and in the name given to that assembly by the election laws: Constituent Assembly.[43] Indeed, the provisional legislature of Israel began carrying out this intention. A special committee, the "constitutional committee," began working on a constitution, taking as the basis of discussion a fully elaborated draft of a constitutional text, prepared by Dr. Leo Cohn.[44] However, soon after the election, doubts began to appear as to the advisability of proceeding in accordance with the original plan, and in the first statute enacted by the newly elected body it significantly changed its name to Knesset *(=Assembly),* dropping all reference to the constitution-writing function. For some time the idea of a single constitutional document, enacted as such and placed in some manner "above" ordinary laws, continued active, but gradually the Knesset and the public lost interest in it.

The provisional solution of settling constitutional questions by means of fragmentary ordinary legislation, after the British manner, appears to have become a permanent feature, and little real significance is to be attributed to the tendency to describe such laws as "basic." And even though a resolution adopted by the Knesset on June 13, 1950, seemingly denotes the beginning of the writing of an integrated constitution, though chapterwise,[45] in truth it denotes the abandonment of any real effort to write one. As for the category of so-called "basic" laws, there is nothing in the text of a statute that proclaims it as "basic," and no unanimity exists therefore as to which laws are included under that heading. Nor would it matter much if this were made certain, since neither in respect of enactment nor in respect of repeal or degree of authority does a "basic" law hold a position differing in any way from any other statute.[46]

The reasons ascribed in Israel for this failure to enact a formal constitution are various.[47] Some of them explain it by the need to wait till the planned large-scale influx of Jewish immigrants shall have been accomplished and till the State shall have settled more firmly its fundamental character and purposes, so that immigrants shall not find their development restricted by a somewhat rigid document drawn up by others. Others recall the sad experience of European and Latin American regimes with constitutions written in a hurry and contrast the badly working Articles of Confederation with the well-functioning Constitution of the United States, adopted after an interval of eleven years. But whereas these arguments merely justify delay, another line of arguments is increasingly used that makes one wonder whether a formal constitution is at all intended. Thus, it is pointed out that enacting a constitution would necessitate clear-cut decisions regarding the social-economic policies of the State and regarding the place of religion in it, matters concerning which opinion in the country is sharply divided; hence, it is argued, a constitution, instead of uniting the country, would be more likely to divide it. Finally, the orderly political evolution of England is often cited in contrast to that of many a country in which a formal constitution was unable to ensure stability.

Presumably, each of the above arguments holds within itself a kernel of truth; but in addition to them, the course pursued may be caused by the same desire for fluidity and freedom of action that often underlines resistance to codification. Only, in the constitutional realm, it is not so much the freedom of action of the judges as that of the parliamentary majority and of its leaders—the Cabinet—that is being protected; for, after all, a formal constitution is primarily a brake on the State's chief legislative and executive agencies. To avoid misunderstandings it is well to point out that individual rights are very efficiently protected in Israel, in the absence of a formal constitution, by the judiciary against anything but statutes and that the legislature, too, has been very careful to avoid abusing its unlimited powers and to foster a tradition of stability.[48] Nevertheless the political climate of Israel is far removed from that of England; for all the admirable qualities traditionally ascribed to Jews, political self-restraint is not one of them; and though a formal constitution is no guarantee of stability, Israel would do well, in the opinion of this writer, were it to join that overwhelming majority of states that thought it more prudent to impose upon themselves the artificial restraint of a constitution.

A similar reluctance to systematize and codify characterizes Israeli attitudes in the sphere of administrative law. Just as in England, a great body of administrative law has come into being, though the very existence of this branch of law has hardly received official recognition. A variety of administrative tribunals and administrative agencies, some of them with quasi-judicial functions, have been set up, each one with a composition and procedure and jurisdictional framework designed *ad hoc,* none of them integrated, but all of them controlled by the civil courts, more particularly by the Supreme Court armed with the triple weapons of *habeas corpus,* of broad "orders directed to public officers or public bodies in regard to the performance of their public duties and requiring them to do or refrain from doing certain acts,"[49] and of contempt-of-court orders. Here adherence to the British pattern seems to constitute the principal reason for the fragmentized character of the measures taken, but, just as in England, the trend toward systematization, albeit in a rudimentary form, begins to assert itself. There are in existence, since 1934 and 1941 respectively, a Municipal Corporations Ordinance and a Local Councils Ordinance, both often amended, which, though far from being either comprehensive or perfect, offer a relatively stable framework for local self-government. Pending before the Knesset is the draft of a "Law of State Service" that, if enacted, would provide a solid basis for government employment relations. Another pending bill, already referred to, the "Law of Military Justice," is meant to replace an admittedly unsatisfactory document enacted by administrative regulation in a hurry, at the height of the War of Independence. The American Administrative Procedure Act is attentively studied in Israel with a view to its possible adaptation. And at times, though not too frequently, one hears discussion of the merits of the Continental systems of administrative law, with their high degree of systematization.

NOTES

[1] To some extent the problems discussed in this paper are not unlike those faced by Turkey after the First World War. However, the approach and solutions adopted by the Turks at that time were quite different. See L. Ostrorog, *The Angora Reform* (London, 1927).

[2] This statement refers to Palestine (*i.e.*, Israel and the Hashimite Kingdom of Jordan) as a whole rather than to Israel specifically. As a matter of fact, most of the Holy Places of Christianity and all of the shrines venerated by Jews and Moslems lie in the part of Palestine held by Jordan.

[3] Declaration of the Establishment of the State of Israel, in 1 Laws of the State of Israel 3 (5708–1948).

For the background of the State and a description of its governmental and social system, see Akzin, The Palestine Mandate in Practice, 25 Iowa L. Rev. 32–77 (1939); Hanna, *British Policy in Palestine* (Washington, D.C., 1942); Joseph, *British Rule in Palestine* (Washington, D.C., 1948); Hurewitz, *The Struggle for Palestine* (New York, 1950); Robinson, *Palestine and the United Nations* (Washington, D.C., 1947); Akzin, *United Nations and Palestine,* in Jewish Yearbook of International Law 87–114 (1949); Dunner, *The Republic of Israel* (New York, 1950); Lehrman, *Israel* (New York, 1951); Bentwich, *Israel* (New York, 1952); de Gaury, *The New State of Israel* (New York, 1952); Sacher, *Israel* (New York, 1952). The best brief survey of Israel's governmental structure, with full bibliography, is Kraines, *Israel* (Washington, D.C., 1954) (also published in 6 Western Political Quarterly 518–42, 707–27) (1953).

A detailed analysis of the country's legal structure is found, for the time being, only in Hebrew. See Tedeschi, *Mekhkarim Bemishpat Artzenu* (Jerusalem, 1952); and the issues of *Hapraklit,* the Law Review published by the Israeli Bar Association. For a descriptive survey, see *Sidre Shilton Umishpat* (Silbiger ed., Jerusalem, 1953). See however, Yadin, *Sources and Tendencies of Israel Law,* 99 U. of Pa. L. Rev. 561–71 (1950–1951); and S. Z. Cheshin, Justice in a New State, 10 Record of the Association of the Bar of the City of N.Y. 12–25 (1955).

[4] This material is published in the Hebrew and Arabic editions of Israel's Official Gazette. The early issues of the Hebrew edition bear the title *Iton Rishmi;* since February 1949 they have appeared under the title *Reshumot.* In English there is available a collection of *Laws of the State of Israel,* published by the Government Printer, of which there have appeared hitherto Volumes 1, 2, and 5. English translations of the more important statutes are also published annually in the *Government Year-Book* of Israel. Peaslee's *Constitutions of Nations* contains translations of a few basic statutes, but these have since been considerably amended.

[5] None of these enactments is statutory in the full sense of the word, since they originate with administrative agencies—the King-in-Council and the High Commissioner for Palestine respectively. The enactments originated with the former are the Orders-in-Council; those originated with the latter are the Ordinances. The ultimate authority for these enactments was, according to the British conception, the (British) Foreign Jurisdiction Act, 53 & 54 Vict. (1890) Ch. 37; according to the Israeli conception, the Palestine Mandate, approved by the Council of the League of Nations in 1922 (44 Stat. 2184).

A consolidated edition of Orders-in-Council and Ordinances down to the end of 1933 is the three-volume collection of Drayton, *Laws of Palestine* (London, 1934). For later material see Government of Palestine, *Ordinances, Regulations, Rules, Orders and Notices,* published annually.

[6] The fullest, though not quite complete, collection of Ottoman law up to the time of its publication is found in Young, *Corps du droit ottoman,* 7 vols. (Oxford 1905–1906). Some more recent material has been published in *Legislation ottomane* (Paris, Jouve, 1912). Various collections of Ottoman laws have also been published in Cyprus and Iraq, where they continue in effect to a large extent.

Not all this material was in effect in Palestine during the Mandate or remains in effect in Israel today. For the general place of Ottoman law in the legal structure of the country, see *infra,* note 7, reproducing Article 46 of the Palestine Order-in-Council, 1922. Under the general reception clause enacted by the State of Israel in Section 11 of the Law and Administration Ordinance, 5708–1948 (see *infra,* note 11), this article still remains in effect. There is a volume (in Hebrew) by M. Laniado, *A Compendium of Ottoman Laws in Force in Palestine* (Jerusalem, 1929). The most important single part of Ottoman law still largely in effect is the *Medjelle,* a code of private law enacted *seriatim* between 1867 and 1877. An English translation of the *Medjelle,* together with notes and comments, forms the contents of Hooper, *The Civil Law of Palestine and Trans-Jordan,* 2 vols. (Jerusalem, 1933, 1936). A particularly important field in which Ottoman law still governs is land law. As to that, see Goadby and Doukhan, *The Land Law of Palestine* (Tel Aviv, 1935), brought up to date and enlarged in Doukhan, *Dine Karkaot* (2d ed. Jerusalem, 1953) (in Hebrew).

[7] Palestine Order-in-Council, 1922, Article 46. The article, in full, states:

The jurisdiction of the Civil Courts shall be exercised in conformity with the

> Ottoman Law in force in Palestine on November 1st, 1914, and such later Ottoman Laws as have been or may be declared to be in force by Public Notice, and such Orders-in-Council, Ordinances and regulations as are in force in Palestine at the date of the commencement of this Order, or may hereafter be applied or enacted; and subject thereto and so far as the same shall not extend or apply, shall be exercised in conformity with the substance of the common law, and the doctrines of equity in force in England, and with the powers vested in and according to the procedure and practice observed by or before Courts of Justice and Justices of the Peace in England, according to their respective jurisdictions and authorities at that date, save in so far as the said powers, procedure and practice may have been or may hereafter be modified, amended or replaced by any other provisions. Provided always that the said common law and doctrines of equity shall be in force in Palestine so far only as the circumstances of Palestine and its inhabitants and the limits of His Majesty's jurisdiction permit and subject to such qualifications as local circumstances render necessary.

As the text clearly indicates, common law and equity are to be regarded as subsidiary sources, and applied subject to various limitations. In practice, recourse to these sources was relatively infrequent during the first two decades of British rule, but became much more frequent during the third decade, and these sources have retained their importance since the establishment of the State of Israel.

[8] Much of the Talmud is available in an English translation, and a translation of the Code of Maimonides is being published *seriatim,* since 1949, by the Yale University Press. The Shulkhan Arukh, though translated into French and German, is not available in English; but an authoritative abbreviated edition of the code has been so translated: Ganzfried, *Code of Jewish Law* (transl. Goldin, New York, 1927). See also Herzog, *The Main Institutions of Jewish Law,* 2 vols. (London, 1936, 1939). A very elementary survey is Horowitz, *The Spirit of Jewish Law* (New York, 1953). Of practical importance is Scheftelowitz, *The Jewish Law of Family and Inheritance and its Application in Palestine* (Tel Aviv, 1947).

[9] For a general survey of Moslem law, see Schacht, *The Origins of Muhammadan Jurisprudence* (Oxford, 1950); S. Vesey-Fitzgerald, *Muhammadan Law* (Oxford, 1931). A brief summary is contained in *A Symposium on Muslim Law* (Washington, D.C., 1953). Numerous books on Moslem law have been published in India and Pakistan, where, before partition, this law was in effect for the large Moslem populations. (It enjoys today, so far as Pakistan is concerned, an especially important status.) An example of this literature is Fyzee, *Outlines of Muhammadan Law* (Calcutta, 1949). Numerous studies have also appeared in France and the Netherlands, where the subject held great interest because of the largely Moslem composition of their colonial populations, and also in Germany.

[10] The denominations specified above are those enumerated in the Palestine Order-in-Council, 1939, Article 16. Not all of them have established their own ecclesiastical tribunals. At present only three Christian denominations—Roman Catholics, Greek Catholics, and Greek Orthodox—have fully functioning ecclesiastical tribunals.

There is a very rich literature on the canon law of the Roman Catholic Church. Authoritative recent texts are Bouscaren, *Canon Law* (Milwaukee, 1946); Cicognani, *Canon Law* (2d ed Westminster, Md., 1947). For sources on the legal systems of the Eastern churches, see Cicognani, *op. cit.,* at 182–207.

Although, in principle, religious law governs proceedings before the ecclesiastical tribunal of the respective community, under Articles 51–55 and 65 of the Palestine Order-in-Council, 1922, as amended, civil courts, too, are occasionally called on to apply it, pursuant to Articles 47 and 58–64 of the Order-in-Council. Naturally, questions of conflict between the religious laws in effect often arise. See Goadby, *International and Interreligious Private Law in Palestine* (Jerusalem, 1926); Vitta, *The Conflict of Laws in Matters of Personal Status in Palestine* (Tel Aviv, 1947).

[11] Law and Administration Ordinance, 5708–1948 (1 Laws of the State of Israel 7), Section 11: "The law which existed in Palestine on the 5th Iyar, 5708 (14th May, 1948) shall remain in force, insofar as there is nothing therein repugnant to this Ordinance or to the other laws which may be enacted by or on behalf of the Provisional Council of State, and subject to such modifications as may result from the establishment of the State and its authorities."

[12] Only once, to this writer's knowledge, has the Supreme Court of Israel expressly refused to take older sources into consideration when faced with later legislation. See *supra* pp. 311–12. But this was definitely a departure from usual practice.

[13] A number of judicial decisions in the federal and state courts in the United States, conveniently assembled in the various digests and textbooks, render homage to this view. This attitude has been summarized in 2 Sutherland, *Statutes and Statutory Construction* 255 (3d ed 1943) as follows: "The omission of previous laws from the code operates as a repeal of the law for after adoption of the code only the acts appearing in it are law." And further: "Where an official code purports to cover the entire field of regulation any prior law not included in the code is repealed. The fact of non-inclusion is sufficient to create the repeal and the law excluded need not be inconsistent with included material. Nor is it necessary that the code expressly repeal omitted materials. The repeal is an implied one resulting from the intent of the legislature to create a single, complete and exclusive body of law in substitution for all previous enactments" (*id.* at 257–58).

In England no such attitude is discernible even in theory, and codes are regarded as but little differing from consolidation statutes. On the whole the importance imputed to them does not go beyond that explained by Lord Herschell in *Bank of England v. Vagliano Brothers* (see *supra* p. 312), in which the codelike statute is taken as a point of departure rather than as an exclusive repository of the law in effect. Cf. *Craies on Statutes* 335 (5th ed. 1952); *Maxwell on Interpretation of Statutes* 26–27 (9th ed. 1946).

[14] The traditional attitude of Anglo-American lawyers toward statutes, including codelike statutes, has been described by Roscoe Pound in his classical paper on Common Law and Legislation, 21 Harv. L. Rev. 383 (1908). Even though the opinion has occasionally been expressed that things have changed since 1908, the attitude described by Pound does not differ much from that which we find in Allen, *Law in the Making* 378 and 412–14 (3d ed 1939). English and American case material abundantly illustrates the unwillingness of courts to look at codes and other statutes otherwise than in the context of common law and of earlier statutes and their readiness to cite precedent in support of the statute, even when following the statute. The melancholic conclusion of Sutherland that "with our Anglo-American legal tradition it is unlikely that we can anticipate the establishment of true codes in the American States" (*id.* at 249) seems fairly realistic. Cf. 52 Mich. L. Rev. 756 (1953–1954).

[15] Paradoxically, the unwillingness of the members of the legislature to forgo the opportunity for a careful scrutiny of "legal" bills goes hand-in-hand with a certain lack of interest in these bills.

[16] There is, in the Ministry of Justice, a Section for Legal Planning especially charged with the preparation of codelike legislation and other long-range bills.

[17] To avoid misunderstandings it should be explained that, in an apparent attempt to

bring about a synthesis of English, American, and European practice, the Ministry of Justice in Israel is headed by two officers instead of one. The Minister of Justice is a Cabinet member, usually a member of the Knesset, and not necessarily a legal expert. The second in command in the Ministry is an official whose title is "Legal Adviser to the Government," loosely translated as "Attorney-General." The position—not a civil service position, but with a tendency toward permanence—is filled by a prominent lawyer, who acts as principal law officer of the government, heads the machinery of public prosecution, often participates in Cabinet meetings (without vote), and has numerous other functions. In certain respects the Attorney-General acts as the Minister's subordinate, in others is independent of him; further definition of the dividing line between these two areas might be useful. There is no office in Israel corresponding to the Lord Chancellor in England: the Minister of Justice is not a member of the judiciary and does not preside over a legislative body, but has a greater measure of control over the department and over the administration of the courts.

[18] Merely an approximate estimate based on personal observation. Attempts to obtain precise statistical material were not successful.

[19] Cf. Salmond's *Jurisprudence* 180 (8th ed 1930); 3 Sutherland, *op. cit. supra* note 13, at 171–76 and American cases cited therein.

[20] The opinion can be ventured that the very preoccupation of American legal scholars, especially those of the "realistic" school, with the problem of the predictability of the law, a problem almost ignored by their European brethren, merely reflects an existing contrast: by definition, court decisions based on codes and statutes are more predictable than those based on common law and *stare decisis*. Hence there is less need in a Continental system to worry about certainty and predictability. Interesting observations on the relative freedom of the courts under the two systems are made by Friedmann, *Legal Theory* 370 *et seq.* (3d ed 1953). Though Professor Friedmann's admonition against exaggerating the freedom of the Anglo-American judge and the limitations on the Continental judge is fully justified, it is equally important not to ignore the very real difference between judges in the two systems in this respect. For a well-balanced view on the place of the courts in the development of civil law see Deak, The Place of the "Case" in the Common and the Civil Law, 8 Tulane L. Rev. 337–57 (1933–1934); and see the literature cited *id.* at 340 n. 6.

[21] The distinction between the motives of legislators and those of lawyers is particularly valid in Israel because, in contrast with most Western-type states, lawyers constitute but a minute element in the legislature. At the time of this writing there are barely a dozen Knesset members with legal training out of a total of 120 members. The nonidentification between politician and lawyer is an important feature of the Israeli governmental system.

[22] One of these enactments, the Criminal Code Ordinance, 1936, even bears officially the title "code."

[23] Quasi-statutory enactments of the High Commissioner during the Mandate are known as "Ordinances," as explained above. The name was retained for enactments made by the first legislature of Israel, the Provisional Council of State, from May 1948 to February 1949. The Interpretation Ordinance itself was subsequently published in a revised form on January 1, 1954, pursuant to Section 16 of the Law and Administration Ordinance, 5708–1948, as amended. Cf. *infra* notes 39 and 40.

[24] *Kvutzat Poalim Lehityashvut Shitufit Veakh. v. Bet Din Lesafsarut Veakh.* (Workers' Group for Co-operative Settlement *et al.* v. Price Tribunal *et al.*) 5 Piske Din (1951) 113, 131–32.

[25] [1891] A. C. 107, 144.

[26] 5 Piske Din (1951) 134–35.

[27] English translations of the text and explanatory notes of two successive versions of the bill, the original 1952 version and a 1953 revision, have been made by the Harvard Law School–Israel Cooperative Research under the name "A Succession Bill for Israel," in 1952 and 1954 respectively. Cf. Yadin, The Proposed Law of Succession for Israel, 2 Am. J. Comp. Law 143–55 (1953).

[28] The text and explanatory comments of the Project have been translated in 1953 by the Harvard Law School–Israel Cooperative Research under the name "An Evidence Bill for Israel."

[29] However, the authors of the Succession Law Project propose to amend the 1922 Palestine Order-in-Council by deletion of the words "succession, wills and legacies, and confirmations of wills" from Articles 51 and 54 of the Order-in-Council (Section 151 of the 1952 Project; Section 149 of the 1953 Project). This deletion would have the effect of altogether excluding these matters from the jurisdiction of ecclesiastical tribunals. The intention of the authors of the Project is, of course, to substitute secular law for religious law. Thus the Comment to Section 151 (b) of the 1952 Project:

> The absence of a law of succession, *i.e.* a secular Israeli law that deals fully with succession matters, is one of the major causes for the division of jurisdiction in these matters between state courts, religious courts and foreign consuls and of the multifarious application of general domestic laws, the laws of the religious communities and of foreign countries. Upon enactment of the new Law there will be neither room nor need for these complexities because "successions, wills and legacies" will be withdrawn from the matters of personal status. . . .

[30] It may be interesting to reproduce here the Comment to Section 151 (c) of the 1952 Project:

> Pursuant to Art. 46 of the Order-in-Council the courts decide cases pursuant to Ottoman law, mandatory legislation and the principles of common law and doctrines of equity in force in England. These three sources of Palestinian law —and pursuant to Sec. 11 of the Law and Administration Ordinance, 1948, also of Israeli law—will no longer apply in matters of succession. Instead, the new law, a basic [wrong translation; "original" is the correct translation of the Hebrew term used] law of the Knesset, will apply exclusively. In this area, therefore, the existing link with the laws which the Ottoman and mandatory powers have imposed on the country will be severed. This does not mean that Palestinian decisions rendered during the mandatory period and Israeli decisions from the establishment of the State until the enactment of this Law or English decisions of any period will no longer serve the courts as guide posts and sources of enlightenment. However, instead of being a part of existing law or serving as binding authority, they will henceforward be only persuasive authority; in other words, they will command the same degree of authority as legal sources of other countries and of Hebrew law, to the extent that these sources are capable of aiding in the interpretation of the new Law.

But in view of the significant change introduced in the text of the 1953 Project, it is more than doubtful whether this far-reaching comment still reflects the meaning of the authors of the project and whether, in any case, it may still meaningfully explain the new text.

[31] Advisory Committee on the Reform of Civil Procedure, Minority Report. Comment:

> However, this Law will not repeal the pertinent chapter of the Rules of Civil Procedure of 1938, for in the opinion of the authors of this Bill, this opportunity, too, should be preserved. . . . (*An Evidence Bill for Israel*, p. 88).

[32] *Reshumot, Sefer Hachukkim* (5714–1954) 74. English translation in Government Year-Book 5715–1954, 249.

[33] *Reshumot, Sefer Hachukkim* (5710–1950) 281. English translation in Government Year-Book 5712–1951/1952, 189.

[34] By no means is the possibility excluded, however, that the issue of capital punishment may be revived in connection with the preparation of a new criminal code. The matter is still regarded as one not intellectually settled, and actual experience may induce second thoughts among either adherents or opponents of capital punishment.

[35] Age of Marriage Law. *Reshumot, Sefer Hachukkim* (5710–1950) 286. English translation in Government Year-Book 5712–1951/1952, 194. Women's Equal Rights Law. *Reshumot, Sefer Hachukkim* (5711–1951) 248. English translation in Government Year-Book 5712–1951/1952, 193.

The prohibition of polygamy has been effected, in Section 8 of the Women's Equal Rights Law, by way of repeal of a section of the Criminal Code to the effect that proof that "the law as to marriage applicable to the husband both at the date of the former marriage and at the date of the subsequent marriage was a law other than Jewish law and allowed him to have more than one wife" constituted a good defense against the charge of the felony of bigamy. This closed the only previously existing gap in relation to polygamy, viz., polygamy among Moslems; for Christians, polygamy being prohibited by church law, its exercise was considered a felony, and so it was among Jews, save in a special instance in which another clause of the Criminal Code left its control to the rabbinical tribunals.

[36] *Khok* is the Hebrew term used both for *law* generally and, more specifically, for *statute*. The term *khukka,* which has come to denote *constitution,* is occasionally used for *code* as well. The only enactment made in Israel that was called *khukka* in the sense of code was the "Code of Military Justice" of 1948, which was not a statute at all, but an emergency regulation made in accordance with Section 9 of the Law and Administration Ordinance; the validity of that document was, however, repeatedly extended by statute. The bill now pending before the Knesset, which is intended to replace the 1948 "code," is entitled *khok,* in the usual manner.

[37] *Reshumot, Hatzaot Khok* (5714) 154.

[38] We deal here with the preparation of government bills only. In fact, the government has monopolized legislative initiative to such an extent that private members' bills play a very minor role on the over-all legislative scene in Israel.

[39] This procedure, twice revised by action of the Knesset, has been outlined in its latest form by the Knesset of June 8, 1954, as follows:

> Section 16.
>
> (a) The Minister of Justice may publish in the Reshumot a project of a new version of any law which existed in Palestine on the eve of the establishment of the State and which is still in force in the State. Such version shall contain all the modifications resulting from the establishment of the State and its authorities and all the amendments, modifications and additions which took place in that law by virtue of legislation after the establishment of the State.
>
> (b) The Minister of Justice shall establish advisory committees of three mem-

bers, of whom one—the chairman—shall be a judge appointed by the Chief Justice of the Supreme Court, one—the Legal Adviser to the Government or his representative, and one—a representative of the Bar Association or a representative of the Hebrew University.

(c) Within a period decided upon by the Minister of Justice, for each project of a new version, by notice published in the Reshumot, an advisory committee shall examine the proposed version and shall bring before the Constitutional and Legal Committee of the Knesset, in writing, its recommendations regarding the amendments required in its opinion in order to make the proposed version correspond with the original law.

(d) The Constitutional and Legal Committee of the Knesset shall decide upon the new version in the light of the recommendations of the advisory committee, and it [this version] shall be in force with its publication in the Reshumot over the signature of the Minister of Justice.

(e) Upon the entry of the new version in force as aforesaid, it shall be binding law, and no other version of the same law shall have any more effect and no argument shall be entertained to the effect that the new version deviates from the original law.

(f) Where a law has been enacted in the State and amended, the Minister of Justice may publish in the Reshumot a version of that law which shall contain all the amendments made thereto, and he may, in this connection, modify the numbers of the sections, divide sections or consolidate them.

(Law to amend the Law and Administration Ordinance (No. 4), 1954. *Reshumot, Sefer Hachukkim* (5714) 126).

The above text has been translated and reproduced here in full because it represents the only legislative provision in Israel that deals with the procedure for the revision and consolidation of laws.

[40] *Reshumot, Dine Israel, Nussakh Khadash* (5714) 2.

[41] A. Goldberg, *Mishpat, Am Velashon* (Law, nation and language), Hapraklit 1954, 139–52.

[42] Declaration of the Establishment of the State of Israel (1 *Laws of the State of Israel* 3).

[43] 2 *Laws of the State of Israel* 24, 56, 61, 64, 80, 81, 87, 93, 94, 114, 116.

[44] 3 Peaslee, *Constitutions of Nations* 743 (1950).

[45] "The First Knesset directs the Constitutional and Legal Committee to prepare a project of a Constitution for the State. The Constitution shall be constructed chapter by chapter in such a manner that each of them shall constitute a distinct basic law. The chapters shall be brought before the Knesset as the committee shall complete its work, and all the chapters together shall comprise the State Constitution." *Reshumot,* 5 *Divre Haknesset* (1950) 1743. The discussion of that resolution, *ibid.,* 1711–22, sheds light on the intent of the legislature.

[46] A good example of the extent to which the "ordinary" character of even the most "basic" constitutional laws precludes the attribution of any higher degree of validity to their provisions is afforded by Sections 12 and 13 of the Law Concerning the Office of State President, 1951. Seeking to prevent undue interference by the Knesset with the President's office, these sections specify that the removal of the President from office requires a decision by the Knesset concurred in by three fourths of the entire Knesset and arrived at after special procedure in committee. But these sections themselves and the whole statute

of which they form part may be amended or repealed by any majority whatsoever, without even requiring that a given quorum be present.

[47] See O. Kraines, *op. cit. supra* note 3, at 31.

[48] The only exception worth mentioning is a certain predilection for retroactive legislation.

[49] Courts Ordinance, 1940, Section 7. Though nothing in the Ordinance required it to do so, the Supreme Court of Palestine has understood this broad power, in conjunction with Article 43 of the 1922 Palestine Order-in-Council, as meaning that the Court in applying it shall be guided by the considerations applying in England to petitions in the nature of Mandamus, Certiorari, Prohibition, Quo Warranto (until its abrogation in England in 1938), and Injunction. Accordingly there is a tendency to relate the order given to one of these specific orders. The Supreme Court of Israel has not yet expressly departed from that position and frequently takes its stand on one of the English orders.

15

Codification and International Law

JACK BERNARD TATE

AT A meeting of the Assembly of the League of Nations in the autumn of 1930 five of the Great Powers of Europe put forward a draft of a resolution to serve as a guide to the League's policy of codification. The resolution proposed by the British, French, German, Italian, and Greek Delegations but not adopted, stated:

"It [is] desirable to recognize a distinction between the gradual formulation and development of customary international law, which should result progressively from the practice of states and the development of international jurisprudence, and the formulation in international conventions freely accepted by the States, of precise rules, whether derived from customary international law or entirely new in character, to govern particular relations between States the regulation of which by general agreement is found to be of immediate practical importance."[1]

The draft resolution goes on to say:

"The Assembly considers that the term 'Codification' as applied to the work for the development of international law undertaken by the League of Nations should be understood as an activity of the last mentioned character, and that, in present circumstances, as was shown by the experience of the Conference at The Hague, it is not for the League or the Conferences convened by it to endeavor to formulate the rules which are binding upon states as part of the customary law of nations."[2]

JACK BERNARD TATE *is Associate Dean of the Yale Law School*

Whether or not the proposal should have been approved by the Assembly, we need not consider for the moment. But the distinction, it is submitted, is valid. The development of international law by convention since 1930 has moved apace where designed "to govern particular relations between States the regulation of which by general agreement is found to be of immediate practical importance." Meanwhile the formulation of "the rules which are binding upon States as a part of the customary law of nations" has been less successful.

Today, we are perhaps somewhat more hopeful of the process of codification of international law than were those who in 1930 had so recently seen the substantial collapse of the hope that had gone into the careful preparatory work for the Hague Conference. We are also somewhat less rigid in our definitions of codification.

Sir Cecil Hurst, in his address before the Grotius Society in 1946, made "A Plea for the Codification of International Law on New Lines." He pointed out: "Codification of international law in the sense in which the term was used in the movement which culminated in the Conference of 1930 embodies two possible ideas, two possible methods."[3] He said that one is limited to the ascertainment and declaration of existing rules. This he considered the strict and proper sense. This was the British view. The other, more prevalent on the Continent, he described as incorporating the idea of amending the law as well as defining it; the statement of the rules as they ought to be.

Sir Cecil came out with the proposal that a formulation of broad rules and principles should be achieved through national and international effort. He suggested that a small body of men in each country should make scientific studies of international law available to an international scientific organization as a basis for work that should commend itself to the world entirely by the weight that would attach to its scientific merit. In brief, as Sir Arnold McNair pointed out in his recent lectures at the New York University Law Center, the kind of codification he had in mind was an unofficial restatement.[4]

The memorandum submitted by the Secretary General of the United Nations, in 1949, entitled Survey of International Law in relation to the Work of Codification of the International Law Commission, repeatedly asserts that practically the entire field of international law can be covered—codified—by the work of the Commission, under the procedure envisaged in its statute. But the memorandum is careful to add that the work of the Commission may be "of various forms and of varying degrees of authority."[5] Perhaps even this is too sanguine. Most likely many areas of codification by convention will remain uncovered by the Commission.

Now, let us sort out the different meanings of the word "codification" as we have used it. It has been said that to many the word code is a "blessed word" of a peculiar attraction.

To some the term "codification of international law" still signifies, as it did in former times, the setting down of the whole international *corpus juris* and its formal adoption by the international community. For his part, the present writer believes that the time has passed, if it ever existed, when this undertaking was possible. Nor does he think it desirable.

Many aspects of international law should not be codified in the sense of being merely registered in conventions. In the first place, we immediately run into the problem of unanimity and disagreement.

The registration of existing legal positions would often be a mere registration of disagreements, foreclosing development and defeating legislative needs. We should neither crystallize the obsolete nor stall growth at the level of the lowest common denominator. In addition there are principles that, if registered in conventions, would open them to the perennial arguments as to whether a particular treaty is declaratory of international law or merely binding on the states party thereto in exception to international law.

This writer would suggest that in these realms of principle we should do well to codify through the procedure of restatement as suggested by Sir Cecil Hurst and, more recently, by Sir Arnold McNair.

Of course there are many aspects of international relations that lend themselves to, and even require, in the words of the draft resolution to which this paper first adverted, "the formulation of international conventions by the States, of precise rules, . . . to govern particular relations between States the regulation of which by general agreement is found to be of immediate practical importance." Certainly the conventions regulating navigation by air and by sea are of immediate practical importance. There detailed regulation by general international agreement is essential. The same is true of many other fields—postal, telecommunications, health, tariffs, trade, etc. These are the fields of vastly expanding international legislation.

But success in this type of legislation does not lead this writer to believe that the legislative method can be applied helpfully to all realms of international law. The formulation of rules binding on states as part of customary international law can be codified better by way of restatement. The purpose of restatement should be to restate international law so as to make it more clear and more readily available. The method should be similar to that employed by the American Law Institute and by the Harvard Research in International Law. The results, in the systematization and development of international law, should be comparable to those of the American Law Institute in clarifying, simplifying, and rendering more certain the jurisprudence of the United States. The result should be at least as helpful as the Harvard Restatements in promoting the understanding and progressive development of international jurisprudence.

Restatements would further the purpose of the provisions of Article 13 of the Charter of the United Nations for the progressive development and codification of international law and would be helpful to the International Law Commission established by the General Assembly to promote that purpose.

It is suggested that codification by restatement would commend itself to the International Law Commission and to the General Assembly.

The memorandum of the Secretary General referred to states: "In the sphere of codification . . . the main purpose of the Commission is not that of an international legislator. Its function is essentially and in the first instance that of a judge. It has to find what the law is and to present it in a form which is precise, systematic and as detailed as the overriding principle of the necessary generality of the law allows."[6]

Restatement through the effort of national groups would facilitate codification by restatement on the part of the International Law Commission with precision, system, and detail.

The results of the work of the Commission would of course go to the General Assembly to be noted or approved and would furnish to the international community a foundation of international law of scientific merit. It would further the rule of law, international understanding, order, and peace.

NOTES

1 League of Nations Official Journal, Special Supplement No. 85, Eleventh Assembly, Ordinary Session, Minutes of First Committee 158–59 (1930).

2 *Ibid.*

3 Transactions of the Grotius Society, XXXIII, 146 (1946).

4 McNair, The Development of International Justice, 31 (1954).

5 Survey of International Law in Relation to the Work of Codification of the International Law Commission, Memorandum of the Secretary General 16 (1949).

6 *Id.* at 64.

16

The Code and The Common Law in Louisiana

JOHN H. TUCKER, JR.

Any program to celebrate the adoption of the Civil Code of France, the Code Napoleon,[1] must necessarily focus attention on Louisiana, the only one of these United States that has always had the civil law and that has had a Civil Code[2] almost as long as France itself.[3]

But New York has something more than an academic interest in Louisiana law, for a native of New York, Edward Livingston, largely charted the course that the laws of Louisiana have followed ever since it became a part of this nation. Coming from the domain of common law, he entered into the spirit of the civil law and fashioned for his adopted state legal institutions that have survived to this date.

There are three important jurisdictions in which the civil law, as exemplified in the Code Napoleon, has been brought into sharp contact with the common law: South Africa, Quebec, and Louisiana.

There is no near relationship between the Code Napoleon and the law of South Africa, which differs from Quebec and Louisiana in that its civil law came from Holland and consisted of an uncodified body of laws, decisions, and doctrine originating in Roman and Dutch law.[4]

Quebec, however, retained its archaic laws derived from the

JOHN H. TUCKER, JR., *is President of the Louisiana Law Institute*

Custom of Paris, the royal ordinances, and a diversity of other more or less uncertain sources until 1866, when it adopted the Civil Code started in 1857.[5] A Canadian jurist has said that the success of the Louisiana Code, established by fifty years' experience, was of inestimable benefit to the framing of the Quebec Code.[6] In fact the law that ordered the preparation of the Civil Code for Quebec declared that "the great advantages which have resulted from codification as well in France as in the State of Louisiana and other places render it magnificently expedient to provide for the codification of the laws of Lower Canada."[7] Though the Quebec Code adheres to the form of the Code Napoleon, nevertheless Quebec did not borrow anything from those parts of France called "countries of the written law," and hence it has not reproduced certain parts of the Code, such as those relating to dowry.[8] Louisiana, on the other hand, adopted its first Civil Code, based on the Code Napoleon, only four years after that monumental work was adopted by France. During the long period since its adoption the Civil Code of Louisiana has been developed by legislation, doctrine, and case law concurrently with some statutory adaptation of the common law of its sister states and of England on a variety of subjects mostly beyond the scope of the Civil Code.

A broad, but critical, qualitative analysis of the content of the law of Louisiana will give some idea of the virility of the Code Napoleon when brought into such close association with the common law.

In view of the source of the law in Quebec at the time of the adoption of the Civil Code and the longer experience of Louisiana with a Civil Code modeled on the Code Napoleon, Louisiana may well furnish the most important example for such an analytical study.[9]

This inquiry should be restricted, however, to those general subjects included in the Civil Code of Louisiana and in the Code Napoleon, which was only one of five codes adopted in the period of codification, the others being the Code of Practice, the Commercial Code, the Penal Code, and the Code of Criminal Procedure.

SOMEWHAT OF LOUISIANA LEGAL HISTORY

The effective extent of the civil law and the common law in Louisiana must be examined in the light of the complex history of the state's legal institutions.

Civil government began in Louisiana with the letters patent issued to Crozat, September 14, 1712, the seventh article of which required that the royal ordinances and the Custom of Paris be observed for its law and custom. This provision was amplified and restated in the 15th article of the charter of the Company of the West, granted in 1717, and these laws prevailed until abrogated by the Spanish in 1769.[10]

During this period France was governed by a multiplicity of laws, of greatly different origin. In the south the Roman law prevailed; in the north the Franks had established a system of customary law resulting from the prolonged public repetition of the same overt practices and usages. These customs were at first unwritten and required that the antiquity, notoriety, and multiplicity of the usage relied on be proved in court in the same way as any other fact. Naturally customs crystallized around localities and acquired a territorial rigidity that greatly increased their number and the uncertainty of their application. This condition inevitably led to their reduction to written form, ordered by the ordinance of Montils-les-Tours, April 17, 1453, during the reign of Charles VII, but the work was not commenced until the reign of Charles VIII. The Custom of Paris was reduced to writing in 1510 and, because of the criticism of Dumoulin and d'Argentre, was revised in 1580. The drafts of the Customs were made by practical men, and the unwritten law, derived from usage, became a written law, with legislative sanction. There were sixty general customs in France, bearing the names of the Districts to which they applied, and about three hundred lesser customs of more restricted territorial application.

The Custom of Paris was predominant, and it was naturally selected as the basic law of French colonies. Paris was the capital of the kingdom, and its *parlement* had great influence on other *parlements*. It was the principal foyer of the study of law, and the Custom of Paris had received great attention from the jurisconsults. Moreover it was considered as the common law of the kingdom, applicable where other customs were silent.[11]

During the period of French dominion over Louisiana several important royal ordinances formed a part of its civil law. The ordinance of April 1667, prepared at the instance of Colbert, under the reign of Louis XIV, sometimes called the Code Louis, or Code Civil, regulated civil procedure.[12] The ordinances of Daguesseau on donations (1731), on testaments (1735), and on substitutions (1747) were remarkable in that they later passed, in a large measure, into the Code Napoleon.[13] To what extent they were actually applied in Louisiana cannot be definitely stated. It is believed that the Code Louis had extended application in matters of procedure, but it is probable that the ordinances of Daguesseau, theoretically in force, had little effect in the colony.

The Custom of Paris is brief. It contains only 362 articles and sixteen titles. Aside from those dealing with fiefs and the relation of lord and vassal, all had application to colonial Louisiana, and some of its provisions are immediately recognizable today in the Louisiana Civil Code. That is particularly true of the community property system, pronounced by Article 220 of the Revised Custom of Paris, derived from Article 110 of the first Custom of Paris, beyond which its origin as a part of the Germanic customs is but vaguely perceived through the misty dawn of legal history.[14]

By a secret agreement made in Paris November 3, 1762, France ceded Louisiana to Spain. This cession was confirmed by the Treaty of Paris, February 10, 1763, but effective transfer of sovereignty was not accomplished until O'Reilly was established as governor in 1769.[15] On November 25 of that year he published an ordinance that had the effect of abrogating French law and establishing the law of Spain in Louisiana.[16] On the same day he published a digest of instructions on the manner of instituting suits and of pronouncing judgments, based on the *Nueva Recopilacion* and the *Recopilacion de las Indias,* practically a miniature code of practice, sometimes called O'Reilly's Code, some of the provisions of which have directly passed into the present Louisiana Code of Practice. From that day until they were finally repealed in 1828, the laws of Spain were the basic laws of Louisiana, and they have left their mark on its jurisprudence.[17]

The laws of Spain in force at this period were multitudinous, for Spain, in the earlier centuries of its jurisprudence, had adopted many codes and abrogated none. We find in the earlier reports of the Louisiana Supreme Court frequent citations of most of these Spanish legal institutions, such as the *Fuero Juzgo, Fuero Real,* the *Siete Partidas,* and the *Nueva Recopilacion.* Even in Spain there was a great diversity of opinion as to which of these should prevail in cases of conflict, and the subject was elaborately discussed in the opinions of the Louisiana Supreme Court of the period in which Spanish law prevailed.

These codes, with other Spanish enactments, constituted a tremendous volume of legislation applicable to Louisiana, comprised in twenty-three volumes of eighty-nine books of 1,543 titles containing 20,225 laws.[18]

It is interesting to note that, in a case involving the cities of New Orleans and Philadelphia and the will of Stephen Girard,[19] the Louisiana Supreme Court even found it necessary to hold that the Council of Trent was never in force in Louisiana.

Spain, by the treaty of San Idlefonso, October 1, 1800, ceded Louisiana back to France, but France did not assume actual sovereignty until November 30, 1803, and then assumed it only to transfer Louisiana to the United States twenty days later. In this short period nothing was done to repeal the Spanish law or to establish the law of France. The Louisiana Supreme Court has held, therefore, that the law of Spain was the law of Louisiana at the time of its acquisition by the United States, and that Louisiana courts would take judicial note of the law of Spain and of those countries deriving their laws from Spain, but that the law of France would have to be proved as the law of any other country, although admittedly the Louisiana Code is based on the Code Napoleon.[20]

Immediately after the cession of Louisiana to the United States there was an influx from the United States of officials, lawyers, and others seeking their fortunes who, because unfamiliar with the laws in force at the time, sought to establish the common law as the basic law of the new territory. In this they were aided and abetted by W. C. C. Claiborne, the first territorial governor.

Edward Livingston, who had only recently come from New York, was one of the leaders in the fight to retain the civil law. Perhaps his common-law antecedents added to the strength of his opposition to adoption of the common law.[21]

The Act of Congress of March 26, 1804 divided Louisiana into two territories, Orleans (now the State of Louisiana) and Louisiana (none of which is now part of the state), and provided for their government, and the Act of March 2, 1805 further provided for the government of the territory of Orleans. These two statutes retained in effect all laws in force at the date these acts were adopted that were not inconsistent with them, until altered, modified, or repealed by the legislature.[22] The first territorial legislature attempted to preserve the Spanish civil law and the Roman law on which it was thought to be based, pending the preparation of a civil code for the territory envisioned by the resolution of the legislative council adopted in 1805,[23] but Governor Claiborne vetoed the act passed for that purpose.[24] The legislature thereupon appointed Moreau-Lislet and James Brown to prepare jointly a civil code for the territory.[25] They completed their work in little less than two years, and it was promulgated by an act approved March 31, 1808,[26] as "A Digest of the Civil Laws now in force in the Territory of Orleans." Generally called the Code of 1808, it is largely taken from the Code Napoleon, promulgated in France on March 21, 1804.[27]

A few years later the Supreme Court held that the Code of 1808 was only a digest of laws in force at the time of its adoption; that those laws must be considered as untouched wherever the alterations introduced in the Code did not repeal them; and that only such parts of laws in force at the date of the adoption of the Code were repealed as were either contrary to or incompatible with the Code.[28] This was a virtual judicial revival of Spanish law, and the legislature first tried to remedy the resulting confusion by authorizing the translation of the *Siete Partidas*.[29] This was entrusted in 1819 to Moreau-Lislet and Henry Carleton, with Edward Livingston appointed to check the translations,[30] but the publication of their work was not sufficient to remove the basic cause of the confusion: namely, the multiplicity of the sources and resulting uncertainty of Spanish law, further complicated by the existence of the Code of 1808 itself.

This complex situation led to a general revision of the law, which was ordered by the legislature on March 14, 1822, with Pierre Derbigny, a native of France, Moreau-Lislet, of Santo Domingo, and Edward Livingston, from New York, appointed to prepare a new Civil Code, a Code of Practice, and a Commercial Code.[31] In 1823 they submitted to the legislature a preliminary report that epitomizes the philosophy with which they approached their task, and shortly thereafter a *projet* of the new code that resulted from the additions and amendments they proposed to be made to the Code of 1808.[32] After much discussion in the legislature the Code was adopted in April 1824[33] and promulgated in February 1825.[34] It is known as the Code of 1825.

It is possible to determine in large measure the source of this code from the *projet* prepared by the commissioners who drafted it. Frequent citation is given to specific authorities for its proposals. Though the Code Napoleon was again used as the basis of the Code of 1825, and its provisions predominate, the code commissioners did not hesitate on occasion to draw from Spanish and Roman sources or to avail themselves of the work of the commentaries both on the Code Napoleon, several of which had already been published at the time of the preparation and adoption of the Code of 1825, and on the customary and Roman law that preceded it.

The Code was originally written in French. The English text is a translation, imperfect in some respects. It has been held that in case of conflict the French text still controls where the identical text has been retained in the subsequent Code of 1870.[35]

In 1805 Louisiana adopted an act to regulate practice in the courts, and this served as a sort of embryonic Code of Practice[36] until the important codification period twenty years later, when the Code of Practice was adopted. It exists today in substantially the same form, little affected by amendment. However, there is considerable procedural law in the general statutes outside the Code.[37]

The Code of Practice was adopted in 1824 and promulgated in 1825, but by reason of omission of the enacting clause it was reenacted in 1828.

The Commercial Code and the Penal Code, prepared at the same time, were not adopted, although the penal code, the work of Edward Livingston, became widely known far beyond Louisiana.[38] Whereas the Civil Code of 1825 was largely a reiteration of the Code Napoleon, the Code of Practice is an original Louisiana code, which, however, in many respects reflects its civil-law ancestry.[39]

The Civil Code and the Code of Practice were revised in 1870. Actually, the revision was essentially editorial, mainly for the elimination of all articles relating to slavery, the integration of amendments made to the Code since 1825 and of extrinsic acts relating to codal subjects, and the elimination of all parts of the codes that had been repealed since 1825.

The Louisiana State Law Institute, under mandate of the legislature, is now nearing completion of a *projet* for a completely revised and integrated Code of Practice and is laying the groundwork for a *projet* for a revision of the Civil Code.

SELECTIVITY OF LOUISIANA LAW

Louisiana was forced by the complex of its legal inheritance to exercise that selectivity or eclecticism that has characterized the establishment of legal institutions in countries of the written law.[40]

In France the customary law was codified by a process of ascertainment, selection, and arrangement of the customs then prevalent, and they were adopted and promulgated and thereafter became in effect true codes with legislative authority.[41]

The Code Napoleon is the result of the fusion of the customary law of the north and the Roman law that prevailed in the south of France.

In the nineteenth century practically all the countries of Latin America recast their civil codes on the model of the Code Napoleon, and most of the countries of Europe in the main have based their codes on that great code.[42] Some countries have even preferred to retain the Code Napoleon as the basis of their laws even though it had been imposed upon them by the conqueror, rather than revert to their old laws when liberated from his yoke.[43]

Some English scholars have said that the common law of England has been extended beyond the dominion of the English crown only as the result of conquest or colonization, whereas the French Civil Code has been freely adopted and voluntarily imitated by more than a score of countries all over the world. They mournfully predict that the common law will not be extended beyond its present boundaries, which nowhere pass outside English-speaking countries—apparently a price that must be paid for the privilege of an uncodified and unwritten law.[44]

The change in the sovereignty of Louisiana in 1803 brought the opportunity and the obligation to survey its laws and remodel them according to the ethnic composition of the region and its new status as a territory of the United States. Making a fresh start as a part of a new country, Louisiana had an opportunity to establish its legal system on the bases that seemed best and proper, unhampered by the tenacious tentacles of an unwritten law. A wealth of legal materials was available to the new territory, and the immigration of considerable "American" legal talent steeped in the common-law tradition furnished the catalyst to refine the process of selection.

CIVIL LAW

It is not surprising that for the basis of its own Civil Code Louisiana chose the civil law of France, only recently formulated into its great Civil Code.[45] The two jurisconsults had been instructed, in preparing a Civil Code for the territory, to make "the civil law by which this territory is now governed the ground-work of the code"[46] (which civil law was Spanish), but nevertheless they used the French Civil Code for that purpose. There is some difference of opinion concerning the state of preparation of the code used by them for a model. One eminent authority says that the Louisiana code commissioners used the first draft of the French Code[47] for the model and characterized the tradition that they used the *projet* of that Code[48] as unfounded;[49] another scholar says that they followed the last Cambacérès *projet*.[50] There has been considerable speculation concerning the reasons why the code commissioners used the French model.[51] Suffice it for this paper to say that Louisiana at that date was predominantly French; it had endured Spanish laws imposed a generation earlier against its will; the civil law that it had known was contained in a multiplicity of legal institutions, from both France and Spain; and both systems had a common ancestry in the laws of Rome. It was natural that the commissioners made use of the recently completed codification of France, certainly the most carefully considered and scientifically constructed restatement of the civil law available at that time.

Their philosophy is well expressed in their preliminary report to the legislature on February 13, 1823, and the *projet* of the Code of 1825 shows the fidelity with which they adhered to it.

Basically the Civil Code prepared is a reiteration of the Code

Napoleon. There are, however, evidences of resort to Spanish and Roman sources, and in a few instances particular common-law rules were adopted where experience had demonstrated them to be more suitable to the needs of the new and growing territory.

For example, in 1816 the court decided that according to the civil law, expressed in the Code of 1808, the perfect ownership of public roads was in the State.[52] Livingston had argued that the State had only a servitude, analogous to the easement that it had at common law. When Derbigny, the judge who decided the case, Moreau-Lislet, who won it, and Livingston, who lost it, joined in writing the Code of 1825, they adopted the rule of the common law that the State had only a servitude. They recognized that in a new country, largely frontier at the time, with change the order of the day, roads would not be permanently located, whereas the Romans, who originated the rule, built their roads to endure forever.[53]

The text of the Civil Code has not lost its essential civil-law essence in the years that have passed since it was first adopted in 1808. The revisions of 1825 and 1870 did not have that effect. In some areas of the code and in its broad application to other fields of the law, not envisioned at the time the code was written, Louisiana has followed its sister states.

There are certain fields of the law, such as bankruptcy, preempted by the federal government under the United States Constitution, in which some provisions of the Civil Code have been rendered sterile, respite being an example.[54]

The commercial, industrial, social, and political development of Louisiana, as one of the United States, has inevitably caused it to adopt legislation in certain fields that are not necessarily in essence either civil- or common-law, using those terms in their most general acceptation, but simply American. The phenomenal development of the corporation as an instrumentality for carrying on business, insurance, the laws relating to public utilities, the expansion of the conflict of laws—all these have caused Louisiana to look largely to and borrow from her sister states in these fields. Louisiana has also adopted a number of uniform statutes on such subjects as negotiable instruments, bills of lading, stock transfers, acknowledgments, and warehouse receipts, in order that there might not be confusion concerning these multitudinous instrumentalities of interstate commerce in daily use.

There are, however, some uniform laws, such as those of sales and partnership, that cannot be adopted because of basic differences between the uniform acts and the Civil Code. Similarly, attempts to prepare annotations to the American Law Institute Restatements on Contracts and Agency were unsuccessful, because of basic differences between these two systems of law.

The most recent and perhaps the most striking example of the fusion of common-law devices into the civil law of Louisiana is the Trust Estates Act of 1938.[55] Trusts, except for special educational, charitable, and religious purposes, were not permitted in Louisiana before 1920, and then for only a period of ten years. The Constitution of 1921, in the furtherance of civil-law precedents applicable to Louisiana, prohibits the passing of laws abolishing force heirship or authorizing the creation of substitutions, fidei-commissa, or trust estates except trust estates created for limited periods. This prohibition does not apply to religious, charitable, or educational purposes.[56] The Trust Estates Act preserves these fundamental civil-law precedents, which are designed to maintain the equality between heirs and to prevent the accumulation and preservation of large, inert trusts, and at the same time secures for Louisiana the operative and administrative provisions of the best of the trust laws of her sister states.

All these developments of the common law, however, extensive they may be when the totality of the law of Louisiana is considered, only go to establish the firm adherence that Louisiana has given to its Civil Code, which is as vigorously and as jealously preserved today as it was bodly and enthusiastically adopted in 1808.[57]

Spanish law in Louisiana has no particular monument, although there are vestigial reminders that Spanish laws once prevailed. That is particularly true with respect to the organization for the enforcement of mortgages. Certain aspects of the provisions of the Code of Practice for the foreclosure of a mortgage *via executiva* were taken almost literally from the ordinance of O'Reilly, the Spanish governor,[58] and the effect of the *pact de non alienando* was drawn from Febrero and the *Curia Philipica*.[59] And where the law is silent the Supreme Court has said that it would refer to those general principles of the Roman and Spanish law that to that extent seem impossible of repeal or eradication.[60]

CODE OF PRACTICE

The necessity for rules of practice adapted to the change in governmental structure, the increase in the "American" element of the bar, and the desire of Louisiana to forestall the wholesale adoption of the common law, substantive as well as procedural, caused the early adoption of an act regulating practice in the Superior Court and of another act[61] subdividing the territory and providing for subordinate courts and rules of practice for them.[62] The first of these acts is generally referred to as the Practice Act of 1805.

The Code of Practice is largely the work of Edward Livingston, the New York lawyer. The Practice Act was his work. It is short and very simple. It is reported that Livingston wrote to Jeremy Bentham that in some fifteen years the Supreme Court of Louisiana decided fewer disputed questions of practice than the appellate courts of New York considered in one year, and that he told a young lawyer, also from a common-law state, that he could master Louisiana practice law in one evening after dinner.[63]

The Code of Practice of 1825 is probably the most original legal institution of Louisiana. Its simplicity and much of its essence have found their way into the Federal Rules of Civil Procedure. An out-of-state lawyer familiar with those rules would not have too much trouble with the Code of Practice in Louisiana.

COMMERCIAL LAW

The *lex mercatoria,* the Anglo-American law merchant, has been recognized in Louisiana from the time Louisiana came under the sovereignty of the United States. The Code of 1808 contained provisions that indicated the supremacy of the law merchant in commercial transactions. Thus it was provided with respect to the privilege on movables (Article 74, pp. 467, 470): "Nothing herein shall alter or affect the established laws and usages of commerce as to the claim of the thing sold." The Superior Court of the territory early held that, although the laws of Spain were not abrogated by the cession in 1803, nevertheless from the time and because of the taking of possession by the United States, the commercial law of the nation became the commercial law of the territory, particularly with reference to bills and notes and insurance.[64]

The "laws and usages of commerce" referred to in the Code of 1808 were early held to be those of sister states unless these conflicted with positive legislation of Spain or were in opposition to local uses prevailing in Louisiana.[65]

And, finally, with respect to the effect of the failure of the legislature to adopt the proposed Commercial Code in 1824 the Supreme Court said it was safe to assume that the framers of the Civil Code intended to leave the commercial jurisprudence of Louisiana as it was before the adoption of the Civil Code, in harmony with that of other states and commercial nations, unless prevented by positive statutory enactments.[66]

CRIMINAL LAW

The citizens of Louisiana were discontent with the Spanish medieval penal law, and shortly after the cession of Louisiana they passed the Crimes Act of 1805, making the common law of crimes and criminal procedure the penal law of Louisiana. But the penal law of Louisiana has always been statutory. In 1942 it was formulated into a Criminal Code, in structure and operation a real code as that term is generally understood in countries of the written law. It was probably the first serious codification of substantive penal law in the United States.[67]

DOCTRINE AND MATERIAL

Doctrine to the civilian means the ideas and opinions of jurisconsults or legal scientists; that is, of those learned in the law. Doctrine is not a primary source of law, and its authority depends on the validity and merit of its intrinsic philosophy. French jurisconsults, however, in every period of French legal history have influenced profoundly the development of French law.

It is said that Louisiana has no doctrine, and we are chided because so small a number of the bench and bar can read the French authorities. Some criticism is leveled at the scarcity of the mechanical means and material, civilian in kind and content, available to the Louisiana lawyer. These observations merit attention here, because they partly constitute the basis for the charge that Louisiana is more nearly a common-law than a civilian state.[68]

Doctrine. It must be confessed that the principal doctrinal writings available to the Louisiana lawyer after the adoption of the Code of 1808[69] were French. But there had not been many commentators on the Code Napoleon by 1825, when Louisiana adopted its Code of 1825. Delvincourt, Maleville, the Pandects, Toullier—these are about the only ones mentioned in the *projet* of the Louisiana Code of 1825. At that time and for many years afterward a large proportion of the bar could speak and read French, and there was no need to develop Louisiana doctrine so long as the French commentaries were available. The reports of the decisions of the Louisiana Supreme Court for most of the nineteenth century are replete with references to these works. After the turn of the century, as the English-speaking population became predominant, the frequency of references to French doctrine greatly diminished, but there never has been a time when appropriate reference to these doctrinal writings has not found a responsive court to listen, and often to adopt their views.[70]

Louisiana had a small bar for many years. It is not very large now. The great modern law schools were not firmly established until something more than a generation ago. It is not surprising that Louisiana did not develop a wealth of doctrine, but that does not justify the conclusion that it is a common-law state.

Actually, it did develop some commentaries of its own and of considerable merit. Judge Martin, on the Supreme Court of Louisiana for many years, translated *Pothier on Obligations.* Moreau and Carleton translated the *Partidas,* and included articular references to corresponding provisions of the Code of 1808, the Roman law, and other Spanish laws, with many annotations. Gustav Schmidt published a compilation of the laws of Spain and Mexico, and his *Louisiana Law Journal* was an outstanding civil-law publication. Henry Denis in 1898 wrote a very fine work on the Law of Pledge, according to both the civil and common law. Judah P. Benjamin, whose miraculous career is well-nigh unbelievable, after years of leadership at the New Orleans bar was able to establish his leadership in England. There he wrote his textbook on Sales, according to the common law, with appropriate references to the civil law. His work was authoritative in the field for many years.

William Wirt Howe wrote studies in the Civil Law and its relations to the laws of England and America. K. A. Cross, of Baton Rouge, published works on Successions, Pleadings, and Practice that have value to this day. Professor McMahon's work on Louisiana Practice and Dr. Harriet Daggett's works on Community Property, Mineral Law, and Louisiana Privileges, published in recent years, are excellent. Judge E. D. Saunders' Lectures on the Civil Code of Louisiana is a true commentary of great value. It was published in 1925.

During the long period from the Code of 1808 until the second decade of this century, the compilations of statutes, digests of decisions, and annotated codes were all prepared by leaders of the bar. Though these works rarely contain philosophical comments similar to those of the French legal scientists, scholarship of a high order is reflected in their excursions into French and Spanish sources.[71]

About thirty years ago the modernization of the law schools and the establishment of the *Tulane Law Review* in December 1929 as a successor to the *Southern Law Quarterly,* and its dedication to scholarly legal research devoted to the preservation of Louisiana's legal inheritance, brought about a virtual renaissance of scholarly interest in the Civil Law.[72] Later the *Louisiana Law Review* and the *Loyola Law Review* were created; so that today there are three law reviews, in themselves a continuing source of doctrinal writings that suffer little by comparison with the works of individual authors elsewhere.

The work of the courts comes under critical examination in the law schools, and ultimately is the source of comment in the law reviews. It is not too much to say of them, in Louisiana as in France, that *au Palais* (court) *on compte les arrêts, tandis qu'à l'Ecole on les pèse,* which is somewhat like the expression that in England one looks to the pedigree of a precedent, whereas in France its philosophy is sought.

It cannot be maintained that Louisiana now has a doctrine comparable to the totality of French doctrine. Neither can it be said that it has none at all. It is perhaps fair to say that for a great many years Louisiana doctrine was French doctrine, with some local assistance, and that in the last generation the law schools, through their law reviews, have brought about a system in which the function of doctrine in civil-law interpretation and development is being very well but not fully performed.

Material. By material is meant the publications or tools available to the Louisiana lawyer, and it is mentioned here because observations have been made that Louisiana law books are common-law in design and not conducive to the maintenance of the civil-law tradition.[73] It is true that the Louisiana Reports and the Southern Reporter containing Louisiana cases are keyed to the National Reporter System, based on common-law principles and couched in common-law nomenclature. That is not unwarranted, for in many fields of the law Louisiana has adopted the common law of her sister states, as has been explained elsewhere in this paper.

But the Civil Law of Louisiana is contained in its Civil Code, and the Code itself is its own primary source book. Recently there has been published an annotated edition in fifteen volumes, which share a common index of two volumes with the Annotated Revised Statutes.[74] In this Annotated Code it is possible to trace the legislative history of each article back through the Codes of 1870, 1825, and 1808, and where appropriate to the Code Napoleon. The annotations include the texts of all appropriate law review articles. Moreover it contains articular citations to Planiol's *Traité Élémentaire de Droit Civil,* which will be of great value when the translation of that treatise now being made by the Louisiana State Law Institute is completed and published.

Louisiana itself has published a reprint of the *projets* of the Civil Code and the Code of Practice of 1825, in both French and English, and also a Compiled Edition of the three Louisiana Codes, with correspondence to the Code Napoleon. This compilation gives in English the text of each article of the Code of 1870 and amendments, with the corresponding articles of the Codes of 1825 and 1808, and of the Code Napoleon, in both French and English, with cross reference to the comments, if any, in the *projet* of 1825.[75]

The Louisiana Citator and the Louisiana Reports provide the means for reference to Code Napoleon citations in the opinions, a finding device not now used so much as formerly.

Considering that the Civil Code is the medium by which Louisiana adopted the civil law based on the Code Napoleon, it would appear that the tools fashioned to preserve and maintain the civil law of Louisiana are not inadequate for that purpose.

TECHNIQUES

The two great forces by which law has been developed have been *jurisprudence,* as contained in the decisions of the courts, and doctrine, contained in the philosophical writings of the scholars, both being in effect techniques of interpretation, although case law at common law has a much larger destiny. The role played by *jurisprudence* in Louisiana is no safe criterion by which to determine the character of its law as being civil law or common law. The manner in which civil cases are dealt with in Louisiana, where there is no express law, does invite inquiry and is much more profitable for that purpose.

JURISPRUDENCE AND STARE DECISIS

One writer who has objectively examined the situation in South Africa, Quebec, and Louisiana has said that the quoting and adhering to precedents is "the most intrusive element of the common law" in those jurisdictions.[76] Another writer had rather boldly declared that Louisiana was a common-law state and based his opinion in large measure on the misconception that *stare decisis* was the rule in Louisiana.[77]

The effect of judicial precedent cannot be accepted as a safe criterion by which to evaluate the effect of common law on the civil law of Louisiana as contained in its Civil Code. The essential difference between the civil and the common law lies in the generating force of authority. In the common law it rests wholly in the decisions of the court; in the civil law it is legislation. A code is not intended to provide for every contingency that might arise. It is a statement of general principles to be applied by deduction or analogy to particular cases. It is the function of the court in the common-law jurisdiction to make the law. In the civil law the function of the court is one of interpretation.

In Louisiana all our law is statutory. There have been instances in which the courts have established rules without specific authority in the written law. To a very great extent such cases have been more often concerned with procedural matters than with substantive law. The decisions of our courts bear little resemblance to the decisions of the appellate courts of France. The American style of decisions differs greatly from the French practice. In Louisiana, in civil matters the appellate courts have jurisdiction of the facts as well as of the law—an incentive to lengthy opinions.

Our appellate courts are prone to refer to prior decisions, but the underlying authority in cases involving provisions of the Civil Code is the Civil Code. That is well illustrated in a fairly recent case in which the court, in referring to one of its previous decisions, said: "we agree with the conclusion therein . . . not for the reason advanced therein, but because the servitude owners were co-proprietors under Article 801 of the Civil Code."[78]

Louisiana decisions on subjects of the law not comprised in the Civil Code contain frequent references to common-law decisions, but that does not make Louisiana any less a civil-law state, for the reason that those subjects, with very few exceptions, are not concerned with matters contained in the Civil Code. It has been pointed out heretofore that Louisiana has adopted or had thrust upon it the common law in many fields with which the Civil Code and the Code Napoleon are not concerned, and this common-law content of the Louisiana reports is not a proper basis by which to evaluate the Louisiana civil law derived from the Code Napoleon.

Reference has heretofore been made to the recently published fifteen-volume Annotated Edition of the Louisiana Civil Code. It contains all the decisions from the beginning of Louisiana *jurisprudence* after it became a part of the United States, up to the time of publication, and all of the doctrinal writings from the law reviews published in Louisiana. There are few, if any, citations of common-law sources.

The rule of *stare decisis* really has no place in Louisiana, although it was once openly charged by one of its professors that the rule was followed. Three of his colleagues, however, replied and clearly demonstrated that "if there is any subject of Louisiana law to which the rule of stare decisis does not apply, it is the subject of stare decisis itself." They pointed out that *stare decisis* most often found advocates in the dissenting opinions of judges not satisfied with the conclusions of a majority of their colleagues, and they said: "It is submitted that the Louisiana doctrine of 'stare decisis' is a myth. Case law in Louisiana has never been anything more than de facto and has never shown the tendency to become law de juri. We have never adopted stare decisis and whatever chance it had of creeping into our system has been reduced to the vanishing point with the passage of time. Our courts have always followed, and show every disposition to continue to follow, the essential civilian judicial technique of never letting today become either the slave of yesterday or the tyrant of tomorrow."[79]

CASES NOT COVERED BY EXPRESS LAW

The commissioners who drafted the Louisiana Civil Code of 1825 realized that they could not foresee every possible situation that might arise and make appropriate provision to meet these contingencies. In their preliminary report to the legislature they suggested that in such cases the court would decide "according to the dictates of natural equity, in the manner that 'amicable compounders' are now authorized to decide, but that such decisions shall have no force as precedents until sanctioned by the legislative will."

In order to provoke legislative action in these cases they suggested that the courts should render reports to the legislature about these unprovided-for cases in order that the legislature might make appropriate provision. No such course of procedure was ever adopted. However, on occasion the Supreme Court of Louisiana has noted inaction of the legislature after a decision of that sort as being in the nature of a tacit approval. It is interesting to note that the commissioners thought that the unrestricted power of the common-law judge to decide a case for which there was no precedent, on the theory that the law had always been in effect but had never been stated, was contrary to the constitutional philosophy of separation of powers.[80]

In this broad field of unprovided-for cases Louisiana has adopted judicial techniques of interpretation in accordance with established civil-law tradition. These techniques include:

(1) The application of general principles to new fact situations by logical deduction;

(2) The extension of the provisions of the Code by analogy to new but similar problems;

(3) The selection from available methods of that which would prevent the denial of justice; and

(4) The practical necessities of the case.

The Louisiana Civil Code, Article 21, says: "In all civil matters, where there is no express law, the Judge is bound to proceed and decide according to equity. To decide equitably, an appeal is to be made to natural law and reason, or received usage, where positive law is silent." The equity mentioned does not refer to the equity of the common law. In fact it was inspired by a corresponding provision of the *projet du gouvernement* of the Civil Code of France. Another borrowing from the same French *projet* is Article 13 of the Civil Code, which provides: "When a law is clear and free from all ambiguity, the letter is not to be disregarded under a pretext of pursuing its spirit."[81]

The most striking example of the application of these civil-law techniques is to be found in the mineral law by which Louisiana's most important industry is regulated, for Louisiana has erected these rules on the basis of provisions of the Civil Code, adapted by analogy to meet circumstances and contingencies undreamed of at the time the Code was first adopted.

The sort of rights created by the sale or reservation of the minerals in a property finally became the focal point of a great debate in the case of Frost-Johnson v. Sallings Heirs,[82] decided in 1922. In that case it was determined that the sale or reservation of minerals separately from the land created a real right in the nature of a servitude, which would be extinguished as any predial servitude by nonuse during ten years under the provisions of Article 789 of the Civil Code. The Supreme Court held that the essence of this right was the right of exploitation.[83] Since the original decision in Frost-Johnson v. Sallings Heirs the court has consistently applied this doctrine, although the name by which this right has been called has fluctuated, the court sometimes referring to it as a predial servitude and sometimes as a personal servitude, and frequently as merely a servitude. The one common denominator, however, in all the decisions is that the mineral right owned separately and apart from the soil constitutes a real right in the nature of a servitude, and the courts have consistently applied to this real right the articles of the Civil Code relating particularly to predial servitudes, so far as they are appropriate.

Lately there has been an increasing use of the term "mineral servitude" to designate this real right, which by its nature is closely analogous to the predial servitude of the Civil Code, the definition of which cannot be wholly applicable to the mineral servitude for the reason that the predial servitude is one that exists in favor of an estate, called a dominant estate, upon another estate called the servient estate.[84]

The contracts under which the oil and gas business is conducted for exploration and production are called mineral leases. These contracts follow to a considerable extent the general form of those obtaining in other oil-producing states, and no doubt the earlier mineral leases used in this state were brought in by oil and gas operators from other states and before Louisiana had developed any mineral law of its own. The Supreme Court of Louisiana has held these contracts to be leases, and to them it has applied a great deal of the law of Louisiana contained in the Civil Code relating to the lease of lands.[85] There is a fundamental difference between the contract of lease at common law, by which the lessee acquires some title or interest in the property lease, and in Louisiana, where the lessee only acquires a right to enjoy. In the logical development of the law respecting mineral leases the court has applied these civil-law rules and, accordingly, has held that the royalty payable under a mineral lease is rent for the security of the payment of which the lessor has the lessor's privilege and pledge contained in the Civil Code,[86] and has applied the prescription of three years, by which a suit for the arrearages of rent is prescribed, to a suit for royalty under a mineral lease.[87]

The expansion that has taken place in this field of law, which is based in the last analysis on analogy,[88] has brought about conflicts and created a measure of confusion because there has been no text specifically applicable to the particular situations that have arisen out of the complexity of a situation with so many facets. A study of the problem has been made by the Louisiana State Law Institute at the request of the Bar Association, and an effort is now being made to arrive at a statutory statement of the basic principles underlying the mineral industry of Louisiana. Whether this would take the form of a Mineral Code, or of general legislation as a part of the Revised Statutes, or of a section on the mineral servitude and mineral lease integrated into the present Civil Code, cannot be even the subject of a prediction. It is hardly probable that a complete Mineral Code would be adopted, because the legislature refused to adopt such a Code in 1938. It is safe to say, however, that whatever may be the solution the basic mineral law of Louisiana will rest on the civil law.

EFFECT OF LOUISIANA CIVIL LAW ON THE LAW OF THE UNITED STATES

It may not be appropriate in this paper, which by its title is restricted to the Code and the common law in Louisiana, to speak of the effect of the Civil Code of Louisiana beyond its own borders, but the widespread effect of the adoption of a civilian principle throughout the entire United States, in the field of federal taxation, with Louisiana showing the way, furnishes a fine example of the permanence and unchangeability of sound legal philosophy.

Louisiana has always had the community property system of *acquets* and gains between husband and wife, which it has inherited from its French and Spanish ancestors. This system was brought to Louisiana in the Custom of Paris as part of its first law. It was continued during the Spanish regime, was adopted in the Code of 1808, and has remained in our law ever since. According to this system the income of the marital community belongs equally to husband and wife. This system had the effect of dividing the marital income for income tax purposes, and when the graduated rates of that tax were so violently increased the system meant great savings to Louisiana taxpayers.

In the case of Bender v. Pfaff[89] the Supreme Court of the United States held that the marital income in Louisiana could not be taxed wholly to the husband, but must be divided between husband and wife. The same result was obtained in other states that had retained some form of community property system as a vestigial reminder of their Spanish ancestry, at least one of which, however, had to adjust its community property system by legislation in order to get the benefit of the ruling.[90] All these states except Louisiana were otherwise common-law jurisdictions. Some states attempted to provide for community property systems, optional in some cases, compulsory in others.[91] But this engrafting of the community property system in common-law states was not very successful, and the inequities of the situation finally led the Congress of the United States to adopt the principle of marital deduction, in effect and substantially distributing the benefit of the community property system in its relation to federal income taxation equally throughout the United States.[92] All those who have benefited by this new principle of marital deduction can give their thanks to the barbarian who brought his wife to the field of battle and gave her half the spoils of war because she had earned them, for there, in the dimly perceived beginnings of our legal history, is the genesis of the community property system that became established in France and in Spain and, through them, into Louisiana and the American states of Spanish ancestry.[93]

CONCLUSION

Louisiana has adopted much of the common law in fields not covered by the Civil Code or the Code Napoleon. Within the ambit of its Code its borrowings have been relatively small and then directly by legislation and not by some imperceptible process of infiltration. In the structure of the Code and the processes whereby it has been developed Louisiana is still civilian. Louisiana is now proposing to revise its Civil Code, for there comes a time when the law, whether in code or reporter, should be re-examined and recast. Its provisions must be examined in the light of the political, social, and economic development of the past one hundred and fifty years. Even now the Code Napoleon is being prepared for reformation in France. But the principles on which the revision in Louisiana will be undertaken have already been announced, and they do not differ from those actuating the commission that drafted the Code Napoleon. In a preliminary *exposé des motifs* the agency charged with the preparation of the *projet* for the reformation of the Louisiana Code has adopted the basic philosophy of one of the chief architects of the Code Napoleon, who said:

"In outlining the plan of this legislation, we have felt it our duty to guard against the spirit of the system which tends to destroy all, and against the spirit of superstition, of bondage and of laziness, which tends to respect all. . . . The scythe may be used with indifference on fallow ground; but in a cultivated field there should be pulled only parasite plants which choke out useful crops. In coming to our civil law, we have thought it sufficient to draw a line of separation between the reforms required by the present state of the republic, and the ideas of real order which time and the respect of the people have consecrated. New theories are only the system of some individuals; ancient maxims are the spirit of centuries."[94]

The *exposé des motifs* adopted also the formula of the dean of American legal scholars, who once said:

"Law must be stable and yet it cannot stand still. In law we rely upon experience and reason. As I have been in the habit of saying, law is experience developed by reason; and reason tested by experience. For experience we turn to history. For reason, we turn to philosophy."[95]

With these guides, Louisiana will surely do nothing to militate against the realization of Napoleon's own prophecy that his Civil Code would live forever.

NOTES

[1] Hereafter referred to as Code Napoleon. In Louisiana law books, e.g., *Compiled Edition of the Civil Codes of Louisiana,* Louisiana Legal Archives, Vol. 3, Pt. 1, citation to the French Civil Code is usually "C. N."

[2] The first Louisiana Civil Code was commenced in 1806 and completed and promulgated in 1808. It is called the Code of 1808.

[3] Planiol, *Traité Élémentaire de Droit Civil,* 138, 143. St. Joseph, *Concordance entre les Codes Civile Etrangères et le Code Napoléon,* Introduction pp. v–viii (1840).

[4] Graveson, *De l'influence de la common law sur les systèmes de droit civil existant dans le Commonwealth Britannique.* 5 Revue Internationale de droit comparé 658 (1953).

[5] See the description of the situation in Lower Canada (now Quebec) by M. Desire Girouard, made in 1859, while its Civil Code was being prepared, quoted by E. Fabre-Surveyer, in *The Civil Law of Quebec and Louisiana,* 1 La. L. Rev. 649. The quotation concludes: "There is nothing more uncertain than the actual law of Lower Canada, nothing more confused than the State of Canadian Law." *Id.* at 651.

[6] Surveyer, *id.* at 649.

[7] "An act respecting the Codification of the Law of Lower Canada relative to civil matter and Procedure" June 10, 1857, 20 Vict. c. 43, preamble (Consolidated Statutes for Lower Canada, C. 2) as quoted in Surveyer, *loc. cit.*

[8] Surveyer, *id.* at 654. Louisiana did "import dowry almost bodily from France . . . and we have it today but it is of no importance." Saunders' Lectures on the Civil Code 81 (1925).

[9] Professor H. F. Jolowicz made such a study the subject of his presidential address to the Bentham Club of University College, London, on February 23, 1954. It has been printed in Current Legal Problems, 1954, under the title *The Civil Law in Louisiana* and has been reprinted in 29 Tulane L. Rev. 491 (1955).

[10] Martin, History of Louisiana 115 (ed. 1882); de Funiak, Principles of Community Property, Vol. 1, 79 (1943).

[11] Generally concerning the Custom of Paris, see Martin, Histoire de la Coutume de Paris, 3 vols. (1922); de Ferrière, Corps et Compilation de tous les commentateurs anciens et modernes sur la Coutume de Paris, 3 vols. (1692). The mechanical excellences of this work are admirable by modern standards. Louisiana, of course, was not the only French territory subject to the Custom of Paris. At least two other states thought it necessary to declare the custom no longer effective: Michigan, by the Act of September 16, 1810, and Florida, by an act passed at the first session in 1822; Dawson, *Codification of the French Customs,* 38 Mich. L. Rev., 765 (1940).

[12] Dart, *Courts and Law in Colonial Louisiana,* 22 La. Bar A.R. 17. See also Tucker, *Source Books of Louisiana Law,* 7 Tulane L. Rev. 82 (1932).

[13] Planiol, Traité Élémentaire de Droit Civil, Vol. 1, No. 58.

[14] De Funiak, *op. cit. supra* note 10, Chs. II and III.

[15] Gayerre, Histoire de la Louisiane, Vol. II, p. 98, 100 (ed. 1847).

[16] For the complete translated text of this ordinance see French, Historical Collections of Louisiana. 246 (Fifth Series, 1853). The ordinance alone without the appended digest is given in de Funiak, *op. cit. supra* note 10, Vol. II, p. 518.

[17] "This publication, followed from that moment by an uninterrupted observance of the Spanish law, has been received as an introduction of the Spanish Code in all of its parts, and must be considered as having repealed the laws formerly prevailing in Louisiana, whether they continued in force by the tacit or express consent of the government." Beard v. Poydras, 4 Mart. 348, 368 (La. 1816); Pecquet v. Pecquet, 17 La. Ann. 204 (1865). See also Dart, *Influence of the Ancient Laws of Spain on the Jurisprudence of Louisiana* 6 Tulane L. Rev. 83 (1931).

[18] Schmidt, The Civil Law of Spain and Mexico 102 (1851).

[19] Patton v. Cities of Philadelphia and New Orleans, 1 La. Ann. 98.

[20] Pecquet v. Pecquet, 17 La. Ann. 204 (1865); Malpica v. McKown, 1 La. 248 (1830), Laws of Mexico; Arayo v. Currel, 1 La. 528 (1830), Laws of South America before the Revolution; Berluchaux v. Berluchaux, 7 La. 539 (1835), Laws of Cuba; United States v. Turner, 11 How. 663, 667 (U.S. 1850).

[21] Hatcher, Edward Livingston 117 (1940).

[22] Thorpe American Charters, Constitution and Organic Law, Vol. 3, pp. 1365, 1371.

[23] Resolution of February 4, 1805. For a description of the events leading up to codification see H. P. Dart, *The Influence of the Ancient Laws of Spain on the Jurisprudence of Louisiana,* 6 Tulane L. Rev. 83 (1931); Wigmore, *Louisiana, The Story of its Jurisprudence,* 22 Am. L. Rev. 890 (1888); 1 So. Law Quarterly 1 (1916).

[24] This act appears in full in Franklin, *The Place of Thomas Jefferson in the Expulsion of Spanish Medieval Law from Louisiana,* 16 Tulane L. Rev. 319–38 (1942). See also Franklin, *The Eighteenth Brumaire in Louisiana; Talleyrand and the Spanish Medieval Legal System of 1806,"* 16 Tulane L. Rev. 514–61 (1942). Professor Franklin's imaginative thesis seems to be that the slave-owning Creoles feared the introduction of the common law would tend to destroy slavery, their principal source of wealth. But the legislature in 1806 wanted to preserve their civil law, which was Spanish, and its Roman bases, against the possibility of the introduction of the common law, which had been attempted, until their Civil Code, ordered by the same legislature, could be adopted. That there was some need for a declaration concerning the laws in force is suggested by Schmidt's article

Were the Laws of France, which governed Louisiana prior to the cession of the country to Spain, abolished by the Ordinances of O'Reilly?" 1 La. L. J., No. 4, p. 23 (1842).

Actually most of the laws referred to in this act, which the Governor vetoed, were to a considerable degree in force in the territory as explained by Schmidt; see note 18.

The purposes of the legislature in adopting the act that Claiborne vetoed were set forth in a manifesto appearing in Carter, Territorial Papers of the United States, Vol. IX, Orleans Territory 643–57. The same legislature provided for the preparation of a Civil Code, and it is to be doubted that slavery had anything to do with these events. The same legislature adopted the *Code Noir* regulating slavery. Act June 7, 1806. Martin, Digest, General Acts of the Legislature, Vol. 1, p. 601. Moreau-Lislet, General Digest of Acts of the Legislature, Vol. 1, p. 100, English ed. Moreover there seems to have been nothing to prevent slavery in the other states in the South in which the common law prevailed. Louisiana was predominantly French at the time, and the Code of 1808, based on the Code Napoleon, witnesses their desire for French and not Spanish law. Moreover, when the Code of 1825 was adopted to correct the conditions resulting from the judicial revival of Spanish law in 1817, its basis was French and not Spanish.

[25] Resolution of June 7, 1906. La. Acts of 1806, pp. 214–18. Tucker, *Source Books of Louisiana Law,* 6 Tulane L. Rev. 280 (1931).

[26] *Ibid.*

[27] For somewhat of a history of this code, see La. Civil Code of 1870, VII (Saunders' Second Edition 1920); Martin, History of Louisiana 344 (1882); W. K. Dart, *The Louisiana Judicial System,* 1 La. Digest Annotated 20 (Bobbs-Merrill 1917); H. P. Dart, *The Influence of the Ancient Laws of Spain on the Jurisprudence of Louisiana,* 6 Tulane L. Rev. 83 (1931). H. P. Dart, *Sources of the Civil Code of Louisiana,* 13 La. Bar A.R. 21, 70 (1911); Also published in Saunders' Lectures in the Civil Code of Louisiana v–xxxlx (1925). Tucker, *supra* note 25, at 281.

[28] Cottin v. Cottin, 5 Mart. (O.S.) 93 (1817).

[29] Act approved March 3, 1819, p. 44. For a description of this work see Tucker, *Source Books of Louisiana Law,* 8 Tulane L. Rev. 396 (1934).

[30] Act of March 3, 1819. This act provided that the manuscript of the translation to be prepared by Moreau-Lislet and Henry Carleton should be examined by a committee of lawyers, two of whom, Debigny and Livingston, collaborated with Moreau-Lislet in preparing the Code of 1825. For a description of this work see Tucker, *supra* note 29.

[31] This resolution appears in full in Tucker, *supra* note 25.

[32] This preliminary report was approved March 22, 1823 (La. Acts of 1823, p. 88), and the *projet* was ordered printed and distributed by resolutions of March 26, 1823, and March 25, 1823, respectively (La. Acts of 1823, pp. 68, 90). The *projet* of the Civil Code as well as that of the Code of Practice have been republished by the State of Louisiana as Louisiana Legal Archives, Vols. 1 and 2, in one book. The book also contains the preliminary report. Both *projet* and report are source books of Louisiana law of primary importance.

[33] La. Acts of 1824, p. 172. See Bank of Louisiana v. Farrar, 1 La Ann. 49–55 (1846).

[34] The delay in promulgation was due to the printer, who was granted additional time by Act of Feb. 18, 1825. The certificate of promulgation was issued by the Secretary of State on May 20, 1825.

[35] Dubuisson, *The Codes of Louisiana* (originals written in French, Errors in Translation), 25 La. Bar A.R. 143; Moreau's argument in rebuttal in Dufour v. Camfranc, 11

Mart. O.S. 675, 701; Phelps v. Reinach, 38 La. Ann. 547 (1886); Straus v. City of New Orleans, 166 La. 1035; 118 So. 125 (1928); Sample v. Whittaker, 172 La. 722; 135 So. 38 (1931).

[36] Act of April 10, 1805, regulating practice in the superior court (Livingston's Practice Act), 2 Martin Digest, 148; Acts of 1804–5, p. 210.

[37] See La. Revised Statutes, Title 13, Courts and Judicial Procedure.

[38] Act approved March 3, 1819, p. 44. For a description of this work see Tucker, *Source Books of Louisiana Law, op. cit. supra* note 29.

[39] Flory and McMahon, *The New Federal Rules and Louisiana Practice,* La. L. Rev. 45 (1938).

[40] Cross, *The Eclecticism of the Law of Louisiana,* 55 Am. L. Rev. 405.

[41] See authorities cited in note 11, also Planiol, Traité Élémentaire de Droit Civil, Vol. 1, ch. II.

[42] Sherman, Roman Law in the Modern World, Vol. 1, sections 278, 308 (2d ed. 1924).

[43] *Id.,* sec. 258.

[44] Amos and Walton, Introduction to French Law 2 (1935).

[45] The Code Napoleon (first called *Code Civil des Français;* it was not called Code Napoleon until 1807) was originally adopted in separate parts that became effective when promulgated. The Code as a whole was promulgated March 21, 1804. With the Restoration its original name was restored, but a degree of March 27, 1852 again designated it the Code Napoleon. This decree has not been abrogated, but since 1870 the Code has generally been cited as *Code Civil.*

[46] Resolution of June 7, 1806.

[47] H. P. Dart, *loc. cit. supra* note 12.

[48] Martin, *loc. cit. supra* note 27.

[49] H. P. Dart, *loc. cit. supra* note 12.

[50] W. K. Dart, *loc. cit. supra* note 27.

[51] Tucker, *loc. cit. supra* note 12. See also Hubgh v. N. O. & Carrollton R.R. Co., 6 La. Ann. 495, 512 (1851).

[52] Renthrop v. Bourg, 4 Mart. 97 (1816).

[53] Hatch v. Arnault, 3 Ann. 485 (1848).

[54] Book III, Title XVIII, Article 3084 *et seq.*

[55] Act 81 of 1938, now La. Rev. Stat. 9:1791–1822.

[56] La. Constitution 1921, Article IV, Section 16. Forced heirship or disposable portion, La. Rev. Civil Code Articles 1493–94, Code Napoleon Articles 913–15. Substitution and fidei-commissa, La. Rev. Civ. Code, Article 1520; Code Napoleon 896. For an interesting discussion of this intrusion of the trust device into the civil law of Louisiana see Wisdom, *A Trust Code in the Civil Law, Based on the Restatement and Uniform Acts: The Louisiana Trust Estates Act,* 13 Tulane L. Rev. 70 (1938).

[57] Since the adoption of the Civil Code of 1825 the only revision, that of 1870, has been editorial; the Code has not been subjected to any major change. A proposed revision was rejected by the Louisiana State Bar Association in 1910. However, since the general revision of all Louisiana statutory law in 1870 there has been built up a body of statutory law that treats of subjects included in the Civil Code, but in such a manner that it has been possible to include them in the Revised Statutes of 1950 under Title IX, "Civil Code Ancillaries," and according to the same arrangement as that of the Civil Code itself. Of

course there have been legislative changes in numerous articles of the Civil Code, but these changes have been gradual and well-nigh imperceptible.

[58] Gayerre, *op. cit. supra* note 15.

[59] Nathan v. Lee, 2 Mart. N. S. 32.

[60] Hubgh v. N. O. & Carrollton R.R. 6 La Ann. 495 (1851), Moulin v. Monteleone, 165 La. 169 (1928). Cf. Keator v. Welsh and Binmore, 41 Rapports de Pratique de Quebec 414 (1938), in which, in interpreting similar texts, the Superior Court of Quebec gave effect to French jurisprudence, whereas in the Monteleone case it reasoned from Spanish and Roman precedents. See comment in 1 La. L. Rev. 204 (1938).

[61] Acts of 1804–5, p. 210. 2 Martins Digest 148.

[62] La. Code of Practice v. (Dart Ed. 1932); Hunt, *Life and Services of Edward Livingston; Cross on Pleading, Introduction* La. Bar A.R. 7 (1903).

[63] Flory and McMahon, *The New Federal Rules and Louisiana Practice,* 1 La. L. Rev. 45 (1938).

[64] Wagner v. Kenner, 2 Rob. 122.

[65] McDonald v. Millandon, 5 La. Ann. 408.

[66] Thompson v. Mulne, 4 La. Ann. 210.

[67] La. Act 42 of 1942, now Rev. Stat. 14:1–142. See Smith, *The Louisiana Criminal Code, Its Background and General Plan,* 5 La. L. Rev. 1 (1942); Bennett, *Louisiana Criminal Law and Procedure, Legislation of 1944,* 6 La. L. Rev. 9 (1943). Morrow, *Louisiana Criminal Code of 1942 and 1945,* 19 Tulane L. Rev. 483 (1945).

It is interesting to compare this code of only 142 articles, contained in Louisiana Statutes Annotated, with the Code of Criminal Procedure, adopted in 1928 (Act 2 of 1928, Rev. Stat. Title 15), which contains 582 articles, comprised in three volumes of the Louisiana Statutes Annotated.

[68] See *supra* note 9 and Ireland, *Louisiana's Legal System Reappraised,* 11 Tulane L. Rev. 585 (1937).

[69] There is a charming article about the law books of the Louisiana colonial period in 25 La. Bar A.R. 12, Dart, *The Library of a Louisiana Lawyer in the 18th Century.*

[70] A compendium of French authorities, in translation, forms the basis of the opinion on the distinction between a sublease and assignment in Smith v. Sun Oil Co. 165 La. 763, 116 So. 379 (1928); the French authorities on the doctrine of immobilization by destination caused the decision of a tax question in Straus v. City of New Orleans, 166 La. 1035, 118 So. 125 (1928).

[71] For a bibliographical descriptive list of Louisiana law books see Tucker, *supra* note 25, Part 1, on the Civil Code; Vol. VII, p. 82, Part II, on Code of Practice; Vol. VIII, p. 396, Part III, on Spanish Laws; and Vol. IX, p. 244, Part IV, on Constitutions, Statutes, Reports and Digests.

[72] 4 Tulane L. Rev. 69 (1929). Editorials "The Law School" by Dean Rufus C. Harris and "The Place of Louisiana Jurisprudence in the Legal Science of America" by Frederick K. Bewtel.

[73] See *supra* note 9.

[74] West's Louisiana Statutes Annotated—Civil Code—Vols. 1–15, Revised Statutes, Vols. 1–28, Index, vols. 1–2; and Concordance Tables, unnumbered volume, West Publishing Co.

[75] Louisiana Legal Archives, Vol. I, *Projet* of the Civil Code of 1825, Vol. II, *Projet* of the Code of Practice of 1825, bound together, and Vol. III, Compiled Edition of the Civil

Codes of Louisiana, published in 2 parts in separate volumes. There are, then, three volumes of Louisiana Legal Archives, published by the State and obtainable from the Secretary of State at Baton Rouge.

[76] Jolowicz, *supra* note 9.

[77] Ireland, *supra* note 68.

[78] Ohio Oil Co. v. Ferguson, 213 La. 183, 260, 34 S. 2d 746, 771 (1947).

[79] Daggett, Dainow and Hebert, *A Reappraisal appraised; a Brief for the Civil Law of Louisiana,* 12 Tulane L. Rev. 12 (1937).

[80] Preliminary Report of the Code Commissioners to the Legislature dated February 13, 1823. It appears in Vol. I, Louisiana Legal Archives at page lxxxv.

[81] Professor Dainow discussed the method by which Louisiana courts have disposed of cases on which the law is silent or insufficient, under the title "Method of Legal Development in Louisiana through judicial interpretation." It appears in French in Travaux de la Semaine International de Droit, Paris, 1950, 411 (1954).

[82] Frost-Johnson v. Salling's Heirs, 150 La. 756, 91 So. 207 (1922).

[83] Keebler v. Seubert, 167 La. 901, 120 So. 591 (1929).

[84] Art. 647 Civil Code. It cannot be a personal servitude (called usufruct), which expires with the death of the usufructuary. (Art. 606, Civil Code).

[85] Spence v. Lucas, 138 La. 763, 70 So. 769 (1916); Logan v. State Gravel Co. 158 La. 105, 103 So. 526 (1925); Tyson v. Surf Oil Co., 195 La. 248, 196 So. 336 (1940). These cases illustrate the philosophy of the Code Commissioners (Code of 1825) by a sort of "tacit reconduction"; that is, the court noted the failure of the legislature to act, although it had met several times after the court had applied the law of letting of things (lease) to oil and gas leases as a sort of tacit approval.

[86] Logan v. State Gravel Co., *supra* note 85.

[87] Board of Commissioners v. Pure Oil Co. 167 La. 801, 120 So. 373 (1929).

[88] The civil-law technique of interpretation by analogy is discussed in Gény, Methode d'interpretation et sources en droit privé positif (2d ed. 1954), Vol. I, Sections 107, 108; Vol. II, Sections 165, 166.

[89] 282 U.S. 127 (1930).

[90] Daggett, The Community Property System in Louisiana, Ch. XXI (1945), which is a comparative study of the community property systems in eight states. Also, de Funiak, *op. cit. supra* note 10, Ch. XI.

[91] These states include Oklahoma, Michigan, Nebraska, and Oregon and the territory of Hawaii. They are discussed briefly in the supplement to de Funiak, *op. cit.,* 243, and de Funiak, *The New Community Property Jurisdictions,* 22 Tulane L. Rev. 264 (1947); *The New Community Property Law,* 16 Okla. Bar Assn. J. 1123; Professor Daggett critically discussed the Oklahoma Act in her Article in 2 La. L. Rev. 575 (1940), reprinted in her book cited *supra* note 90.

[92] Section 305, Revenue Act of 1948; 26 U.S.C.A. Section 12 d; Internal Rev. Code of 1954, Section 2.

[93] De Funiak, *op. cit. supra* note 10, Section 11, and notes 27, 328, Daggett, *op. cit. supra* note 90.

[94] Portalis, Discours, Rapports et travaux inédits sur le code civil (1844) Discours de presentation du Code Civil: p. 90, 94, 97; Locré, Legislation Française, pp. 322, 326.

[95] Pound, New Paths of the Law 1, 13 (1950).

17

The Relations Between Civil Law and Common Law

THIBAUDEAU RINFRET

THE common-law world comprises the United States except Louisiana, Great Britain, and Canada except the Province of Quebec. The French Code predominates in what may be termed the civil-law world, in contradistinction to those areas in which the common law prevails. It is the law in force in, among others, Scotland, France, Belgium, Italy, Spain, South Africa, Ceylon, Malta, Mauritius, and some of the West Indies that were formerly early French or Spanish possessions. It is also the law of the Province of Quebec, Louisiana, Mexico, Cuba, Puerto Rico, the countries of Central and South America, and the Philippines. In South Africa and Ceylon it is known as the Roman Dutch law; in Malta they have kept the Roman law. The island of Mauritius is undoubtedly the most curious of them all. It is a former French possession. It now forms part of the British Commonwealth of Nations. It remained under the Code Napoleon as they have it in France. But, unlike Quebec, which has a Code of its own reproducing in most of its parts the French Code, Mauritius has no code; it is still under the Code Napoleon, with the extraordinary consequence that if the Code is amended by the French Parliament, automatically the amendment applies to Mauritius, although the people of that island have had no say in the matter.

"The life of the law," reads a celebrated passage of Mr. Justice

THIBAUDEAU RINFRET *was Chief Justice of Canada from 1944 to 1954*

Holmes, "has not been logic; it has been experience. . . . The law embodies the story of the nation's development through many centuries, and it cannot be dealt with as if it contained only the axioms or corollaries of a book of mathematics."[1] And, in a similar vein, his noted English correspondent Pollock writes: "We must recognize that law is not an affair of bare literal precepts, as the mechanical school would make it, but is the sense of justice taking form in peoples and races. . . . It must be realized that the laws of every nation are determined by their own historical conditions not only as to details but as to structure."[2] The different laws that they now enjoy have sprung from the tacit consent of their people and have proved to be especially fitted to their habits and traditions.

Might the present writer confess that he has not been able to ascertain whether it is now settled in history if the laws of England had already come to Normandy as a result of commercial interchanges or if the laws of Normandy invaded England under William the Conqueror. There are historians to be found who venture to question whether the law of England had not crossed over to Normandy before the Conquest. However, the majority among historians and commentators incline to the view that the Norman laws came to England with the Conquest. And it seems that such an opinion has decidedly prevailed among the jurists of the United States.

Mr. Justice Sanford, a member of the Supreme Court of the United States, at the meeting of the French, English, and American bars in Paris in 1924, paid this glowing tribute to French influence:

"For it is an historic fact that since the time of the Normans, that valiant and dominant race, the French tongue has set its indelible seal for all times upon the English law, both procedural and substantive. In the countries inheriting the Common Law, almost all the terms that have a definite legal meaning are of French origin, and in using them we render daily, in our procedure and in our thoughts, homage to the indestructibility and authority of the French language."[3] And at the same meeting Mr. Wickersham, former Attorney General of the United States, returned to the same idea. He said: "The Common Law itself is derived from the Norman laws and customs which were carried from France to England at the time of the conquest by William the Conqueror.

"We should remember that, until the sixteenth century, French was the judicial language of England; and the American judicial language still retains many French terms—a corrupt French, it is true, but one which attests its Norman origin.

"Every session of the Supreme Court of United States, even at the present time, is opened by a crier with the words: 'Oyez! Oyez! Oyez!' as in the time of Edward III."[4]

The courts in Canada, it should be noted, are likewise opened with the same words.

William D. Guthrie, the Chairman of the Paris Committee of the American Bar Association, in an address delivered before the bar of the City of New York, deemed it fitting, in connection with his report of the Paris meeting, to recall "some aspects of the impress made by French thought and genius upon English institutions and jurisprudence." In the course of his remarks he reminded his hearers:

"The records available to us show that for several centuries after the Norman conquest the governance of England was essentially French. The King of England and his entourage spoke French; the laws were enacted in French; the leaders pleaded and argued in French; the judges rendered their judgments in French; the famous Year Books were long printed in French; the only literature current, whether legal or otherwise, was French; and even the old British language, so far as it survived down to our days, became two-thirds French. But, in truth, neither Saxon nor English nor Norman French survived, for a new language as well as a new people were born of the all-permeating infusion of French blood and culture into Briton and Saxon. If it be urged that French ideas and language have long since disappeared from the surface of the outward life of Englishmen, the reply must be that not disappearance but absorption is the fact, that French thought and culture have no more vanished than Anglo-Saxon ideas and language have vanished, and that the British nation and the English language today alike are composites of many ancient, excellent and enduring elements."[5]

The view that English law is a mixture of many elements is also urged by Edward Stanley Roscoe, who starts his book *The Growth of English Law* with the following passage:

"Before the time of Edward I English law did not exist. Anglo-Saxon, Danish, Norman and Roman law then partially prevailed, and Norman, ecclesiastical and Roman influences were each at work. . . . The influence of the canon law and of the Roman law is obvious not only in its breadth of view, but in some classical pedantries, occasionally also in some actual rules which supply the absence of authority arising either from English dicta, practice or custom."

Chancery is referred to by Bacon, in his history of King Henry VII, as "the Pretorian power for mitigating the rigour of law, in case of extremity, by the conscience of a good man."[6] Now the version of natural justice of the early chancellors "bore a decided civilian or canonical stamp"; and natural justice, the *jus naturale* of the Roman law, was made the ground of a not very remote English decision,[7] in which the right to running waters was in question, as being "that which is *aequum et bonum* between the upper and lower proprietors." As is pointed out by Sir Frederick Pollock, there is a good deal of identity between the Roman conception of *aequum et bonum* or *aequitas* and the present English doctrine of "reasonableness," reasonable price and reasonable time being among "the most familiar elements in the law of contract."[8]

Sir Lyman Duff, the great Canadian jurist, former Chief Justice of Canada, has aptly stated "that Norman French was the nursing tongue of the Common Law," and he referred to Blackstone's quoting the "ironical observation of the Roman satirist: Eloquent Gaul hath instructed British lawyers." As he informs us, "pleadings in the English courts were formerly all written, as indeed all public proceedings were in Norman or law French, and even the arguments of counsel and decisions of the courts were in what Blackstone called: 'the same barbarous dialect.'"[9]

Not the least interesting result of such a situation is the striking circumstance that Magna Carta was framed at a period dominated by French culture and was wrung from King John by barons who spoke in French.[10]

Two remarkable illustrations of our point may be found in the well-known British decisions in Young v. Grote[11] and Taylor v. Caldwell.[12]

In the first, the Court of Common Pleas had based its judgment on a passage from Pothier and held the drawer of a check liable for his negligence in writing it. Mr. Chief Justice Anglin has shown how much Young v. Grote was discussed for almost a century, until its authority finally triumphed in the House of Lords, in 1918, in a case in which the Lord Chancellor, Viscount Finlay, alluding to the passage from Pothier, said that it appeared to him "to embody the principles of English as well as of the Civil Law."[13]

As for Taylor v. Caldwell, it came prominently before the Supreme Court of Canada in the British Columbia case of Canadian Merchant Marine v. Canadian Trading Co.,[14] where it was discussed by all the judges in their opinions. Mr. Justice Mignault took occasion to point to the interesting reference made by Blackburn J. "to the Civil Law and to Pothier (Obligations, no. 668), as laying down the rule that the debtor *corporis certi* is freed from the obligation, when the thing has perished neither by his act, nor by his neglect, and before he is in default, unless by some stipulation he has taken on himself the risk of the particular misfortune which has occurred."[15]

The present writer would not venture, in an American publication, to enter into an examination of how far the law of the United States has been influenced by the French Code. But Canada is an exceptional area in which to explore such a subject, because of the coexistence within its borders of the civil law in the Province of Quebec and the common law in force in its other nine provinces.

This discrepancy has brought about some notable changes in the principles on which English jurisprudence has been grounded. For instance, the Workmen's Compensation Acts (now adopted by all Canadian provinces) appear to be at least a mitigation of the English doctrine of common employment and somewhat partake of the civilian conception of the responsibility of the master.

In most of the English-speaking provinces there have now been passed legitimation acts for the purpose of legitimizing children born out of wedlock whose parents subsequently marry—a provision contained in the Quebec Code (Article 237 *et seq.)* since 1867; it always formed part of the law expounded by the commentators of the old French law.

The civil-law principle of apportioning damages in cases of contributory fault or negligence has been incorporated in the statutes of the common-law provinces by their respective legislatures. This principle is taken from the French law, and there is this to be noted about it: the French doctrine of contributory negligence as applied in the courts of France or of Quebec is based on no special text and is only the extension made by the case law of the general rule of responsibility contained in Article 1053 of the Quebec Civil Code or Article 1382 of the Code Napoleon. Roman law on that point, it should be noted, was in accord with the common law. We now have, then, this curious result: that contributory negligence, as applied in the civil-law countries of France and of Quebec, is unwritten law and based on case law, whereas, as now applied in the common-law provinces of Canada, it has become *lex scripta.*

But whatever the reciprocal influences of one legal system on the other may be, it is not to be doubted that both systems tend, as they should, toward similar conclusions. A complete and adequate study of the genesis of each would show as kindred much that we might fancy to be foreign and of no immediate relation to what we are thinking, doing, and enjoying today.

This kinship was happily expressed by the distinguished *bâtonnier* of the Paris Bar, M. Fourcade, in his opening address at the 1924 meeting in the Palais de Justice: "Recherche laborieuse et féconde au cours de laquelle les origines communes de législations qui se croyaient étrangères ont été plus d'une fois reconnues.

"N'a-t-on pas démontré déjà qu'au temps de la conquête normande, les lois des conquérants les suivirent, continuant plusieurs siècles durant à se formuler dans la langue originaire et marquant d'une empreinte définitive une législation transportée ensuite par les émigrants au-delà des mers. Quel jour n'a pas alors été projeté sur les analogies de fond de lois qui paraissaient si différentes! Et quel stimulant à multiplier les rapprochements, à resserrer les collaborations, à essayer de restituer dans toute sa vérité l'unité essentielle du droit sous l'apparente diversité des législations."[16]

The same opinion was expressed at the same meeting by Mr. Chief Justice Hughes, then President of the American Bar Association, who said that "under our two systems of law we render similar judgments in similar cases."[17]

And to these statements of men in very high positions may the present writer be permitted to add his humble experience of thirty years on the Bench of the Supreme Court of Canada and of more than ten years as Chief Justice of Canada. The Supreme Court of Canada is perhaps a unique example to be mentioned for the purpose of the present paper. In that court judges trained in the common law sit together with those trained in the civil law. These judges deliver judgment now in common-law appeals from nine of the provinces, and now in civil-law appeals from the Province of Quebec. And Sir Lyman Duff, who sat in that court longer than any other Canadian judge, after having made that remark adds this: "Lawyers of this country [Canada] are coming to think, and, as time goes on, more and more will come to think, in terms not of the civil law only, or of the common law only, but in terms as well of the broader principles upon which both structures are reared."[18]

The experience gathered from this writer's association with that court has been that whether a case is decided under the rules of the civil law or under those of the common law, the result is almost invariably the same. And after all, if one thinks of it, it must necessarily be so. Justice is founded on truth, and truth cannot but be one and the same everywhere.

In Acton v. Blundell,[19] Tindal C. J. in the course of his opinion said:

> "The Roman law forms no rule, binding in itself, upon the subjects of this realm, but in deciding a case upon principle, where no direct authority can be cited from our books, it affords no small evidence of the soundness of the conclusion at which we have arrived, if it proves to be supported by that law, the fruit of the researches of the most learned men, the collective wisdom of ages, and the groundwork of the municipal law of most of the countries of Europe."

And the same opinion is expressed by Brown in the introduction to his great work *The Common Law of England:*

> "Our courts will listen to arguments drawn from the Institutes and Pandects of Justinian, and will rejoice if their conclusions are shown to be in conformity with that law."[20]

The more we think of it, the more we find that the diversity of legislation is more in details than in fundamental principles. And, above all, it does not affect the essential unity of justice.

In being asked to participate in this celebration of the Napoleonic Code, the present writer was told that of particular interest would be his conclusions on the relevancy in the common-law world of the French experience with codification technique.

Of course, the main objection to codification is the rigidity of written law as compared with the flexibility of case law. It is not to be denied, however, that both systems have proved equal to the demands of a changing world.

The present French Code has been known primarily as the Code Napoleon. It was named thus not only because it was initiated by Napoleon, who appointed the codifiers, but also because he actually took part in the elaboration of the Code. M. René Savatier, Professor of Law at the University of Poitiers, has related that General Thibaudeau, a conventional general living in Poitiers—and, by the way, one of the present writer's ancestors—had devised a stenography of his own whereby he was able to preserve *verbatim* the interventions of Napoleon in the drafting of the text by the codifiers. They show that the then First Consul took an active part in the introduction of some of the articles. In most cases his suggestions were for the purpose of enlarging the rights of women. As Mr. Justice Sanford has put it, in referring to the language of the French code, it is "la langue du Code Civil, qui donnera même à Napoléon une immortalité au-delà de ses victoires militaires."[21]

The codifiers of the French Code, in their "Discours Préliminaires," foresaw that they could not "tout régler et tout prévoir" and that it was impossible for the legislator "de pourvoir à tout. . . . C'est au magistrat et au jurisconsulte, pénétrés de l'esprit général des lois, d'en diriger l'application."

Codification presents advantages, even if custom is more in conformity with changing human nature, perhaps more spontaneous and more likely to follow progress and to express it. The present Prime Minister of Canada, Mr. Saint-Laurent, who is a leader of the bar, remarked in his opening address as president of the Canadian Bar Association: "Codified law is not dead law destined to set up a standard which shall know no progress and be considered as ordering a state of permanency."[22]

Some others who have given thought to the question before this day have shown an inclination towards codification. Lord Birkenhead, in his *Points of View,*[23] was in favor of codifying the English law. Sir James Aikins, the founder of the Canadian Bar Association, recommended the adoption of a code. He said: "The multiplicity and conflict of decisions create uncertainty. . . . They are to the legislator, the lawyer and especially to the people a dense and trackless forest, rioting in the luxuriousness of its own riches."[24]

Moreover, the tendency of the common-law provinces of Canada is, in part at least, toward a form of codification such as prevails in the civil-law Province of Quebec. They now have partnership acts, sales-of-goods acts, legitimation acts, that are nothing but codes. The Canadian Parliament has supplied codes on bills of exchange and promissory notes, banks and banking, savings banks, navigation and shipping, patents and copyrights, currency and coinage, bankruptcy and insolvency, and others.

In the words of Pollock: "What is best for one race, one society, at a given stage of civilization, is not necessarily best for other races and societies at other stages. . . . We now realize that the laws of every nation are determined by their own historical conditions not only as to details but as to structure."[25] Immediately before that he had said: "We have long given up the attempt to maintain that the Common Law is the perfection of reason."[26]

The present writer is willing to adopt that statement with regard to the civil law.

A remarkable passage in a book by André Maurois in which he brings out the different characteristics of the Anglo-Saxon and the French may well serve as a conclusion to this paper:

"De Rome, et peut-être aussi d'une longue vie paysanne, la France tient le goût de l'exactitude juridique, des formules et des textes précis. L'Angleterre mène sa vie politique sans constitution, rend la justice sans code, et attend la paix de l'Europe d'expédients contradictoires et d'intuitions hardies. La France veut des chartes écrites et des garanties signées. L'Anglais tient pour dangereux de prétendre endiguer un univers aux crues imprévisibles. Le Français croit aux plans, aux édifices symétriques, aux desseins fermes et bien conçus. L'Anglais, s'il rencontre une résistance doctrinale, semble céder, puis revient à la charge dans une autre formation et reprend le terrain perdu. Obligé de concéder à un pays son indépendance, il reconnaît l'indépendance, et maintient l'occupation. Un Français eût maintenu le principe au risque de perdre le gage. De tels contrastes entre les idéologies nationales naissent les malentendus qui, depuis la guerre, ont rendu difficile la vie de l'Europe."[27]

But the same writer, it should be noted, has also asked himself whether men, although so dissimilar, may not after all, be likened to notes of music that, though all different, are meant to be played together and so to produce the greatest harmony.

NOTES

[1] Holmes, The Common Law 1 (1881).

[2] Pollock, The Expansion of the Common Law 14 (1904).

[3] Quoted in Rinfret, Reciprocal Influences of the French and English Laws, 4 Can. B. Rev. 69, 70 (1926).

[4] *Ibid.*

[5] *Id.* at 70–71.

[6] Bacon's Works, Vol. I, 332 (1844 ed.).

[7] Bradford Corporation v. Ferrand, [1902] 2 Ch. 655.

[8] Pollock, *op. cit. supra* note 2, at 111.

[9] Quoted in Rinfret, *op. cit. supra* note 3, at 71.

[10] *Ibid.*

[11] 4 Bing. 253.

[12] 3 B.S. 826.

[13] London Joint Stock Bank v. McMillan [1918] A.C. 777.

[14] 64 Can. Sup. C. Repts. 106.

[15] Of Pothier, in fact, it should be remarked that his authority is very high in the English courts, as may be seen from the judgment of Best C.J. in Cox v. Troy, 5 B. & Ald. 481, as well as in that of Lord Blackburn in the House of Lords in McLean v. Clydesdale Banking Co., 9 A.C. 105.

[16] Quoted in Rinfret, *op. cit. supra* note 3, at 73.

[17] La Réception du Barreau Canadien à Paris 2.

[18] Rinfret, *supra* note 3, at 70.

[19] 12 M. & W. 324, 353.

[20] Brom, The Common Law of England 20 (9th ed. 1896).

[21] La Réception du Barreau Canadien à Paris 3, 4.

[22] Rinfret, *supra* note 3, at 70.

[23] Birkenhead, Points of View, Vol. I, 151 *et seq.* (1922).

[24] I Can. B. Rev. 14 (1923).

[25] Pollock, *op. cit. supra* note 2, at 10.

[26] *Id.* at 9.

[27] Maurois, *Mes songes que voici* 288 (1933).

18

The Reçonciliation of the Civil Law and the Common Law

ARTHUR T. VANDERBILT

For the past three days we have been comparing the civil law and the common law from many angles. Similarities as well as differences in particular fields have been considered. The topic of the reconciliation of the civil law and the common law has been assigned to me for the closing address of this significant conference. The term "reconciliation," I am sure, is not meant to imply identity or even a dream of identity between these two great systems of law. Rather I think it refers to a reconciliation in the minds of lawyers trained in the common-law system, and perhaps of lawyers trained in the civil law, to the realities of the relationship of these two great systems of law that govern so large a part of the civilized world. So insular and provincial have most of uș of the common-law world been that it will come as a great surprise to us to learn (1) how much the civil law and the common law have had in common for centuries. This surprise will be heightened when we observe (2) that the two systems of law, despite their seeming differences, have much in common in their juristic methods, particularly in the field of private law and in the effect of private law on the relationship of the two systems of law.

I

It is singular how few common lawyers, both English and American, have realized that, in addition to customary law, there

ARTHUR T. VANDERBILT *is Chief Justice of the Supreme Court of New Jersey* were three great bodies of law—feudal, canon, and merchant—that long held sway throughout Central and Western Europe and that these three great bodies of law were quite as much in force in England as on the Continent. Thus, William the Conqueror brought with him to England the feudal law that he had known in Normandy, but he took good care to avoid the disintegrating tendency of Continental feudalism, traceable to the doctrine that "the man's man is not the Lord's man," by compelling "the man's man" in England to take a direct oath of allegiance to him. He had seen how largely independent of the French crown the dukes of Normandy had been, and he had no intention of permitting his vassals in England any such power over their subordinates at his expense. Henry II continued the process. He established royal courts that promptly took jurisdiction of feudal cases, and as a result the lower feudal courts were gradually deprived of all real authority.[1] Aside from these matters the European feudal system prevailed in England, but, as Maitland points out, Lord Coke in presenting the English law of the later Middle Ages reveals no knowledge of the European feudal system.[2] It remained for Coke's contemporary, the antiquarian Spelman, to make the grand discovery that English feudal law was really European feudal law and for Sir Martin Wright to spread the new learning and for Blackstone to popularize it.

Likewise English canon law was of European rather than of English origin. Again it was William the Conqueror who imported this second body of European law into England. He had had the support of the Pope on his crusade to conquer England, and in gratitude he established in England the wide jurisdiction of ecclesiastical law, proclaiming: "Things which pertain to the governance of souls ought not to be in the jurisdiction of secular men."[3] The famous quarrel of Henry II with Archbishop Thomas à Becket served to give the Church courts even more authority in the punishment of clerks than they had on the Continent. The ecclesiastical jurisdiction even survived the Reformation, though

Maitland has shown that the theory that England was governed by a special "King's canon law" before the time of Henry VIII was a legal fiction.[4] The canon law was administered in separate courts by a specialized bar with its own quarters, and even to this day its European origin is attested by a special division of Probate, Divorce and Admiralty in the English High Court of Justice and in this country by special courts of first instance, such as orphans' or probate or surrogates' courts.

Until the Tudor period commercial cases were decided as on the Continent in special commercial courts. When commercial cases were drawn into the royal courts by Lord Chief Justice Mansfield the law merchant, except in admiralty cases, ceased to be a separate body of law, but its European origin was unquestioned. Under Lord Mansfield it not only became integrated into the common law, but it reached a new high point of development by reason of his broad knowledge as a student of Scottish civil law of the several systems of European law.

It does not mean much simply to say that England accepted three bodies of European law, but when we note the wide scope of each of these legal systems and their wide influence on the daily life of the people, we can better understand the similarities of the common law and the civil law. Feudalism was at one and the same time a system of government and so of law, a system of society and a system of land tenure at a time when land was the chief kind of wealth. Not only have we derived much of our land law from feudalism, but it long dominated social and family relations and still does to a considerable degree in England. The expanse of the canon law was equally extensive. It had jurisdiction over the person of the clergy in both criminal and civil suits against them and of suits by them when they could not get justice in the civil suits. Widows, orphans, and the helpless generally had the same privilege. It took jurisdiction over crimes that were mostly sins, such as heresy, witchcraft, and sacrilege. It claimed jurisdiction over marriage as a sacrament whether the marriage was performed in the

Church or not, and decided when it might decree separation or annulment, never, however, granting a divorce. It controlled marriage settlements, though not exclusively. It passed on questions of legitimacy and so came to control in large part the jurisdiction over family relations. By reason of its jurisdiction over marriage it dealt with all sexual crimes. It even had jurisdiction over seemingly secular offenses such as the falsification of weights and measures and of coins, forgery of documents, bearing false witness, libel and slander, and usury. It had cognizance of testamentary instruments, especially those disposing of personal property, and of the administration of estates of intestates. For a considerable time it had jurisdiction over contracts involving oaths, pledges of faith, and usury. The law merchant covered not only admiralty and charter parties, but insurance and bills and notes. One has but to epitomize the jurisdiction of these three bodies of European law to see how much of our Anglo-American law owes its origin to the civil law of Europe.

The chief distinction between English law and European law springs from the fact that in England the customary law grew, especially under strong kings like Henry II and Edward I, into a sturdy body of common law, whereas in Europe the maze of local and national customs did not. There was need on the Continent, however, for a body of customary law such as England had developed; failing to achieve it, the nations of Western Europe turned to the Roman law following its revival in the universities of Ravenna, Bologna, and Padua in the eleventh and twelfth centuries to make up the deficiency. That there was no reception of the Roman law in England in the sixteenth century was due, as Maitland has pointed out in his Rede Lecture, to the thoroughness of the teaching of the common law in the Inns of Court;[5] well might Maitland say that "Taught law is tough law."[6] But even though the Roman law was not received in England as a system, much Roman law found its way into England, in some degree through the writers of the early legal classics, but especially through the development of the equitable jurisdiction of the Chancellor. Not only was its procedure drawn from the canon law and hence Roman in its origin, but its pervading spirit of equity and good conscience may also be credited to the churchly influence of the canon law. Its greatest contribution to our substantive law—the trust—presents in its concept of the obligation of a trustee to the beneficiary the highest standards of good faith and unselfish conduct recognized anywhere in the law or elsewhere. In developing the doctrine of unjust enrichment through the action of general assumpsit, Lord Mansfield carried over into the law courts concepts of equity and of the ecclesiastical law that have exercised an influence far beyond the particular cases in which they were made the basis of decision.

Nor did this process end here. In this country following the Revolution the Jeffersonians favored the reception in France of the civil law, and even among those who were opposed to any such course it was perceived that the civil law had much to contribute to the jurisprudence of a new nation, especially in the field of commercial law. Thus we find Chancellor Kent, a Federalist, writing of his work as Chief Justice of the New York Supreme Court:

> "I could generally put my Brethren to rout & carry my point by mysterious use of French and civil law. The Judges were republicans [*i.e.* Jeffersonian democrats] & very kindly disposed to everything that was French & this enabled me without exciting any alarm or jealousy, to make free use of such authority & thusly enrich our commercial law."[7]

The civil law has also had great influence on our modern procedure. The fundamental concept of equity procedure was discovery, through the process of scraping the conscience of the defendant. By depositions it sought to compel the defendant to tell the truth. Within the last few years this concept of the civil law has been adopted in the Federal Rules of Civil Procedure and in the procedure of the states following its example in suits at law as well as in equity (1) to eliminate surprise and technicalities, and

(2) to permit complete discovery in the interest of the truth and justice.

Although there are these wide fields of common origin in the civil law and the common law with respect to the three great systems of European law that we have been discussing, as well as in the gradual development of equity on both the substantive and the procedural side, there are also vast differences between them—particularly in the realm of public law. Roman law as it was revived in the Italian universities was the law of an imperial dictatorship under which the underlying maxim of public law was *"Quod principi placuit, legis habet vigorem; ut pote cum lege regia, quæ de imperio ejus lata est, populus ei et in eum omne suum imperium et potestatem conferat"*—"The will of the emperor has the force of law; for, by the royal law which has been made concerning his authority, the people have conferred upon him all its sovereignty and power."[8] And this concept has left a deep imprint on the civil law in marked contrast to the constitutional doctrine of England and the constitutional republic of America. Our notions of an independent judiciary, of personal liberty, and of due process of law were unknown to the Romans, and likewise our right to a trial by jury and the prohibition against self-incrimination.

We differ widely, too, in procedure; theirs is inquisitorial, ours accusatorial. In the accusatorial process we developed the law of evidence and trial methods that are unknown on the Continent. Nor does the civil law have anything comparable to our prerogative writs, which are so important a part of our judicial machinery for maintaining the rights of citizens to the orderly processes of government. There are many differences, too, in the field of private substantive law, but from an over-all point of view it may fairly be said that the resemblances outweigh the differences. Our unfamiliarity with the resemblances and differences of the two systems is due in part to our provincialism and in part to our linguistic limitations, especially with respect to German law, rather than to juristic differences.

II

The judicial process in France, in England, and in America is much more alike than many of us suspect. Indeed, in some ways the judicial process in this country is nearer to that of France than it is to that of England today.

Our fundamental misconception as to the civil law is in supposing that the French Code covers everything. The French Code, unlike some American codes, especially some of our codes of civil procedure, does not attempt to cover everything. It deals rather with principles and standards. It makes no effort to cover details.[9] Thus in the French Code what we call torts are disposed of in five brief sections.[10] These five brief sections mean little more than that negligent acts create liability. We all know that the subject matter of torts covers innumerable situations; the four sturdy volumes of the American Law Institute *Restatement of the Law of Torts* is a daily reminder of this fact. With all of the law of torts comprehended in five brief sections of the French Code, it necessarily follows that there is quite as much judge-made law in the field of torts in France as there is with us. The same situation in varying degrees exists in other phases of private law. In the field of public law there is no administrative code;[11] all of the public law of France is judge-made.

What tends to mislead us is our failure to understand that, to the French, legislation is deemed the source of all law and their opinions appear to be merely a construction of legislation and not in any wise the making of law by the judges. We have had until the present century similar ideas with respect to law-finding by judges, and some judges still adhere to it in public; it is only in the present century that lawmaking by our judges as distinguished from law-finding has been frankly discussed.

Seemingly the process in deciding cases in the civil law is merely statutory interpretation, but Professor Munroe Smith has aptly described what actually happens:

"For more than two thousand years it has been an accepted legal principle that, in interpreting the written law, effect should be given, as far as possible, to the spirit and intent of the law. Here again the possibilities of law-finding under cover of interpretation are very great. A distinguished German jurist, Windscheid, has remarked that in interpreting legislation modern courts may and habitually do 'think over again the thought which the legislator was trying to express,' but that the Roman jurist went further and 'thought out the thought which the legislator was trying to think.' Of this freer mode of interpretation Windscheid might have found modern examples. The president of the highest French court, M. Ballot-Beaupré, explained, a few years ago, that the provisions of the Napoleonic legislation had been adapted to modern conditions by a judicial interpretation in 'le sens évolutif.' 'We do not inquire,' he said, 'what the legislator willed a century ago, but what he would have willed if he had known what our present conditions would be.'

"In English-speaking countries this freer mode of interpretation has always been applied to the unwritten or common law, and it is usually applied to the written law with a degree of boldness which is very closely proportioned to the difficulty of securing formal amendment. Thus the rigidity of our federal constitution has constrained the Supreme Court of the United States to push the interpreting power to its furthest limits. This tribunal not only thinks out the thoughts which the Fathers were trying to think one hundred and twenty years ago, but it undertakes to determine what they would have thought if they could have foreseen the changed conditions and the novel problems of the present day. It has construed and reconstrued the constitution in 'the evolutive sense,' until in some respects that instrument has been reconstructed."[12]

This evolutive interpretation of legislation would be impossible in a country that adhered to the doctrine of *stare decisis* in the strict form in which it has developed in England. The English doctrine of absolute authority is stated by Professor Arthur L. Goodhart in his Inaugural Lecture:

"Absolute authority exists only in the following cases:

1. Every Court is absolutely bound by the decisions of all Courts superior to itself.
2. The House of Lords is absolutely bound by its own decisions.

3. The Court of Appeal is probably bound by its own decisions, though on this point there is some doubt.

But, even so limited, the doctrine of the binding precedent is of such importance that it may be said to furnish the fundamental distinction between the English and the Continental legal method."[13]

It is conceded that the English version of *stare decisis* results in injustice in some cases and in far-fetched distinctions in others and, because of the difficulty—one might almost say the impossibility—of getting bills for the improvement of the law through Parliament, in placing justice in a strait-jacket. The subject is probably the most controversial in English law, and the number of articles on the subject is legion.[14]

The English view of the effect of a decision even of a court of last resort is repudiated by the French. Says Professor Lambert of the University of Lyons:

"In France, the judicial precedent does not, *ipso facto,* bind either the tribunals which established it nor the lower courts; and the Court of Cassation itself retains the right to go back on its own decisions. The courts of appeal may oppose a doctrine proclaimed by the Court of Cassation, and this opposition has sometimes led to a change of opinion on the part of the higher court. The practice of the courts does not become a source of the law until it is definitely fixed by the repetition of precedents which are in agreement on a single point."[15]

What is the American attitude toward *stare decisis?* Dean Wigmore took an extreme position, which rivals the French repudiation of the doctrine:

"Is the judge to be bound by his precedent? This part of the question ought not to trouble us overmuch. *Stare decisis,* as an absolute dogma, has seemed to me an unreal fetich. The French Civil Code expressly repudiates it; and, though French and other Continental judges do follow precedents to some extent, they do so presumably only to the extent that justice requires it for safety's sake. *Stare decisis* is said to be indispensable for securing certainty to the application of the law. But the sufficient answer is that it has not in fact secured it. Our judicial law is as uncertain as any law could well be. We possess all the detriment of uncertainty, which *stare decisis* was supposed to avoid, and also all the detriment of ancient law-lumber, which *stare decisis* concededly involves—the government of the living by the dead, as Herbert Spencer has called it."[16]

It is believed, however, that Justice Cardozo more accurately presents the modern American point of view:

"I think adherence to precedent should be the rule and not the exception. . . . But I am ready to concede that the rule of adherence to precedent, though it ought not to be abandoned, ought to be in some degree relaxed. . . . There should be greater readiness to abandon an untenable position when the rule to be discarded may not reasonably be supposed to have determined the conduct of the litigants, and particularly when in its origin it was the product of institutions or conditions which have gained a new significance or development with the progress of the years."[17]

Illustrative of the application of the American view of the doctrine of *stare decisis* is the opinion of Mr. Justice Sutherland in the famous case of Funk v. United States:

"That this court and the other federal courts, in this situation and by right of their own powers, may decline to enforce the ancient rule of the common law under conditions as they now exist we think is not fairly open to doubt."[18]

Clearly the American doctrine is nearer to the French doctrine than it is to the English. Equally it must seem to be more suited to the needs of a time in which the tempo of social change is rapid, indeed revolutionary.

In fairness to the English rule, even though we cannot agree with it, we must recall with Holdsworth the flexibility, in the past at least, of its law, despite the language of its doctrine:

"If we compare the medieval common law with the law of the sixteenth and seventeenth centuries, and the law of the sixteenth and seventeenth centuries with the law of the nineteenth and twentieth centuries, this flexibility is apparent; and it is not difficult to see that this result is the consequence both of the English system of case law and of the reservations with which that system is applied in practice. It is true that the application of that system makes the law bulky and technical, and it is true that it imposes upon the lawyers a high degree of technical skill. But is that too high a price to pay for the benefits of a legal system, which combines the virtues of certainty and flexibility in such a way that it has been found capable of continuous adaptation to the needs of successive ages, of a legal system which has enabled the lawyers to construct a body of scientific doctrine which is matched only by that constructed by the classical jurists of Rome?"[19]

The grave question presented, however, is whether the process Holdsworth outlines is gaited to the needs of a society that is changing more rapidly than any previously known to our system of law. True, the legal systems of England, of France, and of the United States have a common objective: the betterment of the average citizen through providing him with a strong effective government and vouchsafing to him as much individual freedom as is consistent therewith and with similar rights in others. In all three countries the state and the government exist for the benefit of the individual and not, as in the Soviet regime, the individual for the benefit of the state. It would be remarkable if they, having a common goal, did not grow toward each other in the field of private law, but the juristic methods of France and America would seem to lend themselves to a closer and quicker correspondence between their private law than the English doctrine of *stare decisis* would permit.

NOTES

1 Munroe Smith, *A General View of European Legal History* 15, 23 (1927).

2 Maitland, *The Constitutional History of England* 142 (1931); cf. Scruton, *The Influence of the Roman Law on the Law of England* 129–33 (1885).

3 Stubb's *Select Charters* 99 (1913).

4 Maitland, *Roman Canon Law in England* (1898).

5 Maitland, *English Law and the Renaissance* (1901).

6 *Id.* at 18.

7 Kent, "An American Law Student of a Hundred Years Ago," in *Select Essays in Anglo-American Law* 843 (1907).

8 Dig. 1. 4. 1; Inst. 1. 2. 1; Fleta, 1. 1, c. 17, §7; Brac. 107; Selden, *Diss. ad. Flet.* c. 3, §2.

[9] Deak, The Place of the Case in the Common and the Civil Law, *8 Tulane L. Rev.* 337 at 345 (1934).

[10] Cod. Civ. Articles 1382–86.

[11] Schwartz, French Administrative Law and the Common-Law World 1 (1954).

[12] Munroe Smith, "Jurisprudence" in *op. cit. supra* note 7, at 352.

[13] Goodhart, Precedent in English and Continental Law, *50 L. Q. Rev.* 40, 42 (1934).

[14] *Id. passim* and Holdsworth, *50 L. Q. Rev.* 180 (1934) and Goodhart, Case Law, a Short Replication, *50 L. Q. Rev.* 196 (1934).

[15] Lambert and Wasserman, The Case Method in Canada and the Possibilities of Its Adaptation to the Civil Law, *39 Yale L. J.* 1, 14 (1929).

[16] Wigmore, *Problems of Law* 79 (1920).

[17] Cardozo, *The Nature of the Judicial Process,* 149–51 (1921).

[18] 290 U.S. 371 at 382 (1933).

[19] Holdsworth, *50 L. Q. Rev.* 180 at 193 (1934).

THE CODE NAPOLEON AND THE COMMON-LAW WORLD

A Selective Bibliography of Publications in English

Selective Bibliography

JULIUS J. MARKE

I. THE CODE—BACKGROUND, TECHNIQUE, AND EXPANSION

Aghion, Raoul. French law as applied to British subjects. London, Stevens & Sons, 1935. 144 pp.

Allen, Carleton K. Precedent, nature and history, authority and operation. (In his *Law in the Making*. 5th ed., Oxford, Clarendon Press, 1951. Pp. 154–357.)

——— Statutory interpretation. (In his *Law in the Making*. 5th ed., Oxford, Clarendon Press, 1951. Pp. 458–504.)

Alvarez, Alexander. Dominant legal ideas in the first half of the century after the French Revolution. (In *Progress of Continental Law in the Nineteenth Century*. Boston, Little, Brown, 1918. Pp. 3–30.)

——— Dominant legal influences of the second half of the century. (In *Progress of Continental Law in the Nineteenth Century*. Boston, Little, Brown, 1918. Pp. 31–64.)

——— The influence of the Napoleonic codification in other countries. (In *Progress of Continental Law in the Nineteenth Century*. Boston, Little, Brown, 1918. Pp. 251–62.)

——— Methods for scientific codification. (In *Science of Legal Method*. New York, The Macmillan Company, 1921. Pp. 430–97.)

Amos, Sir Maurice S. The Code Napoleon and the modern world. *Journal of the Society of Comparative Legislation*. n.s. 10:222–36 (1928).

——— The Code Napoleon in the modern world. *Law Times*. 162:458–59 (1926).

——— Interpretation of statutes. *Cambridge Law Journal*. 5:163–75 (1934).

——— and Walton, Frederick P. Introduction to French law. . . . Oxford, Clarendon Press, 1935. 393 pp.

Amos, Sheldon. [Codification.] (In his *The Science of Law*. New York, D. Appleton & Co., 1875. Pp. 360–93.)

JULIUS J. MARKE *is Law Librarian and Associate Professor of Law, New York University*

Ancel, Marc. Case law in France. *Journal of Comparative Legislation and International Law.* 3rd ser. 16:1–17 (1934).

——— The revision of the French civil code. *Tulane Law Review.* 25:435–45 (1951).

Bentham, Jeremy. Theory of legislation. . . . London, Humphrey Milford, 1914. 2 vols. (Vol. 1. Principles of legislation. Principles of the civil code.)

Bishop, Crawford M. Legal codes of the Latin American republics. Washington, D.C., Library of Congress, 1942. 1 vol.

Blount, Jr., J. H. The three great codifiers. *Georgia Bar Association.* 1895:190.

Bonnecasse, Julien. The problem of legal interpretation in France: The problem stated, the solution adapted and some illustrations. *Journal of Comparative Legislation and International Law.* 3rd ser. XII:79–93 (1930).

Bourriene, F. de. [Effect of introducing the Code Napoleon in the Hanse Towns.] (In his *Memoirs of Napoleon Bonaparte.* Edited by Edgar Sanderson. Pp. 344–46.) *Illinois Law Review.* 19:701–2 (1926).

Brissaud, Jean. A history of French private law . . . tr. by Rapalje Howell . . . with introductions by W. J. Holdsworth and John H. Wigmore. Boston, Little, Brown, 1912. 922 pp. *(Continental Legal History Series,* Vol. III.)

——— A history of French public law . . . tr. by James W. Garner . . . with introductions by Harold D. Hazeltine and Westel W. Willoughby. Boston, Little, Brown, 1915. 581 pp. *(Continental Legal History Series,* Vol. IX.)

Clarke, R. Floyd. The Code Napoleon. *American Law Review.* 54:391–406 (1920).

The Code Napoleon. *The American Law Register.* 3:641–50 (1855).

Cohn, Ernst J. Precedents in continental law. *Cambridge Law Journal.* 5:366–70 (1935).

Colyar, H. A. de. The great jurists of the world. Jean-Baptiste Colbert and the codifying ordinances of Louis XIV. *Journal of the Society of Comparative Legislation.* n.s. 13:56–86 (1912).

Crabites, Pierre. Napoleon Bonaparte and the Code Napoleon. Part played by the Emperor in the compilation of the Code as indicated by the various Procès Verbaux of the Commission, gathered together in Locré's "Legislation de France" . . . *American Bar Association Journal.* 13:439–43 (1927).

David, René, comp. French bibliographical digest: Law, books and periodicals. [Containing a panorama of French legal literature since 1940.] New York, Cultural Division of the French Embassy, 1952. 103 pp.

Dawson, John P. The codification of the French customs. *Michigan Law Review*. 38:765–800 (1940).

Deak, Francis. The place of the "case" in the common and the civil law. *Tulane Law Review*. 8:337–57 (1934).

Domat, Jean. The civil law in its natural order. Tr. from the French by William Strahan . . . Edited from the 2d London ed. by Luther S. Cushing. Boston, Little, Brown, 1850. 2 vols.

Eder, Phanor J. A comparative survey of Anglo-American and Latin-American law. New York, New York University Press, 1950. 257 pp.

——— Law and justice in Latin America. (In *Law, a Century of Progress, 1835–1935*. New York, New York University Press, 1937. Vol. I. Pp. 39–82.)

Elder, H. T. Interpretation of codes and statutes by civil and common-law courts, the doctrine of ejusdem generis. *Tulane Law Review*. 5:266–71 (1931).

Fabre-Surveyer, E. Centenary of the Code Napoleon. *Canadian Law Review*. 4:395 (1905).

Fisher, H. A. L. [Bibliography on the Code Napoleon.] (In *The Cambridge Modern History*, Vol. IX (Napoleon). Cambridge, University Press, 1906. Pp. 808–9.)

——— The codes. (In *The Cambridge Modern History*, Vol. IX (Napoleon). Cambridge, University Press, 1906. Pp. 148–64.)

Fontein, A. A century of codification in Holland. *Journal of Comparative Legislation and International Law*. 3rd ser. 21:83–88 (1939).

France. Laws, statutes, etc. The Code Napoléon, verbally tr. from the French, to which is prefixed an introductory discourse, containing a succinct account of the civil regulations comprised in the Jewish law, the ordinances of Manu, the Ta Tsing Leu Lee, the Zevd Avesta, the laws of Solon, the Twelve Tables of Rome, the laws of the barbarians, the assises of Jerusalem, and the Koran. By Bryant Barrett. . . . London, Printed for W. Reed, 1811. 2 vols.

——— The French civil code, with the various amendments thereto, as in force on March 15, 1895. By Henry Cachard. . . . London, Stevens & Sons, 1895. 611 pp.

——— The French civil code (as amended up to 1906), tr. into English with notes explanatory and historical, as comparative references to English law. By E. Blackwood Wright. . . . London, Stevens & Sons, 1908. 480 pp.

——— The French civil code, revised edition. By Henry Cachard. . . . Paris. The Lecram Press, 1930. 681 pp.

——— Review of discussions respecting the civil code, in the Council of State . . . on the plan of M. Regnaud (Counsellor of State). *American Law Journal.* 2:472–83 (1809).

Freund, Ernst. Standards of American legislation. An estimate of restrictive and constructive factors. Chicago, University of Chicago Press, 1917. 327 pp.

Friedmann, Wolfgang. Code law and case law. (In his *Legal Theory,* 2d ed., London, Stevens & Sons, 1949. Pp. 332–39.)

——— Code law and case law. (In his *A Re-examination of the Relations between English, American and Continental Jurisprudence*). *Canadian Bar Review.* 20:175, 188–94 (1942).

Gaudemet, Eugène. A century's progress in reshaping the law; the German and the Swiss Codes, compared with the French Code. (In *Progress of Continental Law in the Nineteenth Century.* Boston, Little, Brown, 1918. Pp. 286–307.)

A general survey of events, sources, persons and movements in Continental legal history by various European authors. Boston, Little, Brown, 1912. 754 pp. (*Continental Legal History Series.* Vol. I.)

Gény, François. The legislative technique of modern civil codes. (In *Science of Legal Method.* New York, The Macmillan Company, 1921. Pp. 498–557.)

Goodhart, Arthur. Precedent in English and Continental law. London, Stevens & Sons, 1934. 55 pp. (Reprinted from the *Law Quarterly Review,* January 1934.)

Gutteridge, H. C. A comparative view of the interpretation of statute law. *Tulane Law Review.* 8:1–20 (1933).

Hazeltine, H. D. Some aspects of French legal history. *Law Quarterly Review.* 43:212, 223–29 (1927).

Holmes, Oliver W. Codes, and the arrangement of the law. *American Law Review.* 5:1–13 (1870).

Ilbert, Sir Courtenay. The centenary of the French civil code. *Journal of the Society of Comparative Legislation.* n.s. 6:218–31 (1904).

——— Legislative methods and forms. Oxford, Clarendon Press, 1901. 372 pp.

Ireland, Gordon. The use of decisions by United States students of civil law. *Tulane Law Review*. 8:358–75 (1934).

Lambert, Edouard. Codified law and case-law. Their part in shaping the policies of justice. (In *Science of Legal Method*. New York, The Macmillan Company, 1921. Pp. 251–85.)

——— and Wasserman, Max J. The case method in Canada and the possibilities of its adaptation to the civil law. *Yale Law Journal*. 39:1–21 (1929).

Lee, William T. Napoleon and his code. *Natal Law Quarterly* 2:22 (1903).

Lenhoff, Arthur. On interpretative theories. A comparative study in legislation. *Texas Law Review*. 27:312–35 (1949).

Lobingier, Charles S. Blending legal systems in the Philippines. *Law Quarterly Review*. 21:401–7 (1905).

——— Codification. (In *Encyclopaedia of the Social Sciences*. New York, The Macmillan Company, 1935. Vol. III, Pp. 606–13.)

——— Codification in the Philippines. *Bulletin, Comparative Law Bureau*, American Bar Association (1910).

——— Franco-American codes. *Virginia Law Review*. 19:351–80 (1933).

——— Modern civil law. *Corpus Juris*. 40:1235–1486 (1926).

——— The modern expansion of the Roman law. *University of Cincinnati Law Review*. 6:152–84 (1932).

——— Napoleon and his code. *Harvard Law Review*. 32:114–34 (1918).

——— The Napoleon centenary and its legal significance. Consideration of how far Bonaparte's prophecy that "I will go down in history with the Code in my hand" has been realized. *American Bar Association Journal*. 7:383–87 (1921).

——— A Spanish object lesson in code making. *Yale Law Journal*. 16:411–16 (1907).

MacKenzie, Thomas M., Lord. Studies in Roman law with comparative views of laws of France, England and Scotland. Edinburgh, Blackwood, 1911. 473 pp.

McLaury, Helen. Bibliography of civil and commercial codes. [Showing how widespread these codes have become since the promulgation of the French civil code. Thirty-one countries are represented.] *Law Library Journal*. 44:83–93 (1951).

Maine, Sir Henry S. Roman law and legal education. (In his *Village-communities in the East and West*. 4th ed. London, 1881. Pp. 330–83.)

Maitland, Frederic W. The making of the German civil code. (In his *Collected Papers*. Cambridge, University Press, 1911. Vol. III:474–88.)

Maxwell, Sir Peter B. The interpretation of statutes. 9th ed. by Sir Gilbert H. B. Jackson. London, Sweet & Maxwell, 1946. 445 pp.

Meijers, E. M. Case law and codified systems of private law. *Journal of Comparative Legislation and International Law*. 33 3rd ser. pt. III:8–18 (1951).

Montmorency, James E., de. Robert Pothier and French law. *Journal of the Society of Comparative Legislation*. n.s. 13:265–87 (1913).

Palmer, Thomas W. Guide to the law and legal literature of Spain. Washington, D.C., Government Printing Office, 1915. 174 pp.

Pascal, Robert A. A report on the French civil code revision project. *Tulane Law Review*. 25:205–13 (1951).

Perich, Ivan. The French code of 1804, the Austrian code of 1811, the German code of 1900 and the Swiss code of 1907; a contrast of their spirit and influence. (In *Progress of Continental Law in the Nineteenth Century*. Boston, Little, Brown, 1918. Pp. 263–85.)

Planiol, Marcel. The revolution and the codes. France: [1789–1904.] (In *A General Survey of Events, Sources, Persons and Movements in Continental Legal History*. Boston, Little, Brown, 1912. Pp. 274–305.)

Pomeroy, John N. The true method of interpreting the civil code. *West Coast Reporter*. 3:719 (1884).

Pound, Roscoe. [Bibliography on codification with annotations.] (In his *Outlines of Lectures on Jurisprudence*. 5th ed. Cambridge, Harvard University, 1943. Pp. 134–39.)

——— Codification. *Cyclopedia of American Government*. 1:302–6 (1914).

Randall, A. E. Proposed method of interpretation of the French civil code. [Book review: Gény, François. Methode d'interprétation et sources en droit privé pósitif. 2d ed. Paris, 1919. 2 vols.]. *Law Quarterly Review*. 35:344–51 (1919).

Renton, Sir A. Wood. The retouchment of the code civil. *Virginia Law Review*. 20:188–99 (1933).

Roguin, Ernest. The form of the law. *New York University Law Quarterly Review*. 10:445–67 (1933).

Rose, U. M. The Code Napoleon. How it was made and its place in the world's jurisprudence. *American Law Review*. 40:833–54 (1906).

Samuel, Sigmund. The codification of law. *University of Toronto Law Journal*. 5:148–60 (1943).

Science of legal method. Select essays by various authors. . . . New York, The Macmillan Company, 1921. 593 pp.

Sherman, Charles P. The debt of modern Japanese law to French law. *California Law Review*. 6:198–202 (1918).

_____ Roman law in the modern world. 2d ed. New York, Baker, Voorhis & Co., 1924. 3 vols.

Simons, Walter. One hundred years of German law. (In *Law, a Century of Progress*. New York, New York University Press, 1937. I:83–103.)

Smith, Herbert A. Interpretation in English and continental law. *Journal of Comparative Legislation and International Law*. 3rd ser. 3:153–64 (1927).

Smith, Munroe. The development of European law. New York, Columbia University Press, 1928. 316 pp.

_____ A general view of European legal history. New York, Columbia University Press, 1927. 446 pp.

Smithers, William W. The Code Napoléon. *The American Law Register*. 49:127–47 (1901).

Sperl, Hans. Case law and the European codified law. *Illinois Law Review*. 19:505–22 (1925).

Stumberg, George W. Guide to the law and legal literature of France. Washington, D.C., Government Printing Office, 1931. 242 pp.

Stone, Ferdinand F. A primer on codification. *Tulane Law Review*. 29:303–10 (1955).

Szladits, Charles, comp. A bibliography of comparative and foreign law books and articles in English. New York, Parker School, Columbia University, Oceana, 1955. Approx. 500 pp.

Tucker, John H., Jr. Legislative procedure in the adoption of the Code Napoleon. *Louisiana State Bar Reports for 1934–1935* :26–38 (1935).

Vance, John T. The background of Hispanic-American law—legal sources and juridical literature of Spain. New York, Central Book Co., 1943. 296 pp.

Walton, Clifford S. Civil law in Spain and Spanish America, including Cuba, Puerto Rico, and Philippine Islands, and the Spanish Civil Code in force, annotated and with references to the civil codes of Mexico, Central and South America, with a history of all the Spanish codes, including the Spanish, Mexican, Cuban, and Puerto Rican autonomical constitutions, and a history of the laws of the Indies. Washington, D.C., W. H. Lowdermilk & Co., 1900. 672 pp.

Wheeler, Charles B. The Code Napoleon and its framers. Circumstances leading up to great work of codification, some of the evils it was intended to correct and agencies through which reform was accomplished; with glances at principal authors of this famous code. *American Bar Association Journal*. 10:202–6 (1924).

Yerkes, Harman. Some observations on the practice of the French Code. *Pennsylvania Bar Association Report*. 1908. Pp. 475–505.

II. THE CODE AND CONTEMPORARY PROBLEMS

Alfaro, Ricardo J. The civil law reception of trusts. *Comparative Law Series*. 2:1–12 (1939).

Alibert, Raphael. The French Conseil d'Etat. *Modern Law Review*. 3:257–71 (1940).

Ayer, Joseph C., Jr. Legitimacy and marriage. *Harvard Law Review*. 16:22 (1902).

Bates, Lindell T. Common law express trusts in French law. *Yale Law Journal*. 40:34–52 (1930).

Borchard, Edwin M. Some lessons from the civil law. *University of Pennsylvania Law Review*. 64:570–82 (1916).

Burdick, William L. The principles of Roman law and their relation to modern law. Rochester, Lawyer's Cooperative, 1938. 748 pp.

Cahn, Edmond. Undue influence and captation, a comparative study. *Tulane Law Review*. 8:507–21 (1934).

Caillemer, Robert. The executor in England and on the continent. (In *Select Essays in Anglo-American Legal History*. Boston, Little, Brown, 1909. 3:746.)

Charmont, Joseph. Changes of principle in the field of family, inheritance, and persons. (In *Progress of Continental Law in the Nineteenth Century*. Boston, Little, Brown, 1918. Pp. 147–248.)

Daggett, Harriet S. Civil law concept of the wife's position in the family. *Oregon Law Review*. 15:291–305 (1936).

_____ General principles of succession on death in civil law. *Tulane Law Review.* 11:399–411 (1937).

_____ Legal essays on family law. Baton Rouge, Louisiana State University Press, 1935. 170 pp.

Deak, Francis. Contracts and combinations in restraint of trade in French law—A comparative study. *Iowa Law Review.* 21:397–454 (1936).

Delaume, Georges R. A codification of French private international law. *Canadian Bar Review.* 29:721–47 (1951).

Drake, Joseph H. Consideration v. causa in Roman-American law. *Michigan Law Review.* 4:19–41 (1905).

_____ The old Roman law and a modern American code (Porto Rico). *Michigan Law Review.* 3:108–19 (1904).

Duguit, Léon. Changes of principle in the field of liberty, contract, liability, and property. (In *Progress of Continental Law in the Nineteenth Century.* Boston, Little, Brown, 1918. Pp. 65–146.)

Fabre-Surveyer, E. A comparison of delictual responsibility in law in countries governed by a code. *Tulane Law Review.* 8:53–82 (1933).

Freund, Heinrich. Civil law of the Soviet Union. *Illinois Law Review.* 22:699–723 (1928).

The Future of codification. Essays in honor of the centennial of the Tulane Law School. *Tulane Law Review.* 29: No. 2, February 1955.

Garner, James W. Anglo-American and continental European administrative law. *New York University Law Quarterly Review.* 7:387–414 (1929).

_____ French administrative law. I. The French and Anglo-American systems distinguished. . . . *Yale Law Journal.* 33:597–627 (1924).

Goodnow, Frank J. Comparative administrative law; an analysis of the administrative systems, national and local, of the United States, England, France and Germany. . . . New York, G. P. Putnam's Sons, 1902. Two vols. in one.

Hatoyma, Kazuo. The civil code of Japan compared with the French civil code. *Yale Law Journal.* 11:296–303, 354–70, 403–19 (1902).

Hazard, John N. The future of codification in the U.S.S.R. *Tulane Law Review.* 29:239–48 (1955).

Hogg, James E. French and English land law. *Journal of the Society of Comparative Legislation.* n.s. 9:64–68 (1908).

Houin, Roger, and Verrier, Marcel. The legal marital property regime according to the *Projet* of the French Commission for Revision of the Code Civil. *Louisiana Law Review*. 15:712–21 (1955).

Hozumi, Nobushige. The new Japanese civil code as material for the study of comparative jurisprudence. . . . 2d ed. Tokyo, Tokyo Printing Co., 1912. 73 pp.

Kantorovitch, Jacob. The civil code of Soviet Russia. *Yale Law Journal*. 32:779–89 (1923).

Kelly, Edmond. French law of marriage, marriage contracts, divorce and conflicts of laws. 2d ed. London, Stevens, 1895. 1 vol.

Kühlewein, Robert R. Interpretation of contracts in modern European law. *Tulane Law Review*. 13:592–98 (1939).

Lepaulle, Pierre. Civil law substitutes for trusts. *Yale Law Journal*. 36:1126–47 (1927).

Levy, Ernst. The reception of highly developed legal systems by peoples of different cultures. *Washington Law Review*. 25:233–95 (1950).

Lobingier, Charles S. Administrative law and droit administratif. *University of Pennsylvania Law Review*. 91:36–58 (1947).

——— Civil law rights and common law remedies: A resumé of the progress of legal fusion in the Philippines. *Juridical Review*. 20:97 (1908).

Marx, Fritz M. Comparative administrative law: The continental alternative. *University of Pennsylvania Law Review*. 91:118–36 (1942).

Morandière, Julliot de la. Codification of French conflicts of law [including a draft law on private international law as adopted by the Commission for the Reform of the Civil Code, April 5, 1951, translated into English by Kurt H. Nadelman and Arthur T. Von Mehren.] *American Journal of Comparative Law*. 1:404–32 (1952).

——— The reform of the French civil code. *University of Pennsylvania Law Review*. 97:1–21 (1948).

Nabors, Eugene A. Civil law influence upon the law of insurance in Louisiana. *Tulane Law Review*. 6:369–407 (1932).

New York (State) Law Revision Commission. Rights of adopted children and duties of natural and adoptive parents . . . (3) Adoption under the civil law. (In its *Reports*, 1942:251, 255.)

Parker, Junius. Some aspects of the French law. New York, Charles Scribner's Sons, 1929. 82 pp.

Parker, Reginald. The criteria of the civil law. *Jurist.* 7:140–170 (1947).

Plaisant, Robert. The new French law of nationality. A study of demographic [relating to the statistical study of populations] policy and comparative legislation. Translated by Arthur E. Sutherland, Jr. *Cornell Law Quarterly.* 33:373–390 (1948).

Port, Frederick J. "French droit administratif" in administrative law. London, Longmans, Green & Co., 1929. 374 pp.

Register, Layton B. "Property" rights of the surviving husband or wife under the French civil code. *Yale Law Journal.* 30:23–33 (1920).

Rheinstein, Max. Some fundamental differences in real property ideas of the "Civil law" and the common law systems. *University of Chicago Law Review.* 3:629–35 (1936).

Schwartz, Bernard. French administrative law and the common-law world. Introduction by Arthur T. Vanderbilt. New York, New York University Press [1954]. 367 pp.

Schwenk, Heinz. Culpa in contrahendo in German, French and Louisiana law. *Tulane Law Review.* 15:87–99 (1940).

Sieghart, Marguerite A. Government by decree; a comparative study of the history of the ordinance in English and French law, with a foreword by C. K. Allen. London, Stevens, 1950. 343 pp.

Simon, Manfred. Some aspects of French law. [Summary of a series of lectures delivered in Edinburgh University in May, 1944 depicting French family life as seen through French legal institutions and particularly the "Code Napoleon."] The 4th lecture shows how legislative reaction against the conception of equal law for all, on which is founded the French civil code, has lately become apparent. *Scottish Law Review and Sherriff Court Reports.* 60:106–10 (1944).

Szladits, Charles. The concept of specific performance in civil law. *American Journal of Comparative Law.* 4:208–34 (1955).

Trudel, Gerard. The usefulness of codification: A comparative study of quasi-contract. *Tulane Law Review.* 29:311–27 (1955).

III. CODIFICATION AND THE COMMON-LAW WORLD

Amos, Sir Maurice S. The common law and the civil law in the British Commonwealth of Nations. *Harvard Law Review.* 50:1249–74 (1937).

Amos, Sheldon. Codification in England and the state of New York. . . . London, W. Ridgway, 1867. 37 pp.

——— An English code; its difficulties and modes of overpowering them, a practical application of the science of jurisprudence. . . . London, Strahan & Co., 1873. 237 pp.

Armstrong, Richard H. A code of international law. *Virginia Law Register*. n.s. 12:207–13 (1926).

Atkinson, Thomas E. Codification of probate law. (In *David Dudley Field Centenary Essays*. New York, New York University School of Law, 1949. Pp. 177–203.)

Aumann, Francis R. The influence of English and civil law principles upon the American legal system during the critical post-revolutionary period. *University of Cincinnati Law Review*. 12:289–317 (1938).

Bentham, Jeremy. Codification of the common law. Letter of Jeremy Bentham and Report of Judges Story, Metcalfe and others. New York, J. Polhemus, 1882. 63 pp.

——— View of a complete code of law. (In *Works*, ed. by John Bowring, Edinburgh, 1843. Vol. III, pp. 155–210.)

Brosman, Paul. [Editorial.] A controversy and a challenge [on the present place of civil law substance and juristic method in Louisiana]. *Tulane Law Review*. 12:239–42 (1937).

Brown, Philip M. Codification, international law. *American Journal of International Law*. 29:25–39 (1935).

Buckland, William W. and McNair, Arnold. Roman law and common law. A comparison in outline. Revised by F. H. Lawson. Cambridge, Cambridge University Press, 1952. 439 pp.

Burdick, Francis M. A revival of codification. *Columbia Law Review*. 10:118–30 (1910).

Burdick, William L. The civil law in the United States and Canada. (In his *Principles of Roman Law and Their Relation to Modern Law*. Rochester, Lawyer's Co-operative, 938. Pp. 35–55.)

Butler, William A. The Revision of the statutes of the state of New York and the revisers. . . . New York and Albany, Banks & Bros., 1889. 100 pp.

Cardozo, Benjamin N. The American Law Institute. (In his *Law and Literature*. New York, Harcourt, Brace, [c1931]. Pp. 121–41.)

——— The growth of the law. New Haven, Yale University Press, 1924. 145 pp.

Carter, James C. Law: Its origin, growth and function. New York, London, G. P. Putnam's Sons, [c1907]. 355 pp.

_____ The proposed codification of our common law. A paper prepared at the request of the Committee of the Bar Association of the City of New York, appointed to oppose the measure. New York, New York *Evening Post,* 1884. 117 pp.

_____ The provinces of the written and the unwritten law. New York, Banks & Bros., 1889. 62 pp.

Colvin, H. Milton. The path of the civil law in the United States. Paris, n.p., 1935. 1 vol.

_____ Roman and civil law elements in sources of the law of the United States. Padua, A. Milani, 1935. 1 vol.

Conference on the future of the common law. Cambridge, Harvard University Press, 1937. 247 pp.

Crocker, H. G. The codification of international law. *American Journal of International Law.* 18:38–55 (1924).

Dart, Henry P. Influence of ancient laws of Spain on the jurisprudence of Louisiana. *Tulane Law Review.* 6:83–93 (1931).

_____ The place of civil law in Louisiana. *Tulane Law Review.* 4:163–77 (1929).

_____ The sources of the civil code of Louisiana. (In *Saunders' Lectures on the Civil Code,* 1925. Pp. v–xxxvi.)

Dicey, Albert V. Lectures on the relation between law and public opinion in England during the nineteenth century. London, The Macmillan Company, 1930. 506 pp.

Dillon, John F. The laws and jurisprudence of England and America. . . . Boston, Little, Brown, 1894. 431 pp.

Draft code of the International Diplomatic Academy on the fundamental principles of international law. [Editorial.] *American Journal of International Law.* 30:279–82 (1936).

Fabre-Surveyer, E. The future of codification with regard to the execution of wills. *Tulane Law Review.* 29:210–22 (1955).

Fenner, Charles. The Louisiana civil code as a democratic institution. *American Lawyer.* 12:331 (1904).

Field, David D. The civil code. Reply of Messrs. Field, Swayne, Arnoux, Yeoman, Opdyke, Milbarn, Frankenheimer and Foster to the briefs which Messrs. Carter, Mathews, Hornblower, Adams and Dwight have submitted to the Judiciary Committees of the two houses in opposition to the civil code. 1884. n.p. 51 pp.

—— Codification in the United States. *Juridical Review.* 1:18 (1889).

—— Consideration, simplicity, and uniformity in laws. *New Jersey Law Journal.* 8:203 (1885).

—— Draft outlines of an international code. New York, Diosy & Company, 1872. 2 vols.

—— [History of codification; how the commissioners reduced into a written and systematic code the whole body of the law of the state.] n.p. 1883. *Bar Association Pamphlet.* Vol. 27.

—— Outlines of an international code. 2d ed. New York, Baker, Voorhis & Company, 1876. 712 pp.

—— A short response to a long discourse. . . An answer . . . to Mr. James C. Carter's pamphlet on the proposed codification of our common law. [New York, 1884]. 21 pp.

Fowler, Robert L. Codification in the State of New York. 2d ed. with addenda. N.Y., Martin B. Brown, 1884. 69 pp.

Franklin, Mitchell. [Book review of the restatement of the law of contracts.] *Tulane Law Review.* 8:149–52 (1933).

—— Concerning the historic importance of Edward Livingston. *Tulane Law Review.* 11:163–212 (1937).

—— The historic function of the American Law Institute: Restatement as transitional to codification. *Harvard Law Review.* 47:1367–94 (1934).

—— Some observations on the influence of French law on the early codes of Louisiana. *Journées du droit civil François.* 833 pp. (Barreau de Montreal ed. 1936.)

Goodrich, Herbert F. Restatement and codification. (In *David Dudley Field Centenary Essays.* New York, New York University School of Law, 1949. Pp. 241–50).

Gregory, Charles N. Bentham and the codifiers. *Harvard Law Review.* 13:344–57 (1900).

Greenburg, Leonard. Must Louisiana resign to the common law? *Tulane Law Review.* 11:598–601 (1937).

Grinnell, William M. A comparative glance at the French code civil and the proposed New York civil code. New York, Willis McDonald & Co., 1886. 20 pp.

Hadley, Herbert S. Historic background of plan for restatement of the law. Great works of clarification and simplification accomplished under

Justinian and Napoleon furnish interesting analogies to task undertaken by American Law Institute. . . . *American Bar Association Journal.* 9:203–7 (1923).

Halsbury, Hardinge S. G. 1st Earl of. Introduction to laws of England [on codification in England]. 2d ed. London, Butterworth, 1931. (Vol. I, pp. cclxxvii–ccxciii.)

Hamilton, Peter J. The civil law and the common law. *Harvard Law Review.* 36:180–92 (1922).

Healy, T. H. Codification of international law. *Georgetown Law Journal.* 13:205–26 (1925).

Hepburn, Charles McG. The historical development of code pleading in America and England. Cincinnati, W. H. Anderson & Co., 1897. 318 pp.

Hill, Sidney B. 150th anniversary of the French civil code. Influence of the French civil law on the western hemisphere. [Exhibition.] *The Record of the Association of the Bar of the City of New York.* 9:304–6 (1954).

Holland, Thomas E. Essays upon the form of the law. London, Butterworth, 1870. 187 pp.

Howe, William W. Roman and civil law in America. *Harvard Law Review.* 16:342–58 (1903).

——— Studies in the civil law and its relations to the jurisprudence of England and America, with references to the law of our insular possessions. 2d ed. Boston, Little, Brown, 1905. 391 pp.

Hudson, Manley O. The progressive codification of international law. *American Journal of International Law.* 20:655–69 (1926).

Hurst, Sir Cecil. A plea for the codification of international law on new lines. *Transactions of the Grotius Society.* XXXIII:146 (1946).

Ireland, Gordon. Louisiana's legal system reappraised. *Tulane Law Review.* 11:585–98 (1937).

Jenks, Edward, ed. English civil law. 4th ed. by P. H. Winfield [and others]. London, Butterworth, 1947. 2 vols.

Jolowicz, H. F. The civil law in Louisiana. *Tulane Law Review.* 29:491–503 (1955).

Kirschberger, Hans. Significance of Roman law for the Americas. *Wisconsin Law Review.* 19:249–73 (1944).

Klein, Fannie J. comp. Selective bibliography on David Dudley Field [and codification in the State of New York, U.S. and international law]. (In

David Dudley Field Centenary Essays. New York, New York University School of Law, 1949. Pp. 383–400.)

Kuhn, A. K. Codification of international law and the fifth assembly. *American Journal of International Law.* 19:155–57 (1925).

Lamarche, P. E. French civil law under British rule. *Canadian Law Times.* 31:420–24 (1911).

Lang, Maurice E. Codification in the British Empire and America. Amsterdam, H. J. Paris, 1924. 240 pp.

Lawson, Frederick H. A common lawyer looks at the civil law . . . with a foreword by Hessel E. Yntema. Ann Arbor, University of Michigan Law School, 1953. 238 pp.

Lee, Robert W. The civil law and the common law—a world survey. *Michigan Law Review.* 14:89–101 (1915).

Liang, Yuen-Li. The United Nations and the development and codification of international law. (In *David Dudley Field Centenary Essays.* New York, New York University School of Law, 1949. Pp. 267–79.)

McFarland, Carl. Administrative law and codification of statutes. (In *David Dudley Field Centenary Essays.* New York, New York University School of Law, 1949. Pp. 204–14.)

Maxey, Edwin. Codification of American public and private international law: Proposal to codify the law of the Americas. *American Law Review.* 42:105 (1908).

Morrow, Clarence J. An approach to the revision of the Louisiana civil code. *Tulane Law Review.* 23:478–90 (1949).

——— The future of codification in Louisiana. *Tulane Law Review.* 29:249–53 (1955).

——— Louisiana blueprint: Civilian codification and legal method for state and nation. *Tulane Law Review.* 17:351–415 (1943).

Munro, William B. The genesis of Roman law in America. *Harvard Law Review.* 22:579–90 (1909).

Murdock, James O. The French civil code from an American perspective. *George Washington Law Review.* 23:451–54 (1955).

Nys, Ernest. The codification of international law. *American Journal of International Law.* 5:871–900 (1911).

Oppenheim, Leonard. Louisiana's civil law heritage. *Law Library Journal.* 42:249–55 (1949).

Pollock, Sir Frederick. Essay on codification. [Introduction.] (In his *Digest of Law of Partnership*. London, Stevens & Sons, 1884. Pp. iii–xxv.)

Pomeroy, John N. The "Civil code" in California. New York, Bar Association, 1885. 69 pp.

Pound, Roscoe. The French civil law and the spirit of nineteenth century law. *Boston University Law Review*. 35:77–97 (1955).

_____ The influence of the civil law in America. *Louisiana Law Review*. 1:1–16 (1938).

_____ The influence of French law in America. *Illinois Law Review*. 3:354–63 (1909).

_____ Judge Story in the making of the American law. *American Law Review*. 48:691 (1914).

_____ Legislation [essay celebrating the hundredth anniversary of Edward Livingston's death]. (In his *The Formative Era of American Law*. Boston, Little, Brown, 1938. Pp. 38–80.

Pringsheim, Fritz. The inner relationship between English and Roman law. *Cambridge Law Journal*. 5:347–65 (1935).

Rabel, Ernst. Private laws of western civilization. Part II. The French civil code. *Louisiana Law Review*. 10:107–19 (1949).

Renton, A. Wood. French law within the British Empire. I. Historical introduction. The field of its operation. II. Points on which French law, or the influence of French law, has been maintained. III. Points of departure. *Journal of the Society of Comparative Legislation*. n.s. 10:93–119, 250–60 (1909).

Reppy, Alison, ed. David Dudley Field centenary essays. Celebrating one hundred years of legal reform . . . with an introduction by Russell D. Niles. New York, New York University School of Law, 1949. 400 pp.

_____ The Field codification concept. (In *David Dudley Field Centenary Essays*. New York, New York University School of Law, 1949. Pp. 7–54.)

Rinfret, Thibaudeau. The civil law and the common law. *New York University Law Quarterly Review*. 23:8–13 (1948).

_____ Reciprocal influences of the French and English laws. *Canadian Bar Review*. 4:69–85 (1926).

Root, Elihu. Codification of international law. *American Journal of International Law*. 19:675–84 (1925).

Schwenk, Edmund H. Highlights of a comparative study of the common and civil law systems. *North Carolina Law Review*. 33:382–98 (1955).

Scrutton, Sir Thomas E. Influence of the Roman law on the law of England. Cambridge, University of Cambridge, 1885. 199 pp.

Sims, Henry U. Notes on codifying real property law in the United States. *Harvard Law Review.* 36:987–1006 (1923).

Smith, Marion. The first codification of the substantive common law. *Tulane Law Review.* 4:178–89 (1930).

Smith, Munroe. Codification in the United States. (In his *Elements of Law,* sec. III of Vanderbilt, Arthur T., *Studying Law.* New York, Washington Square Publishing Co. [c1945] Pp. 365–76.)

Story, Joseph. Codification of the common law. (In his *Miscellaneous Writings.* Boston, 1852. Pp. 698–734.)

Symposium. A reappraisal appraised. A brief for the civil law of Louisiana by Harriet S. Daggett, Joseph Dainow, Paul M. Hébert, Henry G. McMahon. *Tulane Law Review.* 12:12–41 (1937).

Takayanagi, Kenzo. Contact of the common law with the civil law in Japan. *American Journal of Comparative Law.* 4:60–69 (1955).

Tucker, John H. Source books of Louisiana law. *Tulane Law Review.* 6:280–300 (1932); *Tulane Law Review.* 7:82–95 (1933); *Tulane Law Review.* 8:396–405 (1934); *Tulane Law Review.* 9:244–67 (1935).

Tullis, R. L. Louisiana's legal system reappraised. *Tulane Law Review.* 12:113–23 (1937).

Two centuries' growth of American law, 1701–1901. New York, Charles Scribner's Sons, 1901. 538 pp.

United Nations. Secretary General. Survey of international law in relation to the work of codification of the International Law Commission . . . Memorandum. . . . Lake Success, United Nations International Law Commission, 1948. 70 pp. (A/CN.4/1.)

Vanderbilt, Arthur T. [Codification in the U.S. and England]. (In his *Men and Measures in the Law.* New York, Alfred A. Knopf, 1949. Pp. 83–89.)

——— [The restatement of the law by the American Law Institute] (In his *Men and Measures in the Law.* New York, Alfred A. Knopf, 1949. Pp. 30–36.)

Wagner, Wienczyslaw J. Codification of law in Europe and the codification movement in the middle of the nineteenth century in the United States. *St. Louis University Law Journal.* 2:335–59 (1953).

Walton, F. P. The legal system of Quebec. *Columbia Law Review.* 13:213–31 (1923).

_____ Scope and interpretation of the civil code of Lower Canada. Montreal, Wilson and Lafleur, 1907. 1 vol.

Whiteman, Marjorie H. The codification of the responsibility of the states. *New York University Law Quarterly Review.* 8:187–237 (1930).

Wickersham, George W. Codification of international law. *American Bar Association Journal.* 11:654–61 (1925).

Wigmore, John H. Louisiana, the story of its legal system. *American Law Review.* 22:890–902 (1888).

Yntema, Hessel E. The American Law Institute. (In *Legal Essays in Tribute to Orrin Kip McMurray.* 1935. P. 657.)

_____ The jurisprudence of codification. (In *David Dudley Field Centenary Essays.* New York, New York University School of Law, 1949. Pp. 251–64.)

_____ Roman law and its influence on Western civilization. *Cornell Law Quarterly.* 35:77–88 (1949).

Index